INSIDE THE APPLE

A STREETWISE HISTORY OF NEW YORK CITY

MICHELLE NEVIUS *and* **JAMES NEVIUS**

Free Press

New York London Toronto Sydney

FREE PRESS

A Division of Simon & Schuster, Inc.

1230 Avenue of the Americas

New York, NY 10020

First Free Press trade paperback edition March 2009

FREE PRESS and colophon are trademarks of Simon & Schuster, Inc.

For information about special discounts for bulk purchases,
please contact Simon & Schuster Special Sales at
1-800-456-6798 or business@simonandschuster.com

Book design by Ellen R. Sasahara

Manufactured in the United States of America

10   9   8   7   6   5   4   3   2   1

Library of Congress Cataloging-in-Publication Data

Nevius, Michelle.
Inside the Apple : a streetwise history of New York City /
by Michelle and James Nevius.
    p. cm.
1. New York (N.Y.)—History. 2. New York (N.Y.)—Tours. 3. Historic sites—
New York (State)—New York—Guidebooks. 4. Walking—New York (State)—
New York—Guidebooks. I. Nevius, James. II. Title.

F128.18.N34 2009
917.47'10444—dc22
2008052481

ISBN-13: 978-1-4165-8997-6
ISBN-10:   1-4165-8997-X

Contents

PART 8 Walking Tours 295

Note to Readers

Walking the streets of New York City, you constantly come face to face with history. Every building has a tale to tell, from world-famous places like the Empire State Building and the Statue of Liberty to sites connected to people and events long forgotten. (How many people today remember the bomb that exploded on Wall Street in September 1920 or the sinking of the steamship *General Slocum?*) There is hardly a façade that doesn't, with a little research, reveal an interesting facet of the city's past.

The goal of *Inside the Apple* is to give you a different pathway into the city's long and rich history. While there are many books that focus on New York's notable events and famous people, ours is instead organized around the places where those events took place. By grounding the narrative in sites that you can see and visit, we provide concrete, tangible connections between the city of today and its intriguing past.

People have long tried to answer the question: What makes New York unique? We feel the answer is deceptively simple: more than any other American city, it is primarily experienced on foot. In fact, the city was designed to be walked; its grid of streets, laid out in 1811, was designed to aid people walking to the commercial piers on the East and Hudson rivers. That design—along with the compact network of roads in the oldest part of Lower Manhattan—means that the city has always developed with the pedestrian in mind. New York is a joy to walk around, and for those who wish to take to the streets, we've included 14 self-guided walking tours at the back of the book to navigate you through the city and its past. But even if you are reading the book chronologically from the comfort of your own home, the fact that it is a "streetwise" history of the city always anchors the narrative in the city of today.

❧

Of the book's 182 chapters, the first 21 cover a wide swath of time—nearly half of the city's entire European history. This isn't for lack of curiosity about the Dutch, British, or early American periods. It simply reflects the fact that in a book where every chapter is tied to an existing, modern-day place, there are few early sites that you can actually go and visit. For the most part, the cityscapes of these early eras have vanished as completely as the earlier landscapes of the Lenape and other indigenous peoples. While New Yorkers have done a fairly good job of preserving notable sites from the 19th century, most 17th- and 18th-century sites are gone.

This is not a new trend. Philip Hone, New York's mayor and one of its most famous 19th-century diarists, noted with melancholy in 1839:

> My poor, dear house, 235 Broadway, is coming down forthwith, and in a few weeks the home of my happy days will be incontinently swept from the earth. Farther up, at the corner of Chambers Street, a row of low buildings has been removed to make way for one of those mighty edifices called hotels,—eating, drinking, and lodging above and gay shops below; and so all the way up; the spirit of pulling down and building up is abroad. The whole of New York is rebuilt about once in ten years.

Even with today's historic-preservation laws, this is almost as true now as it was in Hone's era. It is worth noting that it's easier to take a walk through 19th-century Greenwich Village than it is to get a feel for the neighborhood that Bob Dylan called home in the early 1960s. Most of the important locales from Dylan's heyday are gone. The buildings are still standing, but there's no more Gaslight, Gerde's Folk City, Café Au Go-Go, or Izzy Young's Folklore Center: the list of what's gone from 40 years ago is endless.

As you read, you will notice bracketed cross-references to other chapters in the book. We've included these to aid your exploration, and you may find yourself simply following pathways through the book based on your own interests. For example, you might be reading the chapters on Tammany Hall Boss William Tweed and see that he was intimately tied to the 1876 presidential election and Democrat Samuel J. Tilden. Tilden, meanwhile, was the driving force behind the formation of the New York Public Library; reading about the library might, in turn, lead you to read about the Astor Library (one of its antecedents), which in turn would take you to Joseph Papp's Public Theater, the current tenant in the Astor Library's original home. And you could go on and on from there.

The book's 182 chapters are mostly limited to events that have taken place on Manhattan. For the first three centuries of the City's history, it was limited to the confines of Manhattan island. The story of Brooklyn— once the third-largest city in America—is touched on in these pages, but, alas, the rich histories of Queens, the Bronx, and Staten Island will have to wait for another volume. Likewise, some subjects appear only in passing—or not at all. Rather than write a book that was merely an exhaustive checklist, we have chosen instead to focus on certain places because we feel they paint a comprehensive and colorful portrait of the Big Apple.

∾

Over the years, New York has had numerous names and nicknames: Manna-hata, New Amsterdam, Gotham, the Empire City, the City That Never Sleeps. But perhaps none has had the traction of the Big Apple.

Linguistic historian Barry Popik and etymologist Gerald Cohen traced the origins of the phrase to a horseracing column written by John J. Fitz Gerald in the 1920s. Fitz Gerald had picked up the phrase from a stable hand. The term originally referred to the size of the purse at New York's tracks: to win in New York was to take the "big apple." Though the name caught on in the 1930s—particularly among jazz musicians—our modern usage dates to the 1970s, when the New York City Convention and Visitors Bureau launched two campaigns that have proved incredibly durable. One was Milton Glaser's "I ♥ NY" logo; the other revived the "Big Apple" as a replacement for Mayor John Lindsay's earlier slogan, "Fun City."

In many ways, it's an apt metaphor: like an apple, the city has a sleek, tough skin that protects its sweet interior. (Or, if you're not a fan, you might say it's rotten to the core.) But in fact, the experience of New York comes in every shape, size, and flavor imaginable. One simple truth about the city: there isn't a single, monolithic New York. Instead, everyone's version of the city is different. Moreover, it's a place that's constantly in flux. In these pages, we hope to take you "inside" the apple, to explore what makes New York not just a great city but a place where it's possible to discover the whole history of America along its enticing streets.

PART 1

The Early City: New Amsterdam, Colonial New York, the Revolutionary Era, and the Birth of the New Republic, 1608–1804

New York has long had a romance with its early history, which is often depicted through a gauzy lens of nostalgia: stout windmills line the harbor, able-bodied men in tall hats trade beaver skins with the peace-loving Indians, while their wives stand in half doors (still known as Dutch doors), a gaggle of children at their feet. All of it is overseen by the stern hand of "Peg Leg" Peter Stuyvesant, the colony's curmudgeonly director general.

New York City's seal, ca. 1686

New York City's seal today

This is not just the stuff of children's stories. The city's picturesque past is even enshrined on its great seal, which dates back to 1686. At its center are the arms of a Dutch windmill, surrounded by symbols of the city's economic history: top and bottom are beavers, Manhattan's first great export commodity; left and right are barrels of flour, an important staple during the English period. On either side of the shield are two men: to the viewer's left, a Dutch/English sailor, who not only represents the city's importance as a port, but recognizes the idea that all its non–Native American inhabitants have come from across the sea.* To the viewer's right is a Native American—decked out in true "noble savage" style, with

---

*The Algonquin-speaking Native Americans who lived here called the Dutch *swannekens*, meaning "people of salt." This is generally accepted to mean that the natives recognized the Europeans as people from across the ocean.

1

headdress and bow—representing the people the Europeans displaced. At the top of the seal originally sat a British crown, which was replaced after 1783 with an American bald eagle. Finally, at the bottom of the seal is the date of the city's founding.

It is difficult, however, to pin down the actual year of the city's birth. During the British period, the seal was dated 1686, the year Governor Thomas Dongan received an official charter. Later, the date was changed to 1664, the year the Dutch colony of New Amsterdam was conquered by the English and renamed New York. However, in 1975—on what was dubbed the 350th anniversary of the official establishment of New Amsterdam—the date was changed to 1625 to recognize the Dutch contributions to the city's founding.

But to many, even that date is too late. They push the beginning back to 1609, the year Henry Hudson's ship *Halve Maen* entered Manhattan's harbor, which led to European colonization. (New York has long celebrated this year. It hosted an elaborate Hudson-Fulton Festival in 1909 and a Hudson-Fulton-Champlain festival in 2009.) Of course, by 1609 people had been living in and around what would become modern-day New York City for upward of 11,000 years.

All of which is to say, picking a "beginning" is somewhat arbitrary. For our purposes—since this is a book of history that you can see and experience—we begin with Henry Hudson and the coming of the Dutch. Not only does this reflect the fact that few examples of our geological past are visible, it also points to the more grievous truth that there are hardly any traces left of the city's long and rich Native American heritage. It's somewhat heart-stopping to think that Europeans have only inhabited this area for less than four centuries and in that time have erased millennia of human habitation by the Lenape and others who preceded us.

While these first 21 chapters cover a great span of years—nearly half of the city's European history—each place and story they tell is fundamental to understanding the city. Indeed, examining Manhattan's early history presents in wonderful microcosm the brash history of young America, which had its economic and political roots firmly tied to New York.

1 *Manna-hata*: New York Before the Europeans

Walking through Times Square, surrounded by concrete, traffic, steel, and neon, it can be difficult to conjure up what this same tract of land must have looked like in 1608—a mere 400 years ago—before the arrival of Europeans. What would we see if we could strip away the generations of urbanization and return Manhattan to its pre-contact glory?

New Yorkers often wonder about what was here before. It can be tempting to invoke an Eden-on-the-Hudson, where wild animals roamed freely through tall forests and verdant meadows. And Manhattan did have all those things—but for nearly 11,000 years before Henry Hudson [2] there were also people using the land and altering it for their own benefit.

At the end of the last Ice Age (ca. 20,000 years ago), the Wisconsin glacier began a slow retreat, revealing the deep fjord that we now call the Hudson River. Exerting tremendous pressure as it moved, the glacier also scraped away layers of sediment, leaving parts of the island of Manhattan with exposed bedrock. This bedrock, called Manhattan schist,* is easily seen today in Central Park and Morningside Park [73], where vast pieces of rock rise from the ground dramatically. Other remnants of glaciation can also be seen at the southern end of Central Park's Sheep Meadow [151], where a line of boulders marches from the southwest, crossing the footpath that borders the bottom of the meadow. These are glacial erratics, non-native stones that were deposited here by the ice floe.

As the glacier departed, the first Native Americans were arriving, but very little is known about these settlers. Clovis point spearheads and other stone tools found in Staten Island in the 1950s place people in the area about 11,000 years ago. Scant evidence exists of population migrations and changes over the next 10 millennia, but many archaeologists agree that Native Americans lived in and around the area continuously until the arrival of European settlers. In the 17th century, these inhabitants were part of a larger group of Algonquin speakers; they referred to themselves as Lenape ("the people") or Munsee (their language group). Tribal names, such as Canarsie or Hackensack, are a European creation, and were likely place names or family groups.

Today, though there are still some Lenape descendants in and around the New York region, the most vivid reminder of the city's native past can be found in words. The most common of these is, of course, Manhattan—a word that today is known around the world but which has never been adequately defined. Because of differences in dialect and the general inability of most Europeans to correctly hear and reproduce Algonquin words, we will never know for certain what it signified. One Lenape word, *menatay*, means "island"; another, *mahatuouh*, is "the place for wood gathering"; and a third, *mahahach-*

---

*Schist, a metamorphic rock, is similar to gneiss and marble and often reveals embedded minerals. Manhattan schist is usually rich in mica.

A typical European view of a Lenape settlement

tanienk, is usually translated as "place of general inebriation." But none of these are *Manna-hata*, the first words ever written down by a European to name the island.

In the 19th century, Manhattan was often poetically translated as something along the lines of "island of gentle rolling hills." However, that translation has given way to a pithier definition, "rock island." While today the bedrock is really only visible in the parks and a few other places, 400 years ago it would have been the island's most salient feature, making it distinct from the less rocky, more arable land surrounding it in what we would today call New Jersey and Long Island.

〜 Thinking of Manhattan as "rock island" helps shape our understanding of how the island was used. Conventional wisdom has long held that the Lenape must have been farmers, and that corn, the great American grain, must have been their staple crop. But archaeological evidence, which is undeniably slight, suggests that agriculture did not play a large role in the local diet until after European arrivals. Instead, Manhattan would have been a place of hunting, foraging, and, most important, fishing.*

The rivers that surround Manhattan were central to life, from the wide array of fish to the oyster beds in the harbor (which have recently been estimated to have been the largest in the world). The wide river on the island's western edge—today known as the Hudson—was called Muhheakuntuck ("the river that flows two ways"), and it took on mythic overtones for the Lenape. The legend went that they had been told in a vision to journey until they found such a river and to settle there. At its mouth, as it empties into New York Harbor, the river is a tidal estuary, so affected by the ocean that significant tidal activity reaches 150 miles upriver, all the way to Troy, New York. The river remains brackish for 60 miles, to present-day Newburgh. To casual observers, the river's odd flow is most visible in winter, when it is dotted with ice floes; as the tide goes out, the floes move slowly downstream as one might expect. But when the tide turns, the ice changes direction and begins to float lazily back upstream.

Other rivers and streams were equally important, though the ones

---

*The Wildlife Conservation Society, under the direction of Eric W. Sanderson, is at work on the Mannahatta Project, using computer modeling to return Manhattan to its pre–1609 state and examine what flora and fauna would have been here for the Native Americans.

on Manhattan have all either been obliterated or are now underground. Maiden Lane in the Financial District was once a path along a small stream named for the young Dutch women who went there to do the wash. Even today, walking through this part of town, it is easy to imagine the banks of this little river sloping downward to the vanished streambed.

Perhaps the most famous stream is in Greenwich Village. Just south of Washington Square lies tiny Minetta Lane. Intersecting it is a one-block thoroughfare, Minetta Street, and a century ago, there was also still a Minetta Court and a Minetta Place, all of them coming together to form a strange, serpentine pattern. Those streets mark the onetime course of the Minetta brook, a small stream that still runs in the storm drains below the pavement. (Some claim that Minetta is a Lenape word, but in fact it's an English corruption of the Dutch name for the creek, *mintje kill*, "tiny stream.")

Other nearby streets, like Mac-Dougal Alley, Washington Mews, and Stuyvesant Street, likely made up a Lenape trail that served as a canoe portage so that people heading back and forth between what we now call Brooklyn and New Jersey would not have to row around the southern tip of the island. Likewise, Chinatown's Canal Street—though built in the early 1800s [22]—was originally part of a waterway that may have allowed natives to sail straight through the island at high tide.

↝ But everything ancient is not gone. There are living things, too, to remind New Yorkers of their past. In Washington Square is an old elm tree sometimes erroneously called the "Hangman's Elm" [see 35]. The tree certainly dates back to the Dutch, and may, in fact, be even older, a sentry that has watched over the area since it was a Lenape encampment known as Sapokanikan. In Inwood Hill Park, at Manhattan's northern edge, stands the Clove—an old-growth forest of oak, hickory, and dogwood. In the early 20th century, Lenape artifacts were excavated in the park. A short walk from the Clove, there's a plaque marking the spot where Dutch governor Peter Minuit supposedly purchased the island from the natives for $24 worth of beads [3]. While historians today tend to think the sale actually happened in the vicinity of Battery Park, it is truly moving to come to Inwood Hill Park and stand in the Clove—with not a steel-frame skyscraper or neon sign in sight—and experience, if only for a brief moment, the landscape the Lenape were selling to Minuit nearly 400 years ago.

2 Henry Hudson's Great Voyage

It's hard to decide where to place Henry Hudson in the pantheon of early American explorers. Like all of them, he was essentially sailing blindly into *terra incognita*. Had he missed the entrance to New York Harbor and sailed home, he'd be little more than a footnote, perhaps known better for the way he died than the way he lived. (Hudson was a bit of a boor. On a later voyage in 1611, his crew, sick of him, mutinied and sent him overboard in Hudson's Bay, Canada—but that's another story.)

Instead, Hudson *did* sail into

the harbor, spied Manhattan, and proceeded up the Muhheakuntuck River [1], now known in his honor as the Hudson River. (Hudson himself more grandiloquently called it "the Great River of the Mountains"—a reminder that the Catskills, which he passed as he sailed north, are taller than any mountains in Northern Europe except those in Norway.)

But Hudson wasn't the first of New York's "discoverers." That honor goes to Giovanni da Verrazzano, a Florentine navigator who arrived in the waters off Staten Island in 1524.* Verrazzano was employed by François I, the French monarch who was also Leonardo da Vinci's patron. Like other 16th-century sovereigns, François I dispatched navigators to various corners of the earth to map territorial claims. Maps were exceptionally valuable and jealously protected; they asserted ownership, provided directions for future navigators, and gave access to the precious natural resources the Europeans hoped to find in the New World.

It is unclear how far into New York harbor Verrazzano ventured, but what is clear is that he surprisingly mistook it for a lake and turned back before sighting the Muhheakuntuck. (Verrazzano's most noteworthy contribution was claiming Newfoundland for the French crown.)**

Even less remembered is Esteban Gómez, the Portuguese navigator who was sailing at the same time as Verrazzano. He sighted the Muhheakuntuck in 1525 and named it the Rio San Antonio. In Spain, cartographer Diego Ribeiro used Gómez's information to produce the first reliable map of the entire eastern seaboard. On it, the area around New York is labeled *Tierra de Estevan Gómez*. However, Spain never pressed its territorial claims, no doubt in part because of the map's caption: "Land of Esteban Gómez, discovered by him in 1525, by order of His Majesty; abundance of trees, game, salmon, turbot, and soles, but no gold is found."

⌁ Eighty-four years then passed before Hudson's arrival in the Muhheakuntuck—and it's likely that no European saw the river in the intervening decades. It's equally likely that no Native Americans were still alive who had seen a European ship. In the years between Verrazzano and Hudson, the natives felt the devastating effects of European contact—by some estimates almost 90 percent of the indigenous population had died from European-borne diseases between 1492 and 1600.

What Hudson had come looking for was not Manhattan, but rather the fabled shortcut connecting the Atlantic to the Pacific and thus to the Spice Islands, Europe's largest source of luxury import goods in the 16th century.

Sailing under the flag of his native England, Hudson had twice before tried to find this passage.

---

*The spot where Verrazzano anchored is near the base of the Verrazzano-Narrows Bridge; note, however, that the city spelled the explorer's name wrong when it named the bridge.

**Verrazzano, along with Henry Hudson and other early American explorers, is commemorated in the murals in the rotunda of the old U.S. Custom House on Bowling Green [123]. A statue of Verrazzano, originally erected in 1909 and, as of this writing, stuck in storage, will ultimately be returned to Battery Park.

Each time, he had sailed east in the hope that a northeast passage might present itself beyond Russia's Barents Sea. This time, however, he was employed by the Dutch East India Company, which had established a virtual monopoly on the spice trade, and captained a ship called the *Halve Maen* ("Half Moon"). He would sail toward Russia one more time, but if that failed, he would turn and head west. His friend John Smith (of Pocahontas fame) had written to him about a river connecting the Atlantic and the Pacific that lay at the northern edge of Virginia's territory. So, when the Russian plan failed for yet a third time, Hudson turned the *Halve Maen* around and headed toward North America.

Hudson's arrival in New York harbor was inauspicious; the ship ran aground at Sandy Hook, just south of Staten Island. On September 11, 1609,* the ship headed through the Narrows into the harbor. From there, it entered the Muhheakuntuck, the "Great" River. Hudson sailed as far as present-day Albany before realizing that while he'd found a great river, it was not a passage to the Spice Islands. So Hudson turned around, sailed back to the harbor, out the Narrows, and home. The Dutch East India Company was angry at him—both that he'd disobeyed its orders by gallivanting off to North America *and* that he hadn't found a northeast passage. However, a number of Dutch merchants heard of Hudson's voyage and had a different idea. In 1610 and again in 1613, ships sailed from

the Netherlands to further explore the region. They weren't at all interested in a northwest passage; they were coming instead for a crucial commodity found in massive quantity right there along Hudson's Great River—beavers.

Beaver pelts were a coveted import good in Europe, perhaps second only to spices. Men of status wore beaver-felt hats and trimmed

Henry Hudson's ship, the *Halve Maen*

their jackets with fine fur. In buttoned-down, Calvinist countries like the Netherlands, a lace collar and fur-trimmed jacket were probably the most immediately recognizable symbols of wealth. Hudson's discovery of plentiful beaver on the banks of the Muhheakuntuck solved a growing Dutch dilemma about how to procure enough pelts for the country's burgeoning middle class to properly show off its newfound prosperity.

∼ Today, the best way to get a sense of what Hudson experienced when he arrived, the "very good land to fall in with, and a pleasant land to see"

---

*Some have found it an intriguing coincidence that the hijackers who destroyed the World Trade Center in 2001 [180] chose to do it on New York's birthday. But it is surely only a coincidence—even most well-educated New Yorkers wouldn't have known the significance of this 17th-century September 11.

described in the journal of first mate Robert Juet, is to head to Fort Tryon Park in Upper Manhattan and look across at the Palisades in New Jersey. The view here was preserved by John D. Rockefeller, Jr., who originally had plans to develop the Fort Tryon site for personal use before ceding it to the city. It was somewhere near here that the *Halve Maen* anchored during its journey home. Juet, describing the New Jersey Palisades or the cliffs below Fort Tryon, noted in his journal:

> [W]e saw a very good piece of ground; and hard by it there was a cliff that looked of the colour of white green, as though it were either a copper or silver mine; and I think it to be one of them by the trees that grow upon it; for they be all burned, and the other places are green as grass; it is on that side of the river that is called *Manna-hata*.

Thus, on October 2, 1609, Manna-hata had its name written down by Europeans for the first time and Manhattan was born.

3 $24 Worth of Beads

Perhaps the most enduring story about early New York is its founding myth: In 1626, Dutch governor Peter Minuit bought Manhattan from the local Lenape tribe for $24 in assorted beads and trinkets. And, like many myths, it contains quite a bit of truth.

Between Henry Hudson's arrival in 1609 [2] and Minuit's purchase in 1626, Manhattan shifted from being nominal Dutch territory into an occupied colony. However, the earliest Dutch traders didn't feel the need

to settle on Manhattan. They would come, barter with the Lenape for valuable furs, and leave again. Then in 1620 everything changed, in part because of the Pilgrims.

The Pilgrims' voyage to the New World, which started out from the Dutch city of Leiden, where they'd lived in exile, worried the fur traders. In the common Thanksgiving story, it's usually left out that the Pilgrims weren't en route to Massachusetts at all (which lay outside English territory) but instead had been granted the island at the northern limit of the Virginia colony: Manhattan. (Virginia's claim to Manhattan was long-standing. When John Smith wrote to Henry Hudson about a northwest passage, it was because the river he was describing was part of Virginia.)

After a rocky start, where the Pilgrims were forced to abandon one of their two ships—perhaps because of sabotage by Dutch merchants—they continued on to the New World on the *Mayflower*, disembarking in Plymouth after a halfhearted attempt to sail farther south. When it became clear that the English settlers were not going to move to Manhattan, Dutch traders hurriedly began staking a firmer claim to their territory. In 1621, the Dutch West India Company was chartered by the Dutch government to regularize and promote trade in the New World. Then in 1624, the first full-time settlers arrived on the ships *Eendracht* ("Unity") and *Nieu Nederland* ("New Netherland"). These first arrivals were mostly Walloons—Protestant refugees from modern-day Belgium—and they settled both on Nut Island (today Governors Island) at the mouth of the river and at the northern edge of

Peter Minuit strikes the $24 deal for the island of Manhattan.

Dutch territory, Fort Orange, site of present-day Albany.

The captain of the *Nieu Nederland*, Cornelis Mey, became the de facto first governor of the new colony, which, like his ship, came to be known as New Netherland. (Mey is remembered today as namesake of Cape May, New Jersey.) In 1625, Willem Verhulst, the colony's second leader, made the wise decision to move the settlers to the southern tip of Manhattan and to build a permanent fortification there, Fort Amsterdam, and to name the town New Amsterdam.

～ Some also believe that it was Willem Verhulst who successfully negotiated the purchase of Manhattan—not his successor, Peter Minuit—but there is no evidence of this. Indeed, there is no evidence of the sale at all, as there is no longer any deed. In 1821, an official in The Hague, looking for more cabinet space, auctioned off a vast quantity of the Dutch West India Company's papers. What we have is thirdhand: one letter survives, dated November 1626, from company official Peter Schagen in Amsterdam, relating the news he'd heard from a ship recently returned from the colony: "[T]hey have bought the island Manhattes* from the wild men for the value of sixty guilders."

In 1844, New York State historian John Romeyn Brodhead announced to the New-York Historical Society his discovery of this letter and it was Brodhead who converted 60 guilders into $24, a figure that has had remarkable traction. It is better, however, to think in terms of purchasing power: In 1626, 60 guilders would buy 2,400 tankards of beer—not exactly expensive, but certainly more than an average laborer would have in his pocket at any given time.

---

*There was no accepted spelling of Manhattan in the colony's earliest years: Manhattes, Manhattoes, Manna Hatta, and other variations are all seen in early records.

On the other hand, if you were rich, it was a different story: 60 guilders was less than 4 percent of the fee Rembrandt would soon be paid to paint the famous *Night Watch*. The same was true in 1844 of $24. It was the equivalent of about two months' salary for an average New Yorker. But, of course, Brodhead's audience at the historical society was anything but average, and it likely seemed like small change to them.

The goods Minuit used in trade would certainly have been enumerated in the now-lost deed. To judge from contemporary documents, they would have been similar to what was paid for Staten Island: "Duffels [heavy cloth, as in a duffel bag], Kittles [kettles], Axes, Hoes, Wampum, Drilling Awls, Jews harps, and diverse other small wares." The only item on that list remotely like a bead is wampum, the strings of shells that the natives valued as prestige items and that the Dutch ultimately adopted as their unit of basic currency. (The other currency in New Amsterdam, the beaver pelt, was worth about two guilders and thus too valuable for many day-to-day transactions—not to mention far too unwieldy for grocery shopping.)

By the time Schagen's letter referencing the sale surfaced in the 1840s, it was commonly accepted that the Lenape had been swindled by the Dutch. Not, perhaps, because the Dutch were conniving by nature,* but because the natives simply didn't know any better. It assuaged the guilt of some whites to believe that the Lenape's disappearance from New York wasn't due to disease or European encroachment on their territory but instead because they were inherently inferior—that they were too simpleminded to know that they were giving up Manhattan for a worthless sum of shiny beads.

The Lenape have long had their defenders too. It's reasonable to argue that since they had no concept of individual land ownership, they couldn't really *sell* Manhattan in the first place. Likewise, some scholars believe there were no permanent Lenape settlements on the island (at least not in the parts used by the Dutch), which would mean that whoever transacted the sale with Minuit wasn't a Manhattan resident. In this version of the story, the natives are the clever ones, selling land that people don't live on and that can't be owned in the first place.

It is impossible to know what truly happened at that bargaining table, but it seems likely that both sides were fully aware of the compact they were signing. The natives—whether they lived on Manhattan or not—extensively used the island for hunting and fishing; what they were ceding to the Dutch were certain land-use rights. Peter Minuit, in turn, must have understood that while the natives were allowing the Dutch to settle on the island and use the land, they were not simply going to clear off and disappear.

~ It is also impossible to know where the bargain was struck, though people have tried for years. A plaque in Inwood Hill Park in Upper

---

*It was also commonly accepted that the Dutch had driven such a hard bargain because they were cheap. The pejorative expression "Dutch treat" still persists to remind people that supposedly a Dutchman will never pick up a check.

The Netherlands Memorial Flagpole
in Battery Park

ruffed collar, forever caught in the act of handing over the $24 worth of beads to an anonymous Native American in a loincloth.

4 Peter Stuyvesant

In the 25 years following Peter Minuit's purchase of Manhattan in 1626 [3], the colony transformed from a raw frontier trading post to a quaint Dutch town. (The earliest view of the city, drawn ca. 1651, shows the thriving small port town, with a fort, church, and stepped-gable houses.) New Netherland, as the entire colony was known, stretched all the way from modern-day Hartford, Connecticut, in the north to New Castle, Delaware, on the mouth of the Delaware River. But with the exception of Beverwijck ("beaver town"), on the site of present-day Albany, all the other communities were small Dutch farmsteads, trading outposts, or border fortifications. Manhattan was the colony's true hub and a prosperous, small settlement.

Not that New Amsterdam hadn't been without its troubles. Minuit's successor, Sebastiaen Krol, was only around for a year. Then came Wouter van Twiller, best known for accumulating a small fortune in New Amsterdam property during his four years in charge. He was followed by Willem Kieft, whose disastrous relations with the natives led to Kieft's War—two years of intermittent hostilities that claimed many lives and left the Dutch West India Company and New Amsterdam on the verge of falling apart.

Enter Peter Stuyvesant.

Stuyvesant began his career with the Dutch West India Company as a

Manhattan—over 10 miles north of the New Amsterdam settlement—claims to mark the spot where the deal was done [see 1]. This might be true if Minuit was dealing with the particular community that was encamped there at the time, but it's just as plausible that the Lenape went to where the Dutch lived, not the other way around. That would put the transaction someplace in Lower Manhattan. The corner of Whitehall and State is often cited for no good reason except that it would have been about the southernmost point on the island. (Today it stands opposite Peter Minuit Plaza, a forlorn little tract of land often swallowed up by construction equipment.)

A more fitting tribute to Minuit —and to the myth—stands nearby in Battery Park. The Netherlands Memorial Flagpole was erected in 1926 to mark the 300th anniversary of the sale. Here Minuit can be seen wearing his fancy buckled shoes and

The earliest known view of New Amsterdam (ca. 1651)

clerk and rose quickly. He had many admirable traits in the eyes of his superiors: he was a stern Calvinist with some university education and plenty of ambition. His first posting was as a company agent on the island of Pavonia, a remote outpost 300 miles off the coast of Brazil. In 1635, Stuyvesant was transferred to mainland Brazil and three years after that, he was commissioned to oversee the company's interests in Curaçao.

At the time, Curaçao was the company's prized Caribbean possession. Its sheltered harbors provided protection for the Dutch privateers who attacked Spanish ships;* Stuyvesant found Curaçao desolate and inhospitable, but it was a major step forward in his career. Soon, he was governor of Curaçao, Aruba, and Bonaire and in 1644, the Dutch government dispatched him on a mili-

tary mission to retake the island of St. Maarten, which the Dutch had lost to the Spanish in 1633. Stuyvesant, however, was more of a businessman than a military leader, and his inexperience showed. The Spanish garrison on St. Maarten easily outgunned the Dutch, and on the first day of the siege a cannonball landed squarely on the governor's right leg, crushing it below the knee.

He valiantly—or stupidly—continued his attack for nearly a month before finally retreating. Curaçao's barber/surgeon removed the governor's right leg below the knee and as soon as he could, Stuyvesant boarded a ship back to Amsterdam, where he was fitted with a wooden prosthesis. (It's notable that other passengers—presumably healthier than the wounded Stuyvesant—died of various shipboard illnesses en route to the Netherlands; that Stuyvesant sur-

---

*The Spanish and the Dutch had been at war since the Protestant Netherlands declared its independence from Catholic Spain in 1581.

The Stadt Huis (center) on Pearl Street

vived showed his remarkable physical constitution.)

So, just as Kieft's War was winding down in New Amsterdam, the Dutch West India Company suddenly had to figure out something do with Stuyvesant, their wounded war veteran. In 1646, it appointed him Kieft's successor and a year later, he arrived in New Amsterdam. A later observer commented that when Stuyvesant disembarked from his ship, the *Great Crow*, he strutted around in front of the assembled crowd and promised them, "I will be a father to you all."

Little did he, or they, know that he was also to be Manhattan's last Dutch leader.

5 The Stadt Huis and the City of New Amsterdam

The arrival of Peter Stuyvesant in 1647 [4] brought with it a relative return to prosperity and growth in New Amsterdam. While beaver pelts were still the Dutch West India Company's main commodity, New Netherland boasted farmers, artisans, tavern keepers, shipwrights, bakers, and a host of other tradesmen (and tradeswomen). It also boasted some of the New World's first slaves, many of them imported by the company from the Caribbean or directly from Africa in what was becoming one of the company's most profitable industries.

However, the town was still a company town, and not everybody agreed with Stuyvesant's single-minded way of running things, which included instituting a curfew, adding a second sermon on Sundays, and stepping up the penalties for serving beer on the Sabbath. Soon after he'd arrived, Stuyvesant had appointed a board of nine men to advise him; he didn't have much interest in following the colonists' advice, but knew the value of putting on a show. The board's leader, Adriaen van der Donck,* was a wealthy lawyer who

---

*Van der Donck wrote the most important firsthand description of the colony, *A Description of New Netherland*. He must have been quite a character—he was known as the *johnkeer* ("squire") and his family farm came to be known as the Johnkeer's, or as we call it today, Yonkers.

owned a vast tract of land north of Manhattan.

Under Van der Donck's direction, the board stopped giving Stuyvesant advice and instead proposed severing control of Manhattan from the company—and thus, from Stuyvesant. Seeking to quell this little rebellion, Stuyvesant stormed into the board's headquarters and confiscated its notes and papers. For good measure, he had Van der Donck expelled from the board and refused to give back the documents.

Not surprisingly, this didn't help Stuyvesant's cause. New Amsterdam's pastor began publicly preaching in favor of liberation from company control, and the board prepared a petition that Van der Donck personally delivered to the Netherlands. The petition outlined many reasons the colony was failing, including poor governance, a paucity of farmers, the general scarcity of goods, and what they felt was a growing superiority complex among the Native Americans with whom they traded.

Though Van der Donck made a compelling case, Stuyvesant ultimately prevailed, arguing that relinquishing company control would be ruinous. Then war broke out between England and the Netherlands [6], thus shifting everyone's priorities. The Dutch government's one concession was to grant the citizens of Manhattan a limited municipal government—with Stuyvesant at the helm. On February 2, 1653, New Amsterdam officially became the first legally chartered city in America.

What this meant in practical terms was that Stuyvesant would still rule, but he would be advised by a council of five *schepens* (aldermen), two *burgomasters* (chief magistrates), and a *schout-fiscal* (sheriff and district attorney)—all appointed by him. This body served as a civil court, ruling on everything from petty grievances to capital crimes. Lacking a proper place to meet, Stuyvesant granted them the use of the city-run tavern on Pearl Street, which was renamed the Stadt Huis (City Hall). In 1656, a special bell was added, which rang to signal the beginning of the court's sessions.*

∾ In 1979, the lots facing Pearl Street between Broad Street and Coenties Slip were being developed for a skyscraper. Knowing the area was the site of the Stadt Huis and other early Dutch buildings, the city mandated an archaeological excavation, traces of which can still be seen today. While no remnants of the Stadt Huis were unearthed, the team did find the foundations of its neighbor, the Lovelace Tavern, a 1670 structure built during the administration of Francis Lovelace, the second English governor of New York [see 9], making the foundation stones on view at this site today some of the oldest remnants of European settlement on Manhattan.

Where the Stadt Huis would have stood there is an outline in the pavement in yellow brick. This modest square is all that is left of the beginnings of the political life of America's greatest city.

---

*Most important to the authors, in 1658, the Stadt Huis became the home of Johannes Nevius, James's great-great-great-great-great-great-great-great grandfather, who was the last secretary of the city of New Amsterdam.

6 The Dutch Erect the Wall on Wall Street

Ever since New Amsterdam's founding, the Dutch had been worried about attack. The first major building in the city was Fort Amsterdam, at the base of Broadway;* its four bastions faced the East and Hudson rivers and it housed a garrison of soldiers supplied by the Dutch government. The company's main concern was protecting the harbor—and, by extension, its shipping monopoly—from pirates and foreign invaders, primarily the Spanish and the English.

By 1652, relations between the Netherlands and England had soured to the point that these two Protestant allies were at war. This First Anglo-Dutch War was limited primarily to naval sorties in the North Sea, but the conflict had a global reach, and threatened to upset the political balance in the Far East, the Caribbean, and North America. When word of the war reached New Amsterdam, Peter Stuyvesant and the fledgling city government [5] hastily voted to build a wall.

The wall's primary purpose was to protect the town from an overland invasion from the north. Stuyvesant envisioned English citizens from Connecticut—whose border with New Netherland was poorly defined and a source of contention—marching onto Manhattan and down the island to the city. In March 1653, funds were collected by public subscription to pay for a nine-foot-high wooden bulwark along the northern fringe of the settlement. The path in front of it was soon nicknamed "the wall street." The palisade ran from river to river, from what today is the rear of the Trinity Church graveyard to the corner of Pearl Street. (Everything east and west of those spots is landfill.)

The wall had two major prob-

The original wall on Wall Street

lems: it wasn't needed and it didn't work. The First Anglo-Dutch War didn't spill over into the New World, and so New Amsterdam was spared attack. When the city *was* attacked two years later by Native Americans [8], the attackers simply walked around the wall.

Despite persistent rumors to the contrary, no trace of Wall Street's

---

*This is where Bowling Green Park [13; 15] and the old U.S. Custom House [123] now stand.

wall exists today beyond its name, known worldwide as the Financial District's most famous street. The wall was torn down by the end of the 17th century, its wood used for other construction or kindling.

~ Wall Street is just one of the many street names in Lower Manhattan that recalls the city's Dutch history. Federal Hall National Memorial [18] sits at the corner of Wall and Nassau streets—Nassau being a territory controlled by William of Orange, founder of the modern Netherlands. When Nassau crosses Wall, it becomes Broad Street (not to be confused with Broadway). Broad Street is so wide because it was once the city's canal, the Heere Gracht ("Gentlemen's Canal"), built in the 1650s to remind people of home.

Stone Street, a few blocks south of Wall Street, was the first paved street in the Dutch city. (It runs behind the site of the Stadt Huis.) Mill Lane, which intersects Stone, led to the horse mill [see 7]. And Pearl Street, the commercial hub of New Amsterdam, was so-called because when the Dutch arrived they found it piled with oyster shells, the remains of centuries of Lenape fishing in the area. (American oysters don't actually produce pearls; the street was really being named "Mother of Pearl" Street.)

7 Refugees: The First Jews in New Amsterdam

The first Jews came to New Amsterdam by mistake.

During the Inquisition, a number of Spanish and Portuguese Sephardic Jews had immigrated to the Netherlands to escape persecution. For the Dutch, accepting the Jews was a poke in the eye to Catholic Spain, and the Dutch were, on the whole, a tolerant people. The Jews settled into a comfortable—and mostly quiet—existence.

However, when the Dutch wrested control of northern Brazil from the Portuguese in 1630, about 600 Dutch Jews immigrated there. When Brazil returned to the Portuguese in 1654, these Jews decided, along with most of the rest of the Dutch population, to repatriate to the Netherlands. Sixteen ships were outfitted for the voyage. Fifteen made it back to Europe without trouble; the sixteenth was captured by Spanish pirates and hauled toward safe harbor in the Caribbean. The ship contained a small number of Christian families and 23 Jews.

Before the Spanish could reach their destination, they were set upon by a French privateer, the *Saint Charles*, which captured the vessel. The French captain, Jacques de la Motthe, told the captives he would gladly sail them to New Amsterdam for the fee of 2,500 guilders. Upon arrival in New Amsterdam in the late summer of 1654, Captain de la Motthe demanded his payment, but the Jews, pooling their funds, only managed to pay 933 guilders. An auction was held, and every piece of personal property the Jews owned was sold off—and *still* they owed nearly 500 guilders.

At the request of de la Motthe, New Amsterdam's court [5] arrested two of the Jewish refugees and held them in jail as collateral. It was only when the sailors of the *Saint Charles* agreed to forgo their share of the payment that the situation was resolved.

Penniless, homeless, and stuck in a strange and hostile foreign city, these few families must have been over-whelmed by their predicament.

Peter Stuyvesant [4] wasn't pleased. He was worried that if he accepted Jews he'd be forced to accept everyone else, and he immediately appealed to the Dutch government to have the refugees forcibly removed from his island. To his dismay, the government refused, in part because too many Jewish guilders had financed the Dutch West India Company. Stuyvesant was told to let the Jews live in New Amsterdam, perhaps in a ghetto of their own.

Stuyvesant—always putting the company's interests first—did what he could to ease the Jews into the life of Manhattan. To his credit, he realized that a ghetto was the last thing the small town needed, and the Jews rented, leased, and bought property throughout New Netherland. Stuyvesant also granted them space for a synagogue, the upstairs portion of the old horse mill on what is today South William Street. While some have pointed to this choice of venue as an example of Stuyvesant's anti-Semitism, the space had a long history of religious use—when the first Protestant settlers arrived in New Amsterdam 30 years earlier, the mill doubled as the city's first church.

No trace of the original mill exists, though tiny Mill Lane in the Financial District would have led to it. The congregation, however, is flourishing. Known as Shearith Israel, it worships from a beautiful Gilded Age synagogue on the Upper West Side.

8 The Peach War

Even as New Amsterdam expanded under Peter Stuyvesant's tenure [4], its main export commodity remained beaver pelts, which were trapped almost exclusively by Native Americans. It is remarkable that relations with local tribes were so often hostile considering that natives were doing the important labor. During New Netherland's tenure it had three outright wars with the local tribes: Kieft's War; the Esopus War in the early 1660s;* and the most famous of them all, the Peach War.

Peter Stuyvesant's attitude toward the natives was a marked improvement over that of predecessor Willem Kieft. Established trading partnerships continued, clashes were few, and when they occurred, Stuyvesant attempted to deal one-on-one with the *sachems* (tribal leaders). He also tried to remove guns, ammunition, and liquor from the list of items the Dutch would trade with natives, but those mandates were heeded only sporadically.

In fact, Stuyvesant's time wasn't spent finessing relations with the natives, but instead with his English neighbors to the north and with the Swedes who—with the assistance of Peter Minuit [3]—established a colony in Dutch territory along the Delaware River. In September 1655, Stuyvesant mustered an expedition of soldiers and able-bodied male citizens to sail south to confront the fledgling Swedish colony there.

As soon as they were gone, the Peach War began.

Less a war than a terrorist attack, it was instigated by a coalition of natives

---

*Esopus is in the vicinity of modern-day Kingston, New York.

from the Hudson River valley. They found a pretext for the attack when a colonist named Hendrick van Dyck, who had noticed a Native American woman stealing a peach from his orchard,* grabbed his gun and shot her. However, she was not alone—somewhere between 200 and 1,000 natives had beached their canoes nearby (neatly bypassing the wall that had been built to keep out invaders [6]).

The next morning before dawn, the streets of New Amsterdam filled with Native Americans. They broke into houses, ostensibly looking for Van Dyck to exact revenge, and caused a good deal of property damage, but no serious injuries. When they found Van Dyck later in the day, they shot him with an arrow—though not fatally—and injured another man. They then departed into the Hudson River.

Had the story ended there, the events might have faded from New Amsterdam's history. Instead, the natives headed for New Jersey, where a bloodbath began. One eyewitness wrote:

> In a moment a house at Hoboken was on fire, and the whole of Pavonia** was wrapt in flames. With the exception of Michel Jansen's family, every man was killed, together with all the cattle. A large number of women and children were taken prisoners.

From there, the natives crossed the harbor to Staten Island, where a similar scene ensued around the property of prominent citizen Cornelis Melyn. In the end, somewhere between 40 and 100 colonists were dead*** and at least 100 people—mostly women and children—were prisoners. The amount of property and livestock destroyed was almost unbearable. Scores of citizens from surrounding communities came to Manhattan to take refuge in Fort Amsterdam.

Word of the massacre was sent overland to Peter Stuyvesant, who sped up his negotiations with the Swedes and returned home. The destruction he saw upon his return caused him to write later, "It will not be the same flourishing state for several years."

Immediately, Stuyvesant vowed to do two things: strengthen the town's fortifications, which were obviously useless, and secure the release of the prisoners. It became an arms-for-hostages situation, and Stuyvesant, unwilling to risk the lives of any of the colonists, ultimately gave in to the natives' demands for gunpowder and ammunition. Not only did this earn the natives more munitions that they could have acquired on the black market, it showed the Dutch that Native Americans were still a force to be reckoned with. The colonization of New Netherland was less than three decades old and tentative in its success. The natives probably believed that an attack on the Dutch settlements around Manhattan would send settlers clamoring for return passage to the Netherlands. Indeed, if Stuyvesant hadn't immediately forbidden any ships from weighing

---

*Van Dyck's orchard would have been near the present-day corner of Exchange Alley and Trinity Place.

**In modern-day Jersey City.

***Though there is no hard evidence, it is plausible that Adriaen van der Donck [5] was killed during the Peach War.

anchor, a large percentage of the town might indeed have fled in the wake of the attacks, as they had done during Kieft's War a decade earlier. Had this happened, the Dutch West India Company could easily have decided to shut New Amsterdam down.

As it was, the history of New Amsterdam was already on a downward trajectory and though no one knew it at the time, less than ten years remained for the Dutch colony in America.

9 The Bloodless Coup: New Amsterdam Becomes New York

Throughout most of New Amsterdam's existence, England had not been a particularly grave threat. Mired in civil war from 1642 to 1651 (and under Oliver Cromwell's protectorate from 1653 to 1659), the English government barely had time to deal with its own colonists in Virginia and Massachusetts, let alone worry about a small Dutch port on the Hudson River.

However, the restoration of Charles II to the throne in 1660 changed that. The king's ministers—notably his brother, James, Duke of York*—had great territorial plans for the New World, which included complete English control of the area from Boston to the Carolinas. Hostilities had flared in 1652 during the First Anglo-Dutch War [6], but New Amsterdam didn't really begin to feel the pressure until 1664, when Captain John Scott from Southampton, Long Island, asked English citizens in New Netherland to proclaim him the president of Long Island, serving as a proxy for the Duke of York. For many, this was the first they knew that the duke had any designs on the area.

Despite having been sheltered in the Netherlands during Cromwell's interregnum (or, perhaps, because of it), the duke had a very low opinion of the Dutch. In March 1664, his brother the king granted him a remarkable charter for most of New England, including Massachusetts, Rhode Island, Connecticut, and—most particularly—New Netherland. The duke not only wanted to annoy the Dutch, he wanted to disrupt Dutch shipping, specifically between New Netherland, the Caribbean, and the African (or "Guinea") Coast. The duke was head of a syndicate called the Company of Royal Adventurers Trading into Africa (whose coinage, bearing his likeness, would soon come to be known as guineas) and the Dutch monopoly in African trading ports was hindering his ability to profit from slavery. If the taking of New Amsterdam could drive a stake into the heart of the Dutch West India Company, the duke would be delighted.

To conquer New Amsterdam, the duke dispatched Richard Nicolls, who had fought in the civil war and had, for his service, been elevated to the role of groom of the bedchamber (the knight in charge of dressing the duke). Nicolls was given four ships, approximately 600 soldiers, and instructions to keep New Amsterdam as intact as possible. He was, in effect, to treat the mission more like a hostile takeover by a rival corporation and less like a military attack.

---

*James would later become King James II.

Nicolls arrived in New Amsterdam in late August 1664. He came ashore at Gravesend, an English-dominated town in modern-day Brooklyn, where he was greeted by John Scott (the president of Long Island), Connecticut governor John Winthrop, and other English citizens. Nicolls sent Winthrop to negotiate with Stuyvesant, who was presented with a stark choice: (a) surrender, take an oath of allegiance to Charles II, and let everything else remain status quo, or (b) the English attack.

Stuyvesant, angry but pragmatic, chose option "a." In 23 Articles of Capitulation, he extracted concessions from the English, including forbidding them from quartering soldiers in civilian homes, and making them promise to quit the island if word arrived from Europe that the Dutch had won it back.

On September 8, 1664, with great pomp, Peter Stuyvesant and the Dutch garrison marched out of Fort Amsterdam and the flag of the Dutch West India Company was lowered for the last time. By nightfall, the cross of St. George was in its place and the town had a new name: New York, in honor of the duke, its new patron.

10 Peter Stuyvesant's Final Days on the Bowery

In its first years, the changeover from New Amsterdam to New York [9] had remarkably minimal effect on the day-to-day operations of the city. In 1665, the official language of government switched from Dutch to English, and Governor Richard Nicolls reneged on his promise not

to quarter troops, but the rhythms of daily life continued. Most important, there was not a mass exodus of Dutch immigrants back to the Netherlands. Even Peter Stuyvesant stayed behind. Though he was recalled to Amsterdam to explain why he'd so swiftly capitulated to the English, he eventually returned and settled into his retirement on his farm. Known as Bowery No. 1, it was one of six

Peter Stuyvesant

large farms originally established by the company. (Bowery is simply the English corruption of *bouwerij*, the Dutch word for "farm.") Stuyvesant purchased the northernmost of these farms in 1651, soon after his arrival as governor [4], so that his wife and small children would not have to live full-time in the crowded city. No one knows precisely where the farmhouse stood, but it would have been within walking distance of his private chapel, which was erected in 1660 on what is today the corner of East 10th Street and Second Avenue. The chapel became the final resting place of Peter Stuyvesant when he died on the farm in February 1672.

A century later, when the farm-house burned down, the chapel was donated by Stuyvesant's family to Trinity Church, Wall Street [11]. This was a sure sign that the religion of the Dutch (called the Reformed Church) had ceded its precedence to the religion of the English. Trinity tore down the old Dutch chapel and built St. Mark's in the Bowery in its place, preserving Peter Stuyvesant's grave, which is now marked with a stone slab that reads "In this Vault lies buried/PETRUS STUYVESANT/late Captain General and Governor in Chief of Amsterdam/in New Netherland and now called New York/and the Dutch West India Islands died in AD1672/aged 80 years."

There is one error here. The stone promotes the idea—widespread in the 19th century—that the governor would have been about 55 years old when he took over the colony in 1647 and thus 80 when he died. However, compelling evidence places his birth in 1612, meaning he was just 35 years old when he arrived in Manhattan—and just 60 years old when he died, which is more in keeping with life spans of the day. He must have seemed particularly obnoxious to his elders when he first stepped ashore in 1647 and proclaimed, "I will be a father to you all."

〜 A handful of other commemorations of Stuyvesant are scattered across the area that would have been his original farm. The most famous are the names of the roads that led to it, the Bowery and Stuyvesant Street. The Bowery today runs from Chatham Square to Astor Place, but what is now called Park Row (near City Hall) was part of the original Bowery Lane too. In Stuyvesant's

Stuyvesant's pear tree

day, a spur road would have connected the Bowery to the farm. The section of this road that remains is called Stuyvesant Street, which runs at an odd diagonal to the surrounding street grid, and was likely part of a much older Lenape trail that cut through the island here [1].

In St. Mark's churchyard, near Stuyvesant's grave, there is a portrait bust of the governor; it must hold some sort of record for the most text in the smallest font on a plaque. A few blocks up Second Avenue at Stuyvesant Square is a full-height statue of the governor done by Gertrude Vanderbilt Whitney, who is more famous for her eponymous museum. And a little bit farther north at what was the swampy, northern border of the property, sits elegant Gramercy Park [40].

But perhaps the most intriguing reminder of Stuyvesant's farm sits on the corner of Third Avenue and 13th Street. In the 1650s, Stuyvesant (or, more likely, one of his slaves) planted a pear tree here that continued to bear fruit until 1867, when it was felled in a wagon accident. (Just five years earlier, *Harper's Monthly* had called it the "oldest living thing in New York City," though it obviously didn't know about the Hangman's Elm [**35**].)

In 2003, Kiehl's, the venerable drugstore that has operated at that location since 1851, when the original tree was still in place, replanted a pear tree, and a couple of years later reinstalled the historical marker dedicated by the Holland Society. Inside, you can now buy soaps adorned with the image of the original tree.

11 Trinity Church and the Widow Bogardus's Farm

Arguably the first great change in New York under English rule was the expansion of religious freedom. The famously tolerant Dutch were only tolerant of non-Calvinist religions if they were practiced in secret, with the notable exception of New Amsterdam's Jews [**7**]. After the English takeover in 1664 [**9**], Lutheran, Methodist, and Baptist congregations soon established themselves. However, within a generation the most powerful church in town was Anglican, the official state religion.

In 1696, the first Anglican parish, Trinity, leased the city's burial ground at the rate of one peppercorn per year.* A year later, the church received its royal charter from William III and from that point forward only church members could be bur-

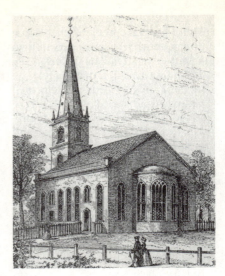

The original Trinity Church, Wall Street (built 1698 and enlarged in 1737)

ied in the churchyard. Not coincidentally, this was the same time that a separate "Negroes Burial Ground" was established outside the city [**12; 178**].

The original church, a simple stone and wood building, was erected in 1698 with both financial and material help from one of its richest congregants, Captain William Kidd, who just three years later would be hanged in London for piracy. Trinity quickly prospered. Six years after its construction, Queen Anne gave the parish an additional 215 acres of the crown's land, stretching from Wall Street north to the village of Greenwich [**30**]. Sixty-two of these acres had been once owned by a prominent Dutch colonist named Anneke Bogardus, the widow of one of the pastors of the Dutch church. In 1671,

---

*Nearby Bowling Green Park [13; 15], was also rented from the colony for a peppercorn per year.

five of the Widow Bogardus's six heirs conveyed the land to the crown, which, in turn, conveyed it to Trinity in 1705. The story should have ended there, but it didn't take long for some descendants of Anneke Bogardus to realize that Trinity was holding the most valuable real estate in the city—and it had once been *their* land. And, since one of the widow's descendants, Cornelis Bogardus, hadn't officially transferred his one-sixth claim in the property to the crown, perhaps there could be legal redress.

Over the next 150 years, the number of claimants—and the sheer audacity of their claims—multiplied. Each time, the courts ruled decisively in Trinity's favor, but that didn't stop other people from rushing to prove their connection to the Widow Bogardus and her land. And, just as people were beginning to lose interest, someone dreamed up the idea that Anneke was actually the illegitimate daughter of William of Orange, founder of the Netherlands, and thus a princess, which only intensified the clamor for the land. (Meanwhile, the claimants now wanted more than Cornelis Bogardus's one-sixth claim to the original property; in their minds, they were now owners of all of Trinity Church's vast holdings.)

Considering Trinity's 19th-century prominence and wealth [**44**], it isn't surprising that there were so many lawsuits. Even today, while Trinity has sold off much of its original royal grant, the church still owns real estate with annual rent rolls in the tens of millions of dollars. This makes it the wealthiest church in New York—and probably the single wealthiest individual parish in the world.

The original Trinity building is gone, burned in the fire that broke out during the Revolution [**16**]. However, there are still visible headstones in the churchyard that date back to the parish's founding. There is even a stone dated 1681, when the yard was still a municipal graveyard, making it one of the only remnants from the heart of the old English colonial city.

12 The Alleged Slave Rebellion of 1741

By 1741, New York boasted a growing economic prominence, an ideal location for shipping goods from Europe, the south, and the Caribbean, and a population of nearly 10,000 people. Approximately one in five of those 10,000 New Yorkers was an enslaved African, most of them house servants or manual laborers. New York was well known for having the most heterogeneous population in America and most of the time, its various national, ethnic, and religious groups got along. However, one observer did call it "too great a mixture of nations," and by 1741, tensions—in particular between slaves and their owners—had reached a crisis point in the small city.

Slavery was not new to New York. The first enslaved men and women had been imported by the Dutch in 1626 and by the end of its life span, the Dutch West India Company's only profitable enterprise was its slave trade. The number of enslaved Africans in New York slowly but steadily increased during the British period, many of them coming as payment from merchants in the Caribbean who wanted to off-load workers who could no longer handle the strain of the sugar plantations. Some owners rented out their slaves for contract work; many others were sent to work on the docks. Those who had skilled trades often plied them, so that New York had enslaved Africans working as butchers, carpenters, and tailors, which gave them a small measure of autonomy. However, a series of laws in the early 18th century sought to curb what few freedoms the Africans enjoyed. A 1705 law expressly outlawed freeing a slave who'd converted to Christianity; in 1712, freed slaves were enjoined from purchasing land.

The first major effort by New York's Africans to organize against their white owners had come in April 1712, when a group of about 25 slaves set fire to an outhouse. When whites came to extinguish the fire, they were ambushed and in the ensuing melee nine whites were killed. The arsonists were eventually captured and eighteen of them were put to death. To quell further rioting, more laws were enacted. In 1697, Trinity Church's acquisition of the city graveyard [11] had pushed the Negroes Burial Ground [178] to the swampy area outside the city limits. In 1731, the city banned nighttime funerals and forbade more than twelve people from attending a burial for fear that any more people than that could be the pretext for a plot.

With this unease as a backdrop, it isn't surprising that when a fire broke out in Fort George [see 13] on March 18, 1741, some people immediately blamed the black population. (Others, citing repairs going on at the governor's house at the time, pointed to the hot coals and a soldering iron.) Then, less than a week later, Peter Warren's house caught fire; three days

after that, two more fires started, and the following Monday brought four more fires. Surely these all couldn't be caused by accident—it seemed clear that someone was trying to burn the city down. An African named Cuffee was seen running away from the scene of a fire at his owner's warehouse and was promptly arrested. Over the next four months, New York Supreme Court justice Daniel Horsmanden would preside over an investigation into the conspiracy to burn the city, an inquiry filled with bribed witnesses, recanted and contradictory testimony, and the arrests of a large portion of the city's black male population. Details of the conspiracy, mostly based on the unreliable testimony of Mary Burton, the Irish indentured servant of white tavern keeper John Hughson, revealed that Hughson had conspired with the slaves in a vast plot to install himself as king of New York and a slave named Caesar as governor.

By the time the trials were over, 17 black people had been hanged and 13 burned at the stake, to the delight of onlookers. Some that were hanged were then gibbeted near the Collect Pond [22] to serve as a warning to others. Over 80 people were banished from the colony. And, when it began to seem as if the conspiracy was just too vast to have been masterminded by the city's enslaved population, a white man named John Ury was accused of being the plot's ringleader. He was convicted of being a Roman Catholic priest in disguise who hoped to ultimately deliver the city into the hands of Britain's great rival, the Spanish. He was hanged in August 1741.

Historian Jill Lepore examined the events of 1741 in *New York Burn-*

ing, concluding that without unbiased evidence it is difficult today to determine if any conspiracy ever existed. Certainly there was no plot to use the city's black population to win the city for Catholic Spain, but it is plausible that one or more of the fires was set by enslaved Africans who were hoping to inflict harm on white New York the only way they could. What is definitely true is that many black New Yorkers were killed who had committed no crime. The fires did have the short-term effect of reducing the city's enslaved population, and fewer Africans were brought to the city in the years after 1741 than in the previous decades. Yet slavery remained a big part of life in New York. By 1799, when New York began the gradual manumission of slavery, it had become the second-largest slaveholding city in the nation. New York State enacted emancipation in 1827, the second-to-last Northern state to do so.

13 Bowling Green Park and the Stamp Act Protests

For years, the land in front of Fort Amsterdam (renamed Fort James by the English, and later Fort George) had been the city's main public gathering spot. As the city gradually anglicized in the 18th century, the fashionable English sport of lawn bowling—similar to Italian *bocce*—became all the rage in New York; on March 12, 1733, the city's Common Council authorized the enclosure of the area in front of the fort as a Bowling Green "for the Beauty & Ornament of the said street as well as for the Recreation and Delight of the Inhabitants of the City." The lease was to last for ten years and—similar to nearby Trinity Church—was for "a yearly Rent of one pepper Corne"* paid by the people to the city.

It's worth noting that when the lease on the Bowling Green was renewed in 1741 (only eight years into the ten-year lease, but who's counting), the rent had been upped to 20 shillings a year, about four times as much as was standard for a half-acre of land. However, it seems that soon the green was abandoned by the bowlers and returned to its original function as de facto town square.

Though the small park would see the most important day in its history in 1776 [15], it got its first taste of revolution in 1765 during New York's protest against the Stamp Act.

The Stamp Act, passed in March 1765, hoped to defray some of the costs of the French and Indian War (1754–63) by taxing colonial documents, which included everything from newspapers to contracts to playing cards. Such taxes had been common in Britain since the 17th century, but it was the first time the crown had attempted to impose them on the colonists. Political leaders in New York, Boston, and Philadelphia, the three largest mercantile centers in the colonies, drew up strongly worded condemnations of the act. (New York's most notable contribution to the effort was to coin the phrase

---

*No spices ever changed hands: this yearly rent of one peppercorn was included to make the contract enforceable. (It distinguished between a leasehold and a freehold.) Thus, the lessees would be given the freedom to bowl on the green, but it was still the King's green.

"taxation without representation.")

On the evening of November 1, the day the act was to have taken effect, a newly organized group calling themselves the Sons of Liberty liberated a battery of cannon near the waterfront (today's Battery Park) and set them up in front of Fort George. Inside the fort was the supply of tax stamps and the colony's acting governor, Cadwallader Colden. As Colden watched from the ramparts, the picket fence that surrounded the Bowling Green was torn down, a bonfire built, and an effigy of

made, the mob withdrew. Two weeks later, Colden's replacement arrived from Britain and agreed to indefinitely suspend the Stamp Act; then, in early 1766, the act itself was abolished by Parliament.

In many ways, this quelled some of New York's revolutionary fervor. In Boston, the next 10 years were marked by an ever-growing sentiment toward independence and war with Great Britain. In New York, by contrast, the grateful citizens ordered a grandiose statue of George III and went back to business.

St. Paul's Chapel

14 St. Paul's Chapel, the Country Church

In 1766, Trinity Church, Wall Street [11], finished construction on its first chapel, St. Paul's, at the corner of Church and Partition streets.* Known as a "chapel-of-ease," it was designed for people who lived north of the city and couldn't as easily reach the "mother" church, Trinity. Built in simple Georgian style, St. Paul's was constructed of schist, Manhattan's local stone [see 1] and featured a high altar designed by young architect Pierre L'Enfant, who would go on to plan Washington, D.C. Though many visitors now enter from the teeming Broadway side, this was originally the back door; the chapel actually faced its churchyard, which in turn faced the eponymous Church Street. The portico on the Broadway side and the bell tower are later additions to what would have been, when it opened, a typically plain church, similar in style to St. Mark's in the Bowery [10].

the governor thrown on top. Then, to add financial injury to that insult, the crowd broke into Colden's stable, stole his sleigh, and threw it into the fire too. Satisfied that their point was

---

*Partition Street is now Fulton Street, named after the engineer of the first viable commercial steamboat [24].

Trinity Church and St. Paul's Chapel are less than a third of a mile apart, and today it seems strange to have built a chapel designed for people who live in the countryside only five blocks away from the city church. But, of course, there was something else at work. St. Paul's may have been ostensibly the "country" church, but it was also the less expensive church. Well into the 20th century, most parishes—regardless of denomination—charged pew rent to all congregants. (The exceptions were the few "free" churches, many of which still bear that description today [see 36].) In theory, the amount of rent paid was not supposed to directly correlate to how far forward a family's pew was situated, but in practice that is exactly what happened, with New York's most fashionable names paying the highest rents to sit in the front rows at Trinity.

This makes it likely that St. Paul's Chapel was built not because people in the country couldn't reach Trinity, but rather because they couldn't afford it. Going to St. Paul's must have seemed quite down-market: the area around the chapel, despite being part of Trinity's land holdings, was the city's red-light district. Thus, once the chapel was built, the red-light district came to be known as Holy Ground.

15 The Revolution Comes to New York

Bowling Green Park is the site of New York's most symbolically potent moment of the War of Independence—the toppling of the grand equestrian statue of George III.

The statue was commissioned in 1766 from British sculptor Joseph Wilton to commemorate the repeal of the dreaded Stamp Act [13], a law New Yorkers saw as an undue restraint on trade. Wilton modeled his work on a

Fanciful depictions of the felling of George III's statue in Bowling Green were typical in 19th-century illustrations. This one doesn't even have the king on his horse.

famous statue of Emperor Marcus Aurelius in Rome, placing George III on horseback, his head enshrouded with a laurel wreath. In 1770, the 4,000-pound, gilded lead statue was erected, and about a year later an iron fence was added to keep the green from becoming a "Recepticle of all the filth & dirt of the Neighbourhood" ("filth and dirt" perhaps being an *entendre* for the rabble-rousing Sons of Liberty). Despite the fence, worries of vandalism persisted, and in 1773, a law was passed to prevent graffiti and other desecration.

But neither the fence nor the law proved much of a deterrent on July 9, 1776.

In April 1776, having driven the British out of Boston, George Washington had hurriedly moved the Continental Army to New York, reasoning that this was Britain's next place of attack. For four months, the Americans waited for the British to arrive. Then, on the evening of July 9, at the Commons, where City Hall stands today [26], the Declaration of Independence was read to New Yorkers for the first time. Led by the Sons of Liberty, civilians and Continental Army soldiers rushed to Bowling Green. They surrounded the statue, attached ropes, and toppled it. They then decapitated the king—surely an act of treason—broke his nose (literally cutting it off to spite his face) and carried the head around for all to see.

As symbolically powerful as this was, there was also an ulterior motive for toppling the statue: the Continental Army was desperate for munitions. The broken statue was shipped to Litchfield, Connecticut, where the family of Oliver Wolcott, one of the signers of the Declaration of Independence, reduced the king to 42,088

musket balls. (Some of the statue clearly never made it into Wolcott's furnace—not only should 4,000 pounds of lead yield 80,000 musket balls, pieces have also turned up over the years. Many are now at the New-York Historical Society, along with the statue's marble base.)

The story of the statue's felling is well documented. For example, Lieutenant Isaac Bangs noted in his diary on July 10, 1776:

> Last Night the Statue on the Bowling Green . . . was pulled down by the Populace. . . . The Lead, we hear, is to be run up into Musquet Balls for the use of the Yankies, when it is hoped that the Emanations of the Leaden George will make as deep impressions in the Bodies of some of his red Coated & Torie Subjects.

The fence that surrounds the Bowling Green today is the original one erected ca. 1771. It is a New York City landmark and one of the city's most significant pieces of pre-Revolutionary architecture. If you walk around the outside of the park, you can easily see that the larger fence posts are uneven and that each is rough-hewn in a slightly different way. It is clear that there were once decorative objects at the top of the fence posts, but it remains a mystery what these finials actually looked like, or when they were removed.

Unlike the king's statue, the fence is not mentioned in any news reports, diaries, or letters of the time. Over the years, it has been posited the finials must have been something round (to be used as cannon balls) or something royal and therefore offensive to Americans. According to

A broken fence post at
Bowling Green

property. Thus, whatever the truth of the story, the Bowling Green fence has become a tangible moment from the Revolution frozen in place—a tactile reminder of the frenzy of war.

16 Washington Retreats—the City Burns

From an American perspective, New York really only had two important years during the Revolutionary War: 1776, at its beginning, and 1783, the year it officially ended [17].

Six weeks after adopting the Declaration of Independence (which prompted New York to attack King George's statue at Bowling Green [15]), the first pitched battle of the war took place August 27–30, 1776.* Today known commonly as the Battle of Brooklyn, it was a terrible loss for the Americans, with over 1,700 members of the Continental Army either killed or taken prisoner. Had the British pressed their attack, it is plausible that the Revolution would have ended in Brooklyn with the Americans hopelessly defeated. However, the British—under brothers Admiral Richard Howe and General William Howe—held back. Taking advantage of a thick fog, Washington evacuated the remaining 9,000 Americans across the East River from Brooklyn Heights to Manhattan in the dead of night [see 157]. (Though the city was still officially under British rule at this point, the Americans had the military advantage on Manhattan.)

the *New York Times*, during the excavations for the foundations of the elevated railroad in 1878, "one of the round knobs struck from the railing" was unearthed. Later that year it was presented to David van Arsdale, the grandson of a Revolutionary soldier who had a direct role in the end of the war in New York [17]. But that is the only time they are mentioned. So unless some new eyewitness account surfaces (or one of the fence posts turns up on *Antiques Roadshow*) we will never know exactly what symbols encircled Bowling Green.

As you walk around the park today, you can see—and feel with your fingertips—the sheer violence required to remove the finials from the iron fence. Doing so, you can easily picture the American rabble, hacksaws in hand, denuding the king's

*During the summer of 1776 only one other significant military sortie took place. On June 28, the British attempted to seize the harbor at Charleston, South Carolina, and were rebuffed by American soldiers from Fort Moultrie on Sullivan's Island.

Fire sweeps through Lower Manhattan, September 21, 1776.

west of Broadway. The churchyard surrounding Trinity Church [11] helped keep the fire from spreading, but neither Trinity was spared, nor anything between it and St. Paul's Chapel [14]. St. Paul's, itself only ten years old, had a bucket brigade manning its roof and was saved. In all, over 400 buildings were gone—nearly 25 percent of the city's structures.

The Americans managed to hold Lower Manhattan for the next two weeks, but on September 15, Washington hurried his men up to Harlem. The next day, the Americans surprised the British by winning the Battle of Harlem Heights (which actually took place in Morningside Heights), but by mid-November, Washington had quit the island entirely, not to return until the war's very end in 1783. During the seven years the city was occupied by the British (though the third of the population still loyal to the king didn't see it as an occupation), it was the center of British military and political operations.

Meanwhile, the city was on fire. The fire started on the evening of September 21, 1776—perhaps in the Fighting Cocks Tavern on the wharf, though that has never been substantiated—and quickly engulfed the city

The British immediately blamed the Americans.* General Howe called it a "horrid attempt" by a "number of wretches to burn the town." As most of the damage happened on Holy Ground and other Trinity Church property, some saw it as an explicit attack on the Church of England's power and influence. In truth, the Americans *had* contemplated the idea of torching the city if it fell into British hands. One of Washington's generals, Nathaniel Greene ("the Fighting Quaker"), had pressed Washington in that direction. However, when Washington floated the idea by John Hancock, the Continental Congress immediately nixed it and it is unlikely that either Washington or Greene disobeyed Congress.**

What is most likely is that, in

---

*One American blamed by the British was Nathan Hale, who was arrested for spying that same day. Hale, however, had nothing to do with the fire.

**It is interesting to note, however, that Washington's motto, *Exitus acta probat* (which can be seen on the memorial arch in Washington Square [102]), means "The end justifies the means," so who knows what private thoughts he had about the fire.

a city filled with nervous citizens, gunpowder, wood-frame construction, and flimsy shingles, any fire that started accidentally would have spread quickly and disastrously without arson. Most galling to those Americans left in the city for the next seven years of British occupation was the British army's refusal to clean up or repair the damage; the entire western side of the city became a barren, squalid area of half-burned structures and shanties. No real work commenced on repairing the west side until the postwar boom.

17 Washington's Farewell

In the summer of 1781, with the War of Independence entering its seventh year, George Washington considered an attack on New York and the 10,000 British troops who had been quartered there since 1776 [**16**]. But when word came of the possibility of defeating the British under Cornwallis at Yorktown, Virginia, the combined American-French force headed south from Philipsburg, New York. The ensuing battle proved to be a decisive victory for the Continental Army and the beginning of the end of the war.

Under the stewardship of New Yorker John Jay, the two sides negotiated the Treaty of Paris, which was signed September 3, 1783. However, British forces still refused to leave New York. Sir Guy Carelton,

commander of the British troops in North America, refused to set a timetable for troop withdrawal. Carelton argued that too many British refugees were coming into New York for him to depart. Thus, to force Carelton's hand, George Washington's last act as commander in chief of the Continental Army was to return to New York for the first time since 1776 to ceremonially retake the city on November 25, 1783.

On the afternoon of November 24, patriotic citizens swarmed through the streets looking for symbols of British rule that they could destroy before Washington's arrival. There's a chance that this is when the Bowling Green fence posts were knocked off [**15**] and we also know of at least one spot they missed: in St. Paul's Chapel [**14**], the pulpit is adorned with a six-plumed coro-

George Washington bids farewell to his officers.

net, the symbol of the chapel's royal patron, the Prince of Wales.

Then, on the morning of November 25, the British officers left the city, sailing out through the Narrows. It is said that the last shot of the Revolution was fired this day—a British musketeer fired off a volley toward Staten Island that fell into the water. Annoyed at the fervor shown by Americans in the city, the British did leave one final insult for Washington: they raised a Union Jack in front of Fort George, cut the halyard, and greased the pole. When Washington and his troops arrived later that day, they would see the British standard flying over the city. However, an enterprising young sailor named John van Arsdale managed to use iron nails to build cleats in the flagpole and carried a Stars and Stripes to the top, hanging it just in time for Washington's arrival.

For the next week, Washington saw to business in the city during the day and attended lavish dinner parties each evening, using Fraunces Tavern on Pearl Street as his home base. Fraunces Tavern was one of Washington's favorite places in the city and Samuel Fraunces, its proprietor, would eventually leave to become Washington's personal steward.

On December 4, he held a banquet there to honor his officers and to say farewell:

> With a heart full of love and gratitude, I now take leave of you; I most devoutly wish that your latter days may be as prosperous and happy, as your former ones have been glorious and honourable . . . I cannot come to each of you to take my leave, but shall be obliged to you, if each of you will come and take me by the hand.

When the feast was over, a tearful Washington headed to the ferry slip, boarded a boat, and sailed to New Jersey. The next day, he began his journey south to turn in his commission and retire to Mount Vernon. For all he knew, it was to be his last day in New York City.

Fraunces Tavern is still a working tavern and features a museum on its upper floors detailing the building and keeping New York's Revolutionary history alive. It has even preserved the "Long Room," where Washington's farewell address took place. However, the building has been altered and renovated many times over the past two centuries—including a complete and not necessarily accurate gutting and facelift in 1907 by William Mersereau—so it is more a re-creation than a preservation of its colonial predecessor.

18 April 30, 1789: America's First Inaugural

Less than six years after Washington's fond farewell to his officers at Fraunces Tavern [**17**], the general was back in New York—this time, as the newly minted first president of the United States.

The years between the end of the war and the inaugural were a frenzy of political activity centered on replacing the Articles of Confederation, which had been adopted by the Second Continental Congress in 1781, with a broader federal constitution. Key among the New Yorkers working on this new constitutional government was Alexander Hamilton, who had come to New York in 1774 to attend King's College (now Columbia University [**101**]) and had risen quickly during the Revolution to become one of Washington's most trusted advisors.

In May 1787, the Constitutional Convention began in Philadelphia, which was America's largest city and had long served as America's political center. But congress itself had not met in Philadelphia since June 20, 1783, when the State House was surrounded by mutinous Pennsylvania soldiers looking for their Revolutionary War back pay. Under the Articles of Confederation, the federal government lacked the power to disperse the mob—and Pennsylvania's executive committee refused to do so—forcing congress to flee to Princeton, New Jersey. Over the next two years, the seat of congress moved a few times until finding a home in New York City.

As part of the new Constitution, the states agreed to have a capital city that was not governed by a state, thus heading off another Pennsylvania debacle, and Alexander Hamilton's preference was for that city to be his own. Pierre L'Enfant, who would achieve great fame as the master planner of Washington, D.C., remodeled the old British City Hall on Wall Street to serve not only as the meeting place for congress and the new chief executive but also continue to house New York City's government offices. On March 4, 1789, congress and the electoral college met there for the first time and unanimously selected Washington as the nation's first president. On April 30, he was sworn in on the second-floor balcony in a short ceremony before retreating inside to address a joint session of congress.

Washington initially made only three cabinet appointments: General Henry Knox became secretary of war, Thomas Jefferson—still serving in France as America's foreign minister—became secretary of state, and

Hamilton was appointed secretary of the treasury and de facto prime minister. When Jefferson returned to America in 1790, he hurried to New York to assume his post—and to see what damage of Hamilton's he could undo. He vehemently opposed Hamilton's ideas regarding a central United States bank and a federal

Federal Hall National Memorial

assumption of the debts the states had incurred during the war. But, it seems, he opposed locating the nation's capital in New York even more.

On June 20, 1790—exactly seven years after the Pennsylvania militia had forced the Continental Congress to flee Philadelphia—the capital was forced to move again, this time at a dinner party. At the dinner, which was hosted by Jefferson and James Madison at Jefferson's home on Maiden Lane, the two Virginians told Hamilton that they wielded such sway in congress that they could block Hamilton's controversial banking measures. Conversely, they promised to ensure Hamilton's bills went through as long as he didn't oppose their quest to move the federal capital to the south. Hamilton, realizing that the needs of the treasury department outweighed his New York City pride, acquiesced. In August 1790, congress met for the last time on Wall Street.

∿ The building called Federal Hall that stands on Wall Street today, with a magnificent statue of Washington by J.Q.A. Ward out front, has no connection to the original structure save for its location. When a replacement City Hall for New York was being constructed in the early 19th century [26], the L'Enfant building was sold at auction, netting only $450. The present structure, by Town & Davis, opened in 1842 as the U.S. Custom House. It served as the U.S. Subtreasury building until the 1920s and was later converted into a museum, today run by the National Park Service. It holds some fragments of the original building, including parts of the balcony on which Washington was sworn in.

19 The Buttonwood Agreement and the Founding of the New York Stock Exchange

Thomas Jefferson had three great objections to New York serving as the U.S. capital [18]: it was too far north, it was too commercial a city, and it was too much the domain of Alexander Hamilton. (Jefferson had his allies start calling the city "Hamiltonopolis" to underscore this point.)

Whether Jefferson was right about the first and third points is debatable; he was undoubtedly correct about the second: New York was fast becoming America's dominant port, and if it had stayed the nation's capital, politics might have taken a backseat to the city's commercial interests. Washington, D.C., by contrast, is too far up the Potomac for easy navigation, thus making the city a prime place to focus on its one industry—government.

When the seat of government left New York in 1790, the city remained the nation's key financial city. Even though the First Bank of the United States was established in Philadelphia (the temporary capital), most financial transactions—including the sale of corporate stock and the exchange of government-issued bonds—centered in New York.

On May 17, 1792, twenty four of the most prestigious traders gathered under the shade of an old buttonwood tree on Wall Street and signed a document formalizing a New York Stock & Exchange Board (later shortened to simply the New York Stock Exchange). The first rule was that they would trade only with each other. The second rule simply stated that they would hold commissions to "one quarter of one percent." (The first rule is today basically still in effect, as the NYSE is an exclusive exchange; oh, if only the second one were still true.)

For many years, the stock exchange did not have a formal home of its own. It met in Tontine's Coffee House, a popular hangout near Pearl Street, and later moved into the Merchants Exchange building at 55 Wall Street (today Cipriani, whose ballroom is the old trading floor), and ultimately to its current home at Broad and Wall streets [114].

20 New York's Country Mansions

In the 18th century, New York's growing prominence as a port was reflected not only in financial pres-

Hamilton Grange

Today, the best-known early mansion is the home of Scottish merchant Archibald Gracie, built in 1799 on a spit of land called Horn Hook overlooking the East River. Owned by the city since the late 19th century, it has served, since 1942, as the official mayoral residence. Horn Hook is now known as Carl Schurz Park.

tige [19], but in the number of country mansions built as weekend or summer retreats. Remarkably, some of these homes still stand.

Those mansions closest to the city's northern limit—which was then around Chambers Street—have not fared as well. Perhaps the most famous of these demolished estates was Richmond Hill, which served as one of Washington's headquarters in the Revolution, and then both as John Adams's official vice presidential mansion during New York's brief tenure as capital [18], as well as Aaron Burr's home when he was Jefferson's vice president [see 21]. Richmond Hill stood near the modern-day intersection of Varick and Charlton streets. However, one grand Greenwich Village mansion remains, albeit from a slightly later era: Samuel Whittemore's 1830 home on Grove Street, near Bleecker Street. This house, converted into apartments in the 19th century, is more famous for the legend that John Wilkes Booth planned the Lincoln assassination there. Booth *was* friends with tenant Samuel K. Chester, but that is the only link to the Lincoln plot.

The home Gracie Mansion replaced, owned by Loyalist Joseph Walton, was also briefly George Washington's headquarters and was bombed out of existence by the British in September 1776. Washington retreated north to another mansion that still stands, which is today called Morris-Jumel after its first prominent owner, British colonel Roger Morris, and a later inhabitant, Eliza Jumel, whose second husband, Aaron Burr, shared the home with her in the early 1830s. Built in 1765, it is the oldest home in Manhattan.

Burr's political nemesis, Alexander Hamilton, built his own country home in Harlem about a mile south of the Morris-Jumel home. Hamilton enjoyed his new house—which he called the Grange—for only two short years before his untimely death at Burr's hands on the field of honor [21].

Even farther uptown, not far from Manhattan's northern border, stands the farmstead of William Dyckman. Erected immediately following the Revolution on a broad street then called Kingsbridge Road (but now part of Broadway), the home may also have served as an inn for travelers heading to and from the city.

With the exception of the Whittemore house, each of these homes is today open for visitation, and together they provide a rare glimpse into an era that was vanishing even as the homes themselves were being built—Manhattan as countryside. Within a generation or two, it would be rare to find someone's country retreat still on Manhattan; within 50 years, the formal city would stretch all the way to the Harlem River.

21 The End of the Revolutionary Era: Aaron Burr Slays Alexander Hamilton

To say that Alexander Hamilton and Aaron Burr were enemies is to oversimplify the rivalry between the two men. There was personal animosity between the two, certainly, but more than that there were deep, fundamental political differences that demonstrate how, within a generation after the Constitutional Convention [18], American politics had evolved into a de facto two-party system. (That system would be enshrined in the 12th Amendment, introduced during his brief stay in Washington by Senator DeWitt Clinton [25].)

Hamilton was the last great Federalist and, indeed, after his death his Federalist Party would soon fade from the national scene. He was also one of the last true journalist-politicians, who committed every argument to paper. He founded what is now New York's oldest paper, the *New-York Evening Post*, to further the aims of the party and as a platform from which to attack Republicans like Burr.

After the Revolution, Aaron Burr had risen quickly in New York State politics, serving as a U.S. senator and then a member of the New York legislature. His growing stature was in part tied to his influence at the Society of Tammany—later famous as William "Boss" Tweed's Tammany Hall [70]—which he used to engineer Thomas Jefferson's success with New York's voters in the presidential election of 1800 and his own spot as vice president.

(In 1800, the factionalism of early American politics led to the first major test of the electoral college. Because the electoral college had no mechanism for electing "running mates," Jefferson and Burr each received equal votes, and thus Jefferson was not clearly elected president,

Alexander Hamilton

even though Burr was supposed to be on the ticket as the vice president. This threw the contest into the House of Representatives, where those Federalists with a particular hatred of Jefferson attempted to convince members of the House to vote for Burr as president instead. Only after 36 deadlocked ballots was Jefferson finally confirmed as president. While Burr didn't actively pursue the presidency during this conflict, neither did he try to broker a deal to ensure Jefferson's victory. This essentially forced Burr out of the president's inner circle.)

Left off the ticket in 1804 in favor of New York's governor, George Clinton, Burr chose to run for governor himself. When he lost, he blamed it, in part, on the conniving of people like Alexander Hamilton. While politicians often attacked each other in print, it was done using pseudonyms or by attacking the party rather than the person. However, at a dinner party in Albany in March 1804, Hamilton and other anti-Burr Federalists had a grand time describing why Burr was incapable of being "trusted with the reins of government." One guest at the dinner, Dr. Charles Cooper, wrote a letter to a friend recounting the event; the letter was leaked, and before long Hamilton's *Evening Post* was refuting its contents publicly. This caused Cooper to write a follow-up, published in the Albany *Register*, in which he declared that everything he'd said was true—and there was more. Had he wished to, Cooper could have recounted Hamilton's "still more despicable opinion . . . of Mr. Burr." It was these words—"despicable opinion," which were not even Hamilton's—that would eventually get him killed.

In a series of letters, Burr insisted that Hamilton retract his statement and Hamilton insisted that he didn't know what Cooper was talking about and that he shouldn't be asked to retract another man's words. Burr demanded satisfaction and in early 19th-century America, soldiers and statesmen preferred pistols to libel lawsuits. Since dueling was illegal in New York, the men and their seconds rowed across the Hudson River to Weehawken, New Jersey, on the morning of July 11, 1804.

There is great debate as to each man's intentions that morning, but

Hamilton lies wounded in Weehawken.

many historians believe that Hamilton purposely threw away his first shot; indeed, Hamilton indicated this in papers discovered after his death. If both Burr and Hamilton had discharged their pistols into the ground (or air), they would have satisfied the *code duello* and could have parted, honor intact. As it was, Hamilton's shot missed Burr completely, hitting a tree limb behind the vice president. However, Burr then fired directly into Hamilton's torso, puncturing both his liver and his spine. Hamilton was taken to the Greenwich Village home of his friend Nicholas Bayard, where he died the next day.

Though he was often a controversial figure in life, New York made Hamilton a martyr in death and brought out all the appropriate pomp for the funeral of a fallen soldier and statesman. Thousands gathered along Broadway to watch the funeral procession. Trinity Church was packed for the service, where his friend Gouverneur Morris eulogized him as New York's greatest Founding Father. Hamilton was laid to rest in the south side of Trinity's churchyard, where his grave is still the most visited spot in the cemetery. (Many visitors leave money on the grave to honor America's first treasury secretary.) Buried next to him is his wife, Eliza, who outlived him by nearly five decades. She died in her home in Washington, D.C., in 1854, making her one of the last links to the heroes of the Revolution. It is incredible to think that Eliza Hamilton died only six years before Abraham Lincoln's election and the start of the Civil War, and it serves as an excellent reminder of just how close those two wars were to each other.

PART 2

The Great Port: 1805–1835

There now is your insular city of the Manhattoes, belted round by wharves as Indian isles by coral reefs—commerce surrounds it with her surf. Right and left, the streets take you waterward. . . . Circumambulate the city of a dreamy Sabbath afternoon. Go from Corlears Hook to Coenties Slip, and from thence, by Whitehall, northward. What do you see?—Posted like silent sentinels all around the town, stand thousands upon thousands of mortal men fixed in ocean reveries.

—HERMAN MELVILLE, *Moby-Dick*

New York entered the 19th century as the largest and most economically vital city in the country. With the seat of the U.S. government now permanently in Washington, D.C., New York could concentrate on its strength: commercial shipping. It is not an exaggeration to say that every job in New York was based on the sea. Some made their living directly on the water as captains and crew; others outfitted those ships in the chandleries that lined the waterfront. Others built the warehouses and countinghouses to store and enumerate the goods passing through the city; and still others ran the nearby boardinghouses, saloons, and brothels that served the city's transient population.

Beyond the waterfront was New York's growing merchant class, the men who financed these long voyages and reaped the ample rewards—or suffered the consequences when a ship went down or lost its cargo. New York had always been a city of traders, but it was in the early 19th century that they elevated themselves into an elite social class, with their own churches (Trinity on Wall Street—always the city's richest church—first among them) and, soon, their own neighborhoods, like Greenwich Village and Gramercy Park.

But the same ships filled with cargo were also bringing in people, and New York's greatest change—and its greatest challenge—during the first third of the 19th century was housing and feeding its ever-expanding population. In 1790, when the first constitutionally mandated census was taken, the city's population stood at around 33,000 people. By 1800, it had nearly doubled to 60,000, and in 1830—just after the opening of the Erie Canal—it had risen to over 200,000, making it not only the largest city in the United States, but one of the fastest-growing cities in the world. A portion of this new population had migrated from other parts of the country, lured by New York's jobs. But there was also an ever-growing number of immigrants from Ireland, Germany, and other Northern European nations. New York's immigrant population so dominates its later 19th-century history that it is easy to forget that the city was already fast becoming a melting pot before the century was even a third over.*

The chapters in Part 2 trace the city's growth not just in terms of population but also geographically. In 1805, the city still hewed to a northern border, Chambers Street, that had essentially remained unchanged since the British colonial era; by 1835 not only had rural villages like Greenwich been swallowed into the growing city, but entire sections of the island had been transformed from unusable swampland into viable—if wretched—property. As the richest New Yorkers were moving northward to fashionable streets like Lafayette Place and Washington Square North (aka the Row), newly arrived immigrants and the city's recently freed black population were being pushed together into the Five Points, a barely livable slum just north of the city's architectural crown jewel, the brand-new City Hall. New York has always been a city of contrasts, but this was perhaps never more visible than in these years of rapid growth at the beginning of the 19th century.

---

*And, it is worth noting, the city had always been a melting pot; Dutch governor Willem Kieft told French missionary Isaac Jogues in 1646 that "there were men of eighteen different languages" in Manhattan.

22 The Draining of the Collect Pond

As New York's population began to grow in the 19th century, its first challenge was to find a place to put everyone. The primary means of locomotion was on foot, which limited the city to the area south of modern-day Chambers Street. In any case, the area just north of the city was mostly uninhabitable, filled with mosquito-ridden swamps and, in the center, a large fresh-water pond called the Collect (a corruption of *kolk*, the Dutch word for "pond").

Today, no one is certain how big the Collect was—estimates range from 6 acres (surely too small) to 75 acres (probably too big). It took up the area around what is now Foley Square, the city's courthouse district, and had for years been the city's best source of potable water. Nearby were "tea wells," which, as the name suggests, were the only places to draw water soft enough for brewing good tea.*

The Collect's importance as a water source did not, however, stop the city from ruining it.

In order to protect its citizens from the noxious (and potentially disease-causing) fumes of cattle slaughtering, the Common Council had attempted, as early as the 1730s, to regulate how and where cattle could be killed. The slaughterhouses (and tan yards that accompanied them) found the Collect an excellent place to relocate. It was just far enough away from the population to limit the smell, and the refuse and offal could just slough off into the pond. By 1800 the Collect was a stagnant mess.

Now the city faced a new set of problems. The removal of the slaughterhouses hadn't really lessened disease—which was most frequently mosquito-borne yellow fever [**see 31**]

The Collect Pond as it looked in the late 18th century

or sewage-inflicted dysentery. But the city *had* ruined its best water source. In 1803, the Common Council voted to drain the Collect. By 1805, a canal was dug from the pond to the Hudson River (enlarging a preexisting waterway that had once been used by the Lenape to sail into Manhattan's interior) and gravity was supposed to do the work.

*The eastern flank of today's Canal Street was once Pump Street, named for one of these wells.

Early signs weren't encouraging. Before work on the canal commenced, an astute writer in the local *American Citizen* noted that the water level in the canal wouldn't always be higher than the Hudson River into which it was draining. More important, the Collect would constantly be refilled by its own underground source. Still, the city persisted, and eventually the pond was filled with earth reclaimed from the area that is now Chinatown. The city filled the canal by the 1820s and Canal Street was born.

But, just as the *American Citizen* correspondent had predicted, the aquifer filling the Collect continued to flow, turning the area into a boggy quagmire—and making the newly reclaimed land some of the worst real estate in New York. This, in turn, gave rise to the Five Points [**37**], the most notorious slum in the city's history. Houses there soon began sinking into the ground and property values plummeted. (Even today, buildings that stand in what was once the Collect—such as the Supreme Court Building on Foley Square—have sump pumps to keep the pond's aquifer from flooding their basements.)

23 Elizabeth Ann Seton, First American-Born Saint

Religious pluralism in New York developed slowly during the English colonial period, and only after the Revolution was the first official Catholic parish founded, the French-dominated St. Peter's on Barclay Street (which still exists in an imposing Greek Revival building from the

St. Elizabeth Ann Seton
(as depicted on the front doors
of St. Patrick's Cathedral)

late 1830s). However, Catholicism was given little standing by the city's Protestant establishment. It is an unfortunate truth that New York's history is marred by a virulent strain of anti-Catholicism [**see 12**]. Often this went hand in hand with anti-Irish and anti-Italian sentiment [**see 43 and 98**], but as can be seen in the story of St. Elizabeth Ann Seton, it was not limited either to immigrants or to the poor.

Born Elizabeth Ann Bayley, Seton was the daughter of Columbia College's renowned professor of anatomy, Richard Bayley, and a member of the de rigueur Episcopal parish, Trinity [**see 11**]. In 1794, the Episcopal bishop of New York officiated at her marriage to merchant William Seton, and in 1801 the Setons moved into a waterfront house on State Street near the Battery. However, William Seton's health was failing and just two years later the family moved out, embarking on what they hoped would be a restorative trip to Italy.

Sadly, William died in Pisa shortly after their arrival. Rather than turn right around (for what was an exceptionally long sea voyage), Elizabeth stayed in Italy for a few months grieving—and discovering the Catholic Church. After returning to New York the next year, she began seriously considering conversion, and in 1805 she was received into the Catholic faith—much to the chagrin and embarrassment of her friends and relatives.

Had Elizabeth contented herself to be privately Catholic, it perhaps wouldn't have mattered so much, but soon her sister-in-law came to her with an interest in conversion. When that happened, Elizabeth's family began threatening to have powerful allies in the state legislature kick her out of New York for proselytizing. (Or so the story goes—they never followed through.) Elizabeth didn't give them the satisfaction; instead, she moved to Baltimore in 1808 to open a school and then founded America's first convent, the Sisters of Charity, the next year. She died at the convent in Emmitsburg, Maryland, in 1821. In 1963, she was beatified by Pope John XXIII, and in 1975, she was elevated to sainthood for her posthumous miracles, making her the first American-born saint.*

❧ A shrine to St. Elizabeth Ann Seton now occupies the building at 7 State Street. It takes up two lots, the southern portion of which (6 State Street) is the only 18th-century home left in the area. Built by merchant James Watson ca. 1792–94, it was probably designed by John McComb, Jr., who later built City Hall [26]. A curved addition at 7 State Street was added in 1806 with a double-height wooden colonnade. (There is a story passed down that says that these columns were once masts on cargo ships owned by Watson, which is possible, but unlikely.) In 1883, the house was taken over by the Mission of Our Lady of the Rosary to become a home for what were called, in the language of the day, "wayward Irish girls."

Because the home is a shrine, most people make the obvious assumption that this is where the Setons lived from 1801 to 1803. However, they actually lived next door at No. 8. That home, which stood until 1963, the year of Elizabeth Seton's beatification, was torn down in order that a chapel in her honor could be built in its place. At the same time, the interiors of the Watson house were gutted, leaving only the original Federal-era façade intact.

It is worth noting that the same year the Setons moved to State Street, 1801, William Seton had declared bankruptcy. We see the Watson house today, wedged in between two modern skyscrapers, as a reminder of a more elegant, refined era. But even before the grand colonnade was added to the home in 1806, this part of the city was beginning its transformation into a more commercial—and thus, less desirable—neighborhood. Herman Melville was born in this same block (in a now-demolished house on Pearl Street) in 1819 during a period when

---

*This is an important semantic distinction. Seton is not the first American saint—that honor goes to another New Yorker, Mother Cabrini, who was sainted in 1946. However, Cabrini was born in Italy.

his once-comfortable family was suffering financial difficulties.

Even more famous than Melville in his own lifetime was the man who lived nearby (in a house now also gone) who almost single-handedly caused the area to change from a residential to a commercial precinct: Robert Fulton.

24 Robert Fulton, the *Clermont*, and the Age of Steam

The sustained growth of New York harbor—and, for that matter, of shipping in general—had been hampered for generations by the technical drawbacks of sail-powered navigation. While clipper ships could navigate the open ocean with little difficulty, they were nearly useless for domestic river-bound commerce and they were often trapped in port by their inability to sail out of the harbor if the prevailing winds and tides did not align perfectly.

During the 18th century, a number of attempts were made to solve this problem by equipping boats with steam engines. In America, the most successful of these attempts was by Pennsylvania inventor John Fitch, who successfully demonstrated steam-powered locomotion on the Delaware River in August 1787. In the summer of 1790 he launched the first commercial steamboat service, which traveled every other day between Philadelphia and Trenton. However, Fitch's steam service soon failed. The route was already well served by coach and the ship probably had an engine so big that its cargo

capacity was limited. By autumn, it was in dry dock, never to sail again. Fitch went to New York in 1793 and demonstrated a steamboat on the Collect Pond [22]; while this didn't net him any backers, one of his passengers that day was Chancellor Robert Livingston, and his presence at the demonstration would later have a profound effect on the life of Robert Fulton.

At the time, Fulton was living in England and studying painting. However, he had a penchant for mechanical engineering and was beginning to turn away from portraiture and toward invention, with a particular interest in canals and navigation. In the late 1790s he relocated to Paris, where Napoleon's government was keen on his idea for a submarine that could torpedo the English fleet. By 1801, he had successfully demonstrated the first practical submarine, the *Nautilus*, at a depth of 25 feet. Napoleon, however, declined to finance the project, and when Fulton tried to switch sides and sell the submarine to the British, he made little headway.

While in France, Fulton was introduced to Robert Livingston, who was serving as U.S. foreign minister. Livingston was a member of the Committee of Five that drafted the Declaration of Independence, he was the chancellor of the state of New York who swore in George Washington on the balcony of Federal Hall [18], and as Jefferson's minister to France he successfully negotiated the Louisiana Purchase, doubling the size of the United States with the stroke of a pen. Because of his close ties to New York politics, he was generally known by his New York title, "the Chancellor." Livingston had been impressed by Fitch's steamboat demonstration eight years earlier, and was now hoping to bolster U.S. navigation—and, in particular, New York's preeminence as a port—with a practical steam engine. So, Fulton turned his attention to steam navigation.

The first steamship Robert Fulton built for Chancellor Livingston promptly sank in the Seine, but a second prototype proved seaworthy and Livingston bankrolled Fulton, sending him to New York City to build a commercial vessel. Simultaneously, Livingston was able to secure a monopoly on Hudson River steamship navigation, thus ensuring that as long as Fulton's steamboat stayed afloat it would also be profitable.

On August 17, 1807, the boat, christened with the rather prosaic name *North River Steamboat*, left New York harbor en route to Albany. It arrived 52 hours later: 32 hours of that was steaming, and 20 hours was a diversion to Robert Livingston's Hudson River estate, Clermont (where, presumably, the chancellor took a long nap). The return trip, the next day, took just 30 hours and within a month twice-weekly service was scheduled between the two cities, averaging 36 hours per trip. (Hudson River sloops, by contrast, averaged a week for the same trip.)

In its own day, the boat was only called by its own name, *North River Steamboat*, or simply "the Steamboat" (since it had no competition). It was only after Fulton's death in

1815 that the name of Livingston's estate, Clermont, became commonly associated with the vessel.

Steam travel had massive repercussions for the remainder of the century. Only three years after Fulton's success, New York's mayor, DeWitt Clinton, proposed the world's longest canal [34], a project that would not have been possible without reliable steam navigation on the Hudson.

Perhaps the greatest measure of Fulton's fame came in 1909, when New York celebrated the 300th anniversary of Henry Hudson's voyage of discovery [2], linking him with Robert Fulton in a joint Hudson-Fulton Festival, one of the largest parties the city has every thrown. (And, in 2009, New York State is marking its 400th

Robert Fulton's *North River Steamboat* (aka the *Clermont*)

anniversary with a Hudson-Fulton-Champlain celebration, continuing Fulton's legacy into a new century.)

A large monument to Fulton stands in the south side of Trinity Church's graveyard, right next to the grave of Alexander Hamilton

[21]. Fulton, however, isn't buried here. Because he married Chancellor Livingston's niece, he's buried in the nondescript Livingston family plot in the north side of the churchyard. This grander monument was erected by the Society of Mechanical Engineers in 1901 to stand in a high-traffic part of the graveyard and draw attention to its hero.

25 DeWitt Clinton and the Manhattan Street Grid

DeWitt Clinton

Perhaps the greatest unsung hero of 19th-century New York is DeWitt Clinton, one of the city's most influential citizens but now little known even in the city he helped create.

Clinton's political career began in the office of his uncle, Governor George Clinton, who was known as "the Old Incumbent" because few could remember a time that he hadn't been the state's governor. (George Clinton was also Thomas Jefferson's second vice president—he replaced Aaron Burr not long after the Burr-Hamilton duel [21].)

Young DeWitt Clinton quickly climbed the political ladder, becoming a state assemblyman, state senator, and then a U.S. senator. However, he left Washington, D.C., after just one year, appalled at the living conditions in the young city, and was appointed mayor of New York in 1803, serving as the city's chief executive off and on for the next twelve years.

As mayor, Clinton's most lasting and visible legacy is surely the Manhattan street plan—known officially as the Commissioners' Plan of 1811—which overlaid a Cartesian street grid onto the undeveloped land north of Houston Street. (Clinton's desire to superimpose order on chaotic New York was perhaps influenced by his year in Pierre L'Enfant's master-planned Washington.) The Manhattan street grid, lauded by some as efficient and practical and derided by others as monotonous and soulless, has come to thoroughly define one's experience of the city. It isn't an exaggeration to argue that the city's history exists in two sections: before the grid and after.

With the population rapidly increasing and without any plan for regulating property sales and population growth, it seemed very possible that the city would simply collapse underneath its own weight, with too many people crammed into the area of the city below Chambers Street but not enough food, water, or sanitation to go around.

The grid plan was overseen by a commission headed by Gouverneur Morris, the eminent politician who'd written the Preamble to the

Constitution. The survey itself was carried out by John Randel, Jr.; he and his team walked out every block of the city from Houston Street to 155th Street in Harlem, charting over 2,000 city blocks in all. It was enough room, as was noted at the time, "for a greater population than is collected at any spot this side of China."*

The goal was to create a regular pattern of east-west streets; along the avenues, exactly twenty of the blocks made up a mile. In turn, these blocks could be divided into regular lots, 25 feet wide by 100 feet deep. Each lot would back up precisely to its neighbor, with no room behind for service alleys or carriageways. Not only did eliminating alleys allow for bigger, more desirable lots, it reflected the reality that very few in New York would ever have the means to own a horse and carriage. Thus, there was no need for rear stables.

(This aspect of the grid later became a sort of self-fulfilling prophecy: since there's no place to park, today, fewer than 20 percent of Manhattan residents own cars.)

As so few people had access to horses and carriages, the Commissioners' Plan reinforced that New York was a city for walking. The plentiful east-west streets connected the two rivers where most commerce took place, with the wide north-south avenues designed for transporting goods and people over longer distances. Until the opening of the subway in 1904 [**119**], the grid served this

original purpose well. Even with the coming of horse-drawn omnibuses, trolleys, streetcars, and private vehicles, New York was simply easier to walk, and the vast majority of the city's workers lived within relatively easy walking distance of their jobs.

Today, the grid is such an integral part of the New York experience that it's easy to take it for granted and, indeed, most people only really think about it in those places where it is somehow off-kilter as when, for instance, older, named streets intrude into the grid (such as Stuyvesant Street [**see 10**]) or when streets like Broadway intersect the grid at odd angles [**see 111 and 124**].

While the grid may be omnipresent, DeWitt Clinton, meanwhile, has faded from view. He has a fort [**27**], a park, and a few schools named for him, but little else. (The neighborhood that city planners would like people to call Clinton is better known as Hell's Kitchen and the people who live there have no intention of changing the name; even those who do call it Clinton probably don't know why.)

A year after the Commissioners' Plan was published in 1811, Clinton ran for president as a "Fusion" Federalist/Republican and lost to incumbent James Madison. However, he would go on to achieve even greater fame in his day—and have a slew of towns and streets in the Midwest named for him—as governor of New York and champion of the Erie Canal [**34**].

---

*Randel's survey extended work that had been done in the late 18th century by Joseph-François Magnin (co-architect of City Hall [26]) and Casimir Goerck. The men named two streets for themselves on what is now the Lower East Side; Goerck Street is long gone, but a tiny section of Magnin Street still exists underneath the Williamsburg Bridge.

26 A New City Hall

When the federal capital moved to New York in 1785 [**18**], the old British City Hall became the first U.S. Capitol building, while at the same time continuing to house city government offices. To ease the overcrowding in the old building, plans were drawn

City Hall

up to move the city's executive offices to the old Commons at the junction of Broadway and the Bowery. (As in many cities, the Commons had started as common grazing land for livestock; when pasturage moved northward, it became a public gathering spot. This is where American troops first heard the Declaration of Independence on July 9, 1776, leading to the attack on Bowling Green [**15**].)

In 1802, Joseph-François Magnin and John McComb, Jr., won the $350 first prize in the competition for the new City Hall. Their French-inspired Federal building was planned to be not only the grandest building in the city but one of the finest pieces of architecture in the country.

Magnin and McComb's plans were trimmed down almost immediately. The size of the overall building was reduced and while the Common Council "strongly recommend[ed]" that the building be faced in marble, they thought it would be fine to cover only the front and the east and west ends with the expensive stone. The back was left cheap, plain brownstone. Since the building would be farther north than any proper homes, its rear wall would therefore "be out of sight to all the world." Despite these cost-cutting measures, construction soared to $500,000 at the same time that the Embargo Act of 1807 [**see 27**] was laying waste to the city's economy.

The construction of City Hall took place simultaneously with the survey of the Manhattan street grid [**25**] and it reveals the city's ability to balance its short- and long-term goals. Clearly, the city was going to grow—the expanding population had to go somewhere, after all—and the grid being planned would inevitably lure people northward. But that was a problem for the future. For now, City Hall had to be built—as elegantly as possible, but as economically as possible too. So, the back façade was left unadorned, a true symbol that once you'd passed Chambers Street you were no longer in New York, but out in the countryside. (Or, more precisely, in the slum, as what lay just behind City Hall was the emerging Five Points district [**37**].)

City Hall held its first event on July 4, 1811, and became the official seat of city government the next year. Mayor

DeWitt Clinton moved his office into the Blue Room in April 1812—where a handsome portrait of him by John Trumbull still hangs. By the 1950s, the marble facing on the buildings' three sides had begun to deteriorate badly and it was replaced by Alabama limestone. During the replacement process, a rear façade was fabricated so that, 144 years after it opened, City Hall finally got a proper backside.

27 Castle Clinton and the War of 1812

At the same time the Manhattan street grid [25] and City Hall [26] were being completed, Mayor DeWitt Clinton had other, more immediate concerns—specifically the imminent threat of a British invasion.

Tensions between Great Britain and America had been growing throughout President Thomas Jefferson's second term. In order to punish the British for violating the neutrality of the seas (and for impressing American sailors into service in the British navy), Jefferson introduced the Embargo Act of 1807, which sought to keep American ships from trading in British ports. When the act proved unenforceable, the law was strengthened to prohibit all American exports—which brought New York's port to a virtual standstill. The end of Jefferson's presidency in 1809 and the repeal of the worst of the embargo measures did little to improve relations with Britain and in June 1812, America declared war.

Because of DeWitt Clinton, New York was prepared. Clinton perceived that the city's greatest challenge was protecting its expansive and vulnerable harbor. If the British could be convinced the harbor was impenetrable, the city would probably be safe. To achieve this, Clinton ordered the construction of a number of forts in the harbor, including ones on Bedloe's (now Liberty) Island, Governors Island, and on an artificial spit of land just off Manhattan's southern tip. This last fort, today known as Castle Clinton, was built between 1807 and 1811 by volunteers, many of them students at nearby Columbia College, out of rough-hewn brownstone, the local, cheap material.*

Clinton's gambit paid off. Brit-

Castle Clinton

ish naval intelligence realized that an attack on New York from just about any position would be fruitless. The British navy bypassed the city in favor of less-well-defended cities, such as Baltimore

---

*There is a story that because these Columbia students studied by day and worked on the fort by night that their labor originated the term "moonlighting." This is all but impossible; the term (in the modern sense of holding a second job) didn't enter the language until the 1950s.

(where Francis Scott Key watched the bombardment and wrote "The Star-Spangled Banner") and Washington, D.C. (where British troops burned the White House).

By the end of the war in 1815, it seemed that if any attack were to come, it would be overland, so New York hastily erected fortifications north of the populated area in what is now Central Park. (One of these forts remains, known as Blockhouse No. 1, near the park's entrance at 110th Street and Adam Clayton Powell Jr. Boulevard.) But by the time these forts were finished, the war was over, and America never again faced Britain as an enemy. With the cessation of hostilities and a return to the status quo, America was free to trade again with both Britain and France. Due to New York's ample protection of its harbor, the city was immediately ready to open for business—and trade with Britain flourished.

Castle Clinton, which had never fired a shot, was decommissioned in 1825. It eventually became a theater [53] and the city's first immigrant processing station [59].

28 Catholic New York: St. Patrick's (Old) Cathedral

When Elizabeth Ann Seton converted to Catholicism in 1805 [23], she had no choice about where to go to church—there was only one Catholic parish in the city, St. Peter's on Barclay Street, which was operated under the aegis of the Diocese of Baltimore.

In 1808, a separate diocese for New York was created, which covered the entire state as well as parts of New Jersey. The following year the cornerstone was laid for St. Patrick's Cathedral on Mott Street near Prince Street. The cathedral, made of schist and designed by Joseph-François Magnin, who was at the same time working on City Hall [26], was dedicated on May 14, 1815. The building was one of the largest churches in its day—120 feet long from the entrance to the apse, with a vaulted ceiling rising 85 feet above the floor. It was also the first church in the city to have Gothic elements, though Magnin's tentative use of the style doesn't qualify it in many experts' eyes as a true Gothic Revival structure.

Locating the church this far north of the city was strategic. In 1815, the cathedral's property on Mott Street was still in the countryside, far beyond the day-to-day reach of most New Yorkers. (It is a little over a mile north of City Hall.) With Catholicism treated with a mix of skepticism and hostility, building the cathedral far from the eyes of the Protestant establishment was simply a measure of safety.

Today, people sometimes wonder why St. Patrick was chosen as the patron of this cathedral when New York wouldn't see a great influx of Irish until the potato famine in 1845 [see 64]. However, when the cathedral opened, the first bishop of New York, John Connolly, described the 17,000 Catholics in the city as already being "mostly Irish." The city even had an Irish paper, the *Shamrock*, which had started publication in 1810.

In 1866, a fire swept through St. Patrick's, destroying much of the interior as well as the Mott Street façade. The church was repaired and continued to serve as the diocesan seat until the new St. Patrick's uptown was finished in 1876 [**83**]. At that time, the Mott Street church was reborn as a local parish and dubbed St. Patrick's (Old) Cathedral.

The high walls of the churchyard have served over the years not only to protect the graves but also to shield the parishioners from occasional outbreaks of anti-Catholic street violence. For many years, the most famous person buried at the church was Pierre Toussaint, the Haitian-born former slave who became one of America's first prominent black Catholics. But in 1990, Cardinal John O'Connor had Toussaint's remains dug up and reinterred at the cathedral on Fifth Avenue. A few years later, Pope John Paul II declared Toussaint to be a venerable person, which is a first step toward sainthood.

The original St. Patrick's Cathedral (seen from Mulberry Street)

29 Episcopal New York: The General Theological Seminary

Clement Clarke Moore is best known today for a children's poem that appeared in the Troy *Sentinel* in 1823, "A Visit from St. Nicholas"—otherwise known as "'Twas the Night Before Christmas."* However, Moore's stature in his own day was as a wealthy landowner and a key founder of the first Episcopal theological seminary in America.

Moore was descended from distinguished New York families: his large family estate, Chelsea, which gave rise to the modern-day neighborhood, had originally been owned by his grandfather, Major Thomas Clarke, a veteran of the French and Indian War. Moore's father, Bishop Benjamin Moore, was the head of the Episcopal Diocese of New York and twice president of Columbia College [**101**].

In 1817, soon after Bishop Moore's death, the Episcopal Church convened in New York to establish the General Theological Seminary. Jacob Sherred, a member of the Trinity Church [**11**] vestry, donated $70,000 and Clement Clarke Moore agreed to donate 66 lots from his Chelsea estate to house the school. (The seminary met elsewhere until construction could begin in the 1820s.) Moore, already the author of a well-regarded

---

*There has been controversy in the last decade about whether Moore actually wrote the poem (which was initially published anonymously). While the jury is still out, it at least seems plausible that it is Moore's creation.

Hebrew lexicon, was also hired to serve on its faculty, teaching biblical languages until 1850.

In the 1880s, the campus was redesigned by Charles Haight in a more insular fashion, with its buildings ringing a central close. The centerpiece of this redesign, Haight's 1888 Chapel of the Good Shepherd, is considered by many to be one of the finest Victorian Gothic buildings in New York.

30 The Last Days of the Village of Greenwich and the Building of St. Luke in the Fields

While portions of Clement Clarke Moore's estate in Chelsea were being prepared to house the General Theological Seminary [29], Moore himself had more pressing religious matters on his mind: where to go to church.

Even for someone of Moore's social station and wealth, commuting from Chelsea to the city was difficult. The best route was via the Hudson River by sloop, but this wasn't always possible or practical. Overland, there were two options: the longer route via the Albany Post Road on the east side of the island, which connected to the Bowery and then to Lower Broadway, or the shorter "Road to Greenwich," which ran up the Hudson side of the island to the vicinity of 14th Street. However, this road (today called Greenwich Street), was so close to the river—and had to go through at least one swamp—that it was rutted, muddy, and frequently impassable.

Moore's solution to this quandary was to ally with residents of the nearby village of Greenwich and convince Trinity Church to sell off part of the northern section of its land [11] so that an independent Episcopal church could be established. The cornerstone for the church was laid in 1821 at a site on the corner of Hudson and Burrows streets.* The name of St. Luke, the healing evangelist, was chosen to reflect Greenwich's role as a place of refuge for New Yorkers during summer outbreaks of yellow fever and other pestilence. Due to its rural location, the parish was soon dubbed St. Luke in the Fields and it became the center of religious life for the residents of Greenwich, Chelsea, and other outlying areas.

~ The history of the village of Greenwich goes back to the Lenape, who established at least a part-time encampment called Sapokanikan.** The Dutch dubbed the small village here Noortwyck ("north village") and it isn't until 1713 that the city first referred to it as Greenwich; it is no doubt named in honor of Greenwich, England, but when exactly the name was changed is unknown.

The population of the village centered on the junction of Hudson and Christopher streets. The oldest

---

*Burrows Street is now called Grove Street.

**Sapokanikan has been translated as "tobacco fields," and tobacco perhaps grew wild here. However, it's quite likely that the first people to attempt tobacco cultivation were the Dutch; if that's the case, Sapokanikan is the word the Lenape used to describe the Dutch settlement, not an older term.

home still standing dates to 1799 [see 140] and a school had been established by 1806.* Most of the property, however, was in the hands of a few wealthy landowners, including noted New York families like Warren, Hammond, and Burr. Aaron Burr's home here, Richmond Hill, was his vice presidential residence [20].

The most notorious place in Greenwich, however, was Newgate Prison, which sat on the Hudson near the Christopher Street pier. In an era when few people were jailed for their crimes (one normally just paid a fine), being sent to prison was an extreme sentence. Because Newgate lay a few miles north of the city—and because it was usually reached by boat—an expression was born that convicted criminals were being sent "up the river." (In 1825, the prison relocated to Ossining, New York, much farther up the river, and the expression stuck.) Since some of Newgate's tenants would ultimately be hanged nearby for their crimes (in what would later become Washington Square [35]), being sent "up the river" was a particularly dreaded outcome.

In May 1822, when St. Luke in the Fields opened its doors, the population of the village of Greenwich was probably only a few hundred people. However, by the end of that summer, the population had shot up dramatically, fueled by the worst yellow fever outbreak in the city's history. And soon, the little church of St. Luke's would find itself no longer at the center of the village of Greenwich but on the fringes of a new neighborhood: Greenwich Village.

31 The First Days of "Greenwich Village" and the Building of the Hyde House

Like all early cities, New York had been plagued by disease since its founding. Inadequate sanitation coupled with a lack of clean drinking water and rapid population growth made the city ripe for outbreaks of everything from cholera to smallpox. However, the city was hobbled by its lack of understanding about how diseases were transmitted; New York did try some preventive measures, including banning cattle slaughtering [22], but without knowing that

The William Hyde house

yellow fever was spread by mosquito rather than pestilent vapor, their efforts were fruitless.

Instead, every time there was an outbreak, the richest members of the population simply fled. (It was probably a yellow fever outbreak in the late 1790s that caused Alexander Ham-

---

*P.S. 3, at the corner of Grove and Hudson, stands on the spot of the original school.

ilton to decide to move his family permanently to Harlem [20].) In the summer of 1822, yellow fever was so widespread that the Common Council voted a general quarantine. A chain was dragged across the island near Beekman Street and those citizens who were well enough and wealthy enough were encouraged to head to the safety of the village of Greenwich and the surrounding countryside [30].

The immediate growth in Greenwich was staggering. One writer noted that he "saw corn growing on the present corner of Hammond and Fourth streets* on a Saturday morning and on the following Monday 'Sykes and Niblo' had a house erected capable of holding three hundred boarders." Business relocated en masse to the area, leading to new street names like Commerce and Bank to describe what only a few months earlier had been sleepy village roads. Soon it was no longer a village at all, but simply a northerly extension of the city—transformed into a neighborhood we still call Greenwich Village.

One resident who took advantage of the boom was William Hyde, a window-sash maker, who built a two-story wood-frame home at the prominent corner of Bedford and Grove streets, one block from St. Luke in the Fields. The home, which essentially served as a giant advertisement, showed off his lovely windows and shutters to full effect, and his small workshop behind the house was probably quite busy.

However, wooden houses were quickly going out of style. While country homes were often wood frame, more expensive—and therefore more fashionable—city homes were made of brick. The sudden migration of the downtown elite to Greenwich Village—turning it overnight into city, not country—meant that wood-frame construction on these streets would soon disappear. Today, William Hyde's house—which was enlarged in the 1870s to include a third story—is not only the last large wood-frame house in the Village, it is one of the only large wooden houses still in private hands in Manhattan. His original workshop (also enlarged later in the 19th century) is still visible behind the home.

32 The First New York Tenement

While genteel New York was moving uptown to Greenwich Village in response to disease and overcrowding [31], New York's poorest residents were getting a new neighborhood all their own.

By 1820, the area where the Collect Pond had once stood had been reclaimed [22]. However, it was without a doubt one of the worst public projects the city had ever done. Early on, the filling was accomplished by indiscriminately paying anyone five cents for a cartful of dirt. As city surveyor John Randel, Jr., noted at the time, this meant that people were simply bringing any household rubbish that could fit in a cart. In the years it took to complete the project, property values surrounding the pond—which were already low

---

*Today, this is the corner of West 11th and West 4th streets.

due to the high concentration of butchers, tanners, and cattle pens—plummeted.

While the pond was being drained and filled in, New York was experiencing its first real surge of post–Revolutionary War immigration. The two most significant populations were rural Irish (which helped spur the growth of the Catholic diocese [28]) and Germans. Though this had never been the city's intent, it was almost as if New York—already hemmed in by its 18th-century borders—was filling in the Collect just for these new arrivals.

Certainly, this is where the immigrants went, into one- and two-story wood-frame houses that lined streets like Orange, Mulberry, and Mott.* Usually, these homes were turned into de facto apartment buildings or rooming houses, with multiple families sharing what had only a few years earlier been a single-family home. When the number of Irish arriving spiked after 1820, the population density rose; quickly, it became apparent that without expansion, there would be no place for these new arrivals to live. And, since most people relied on being able to walk to their jobs (mainly on the nearby waterfront piers), moving northward toward Greenwich Village or Chelsea was not an option.

Circa 1824, one enterprising developer—whose name is unfortunately lost to us—found a solution. If the neighborhood couldn't expand outward, it could grow upward. At 65 Mott Street he constructed the first

65 Mott Street, New York's first tenement

example of New York's most ubiquitous form of architecture: the tenement. (Though records are scarce, 65 Mott Street may be the first modern tenement apartment building ever constructed in the United States.)

Originally known as a tenant house ("tenant" and "tenement" both come from the Latin *tenare*, "to hold"), the building at 65 Mott pioneered the style for most future tenements, though it had a smaller footprint than many later tenements. There were two apartments on each floor: a front apartment with parlor, living room, and two bedrooms, and an identical rear apartment, overlooking the "yard" where the outhouses would have been located. If the small interior bedrooms had windows

---

*A few years later, this neighborhood would get a name—"Five Points" [37].

when they were built, they soon disappeared as other tenements sprang up in the neighborhood.

Sixty-five Mott Street, being seven stories tall, would have had 12 apartments, with the first floor dedicated to retail. As more tenements were built, developers found better ways to cram people into the same amount of space. A classic pre–Old Law tenement* had four apartments on a floor—two in the front with windows overlooking the street, and two in the rear facing the yard. In these tenements, the interior bedrooms were built without any windows at all. Because no natural light could penetrate from the front windows, these dank bedrooms were lit by oil lamps or, just as likely, were rarely lit at all and used only for sleeping.

As New York's immigrant population expanded over the next thirty years, the tenement became the preferred mode of building not only in this Irish/German neighborhood, but also in the rapidly expanding immigrant sections of Greenwich Village, Lower Manhattan, and what would soon come to be known as the Lower East Side.

33 John Jacob Astor and Lafayette Place

Only 18 years old when the American Revolution began, Marie-Joseph-Paul-Yves-Roch-Gilbert du Motier —better known as the Marquis de Lafayette—traveled to America in 1777 to fight for the Continental Army and became one of the war's chief boosters in France. He was appointed a major general in the American army and for the next two years he fought in a variety of campaigns, including the Battle of Brandywine, during which he was shot in the leg. Lafayette quickly became a trusted friend and ally of George Washington, who came to treat the marquis as a surrogate son.

After a six-month stay in France in 1779, Lafayette returned to America for the remainder of the war. Given the task of defending Virginia, it was Lafayette who summoned Washington south from West Point to Yorktown in September 1781. There the combined forces of Washington, Lafayette, French general Rochambeau and Admiral de Grasse (who blockaded the Chesapeake) defeated British general Cornwallis and ended the war.**

Lafayette's exploits during the war—and his subsequent role in the French Revolution—made him a remarkable celebrity in America. When he returned to America in 1824 for a yearlong "farewell tour," he was treated like visiting royalty. In the places Lafayette visited—at least one in all 24 states then in the union—he was celebrated with parades and parties. Towns presented him with tokens of their esteem and often roped him into laying cornerstones for civic monuments and cutting ribbons. Sometimes he simply

---

*Early tenements were known as pre–Old Law because they were built before the first, or Old, tenement law went into effect in 1879 [84]. Tenements built from 1879 to 1901 are Old Law tenements, and those built after 1901 are New Law tenements.

**The British, however, would not leave New York for another two years [17].

stood in the town square for hours, shaking hands.

Lafayette's sojourns brought him through New York many times: he arrived in the harbor on August 15, 1824; later in the tour he was feted at Castle Garden [**53**]; he paused in the city before and

La Grange Terrace (aka Colonnade Row)

after a trip up the Hudson; and he celebrated Independence Day, 1825, in New York. It was during this visit to the city that he may have met John Jacob Astor, a fellow Freemason, who soon thereafter created Lafayette Place (today called Lafayette Street).

Astor was one of the richest men America had ever produced. Born in Germany in 1763, he came to the United States just after the Revolution and made his first fortune in the fur trade—places as far-flung as Astoria, Oregon, and Astoria, Queens, are named for him. Even before the Commissioners' Plan of 1811 laid out the city's street grid [**25**], Astor saw the possibility of enlarging his fortune further by buying large swaths of real estate outside the city limits and waiting for Manhattan's population to move uptown. He rarely developed the land himself, simply waiting for demand to drive the prices up. (It is said among Astor's last words were, "Could I begin life again, knowing what I now know, and had money to invest, I would buy every foot of land on the island of Manhattan.")

One of Astor's tracts had been leased since 1805 to Jacques Delacroix, who operated a "pleasure ground" called Vauxhall Gardens.

It featured tree-lined gravel walkways festooned with paper lanterns, refreshment stands and a restaurant, and an odd collection of statuary that Delacroix called "a choice selection of Statues and Busts, mostly from the first models of Antiquity, and worthy of the attention of Amateurs." Subjects ranged from Cleopatra to Alexander Hamilton.

In 1825, Delacroix's lease expired and Astor had a broad street—the same width as Fifth Avenue—laid out through the middle of the garden running from Art Street (today's Astor Place) to Great Jones Street. Though a story is sometimes told that Astor invited Lafayette to open the street in July 1825 from a dais erected on Great Jones Street, there seems to be no evidence to support this. At best, Astor may have told Lafayette of his intentions, but there was no formal ribbon cutting and, indeed, lots on the street did not come available until the next year.

The area around Lafayette Place was already becoming a popular place to live, with elegant townhouses lining streets like Prince, Bond, and St. Mark's Place. The next year, Mayor Philip Hone would oversee the transformation of a nearby graveyard into

Washington Square [35], and the center of the city's mercantile elite would forever leave downtown Manhattan.

In 1833, developer Seth Geer erected the finest homes on Lafayette Place, a row of marble townhouses called La Grange Terrace, which were named for Lafayette's country estate. Rivaling Washington Square's "Row" [39] for prestige, the homes had such innovations as central heating and indoor plumbing. What impressed viewers was the unity of design: each of the original nine homes was identical, and the row featured an integrated marble colonnade that ran the entire length of the development on the second and third floors. Among those who lived in the development were John Jacob Astor's son, John Jacob II, and future first lady Julia Gardiner [48]. After the Civil War, as the area began to rapidly industrialize, many of the original homes were altered or torn down. Today, only four original homes remain (428–434 Lafayette Street, usually known as Colonnade Row); they are in poor condition and offer only a pale reflection of what the grand street must have looked like in its heyday.

When John Jacob Astor died in 1848, the bulk of his fortune went to his son William Backhouse Astor, who lived in a home facing La Grange Terrace. (His son John Jacob Astor II was considered too mentally unbalanced to carry on the family legacy.) A portion of the estate, however, went to establish one of New York's first public libraries. Built 1849–53 on the site of William Astor's home, the Astor Library was one of the three founding institutions that combined in 1895 to form the New York Pub-

lic Library [128]; the building today houses the Public Theater [165].

In the first decade of the 20th century, Lafayette Place was connected through to Elm Street near City Hall and the entire length of the road renamed Lafayette Street. There is also a Lafayette Avenue and Lafayette Gardens in Brooklyn, and Lafayette Square in northern Manhattan, which abuts Morningside Park [73]. In this small square is a statue by Frédéric Auguste Bartholdi that shows Lafayette and Washington shaking hands; the work was commissioned by Joseph Pulitzer following the success of Bartholdi's more famous statue in New York—the Statue of Liberty [93]. Indeed, this was actually the second statue of Lafayette that Bartholdi had created for New Yorkers; the other was dedicated for the American centennial in 1876 and stands on the east side of Union Square Park.

34 Opening the West: The Erie Canal

In 1820, New York's population of nearly 124,000 equaled that of the next two largest cities, Philadelphia and Baltimore, combined. A decade later, Philadelphia and Baltimore had each added only 20,000 people to their respective populations, but New York had shot up to 202,000, in large part thanks to the creation of the Erie Canal.

America's westward expansion during the Jeffersonian period—most notably with the Louisiana Purchase of 1803—was driven by a desire not only for new territory but for the raw materials needed in the country's industrializing east coast.

However, the great forests of the west were virtually inaccessible to eastern cities like New York: it took 30 days and over $30 just to move a ton of raw materials from Chicago to New York. (It was faster and cheaper to send goods to Liverpool on a packet boat than to get them from Chicago.) Mayor DeWitt Clinton became the first champion of creating a canal to link New York, via the Hudson, to Lake Erie; as governor, he became the man who made it happen.

The idea of connecting the Hudson to the Great Lakes was not new. As far back as the 1720s, Cadwallader Colden* had suggested using the Mohawk River valley, one of the only natural passes through the Appalachians, as the basis for a canal. However, no one had ever built a canal as long as the Erie would need to be (over 360 miles), and there was an immense elevation gain between the Hudson and Lake Erie, meaning a minimum of 50 locks. President Jefferson saw the engineering problems as insurmountable. He wrote that perhaps it could be "carried out in a hundred years, but it is a little short of madness to think of it at this time."

But in 1811, a committee led by DeWitt Clinton and Gouverneur Morris (who was, at the same time, heading the commission to lay out the Manhattan street grid [25]) reported that a canal was possible. It would cost an exorbitant $5 million but would more than pay for itself within a few decades. As the nation edged toward the War of 1812, enthusiasm for the canal (or, more precisely, for spending $5 million on it) waned. It was only after the war ended—and DeWitt Clinton lost his bid for the presidency—that the mayor turned his attention to advocating for the canal full time, despite the fact that people began calling the project "Clinton's Folly" or "Clinton's Ditch."

Perhaps the greatest obstacle to breaking ground—the objection of New York's governor, Daniel Tompkins—was removed in 1816 when Tompkins was elected vice president. A special election to fill the vacancy led to DeWitt Clinton taking office on July 1, 1817. Three days later, in his first act as governor, he took part in the groundbreaking for the canal in Rome, New York.

Remarkably, the canal was finished in only eight years. On October 26, 1825, Clinton boarded a boat at Lake Erie; five days later, he ceremonially dumped a container of water from Lake Erie into New York Harbor, presiding over what the press called the "wedding of the waters."

With the completion of the canal, a ton of goods could now travel from Chicago in a week at a cost of roughly $8. Cities like Philadelphia, Boston, and Baltimore, which had no access to the heartland, suddenly found themselves at a grave disadvantage, and within a generation New York was handling more cargo than all the other American port cities combined.

Clinton died unexpectedly on February 11, 1828, less than 18 months after the completion of the canal. So crucial was the Erie Canal to development of the west that a slew of Midwestern towns and counties were named for DeWitt Clinton, including two separate Clinton counties in Illinois (the only place in

---

*It was Colden who was burned in effigy during the Stamp Act protests in 1765 [13].

the United States where two counties in a state are named for the same person), and multiple towns, villages, and parks.

35 July 4, 1826: Washington Square

Hot on the heels of the Marquis de Lafayette's triumphal 13-month sojourn through the states [33], America approached the 50th anniversary of the Declaration of Independence in a heady frame of mind. In New York City, the celebrations of the Fourth of July centered on the creation of a new public square in Greenwich Village, to be named for George Washington.

This was an admirable sleight of hand by Mayor Philip Hone, who wanted to raise property values in the Village without the need for great capital investment.* In the four years since the yellow fever quarantine had sent city residents fleeing northward [31], the streets of the old Village had filled with newly built middle-class townhouses. However, without a plan, the mayor and his allies feared that Greenwich Village would become as overcrowded (and thus as potentially disease-ridden) as the downtown from which they'd escaped.

The solution was to build open space. Not only would a park provide a healthful respite from the city streets, but parkland would have the side benefit of raising real estate values. In short, it would become the nicest part of Greenwich Village, which would make it simply too expensive for the working class. The only problem with this plan was that on the new street grid [25], there were no parks at all, only one square for a military parade ground near 23rd Street. After all, in a city where the vast majority of the land was still undeveloped, who really needed a park anyway?

To gain approval for his plan, Mayor Hone proposed doing away with the as-yet-unbuilt parade ground uptown, instead turning a portion of Greenwich Village into the Washington Memorial Parade Ground. Moreover, he would open the new parade ground on July 4, 1826, as a culmination of a gigantic Independence Day celebration. Wrapping this land grab in a cloak of patriotism, Hone staved off controversy while at the same time making New York the center of a national celebration of the country's birthday.

Then, to ensure that no one complained that the city was seizing their land for the project, Hone instead chose an easily accessible tract on the eastern edge of the village, most of which the city already owned: the recently defunct potter's field. From 1797 to 1825, this graveyard had been the final resting place for New Yorkers who had either died of epidemic diseases, were too poor for a church burial, or who were hanged for their crimes. (To save time and trouble, a gallows had been erected in the graveyard.** While there is an

---

*Hone's desire sprang, in part, from his responsibilities as a board member of Sailors' Snug Harbor, which owned a large tract of Greenwich Village [39].

**A story is often told that the Marquis de Lafayette witnessed the hanging of 24 highwaymen here during his 1824–25 American visit. That must have been an odd invitation: "Welcome to America, Marquis—would you like to see how we kill people?"

old elm tree near the northwest corner of the park that is marked "Hangman's Elm," this couldn't possibly be the place where the hangings took place. First of all, city law required the use of a gallows; second, the elm was on private property, not part of the potter's field. The tree, however, is at least 350 years old, making it the oldest living thing in Greenwich Village.)

While estimates vary, it seems likely that over 20,000 people were buried in the land that Hone wanted for the parade ground, both in the potters' field and in a couple of adjoining church-owned burial grounds. The bulk of the bodies were never disinterred, which means they remain to this day under the grass and pavement of Washington Square.

The celebration that Hone engineered on July 4, 1826, was indeed a grand one. Ten thousand people gathered to review the troops, hear the Declaration of Independence read, and consume vast quantities of meat. Wrote one participant:

Immense awnings were erected, beneath which two tables, each four hundred and fifty feet long, groaned under vast quantities of substantial viands . . . [with] two oxen, roasted whole, two buttered hams, immense piles of bread, innumerable barrels of beer.

The troop review, however, may have been the only time the parade was used for military purposes. By 1827 it had been enlarged to its current boundaries; by 1828 landscaping had added (according to the *New-York Evening Post*) a "handsome fence," "green turf," and "neat gravel foot paths." In the coming years a fountain would be added, completing the square's transformation into the city's most important park.

As for Hone's plans to raise property values, this had worked too. When the University of the City of New York (today's NYU) bought its first tract facing the square in 1832, it paid $40,000 for one block of land between Waverly Place and Washington Place, an average of $5,300 per lot. This nearly bankrupted the new institution; after the purchase it was left with only $6.40 in the bank. Had it acted sooner, it would have saved a great deal; six years earlier, those same lots had been assessed for just $537.50 each.

36 The Abolition of Slavery and the Construction of St. Augustine's Church

Slavery had been a contentious issue through America's brief history as a nation,* in no place more than New York. By the turn of the 19th century, it had become the largest slaveholding city in the north—and the nation's second-largest slaveholding city, after Charleston, South Carolina. New York's Manumission Society, whose founders included John Jay and Alexander Hamilton, was instrumental in banning the sale of enslaved Africans in the state and instituting a gradual manumission

---

*Slavery, of course, was not just an American problem; the Dutch had first imported slaves to New Amsterdam in 1626, and the British had continued the practice [12].

Looking down toward the sanctuary from the west slaves' gallery at St. Augustine's Church

Saints Free Episcopal, an indication that it did not charge pew rent. It was the outgrowth of a mission started by seminarians from the General Theological Seminary [29], and was run in its earliest years as a chapel of Trinity Church, Wall Street [11]. The building, like many of its contemporaries, was built of schist, in this case quarried from nearby Pitt Street, where Mount Pitt had once served as a redoubt during the Revolutionary War.

beginning in 1799. However, by 1817, slavery was still abundant and Governor Daniel Tompkins prompted the state legislature to set a date for total emancipation. The date selected—a decade away—was July 4, 1827, when all slaves in the state were freed.

At the same time that slavery was winding down, an Episcopal church was being erected on Henry Street in the newly fashionable area on the city's east side. Much of the area, known as Corlear's Hook after an early Dutch resident, had been owned by the Rutgers and Delancey families. The Delanceys, ardent Loyalists, had fled the city after the Revolution and their land was confiscated by the state legislature to be sold in lots as a countryside development. Henry Rutgers, a patriot and colonel in Washington's army, soon leased his land, too, and the area developed in the early 19th century as a relatively prosperous rural community.

The church is today called St. Augustine's, but was originally called All

However, while the church may have been called "free," it was, in truth, one of the last vestiges of slavery in the city. In rooms above the balcony were two small slaves' galleries where black people—both free parishioners and those still enslaved—were forced to sit during Sunday services.

These galleries present a historical conundrum. All Saints was consecrated in 1828, months after New York's emancipation. So how did it get built with slaves' galleries? After all, manumission was not a sudden event, but rather the culmination of 28 years of incremental, well-known change. Who would have owned the people put in these rooms?

Since New York was the dominant economic hub of the country, it stands to reason that the ebb and flow of visitors to the city included a large number of slaveholders, many of whom traveled with their slaves.

Perhaps All Saints was providing an amenity for its out-of-town guests. (Notably, these could have included visitors from the other side of the Hudson River in New Jersey. While New York became the second-to-last northern state to free its enslaved population, New Jersey held out until the bitter end, not officially freeing people until 1846, and even then making children born to slaves before emancipation "lifetime apprentices." Slavery was not fully abolished in New Jersey until the 13th Amendment passed in 1865.)

But building these rooms simply to serve visitors doesn't seem like a strong enough motivation. After slavery ended, the city remained extremely segregated. In all likelihood the church's free black parishioners were made to sit up in the galleries.

There is, however, the third, more sinister, possibility that some people of Henry Street and environs simply didn't emancipate their slaves in 1827. They would not have been alone. The most famous New York State slave not to gain his freedom was Caesar, who died in 1852 as a "house servant" at Bethlehem House, the estate of the Nicoll family, descendants of New York's first English governor, Richard Nicolls [9] (somewhere along the line, the final "s" was dropped from their surname). Caesar was born in the house in 1737 and served his entire 115-year life in service to three generations of the Nicoll family, totally unaware that after 1827 he was a free man. Caesar's fate is only known because a later Nicoll descendant wrote up the story of his life. How many other Africans continued in enslavement or indentured servitude because their owners hid the truth from them?

37 "Five Points" Gets Its Name

In June 1829, an editorial in the *New-York Evening Post* pointed to the area where the old Collect Pond had once stood [22; see also 32] and lamented that it had "become the most dangerous place in our city." The article used the term "Five Points" for the first time, and the name would soon become synonymous with the decrepit square mile stretching north from the old Collect to the new Canal Street. However, it is unclear whether the *Evening Post* was referring to the entire neighborhood or just to the intersection of three streets—Orange, Anthony, and Cross—which formed an irregular five-cornered junction.

Before the draining of the Collect, Anthony Street, named for colonial landowner Anthony Lispenard, had only existed on the west side of Manhattan. As the pond disappeared, the street was run farther east, eventually connecting to the intersection of Orange and Cross in 1817. In extending Anthony Street, the city created an odd triangle of land with buildings whose corners had been lopped off to make way for the street. It was this triangle of rundown wooden houses that the *Evening Post* was targeting in its editorial, at least in part because they were in such blighted condition. But it is also likely that the soaring number of black residents in the neighborhood—a direct result of emancipation two years earlier [36]—discomfited the paper. At around 14 percent, the black population of Five Points was almost double the city average, and the newspaper may have been advocating the destruction of the houses in the Five

Points triangle in order to force the black people to move elsewhere.

In the coming year, the city took up the measure, at first contemplating a jail on the site (which it nixed because it envisioned "great Mortality in a crowded prison located at the Points"), but then decided to purchase the houses, tear them down, and replace them with a public square. The dwellings were, in the words of the Common Council, "of but Little value and occupied by the lowest description and most degraded and abandoned of the human Species." (It also labeled them a "sink of iniquity," just for good measure.)

The resulting triangle of land was dubbed Paradise Park (often called Paradise Square) and the square quickly became the centerpiece of the neighborhood; the nickname for the streets leading into it, Five Points, was adopted as the term to describe the entire area. Today, the site of Paradise Park and the original Five Points intersection sits behind the city's courthouses, where Columbus Park [**105**] creates a divide between the Civic Center and Chinatown.

This would not be the last time the city attempted to improve this neighborhood's fortunes by simply changing some names. Orange, Anthony, and Cross streets are all now gone. Both Orange and Anthony were renamed in the wake of the Mexican-American War: Orange is now called Baxter, after Lieutenant Colonel Charles Baxter, who died at Chapultepec; Anthony is now known as Worth, after General William Jenkins Worth, perhaps the greatest New York hero of that war. (Tiny Cross Street became Park Street and then, years later, was shortened even more and renamed Mosco Street.)

It's amazing to think that Five Points has been reduced to such a shadow of itself that only one "point" of the original five-cornered intersection that gave the area its name is visible: the corner of Baxter and Worth, behind the courthouse district. Indeed, so thorough was the city's decimation of the area that when Herbert Asbury published *The Gangs of New York* in 1928, he didn't know where it was and placed the intersection one block too far east. (And, of course, so did Martin Scorsese when he made the film *Gangs of New York* in 2002.)

38 The Working Poor and the Northern Dispensary

Within a year of the opening of Washington Square [**35**], the transformation of Greenwich Village into a posh residential neighborhood was almost complete.

The creation of the square had also caused an interesting flip in land values. In the early 18th century, the most desirable land in the Village was close to the river [**30**]. The bulk of Greenwich's estates lay in the area between Hudson Street (then just a block from the river) and what was to become Sixth Avenue on the Commissioners' Plan of 1811 [**25**]. However, the creation of Washington Square and the resulting shift away from country homes and toward city townhouses pushed the wealthiest residents inland. Sixth Avenue soon became the border between the two districts, with the area close to Washington Square and Fifth Avenue as the high-value district and the area west of Sixth Avenue—which was not part of the street grid—quickly becoming more working class. Soon this split would regularize into two voting districts (known as wards), with a common border along Sixth Avenue. The area around Washington Square was nicknamed "the American Ward"— that is, no immigrants need apply.

The economic divide between the two wards was confirmed in 1827 with the establishment of the Northern Dispensary in temporary headquarters on an odd piece of land at the intersection of Eliza, Factory, and Christopher streets. The Northern Dispensary was an offshoot of the New York Dispensary, a private institution located near City Hall that had been founded in the 1790s to provide subsidized health care to New York's poorest citizens. The establishment of this Greenwich Village outpost not only acknowledged the area's growing population, but also underscored just how far away from the city it was. A working-class resident of Greenwich Village simply didn't have the luxury of time or money to travel down to City Hall for medical care. (And while the American Ward was filling up with doctors at this time, working-class Villagers couldn't, of course, afford to see them either.)

In 1831, the Common Council granted the Northern Dispensary $2,000 to build a permanent structure on the lot; since it was a triangular plot of land, they constructed a handsome triangular Greek Revival building, which still stands today. Two years after it was built, Factory and Eliza streets were renamed Waverly Place, in honor of the recently deceased Scottish poet and novelist Sir Walter Scott. Though today Scott's fame is mainly connected to

Ivanhoe, he was the best-selling author in America in his own lifetime. His romantic series of Waverley novels were particularly beloved and are commemorated—sans the final "e"—in the street's name.

The Northern Dispensary

This street renaming, however, produced a cartographic conundrum: not only did Factory and Eliza streets run at odd angles to each other, a spur of Eliza Street continued along the front of the Northern Dispensary to Christopher Street. Today, what this means is that there is an intersection of Waverly Place and Waverly Place and, technically, two sides of the Northern Dispensary are on the same street.

The people who availed themselves of the Northern Dispensary would have been the tradesmen who were quickly moving into the neighborhood to provide services to the wealthier residents of Washington Square. Nearby Gay Street, which first appeared in 1827, featured small homes for tailors, tinkers, and the like. However, the most famous patient at the Northern Dispensary was Edgar Allan Poe, who was treated for a head cold in 1837. He had moved to Waverly Place in 1837 with his new bride, his 14-year-old first cousin, Virginia Clemm. They chose Greenwich Village not because it was a literary bastion—that wouldn't happen for many decades—but because it was cheap. And, possibly, the lure of free health care at the dispensary influenced their decision.

Poe's Waverly Place home, a boardinghouse at Sixth Avenue, is gone. Poe would ultimately live many places in New York (including on West 3rd Street in the Village and on 85th Street on what is now the Upper West Side), but the only one that still remains is the small cottage where Virginia died of consumption in 1847. It stands in small Poe Park in the Bronx, just off the Grand Concourse, in what was then a rural setting, far removed from the city.

39 "The Row" and Genteel New York

When New York laid out Washington Square atop the old potter's field [35], this not only raised property values generally throughout the area, but specifically helped Sailors' Snug Harbor, a pet project of Mayor Philip Hone.

The land to the north of the potter's field had once been owned by Thomas Randall, a New York ship captain who, like William Kidd

before him, made his money through privateering, then still a respectable profession. In the years leading up to the Revolution, he built a grand home on Whitehall Street and bought a large farm just north of what would soon be the potters' field. Upon his death, the land was inherited by his son, Robert Richard Randall; Robert drew up his will in June 1801, just four days before he died.* Instead of leaving the farm to his far-flung cousins, he created a philanthropic foundation—America's first—to house "aged, decrepit, and worn out sailors." In other words, Robert wanted the farm to become an old-age home for his father's privateering crew. The name for the new home was to be Sailors' Snug Harbor.

One thing the will did was to appoint a board of trustees that automatically included, by virtue of their posts, the rectors of the First Presbyterian Church, Trinity Church, and the mayor of New York City. However, setting up the Randall farm as Sailors' Snug Harbor proved difficult. The trustees of the foundation had trouble reaching a quorum and, more important, Randall's far-flung cousins appeared, lawsuits in hand, to challenge the validity of the will. Throughout the first three decades of the 19th century, the foundation rented out portions of the farm to make money. Then, in January 1826, Philip Hone entered the picture; when he began his term as mayor, his post granted him a seat on the Sailors' Snug Harbor board, and he began to see the benefit that creating Washington Square would have for them.

*It's often said that the will is so cleverly written that it had to be the work of Alexander Hamilton, but there's no firm evidence of this.

Rather than housing the sailors in Greenwich Village, the foundation could instead lease their park-facing land at a premium and use that revenue to build a rural complex for the seamen on Staten Island. At the same time, this would guarantee that the land on the north side of the square became some of the nicest property in the city.

In 1831, Sailors' Snug Harbor leased the lots at No. 1–13 Washington Square North to a trio of prominent businessmen. In order to ensure the maximum income for the foundation, the lease on each lot ran 99 years and stipulated that within two years, each lot contain "a good and substantial dwelling house, of the width of said lot, three or more stories high, in brick or stone, covered with slate or metal." The houses were to be set back a uniform 12 feet from Waverly Place and behind each lot, space was apportioned for a stable. Neither the homes nor the stables could be used for "nuisances" or any "trade business which may be noxious or offensive to the neighbors." (These included slaughterhouses, tallow chandleries, blacksmiths, and foundries.)

The 13 homes of the row were built as a piece, probably by builder Samuel Thomson, who lived in No. 4, and were the first major houses to embrace the Greek Revival as a domestic architectural style. Along with John Jacob Astor's more exclusive Colonnade Row [33], they were among the first homes to successfully mimic the elegant London "terrace" style, in which each home along the street matched its neighbors. An advertisement for No. 2 appeared in 1833, touting it as "inferior to no house in the United States, either in workmanship or convenience." Immediately they were nicknamed "the Row," and, for the first time in the city's history, an address immediately conveyed status. To be able to say, "I live on the Row," was all the calling card one needed, and walking through Washington Square became a pastime as much for admiring the elegance of the houses as for enjoying the park.

The stable road behind the homes, now called Washington Mews, was the oldest street on the property, having once been part of a Lenape trail that connected the East and Hudson rivers [1]. It is still paved today with many of its 1830s blocks, which cant toward what would have once been the gutter (now filled with large stones). This is a rare street in the city that still shows its pre-1842 central sewer. After the establishment of the Croton Aqueduct System [46], gutters were moved to the sides of streets to better accommodate indoor plumbing.

40 Samuel Ruggles's Gramercy Park

The success of Washington Square [35] and the Row [39] proved to be a catalyst for the city's northward development. In addition to Washington Square, the city had two other residential developments, one public and one private. The public square—one of few on the Commissioners' Plan of 1811 [25]—was Union Place (today Union Square), named for the junction of Broadway and the Bowery, two roads that were to terminate at 14th Street in favor of the new, numbered avenue system.* The other, Hudson Square, was located on land that had been donated to Trinity Church by Queen Anne in 1705 [**11**], and was a private residential development. The square itself was owned and maintained by the church through

Gramercy Park

its nearby chapel, St. John's Hudson Square.**

It was this latter square that was the model for a developer named Samuel B. Ruggles. In 1831, he acquired the parcel of land once owned by James Duane (New York's first post–Revolutionary War mayor) called Gramercy Farm. Gramercy is the English corruption of the Dutch name for the area: *krom moersje* ("crooked little swamp"), an apt description of the marshy terrain. It had previously been the northernmost part of Peter Stuyvesant's immense farm [**10**]; by the time Ruggles bought the property, Gramercy Farm had shrunk to cover the area on the grid roughly bounded by 20th and 21st streets and Third and Fourth avenues. Encouraged by the high property values on Washington and Hudson squares, Ruggles decided that the center of his property would also become a park, fenced in as a private refuge. Most remarkably, unlike Hudson Square (where the park and the surrounding lots were still church property) or Washington Square (where the best lots were owned by Sailors' Snug Harbor), Gramercy Park's land would be owned and administrated as a cooperative by the 66 house lots surrounding it. Ruggles set up a trust for the park, designating five lifetime trustees, and giving each surrounding lot one vote in trustee elections that would be trig-

---

*While the Bowery (also today known as Fourth Avenue for a few blocks) does end at 14th Street, the city was unable to convince people to curtail Broadway. Today, people often refer to Broadway as the only road that runs the entire length of Manhattan, but technically this isn't true—Broadway ends at 14th Street, as it did on the Commissioners' Plan, and then starts up again on the other side of Union Square.

**St. John's and Hudson Square are now gone. What remains is a traffic rotary guiding vehicles into the Holland Tunnel.

gered if the number of living trustees dropped to three.

Almost immediately, Ruggles hit up against his property's biggest drawback: it did not actually reach all the way to either Third or Fourth avenues, and thus the only access roads were 20th and 21st streets. While he was interested in creating a private enclave, this was a little *too* private. He appealed to the city of New York for the right to run access roads from the north and south that would bring people to the edge of the new park. The fact that the Common Council cheerfully acceded to this request shows that by 1830, the city was aware of the limitations of the Commissioners' Plan. It had plenty of east-west streets, but it didn't have nearly enough north-south avenues to meet the demand of the growing city.

Ruggles was given the honor of naming the two roads that led into his property; the one running north from 21st Street he dubbed Lexington Avenue after the first battle of the Revolution; the street leading up from 14th Street he named after his friend Washington Irving.

Though the evidence is circumstantial, it seems likely that Ruggles chose Irving because of the contemporary movement to rename Eliza and Factory streets in the Village after Sir Walter Scott's novel *Waverley* [38]. If a Scotsman was good enough to honor, why not an American writer? And if a street was to be named for an American, there was no better choice than New York's homegrown literary hero, Washington Irving, author of "The Legend of Sleepy Hollow," "Rip Van Winkle," *Tales from the Alhambra*, and perhaps most important, the satirical *History of New York* that not only coined the term "Knickerbocker" to describe the city's first inhabitants, but launched the first real New York literary circle, also called Knickerbocker. (Irving also coined the term "Gotham" to describe New York City.)

One thing Irving did not do, however, is live at the quaint house on the corner of 17th Street and Irving Place that bears a large plaque declaring it to have been his home. Later generations, certain that the street could only have been named for Irving if he was a resident, basically picked the oldest house on the street and assigned Irving to it.

⁓Adding Lexington Avenue and Irving Place cut the number of lots surrounding Gramercy Park from 66 to 60; despite the new roads, sales remained sluggish for the next decade. However, development took off after 1842 with the opening of the Croton Aqueduct [46], which allowed the houses of Gramercy Park to be built with indoor plumbing. Posh as the homes of the Row were, they had rear gardens with privies. Faced with the choice of retrofitting those townhouses or building new homes uptown, the richest New Yorkers decided it was easier to move, either to Gramercy Park, to nearby Union Square, or to new Stuyvesant Square, which had been created by a bequest from the Stuyvesant family in 1836.

Over the years a number of legal challenges have been brought against Gramercy Park for its exclusivity. Some have claimed that as a park, it should be open to all people, regardless of who owns it. Others have pointed to the annoyance of having to go around the park when driving down Lexington Avenue and have lobbied to cut the avenue straight through to join up with Irving Place. None of these efforts have ever been successful and Ruggles's original deed and trust have been reconfirmed by courts each time. Indeed, the only time the park has ever seen a truly public use was in July 1873, when Union troops were billeted there during the Civil War draft riots [**67**].

41 The Great Fire of 1835

On the night of December 16, 1835, a gas line broke in a dry-goods store near Hanover Square in the Financial District; the gas, ignited by a coal stove, caused the store to explode and the ensuing fire quickly fanned southward along Stone Street and northeast toward Wall Street. Not only was it the worst fire in New York's history, it wiped away almost all of the remaining traces of the old Dutch and British colonial city.

New York had some of the nation's strictest fire codes; buildings were never erected with common walls, and brick and stone were favored over cheaper wood (though this was as much about status as safety). Every home was required to have a leather fire bucket affixed to a hook by the door and every business had to have at least two. At the sound of the first alarm, the city's volunteer fire companies turned out in force. As per instructions, every fire bucket was made ready, and bucket brigades formed to nearby wells and cisterns. Unfortunately, it had been so cold for so many nights that the wells were frozen solid. When the firefighters changed tack and headed for the East River instead, they found to their chagrin that the river was frozen too. With no other source of running water, they were forced to improvise. At the ends of the piers, holes were hacked in the ice and fire engines lowered down to pump water. However, by the time they were able to get any water flowing, the hoses had frozen, and when they did manage to get water up, most of it was blown back as frozen ice into their faces. In some places, the only way to stop the fire's spread was to blow up buildings in its path to create a makeshift firebreak.

The blaze raged for over a day, destroying over 600 buildings in about 50 acres of the old city, including the home of the New York Stock Exchange, the old city post office, and many warehouses and countinghouses on which the city depended. Though the neighborhood was still a mix of commercial and residential structures, fortunately only two people died. Because the city's economy had been buoyed for nearly a decade by the opening of the Erie Canal [**34**], it was both necessary and possible to rebuild the commercial buildings almost immediately. Today, the best stretch of these replacement buildings can be seen along Stone Street between Hanover Square and Coenties Slip. Almost every building along this row was built in 1836 as a countinghouse for goods being shipped in and out of New York. Because New York took a cut of every durable good that passed through its harbor, being able to accurately account for everything was crucial. The entry-level jobs at these firms were for bean counters—literally people who counted to see how many dried beans were in a barrel. Those who were meticulous at this were soon bumped up to more complex accounting jobs, but the term "bean counter" still persists for their profession.

There are no memorials to the Great Fire, despite the fact that it was the largest urban fire since London's Great Fire in 1661. A valiant attempt was made to rescue a 15-foot statue of Alexander Hamilton from the floor of the exchange, but just as the statue reached the doorway, the roof collapsed, destroying it. The statue, by Robert Ball Hughes, was the first marble statue created in the United States and had been installed only eight months earlier. Though it took 45 years, the statue was ultimately replaced by Hamilton's youngest son, John C. Hamilton, and it stands in Central Park behind the Metropolitan Museum of Art. This statue in the park is remarkable in that it is made entirely of granite—not the easiest stone to carve—and it has long been thought that John C. Hamilton commissioned the work out of this durable stone so that no matter what calamities might befall Central Park, his father's statue would endure.

PART 3

The Growth of the Immigrant City, 1836–1865

New York in the middle of the 19th century underwent such a profound change that in the space of one generation it became a completely different city. In 1830 only 9 percent of the city's population was foreign born. (Some of the remaining 91 percent who had been born in America would soon take to calling themselves "nativists" or "Native Americans.") By 1855, when New York began formally processing immigrants at Castle Garden in Battery Park, 51 percent of the city had been born in another country—nativists were suddenly in the minority.

This rapid change was brought on primarily by two events: the Irish Potato Famine (known in much of the world simply as the Great Hunger), which laid waste to Ireland from 1845 to 1851, and the revolutions that swept across Europe in 1848.

By 1845, when a fungus-like blight began to kill the potato crop in Ireland, the large majority of poor Irish were tenant farmers, crowded onto tiny plots of land that they worked entirely on behalf of their landowners. Because their meager supply of good land was given over to cash crops, like wheat and barley, often the only food these farmers could grow for themselves was potatoes. It's been estimated that the poorest Irish families—who made an average of $14 per year—ate potatoes three meals a day, 364 days a year, supplemented by meat on Easter. So, when the potato crop failed, families were given the harsh choice of starving or leaving. During the worst year of the famine, 1847 (or "Black '47"), over 200,000 people left Ireland for New York, where, often penniless, they settled in the slum behind City Hall called Five Points. Typically, it was the younger men and women in the family who were sent to the States to earn money for the family; knowing that these children would never return to Ireland, a tradition arose of holding an "American wake"—not for the departed but for the departing.

Though politics certainly played some role in Irish immigration—the Act of Union in 1807 had placed Ireland under British rule, deepening economic and religious divisions throughout the country—political unrest was central to most other immigration after 1848. That year, a series of revolutions erupted thorough Europe, from southern Italy to France to the Austro-Hungarian Empire and the German states. Many Germans—both educated young men caught on the losing side of the uprising and farmers who'd lost everything backing the revolutionaries —flooded into New York after 1848, and some new German residents rose to the highest levels of the city's merchant elite.

As new immigrants, the Irish and Germans shared many traits and were thrown together into working-class New York City under relatively similar circumstances. But where at least some Germans found opportunities to leave the Five Points—or to avoid living there altogether—the Irish had to work much longer and harder to gain acceptance into American society. The most profound difference between them was religion; it would take over a century for the Irish in America to gain the same level of acceptance as the Germans, if, indeed, they have ever received the same approval. It is worth noting that the presidential election of 1928 pitted German-American Herbert Hoover against Irish-American (and New York City–born) Al Smith. For many, the election became a referendum on religion, and Hoover won handily. (Soon the two world wars would take their toll on the reputation of German-Americans, but in 1928 that hadn't fully happened yet.)

These chapters paint a picture of a growing immigrant city, but what also emerges is a New York that's more recognizable to modern eyes. It was the middle of the 19th century that gave us Central Park, for example: conceived in 1844, work began in 1853, and the architects drew up their plans in 1857—plans that are remarkably close to the park we see today. Similarly, department stores, like A. T. Stewart's Marble Palace, sprang up mid-century on Broadway, and while that venerable old store is gone, many of its competitors—like Brooks Brothers and R. H. Macy—thrive. Churches from this era, like Trinity on Wall Street and the Plymouth Church in Brooklyn, are still active and many of the grand townhouses that line the streets of Brooklyn Heights and Greenwich Village were built during this era of commercial and domestic growth.

42 The New City of Brooklyn

The first settlements in what is today the borough of Brooklyn were five small Dutch farming villages: Breuckelen, New Utrecht, Boswyck (today's Bushwick neighborhood), New Amersfoort, and Midwout (Midwood). A sixth village, Gravesend, was founded by religious dissenter Lady Deborah Moody in 1645 so that she and her followers could worship in peace. Having fled religious persecution—first in England and then in the equally rigid Massachusetts Bay colony—Moody was granted a patent of land by Dutch governor Willem Kieft. Moreover, Moody's Anabaptists were permitted to worship freely, even though Dutch West India Company policy expressly forbade any religion other than Calvinism. (This English community set in the midst of the Dutch would later come back to haunt them; when Richard Nicolls came to conquer the colony for the Duke of York [9], he was warmly welcomed at Gravesend.)*

Through the seventeenth century, Brooklyn remained a predominantly rural area—by 1800, the entire county had only 4,495 residents—and its six original villages served as population hubs in the midst of some of the best farmland within easy distance of New York City. However, in the first years of the 19th century, Brooklyn's waterfront began to emerge as a commercial hub to rival Manhattan. These piers and warehouses would later become so numerous that Brooklyn was sometimes called "the Walled City." As Brooklyn began to grow, developer Hezekiah Pierrepont

Brooklyn City Hall (today known as Borough Hall)

turned what had once been farmland on the bluff overlooking Lower Manhattan into a residential enclave called Brooklyn Heights. The neighborhood was made possible by Robert Fulton [24], who in 1814 opened a commercial ferry that could whisk people across the East River in 5 to 10 minutes in good weather.** This small neighborhood was the catalyst for a radical change in how New Yorkers thought about their lives. If you lived in Brooklyn Heights and worked in Manhattan, there was now a work sphere on one side of the river and a home life on the other—and they were no longer intimately connected. Not only had Pierrepont cre-

---

*The square of streets in the Gravesend neighborhood today bounded by the three Village Roads (north, south, and east) and Van Sicklen Street still adheres to Deborah Moody's original, egalitarian town plan.

**The two ends of this ferry line are now Fulton Street in Manhattan and Old Fulton Street in Brooklyn; it was the only road that began in one city and continued in the other.

ated the first American suburb, he'd created the commuter.

In 1836, many of the waterfront communities of Brooklyn incorporated into a city of their own, in part to regularize and oversee the port. The new city held a design contest for a grand city hall to stand just up the hill from the ferry. However, the contest's winner, Calvin Pollard, got no further than laying the foundations before Brooklyn had to quit the project due to lack of funds. By 1845 funds had been secured and builder Gamaliel King (who'd been the runner-up in the contest) was brought on to finish the job as long as he could make his building fit into Pollard's foundations. The resulting City Hall, opened in 1848, is one of the most impressive Greek Revival buildings of its era. A fire destroyed its original cupola in 1895, but a replacement was built in 1898, the same year the independent city of Brooklyn ceased to exist and was absorbed into the Greater City of New York [107].

During Brooklyn's 62 years as a city, it grew tremendously. When it was incorporated it had about 30,000 residents. Though this was only 10 percent of Manhattan's population, it still made Brooklyn the seventh-largest city in the country. In 1854, it annexed the city to its north, Williamsburgh (today the neighborhood of Williamsburg, without the "h"), and by 1898 it had spread out to fill the present borough's boundaries. It had also grown to a population of well over one million, making it the third-largest city in the country, behind only New York and Chicago.

43 The Burning of St. Mary's and the Ancient Order of Hibernians

In November 1831, New York witnessed one of the most brazen acts of anti-Catholic violence it had ever seen: the burning of St. Mary's Church on Sheriff Street.* The fire signaled a rising tide of hatred against immigrant Catholics. No arrests were made in the arson and no real investigation undertaken, but it seemed clear that it was nativists at work. The 1830s saw a rise of "Native American" (i.e., born in America) sentiment in the city. Their venom was aimed at all immigrants, but mostly targeted at the Catholic Irish, whose religion was considered more dangerous than that of Protestant or Jewish Germans.

With the help of parishioners and sympathetic non-Catholics, St. Mary's was immediately rebuilt—out of tough Manhattan schist—on a new lot on Grand Street. In 1837, fear that growing nativist feeling would prompt other acts of violence led to the creation of one of the first unified civic organization within the Irish community, the Ancient Order of Hibernians ("Hibernia" is Latin for Ireland). Founded in part to protect Catholic life and property, it also provided Irishmen with a sense of community and the opportunity to join an exclusive organization. (New York's traditional organizations, like the Freemasons, excluded them on the basis of their religion.) After the Irish Potato Famine began

---

*St. Mary's was only the third Catholic parish church in the city; the older St. Peter's on Barclay Street served the city's wealthier Catholics, while St. Patrick's Cathedral [28] and St. Mary's were for the growing working-class Irish population.

in 1845, the Hibernians' focus shifted toward helping immigrants navigate through the strange new city, providing job placement, housing, and financial assistance.

The home parish of the Ancient Order of Hibernians (AOH) was St. James, a small Greek Revival schist-and-brownstone structure on James Street. The church, built sometime in the mid-1830s, is possibly the work of Minard Lafever (a rival of Richard Upjohn and James Renwick [**44**]), but records of its construction are scarce. The church is remembered today not only as the birthplace of the Hibernians, but also for its most famous altar boy, Alfred E. Smith, who became New York's governor in 1919, and was the 1928 Democratic presidential candidate [**144**]. Though AOH continues as a fraternal organization, its most visible contribution to New York is organizing the annual St. Patrick's Day Parade.

To give some sense of what AOH was combating, consider what once stood directly across the street from St. James. Today it is the parish's school, but in the mid-19th century there was a Protestant mission here, opened specifically to lure Catholic children away from the "clutches" of the Roman church. As one contributor to the *New York Times* put it in 1855, he and his fellow Protestants believed that "the dispersion of the Irish race to strange lands is one of the inscrutable agencies of Providence for the spread of Catholic doctrines among the benighted heretics with whom they are forced into contact." To counteract these "heretics," the mission here on James Street placed candy and trinkets out front on Sunday mornings in hope of convincing the local Irish children to

The Church of St. James

come inside and hear about the evils of the pope and the joys of the Reformation.

44 The Gothic Revival: Richard Upjohn vs. James Renwick

Just 37 years old in 1839, Richard Upjohn was soon to become the most significant church architect in America. That year, he was chosen by the vestry of Trinity Church, the city's wealthiest and most influential parish [**11**], to build a new church. At the same time, 21-year-old James Renwick—who had never studied architecture or built a church in his life—was about to receive the commission for Grace Church in Greenwich Village, which would soon rival Trinity for its architecture and prestige.

∾ Upjohn's Trinity was the third version of the church to stand at the junction of Broadway and Wall Street. The original Trinity had burned down on September 21, 1776, in the fire that swept through the city

Trinity Church

Grace Church

as Washington's army retreated [16]. A second church was consecrated in 1790, but a series of heavy snowstorms in the winter of 1838–39 so badly damaged the roof that the vestry voted to tear down the building and start again. The snows came at an opportune moment. Already, neighborhoods like Greenwich Village had pulled prominent churchgoers northward. When churches like Grace (and its Village rival, Ascension [48]) were erected, trendy uptown residents had to decide whether it was worth traveling all the way downtown on Sunday morning. Trinity needed to do something to return itself—in its own eyes, at least—to its rightful place as the city's premier religious institution.

Upjohn's grand Gothic Revival building quickly restored Trinity to the forefront of the city's social and architectural scene. In 1844, architect Albert Gilman wrote of the almost-finished church: "[It] surpasses any church erected in England since the revival of the pointed style." Its spire, at 281 feet tall, made it not only the tallest church in the city, but New York's tallest building, a title it would retain for nearly 50 years. Part of what made the church so perfect was that Upjohn had copied it, almost exactly, from the design for "An Ideal Church" in the book *True Principles of Pointed or Christian Architecture* by A. W. Pugin, the leading English proponent of the Gothic Revival. And unlike many of Upjohn's successors and imitators, he had an attention to detail—overseeing everything from the stained glass to the exterior carvings—that gave Trinity an unequaled aesthetic appeal.

The building was also controversial, however, both inside and out. A devout "high church" Anglo-Catholic, Upjohn introduced architectural elements that were utterly foreign to most Americans, including a chancel at the west end of the church complete with a high altar and rows of choir stalls. (At first, this was deemed too Roman Catholic, and the stalls weren't used.) Outside, the building was constructed of brownstone, a locally quarried, soft sandstone. The stone was chosen for its outward resemblance to materials used in medieval English architecture, but not only did it lack the strength of schist, it was also commonly considered a cheap building material. Though many people tend today to call all single-family townhouses in New York "brownstones," in the 19th century no one would have conflated cheaper brownstone buildings with their more expensive brick cousins. (In her autobiography, Edith Wharton deplored the look of New York, claiming it was bathed in a "universal chocolate-coloured coating of the most hideous stone ever quarried.") Both at Trinity and at Ascension in Greenwich Village, Upjohn had to convince his employers that the look of brownstone outweighed its *déclassé* associations.

~ As work was getting under way on Trinity, a wealthy landowner in Greenwich Village, Hendrick Brevoort, sold a portion of the family's old farm to erect Grace Episcopal Church on Broadway at 10th Street.

Brevoort was from a Dutch family that had once owned most of the land between Washington and Union squares. He was so powerful, it was said, that he forced the Commissioners' Plan of 1811 [25] to remove one block of 11th Street between Broadway and Fourth Avenue so that his favorite tree would not be disturbed. While historians tend to dismiss that as a tall tale, there could be some truth to it. Brevoort may not have cared about his tree at all, but by stopping 11th Street, what he got was a large, unbroken tract of land that he could do with as he pleased. In 1843, Brevoort sold it to Grace Church, and in a case of genuine nepotism, his nephew, James Renwick, immediately won the architectural competition, despite being only 21 years old and having a résumé that included only work as an engineer on the Croton Aqueduct [46].

Unlike Upjohn, who relied heavily on Pugin's *True Principles*, Renwick was freer with the design details. Also unlike Trinity, Grace Church was built of marble, so that there could be no question of the social standing of its parishioners. Former mayor Philip Hone, now living on nearby Great Jones Street, soon tweaked the new parish's congregants in his diary:

This is to be a fashionable church and already its aisles are filled . . . with gay parties of ladies in feathers and "mousseline-delaine dresses" and dandies with moustaches and high heeled boots; the lofty arches resound with astute criticisms upon "Gothic Architecture" from fair ladies who have had the advantage of foreign travel, and scientific remarks upon "acoustics" from elderly millionaires who do not hear quite as well as formerly.

The other great New York diarist of the time, George Templeton Strong, took issue with the city's sudden love of all things Gothic and levied his criticism squarely at Renwick:

If the infatuated monkey showed the slightest trace or germ of feeling for his art, one could pardon and pass over blunders and atrocities. ... [Renwick is] caught up in the prevailing romantic preoccupation with keeps and dungeons illuminated by flashes of lightning and ringing with the clash of sword on shield.

Over the next 70 years, both Grace and Trinity would exert enormous influence on polite society. If you visit Grace today, the names of the families who rented pews are still attached. The front row is for the Schermerhorns, one of the most successful old Dutch trading families.* At Trinity, the names have been removed, but in their front row sat the most successful Schermerhorn of them all: Caroline Schermerhorn Astor, the doyenne of New York's elite. It was the size of her ballroom, which held 400 people, that determined the city's roster of socially acceptable families, which came to be known simply as the Four Hundred.

45 Charles Dickens Visits the Five Points

Historian Tyler Anbinder has posited that Five Points [37] was the most contemporaneously written-about neighborhood in American history. But most New Yorkers didn't *know* it in any real sense until the 1842 publication of Charles Dickens's travelogue *American Notes*, still one of the best of pieces of reportage about the United States in its adolescence.

The impetus for Dickens's work came not from a keen desire to know America better, but rather from a more pragmatic need to make money from his American audience. By 1840, Dickens was the best-selling author in the United States, but he realized no profit from any of his North American sales—the idea of international author royalties was still far in the future. So in 1842, he embarked on a lecture tour of the States, recording his observations in a journal with an eye toward later publication. In New York, he was wined and dined at Delmonico's, taken to the trendiest theater—and then brought to Five Points. His hosts reasoned that he was, after all, the world's foremost expert on slums, and therefore he'd be interested in our homegrown variety.

Dickens's reaction to Five Points is biting:

Poverty, wretchedness, and vice, are rife enough where we are going now. This is the place: these narrow ways, diverging to the right and left, and reeking everywhere with dirt and filth. Such lives as are led here, bear the same fruits here as elsewhere. The coarse and bloated faces at the doors, have counterparts at home, and all the wide world over. Debauchery has made the very houses prematurely old. See how the rotten beams are tumbling down, and how the patched and bro-

---

*The beautifully restored mercantile buildings at South Street Seaport are known as Schermerhorn Row.

ken windows seem to scowl dimly, like eyes that have been hurt in drunken frays. Many of those pigs live here. Do they ever wonder why their masters walk upright in lieu of going on all-fours? And why they talk instead of grunting?

New Yorkers reacted to these scenes from *American Notes* not by recoiling in horror—or by organizing social services or charity—but by becoming tourists. Indeed, the term "slumming" may have first been used to describe rich New Yorkers hiring Irish policemen to take them on guided tours of Five Points.

And the neighborhood wasn't even near its peak. This was still 1842 and no one knew that just around the corner lay the Irish Potato Famine, which would, within twenty years, make New York the second-largest Irish city in the world [**see 64**].

∽ In 1991, archaeological excavations underneath the site of the Daniel Patrick Moynihan U.S. Courthouse (which stands near what would have been one of the five points of the intersection) provided a revealing glimpse into the lives of the men and women who lived in the center of the neighborhood. The quality of some of the finds, including china teacups, imported glass, and children's porcelain dolls, rivaled what one would expect to find in any middle-class home of the time. While the neighborhood had more than

its fair share of poor residents, it was not home exclusively to the "poverty, wretchedness, and vice" that Dickens reported (though evidence of at least one brothel was unearthed in the same excavation).

The courthouse dig was the most complete modern, scientific exploration into the Five Points neighborhood; unfortunately, all but a handful of the finds from the site were stored in the basement of World Trade Center 6 and were destroyed on September 11, 2001 [**180**].

46 The Croton Aqueduct System

By the early 1840s, New York was facing a crisis. The population had surpassed 300,000 and was in danger of doubling every generation, which put the city's antiquated water supply in grave danger.

The polluting and subsequent draining of the Collect Pond [**22**] had robbed Lower Manhattan of its only viable source of good drinking water. Entrepreneurs brought water

Commemorative print celebrating the opening day of the Croton Aqueduct system

to the city from Greenwich Village and Long Island, but without a constant source of water for plumbing, the city was surely on the brink of failure.

Thus, it was with great relief that the Croton Aqueduct system opened on October 14, 1842. The system was built following ancient Roman principles, with water descending by gravity from the Croton River dam, 40 miles north of the city in Westchester County, in elevated iron pipe. The city had two large reservoirs: the receiving reservoir, where Central Park's Great Lawn now stands [151] and a distributing reservoir on 42nd Street, future home to the New York Public Library [128]. The system came to a grand, ceremonial terminus in City Hall Park at the Croton Fountain, the first fountain the city had ever been able to build that sprayed jets of water throughout the day.

If you look closely at the print commemorating the Croton Aqueduct's opening day, you'll see that taking pride of place at the front of the fountain is a horse-drawn fire engine. Despite the city's grave need for water for basic human consumption, what actually convinced the public that an aqueduct system was needed was the Great Fire of 1835 [41], which had destroyed most of the old city. Thus, New Yorkers weren't just celebrating their ability to drink a clean cup of water—they were glad that the next time fire struck, the volunteer firefighters would be able to vanquish it quickly.

However, when you stand in City Hall Park today and look at the fountain, you are not looking at the original, which stood less than 30 years. The gorgeous replacement by Jacob

Wrey Mould [**see 68**] was installed in 1871 at the behest of William "Boss" Tweed [**70**] in order that he and his cronies might make a little extra cash.

(An aside: the ubiquitous German cockroach was introduced to the city—quite coincidentally—around the same time, and people took to calling it "the Croton bug" on the assumption that it swam down from Westchester in the water supply.)

47 On the Outskirts: Bloomingdale Asylum and the Leake and Watts Orphan House

It is easy to forget when talking about the hustle of mid-19th-century New York that the city still barely reached 23rd Street. Everything north of 59th Street would have been considered the countryside. Not only were the areas of Manhattan outside the city still ideal for country homes, but the more remote parts of the island were also good for large-scale institutions that wanted both room and peace and quiet, such as the Bloomingdale Asylum for the Insane, established in 1821. The asylum, an offshoot of New York Hospital, stood on an undeveloped promontory just north of what had once been the old Dutch village of Bloomingdale ("valley of flowers"). It was here that George Washington's troops had won the Battle of Harlem Heights. The location was ideal for an asylum in that it was far enough away from the city to allow the hospital to create the sort of bucolic country landscape that was seen as crucial for the rehabilitation of the mentally ill. As Bloomingdale's historian would write in the 1840s:

> About thirty acres of it is under high cultivation, portions being devoted to grass, vegetables and ornamental shrubbery. The part last mentioned includes a liberal space, which is laid out and planted in one of the most approved styles of English gardening. . . . In short, there are but few, upon this side of the Atlantic, which bear so strong a resemblance to the beautiful homesteads of the wealthy, in the rural, cultivated districts of England.

The majority of the Bloomingdale property is now home to Columbia University [101]; however, in 1832, the eastern portion of the asylum's land was sold to the newly founded Leake and Watts orphanage, which was created from the fallout of a strange inheritance.

John Watts and John George Leake, both well-regarded downtown merchants, were best friends. Thus, when John George Leake died, childless, it wasn't that strange that he left his fortune to John Watts's son, Robert. What was a little more unusual was that, under the terms of the will, Robert Watts could only inherit if he was willing to change his last name to Leake, thus becoming John George Leake's de facto son and heir. Though it sounds strange today, at the time it wasn't unheard-of; for example, in 1847, Stuyvesant Rutherfurd inherited his great-uncle Peter Gerard

Stuyvesant's fortune by changing his name to Rutherfurd Stuyvesant, though in that case they were still keeping the money in the family.

John Watts was crushed when his son decided to go through with it and take the money by becoming Robert Leake. But he was even more devastated just a few months later when Robert died. And because he died intestate, John Watts suddenly found himself inheriting his friend John George Leake's money, which he absolutely did not want.

Had Robert turned down the money in the first place, it would have gone to provide a home for orphaned children. So, John Watts went to the courts and asked them to take the inheritance and apply it to this use, which they did, creating the Leake and Watts Orphan House. They negotiated the purchase of land from the Bloomingdale Asylum not only to give children access to fresh air and open space, but also to take them away from the lures and pitfalls of neighborhoods like Five Points [45].

The orphanage's main building opened in 1843. It was designed by Ithiel Town, whose firm also did Federal Hall National Memorial on Wall Street [see 18], and is the oldest building that still stands in the neighborhood now known as Morningside Heights. It is an outstanding example of the sort of Greek temple architecture then in vogue. Many years later, the orphanage moved to Westchester County and the land was purchased by the Cathedral of St. John the Divine [100].

48 "His Accidency": John Tyler and the Church of the Ascension

By the late 1830s, Trinity Church's virtual monopoly on good pews (where one could "see and be seen") was undermined when its vestry decided to tear down the church and build a new one [44]. But even before construction on the new Trinity could begin, its architect, Richard Upjohn, had been hired by the fledgling Church of the Ascension in Greenwich Village to build it a parish church as fast as possible.

The resulting structure, on Fifth Avenue at 10th Street, opened five years before Trinity and is one of the earliest examples of English Gothic Revival architecture in New York. It also served as a way for Upjohn to test his designs before constructing the larger Trinity downtown. Prior to this point, churches in the city had either been designed in a neoclassical style (such as at the Church of St. James [43]) or, more commonly, as plain Puritan-inspired boxes. (For examples of this, see the original St. Paul's Chapel [14] and St. Augustine's [36].)

Soon after it opened, Ascension became internationally famous as the site of the first marriage of a sitting U.S. president. President John Tyler wed Julia Gardiner here in June 1844 and it was one of the juiciest pieces of gossip of its age, not least because it was, for all intents, an elopement.

Neither Tyler nor Gardiner was a stranger to scandal and public scrutiny. Tyler is best remembered today as the first vice president ever to ascend to the presidency. The president, William Henry Harrison, caught pneumonia at his own inaugural while delivering a nearly two-hour address in the freezing cold; thirty days later he had succumbed to the disease. Tyler immediately assumed the presidency, despite the fact that the U.S. Constitution did not explicitly give the vice president the right to serve out the president's term. (Indeed, this right of succession wasn't spelled out until the 25th Amendment passed in the wake of John F. Kennedy's assassination.) Some took to calling the new president "His Accidency."

Meanwhile, Julia Gardiner was considered one of the most eligible young women in New York. A descendent of Lion Gardiner, one of the earliest English settlers on Long Island, she was both beautiful and astonishingly rich. Today, Gardiners Island, off the east coast of Long

"The Rose of Long Island," Miss Julia Gardiner and Gentleman in front of Bogert & Mecamly's.

Island, is still the largest privately owned island in America.

Julia was also clearly a rebellious and bored young woman. In 1840, she appeared in a handbill advertisement for Bogert & Mecamly, a dry-goods store. Julia stands clutching a handbag that is actually a sign:

I'll purchase at Bogert & Mecamly's, number 86 Ninth Avenue. Their goods are beautiful and astonishingly cheap.

Julia's family was horrified. Not only was she shilling for a middle-class department store while wearing a gaudy frock, she was doing it on the arm of a man who was not a male relative. Of all the social faux pas in Victorian New York, the unchaperoned female was high on the list.

Julia was immediately sent to Europe to learn her social graces. Soon upon her return, she met President Tyler—who was less than five months a widower—and the two began an oblique romance. Within a few weeks, he had proposed to her. Julia demurred, but Tyler was not easily dissuaded. In February 1844, he invited Julia and her father, David, to see the first demonstration of the U.S. Navy's new twelve-inch gun "the Peacemaker." The gun exploded in the breech, killing four people—including David Gardiner—and further marking Tyler's presidency for ignominy.

Four months later, Julia and the president were married at a secret ceremony at the Church of the Ascension, near the Gardiners' New York City residence on Lafayette Place [33]. Tyler was loath to tell his children about the wedding. His el-

dest daughter, Mary, was five years older than Julia, who was 24—and the president was himself only nine years older than Julia's mother.*

However, word soon spread of the nuptials—not least because Julia took Washington by storm, spending her nine months as first lady in a whirl of social engagements and state functions. She established new, more rigid protocols (including the tradition that "Hail to the Chief" be played every time the president made an appearance) and catapulted herself into a lifetime career as Former First Lady Julia Tyler.

49 July 3, 1844: William Cullen Bryant and Central Park

One of most important turning points in New York's history came on July 3, 1844, when celebrated journalist William Cullen Bryant penned an editorial in his *New-York Evening Post* entitled, quite simply, "A New Public Park."

Bryant was one of the great cultural icons of his day. In addition to running the *Evening Post*, which he did for 50 years, he was a lawyer, an early champion of the Republican Party, a philanthropist, and a noted poet. (His best-known work, "Thanatopsis," was a meditation on death. Mostly composed when Bryant was 16, it launched him into the top ranks of American poets.)

But for most New Yorkers, Bryant's greatest contribution has to be planting the seed for Central Park. Bryant chose the date of his editorial

---

*Tyler was 54 years old but looked "ten years older" according to Philip Hone.

carefully. It was eve of Independence Day and in the mid-19th century this was the only public holiday of the year.* The editorial began:

> The heats of summer are upon us, and while some are leaving the town for shady retreats in the country, others refresh themselves with short excursions to Hoboken or New Brighton, or other places among the beautiful environs of our city. If the public authorities who expend so much of our money in laying out the city, would do what is in their power, they might give our vast population an extensive pleasure ground for shade and recreation in these sultry afternoons, which we might reach without going out of town.

For the city's wealthiest citizens, a public park wasn't high on their list of priorities. For a stroll in the garden, there was Washington Square [35]. And just a few hours by steamboat up the Hudson lay pristine wilderness. Indeed, Bryant was very familiar with the Hudson River valley, where he traveled frequently with his friends, many of them members of the Hudson River School, America's first indigenous art movement. But Bryant was keenly aware that his enjoyment of nature was beyond the reach of the average working-class New Yorker.

His plea was subtle but pointed. People of his social station had the ability to go to "shady retreats in the country." "Others" (i.e., the middle class) had the option of going to Hoboken for the day. But a green place was needed in the city for the "vast population"—the newly arrived immigrants. And it was crucial that this pleasure ground be on Manhattan, for even a day trip across the Hudson could be prohibitively expensive.

Bryant, in fact, had already picked out a spot: a "striking and picturesque" area on the east side between 68th and 77th streets. Though he did not mention it by name in his editorial, this was Jones Woods, a thickly forested area already popular with pleasure seekers looking for a quick retreat from the crowded city. But as Bryant did note, one stumbling block would be the "difficulty of persuading the owners of the soil to part with it."

Over the next few years support for the project grew quickly. The *Evening Post*'s great rival, Horace Greeley's *Tribune* [see 58], endorsed the idea, warning that the city should learn from past mistakes: "[I]n a few short years, the lovely waste may be covered with close, dusty, dingy streets and endless piles of bricks and mortar." The grandest champion was landscape architect Andrew Jackson Downing, who tirelessly campaigned for a "people's park." However, Downing realized that there was more wrong with Jones Woods than just convincing its owners to sell. At just over 150 acres it was too small; it was too densely wooded to be properly sculpted into a park setting; and it was too far on the east side, making it difficult for half the city to access. And the lovely waterfront—where Bryant hoped "the tides may be allowed to flow pure"—would surely

---

*New York's long history of Calvinism, which discouraged the celebration of Christmas, meant that if December 25 didn't fall on a Sunday, it was a workday.

soon become docks and piers like the rest of the island. Instead of Jones Woods, Downing advocated a spot more central to the rest of the city—and thus took to calling his proposed area "the Central Park."

Little did Bryant know when he penned this editorial how quickly Central Park would be needed. As famine and revolution brought in Irish and German immigrants, the population skyrocketed; by the time the park was open to the public in 1858, the city's population had almost reached 800,000 people.

50 A. T. Stewart Invents Modern Shopping

It's hard to imagine in a city as shopping-obsessed as New York, but for all of America's history up to the 1820s—both as a colony and an independent nation—the modern concept of shopping didn't exist. (This was true outside America as well.) While you might go to the market for perishables on a frequent basis, there was no sense that you went browsing for other goods. Indeed, in the first years of the 19th century most Americans had their clothes tailored or made their outfits themselves. Pattern books and fabric were essential to being well dressed, and the process of haggling with wholesale dealers for the right cloth and accoutrements was arduous and time-consuming.

In the course of a few short years, Scotch-Irish immigrant Alexander T. Stewart changed all that. Like many immigrants, Stewart got to America with little money in his pocket. Arriving in 1818, he worked a vari-

ety of jobs, including in warehouses and wholesale dry-goods stores. He went to Belfast in 1823 to collect a small inheritance (which evidently he couldn't get his hands on); however, he was still able to return to the United States with lace and other

A. T. Stewart's Marble Palace

material and go into business for himself. When his initial supplies ran low, Stewart began visiting auction houses, buying wholesale and used merchandise that he and his wife would meticulously repair and iron, and then showcase as if new.

We take so much of what Stewart did for granted that it's remarkable no one had operated a store quite like his before. First, he sold items complete and ready-to-wear. Second, he prominently displayed all those items, both arranged throughout the store and in the shop window itself, so that all customers could readily see what was on offer. Third, every item had a price tag. Fourth, that price was firm—Stewart might lower it for an "end of season" sale (another of his innovations), but you weren't expected to barter with him for a better price. Fifth, he made note of the market fluctuations and consistently changed his prices to beat his competitors. In short, he revolutionized the way people thought about buying clothes, inventing the modern department store and making himself a fortune in the process.

In 1846, he invested a great deal of that fortune in a new store at the corner of Broadway and Chambers Street. The building was the first store ever built of marble. The *New York Herald* soon dubbed it "the Marble Palace" and it instantly became the fashionable shopping destination.

As Philip Hone noted in his diary: "There is nothing in Paris or London to compare with this dry-goods palace." He was worried, however, about the windows.

My attention was attracted, in passing this morning to a most extraordinary, and I think useless, piece of extravagance. Several of the windows on the first floor, nearly level with the street, are formed of plate-glass, six feet by eleven, which must have cost four or five hundred dollars each, and may be shivered by a boy's marble or a snow-ball as effectually as by a four-pound shot.

While Stewart's windows stayed intact, he soon faced the greater challenge of a host of competitors lining Broadway. Stewart, however, would not lose his primacy as the city's shopping king until his death in 1876 [82].

51 Pilgrims in Brooklyn

As New York and Brooklyn [42] developed along separate, parallel trajectories, one of the marked differences between the two cities was religion. While the Episcopal Church remained the elite church in both cities, Brooklyn had a much greater affinity for the denominations popular in New England: Universalism, Unitarianism, and, most important, Congregationalism. At its peak, the wealthy Brooklyn Heights neighborhood supported two major Congregational churches, the Plymouth Church on Orange Street, and the Church of the Pilgrims on nearby Henry Street. The first pastor of the Plymouth Church, built in 1849, was Henry Ward Beecher, who was not only the most famous person ever to call Brooklyn home, but was also, at the peak of his fame, probably the most famous person in America.

Beecher came from a distinguished family. His father, Lyman Beecher, was a well-known preacher, and his sister, Harriet Beecher Stowe, authored the most famous anti-slavery novel, *Uncle Tom's Cabin*. Henry Ward Beecher, also an ardent abolitionist [65], became known for his lengthy, often extemporaneous sermons, which covered a host of reform-minded topics from the evils of slavery to the benefits of temperance to the need to enfranchise women. Steam ferries nicknamed "Beecher Boats" would bring hundreds of people over from Manhattan each Sunday to hear him. Mark Twain described his experience seeing Beecher at Plymouth Church:

[Beecher was] sawing his arms in the air, howling sarcasms

this way and that, discharging rockets of poetry and exploding mines of eloquence, halting now and then to stamp his foot three times in succession to emphasize a point.

At the peak of his fame, Beecher was such a household name that he was paid handsomely to shill for products like throat lozenges and soap. (The soap advertisement began, "If cleanliness is next to godliness, soap must be considered as a 'means of grace.'") These endorsement deals probably made him the highest-paid clergyman in America.

But Beecher did much more than simply preach. As a supporter of the Free Soil movement,* he sent rifles to settlers in Kansas in boxes marked "Bibles" and from that point the guns used to fight slavery in the west were known as Beecher's Bibles. After the passage of the Fugitive Slave Act in 1850, the basement of the Plymouth Church became such a key stop on the Underground Railroad that it was known as "Grand Central." In 1860, Republican presidential candidate Abraham Lincoln visited the church, which was, in effect, an endorsement of the candidate by one of the country's most respected abolitionists. In fact, Lincoln had been invited to address the congregation, but fearing he would draw too large a crowd, the lecture was moved to Manhattan's Cooper Union the next day [66].

∾ The nearby Church of the Pilgrims on Henry Street, designed by Richard Upjohn and completed in 1846, is actually the older of the two Congregational churches in Brooklyn Heights. The heavy, unadorned Romanesque church was out of character for Upjohn [44]. No doubt he was in part bowing to the demands of his Puritan clients, but

The Remsen Street doors of the Church of the Pilgrims (today Our Lady of Lebanon)

there may be more at work here. Upjohn was an "ecclesiological" architect and firmly believed that his Episcopal churches were bringing their parishioners closer to God. He may have changed from his normal Gothic style here because he didn't

---

*Free-Soilers advocated keeping the western territories and states free from slavery, in particular after the passage of the 1854 Kansas-Nebraska Act, which would permit slavery in new states north of the line established by the Missouri Compromise through a notion known as popular sovereignty.

want to help the Congregationalists get any closer to heaven than was necessary.

In order to give the structure a genuine connection to the Pilgrims and establish the congregation's Puritan bona fides, a piece of the Plymouth Rock was chiseled off and set into the tower. For 54 years, the parish was led by Richard S. Storrs, who in his own day rivaled Henry Ward Beecher in popularity in Brooklyn, but who never achieved Beecher's national prominence.

In the 1940s, with the size of their congregations shrinking, the Church of the Pilgrims merged into the Plymouth Church. The building on Henry Street was sold (after the chunk of the Plymouth Rock was extracted from the wall), and the doors and Tiffany stained-glass windows stripped from the church to be taken to the parish hall at Plymouth (which is today known as the Plymouth Church of the Pilgrims). The Henry Street building was bought by the Lebanese Catholic Church and rechristened Our Lady of Lebanon. However, it had one small problem: no windows or doors.

If you visit the church today and look at the doors on both the Henry and Remsen Street sides of the building, they don't, at first glance, seem out of place. But when you examine them closer, you see that the scenes depicted are not typical ecclesiastical motifs, in particular the large cruise ship, *Ile de France*, being towed into port on the Remsen Street entrance. In

fact, these doors were purchased secondhand—they once adorned the formal dining room of the SS *Normandie*. The ship's interiors were stripped when the *Normandie*, seized by the United States after Hitler invaded France, was in New York being refitted as a troop transport. During the conversion, an acetylene torch caught fire and the ship sank on its moorings in the Hudson, which meant that the furnishings could never be reinstalled. Instead, they were sold at auction, and these grand doors, which feature Norman churches and Crusader castles, found a home here.

52 The Astor Place Riot and the Central Park Arsenal

By the late 1830s, a popular entertainment district had arisen along the Bowery north of Chatham Square with theaters, opera houses, and beer gardens.* Because this stretch of the Bowery bordered Five Points [45], some theaters began to lose their "uptown" audience and in 1847, the subscription-only Astor Place Opera House opened for the residents of Greenwich Village and Gramercy Park.

After a successful first season, the opera house began to falter (a season of nothing but Donizetti operas didn't help), and in 1849 it invited acclaimed British tragedian William Macready to perform *Macbeth* dur-

---

*In 1836, the city still only had a total of five theaters. The *New York Mirror* complained this was too many. "The resident population would not more than adequately support one" and visitors "might possibly eke out a respectable audience for two more—but for five! that's too great a supply for the demand."

ing his tour of the United States. This annoyed the champions of American actor Edwin Forrest. Forrest had recently returned from a disappointing European tour (where he'd been hissed and booed in London), so to tweak Macready, Forrest had embarked on a tour of the same cities Macready was playing in the States, doing his rival version of *Macbeth*. Thus, when Macready was scheduled to appear at the Astor Place Opera House, the Bowery Theater downtown would mount Forrest's production of *Macbeth*.

Had this been nothing more than two rival Shakespearens treading the boards, things might have remained calm. However, the audience at the Bowery Theater, led by the rowdy Bowery B'hoys (a quasi-gang), turned it into a violent clash over class and values. Was Macready, an imported British actor, better than Forrest, his American rival? They set out to prove he was not.

It is worth noting that most Bowery B'hoys were Irish and thus some of their desire to see Forrest triumph was likely the result of their own anti-British sentiments. But beyond that, their embrace of Forrest shows acknowledgment of their connection to their new home and their attempt to self-identify as Americans. Moreover, the Bowery Theater, where Forrest's *Macbeth* was set to play, was clearly hoping to reap the financial benefits of hiring an American actor with mass audience appeal.

This was a great contrast to the elite Astor Place Opera House, which was so upper crust that it had a dress code mandating kid gloves for men. To Five Pointers, the opera house's hiring of Macready was a sign that there must not be an American actor good enough to perform for high society. (While the opera house had, in fact, consistently hired Americans, it was true that New York society still took its cultural cues from Europe.)

On May 7, 1849, Macready fled from the stage at the Astor Place Opera House when he was greeted with rotten eggs, old shoes, and other objects smuggled into the theater by Five Pointers who'd infiltrated the audience (with or without kid gloves is unknown). Macready refused to go on the next two nights, but on May 10, he agreed to continue. All the day before, Bowery B'hoys and Isaiah Rynders—a political heavyweight in the Five Points and personal fan of Edward Forrest—had posted flyers around town encouraging people to come to Astor Place at performance time. As the flyer announced in capital letters: SHALL AMERICANS OR ENGLISH RULE IN THIS CITY?

By the time the performance began, a crowd of between 10,000 and 20,000 people surrounded the theater, pelting it with bricks and paving stones. New York's elite militia, the Seventh Regiment [85], was called in to quell the riot—the first time a military unit had been asked to do so in peacetime. When the crowd did not disperse, the soldiers were given the order to fire, and by the end of the evening scores had been injured and eighteen people had been killed; four more people would die from their injuries over the next few days.

Though the rioters reconvened the next night, it was a peaceful protest—now no longer aimed at the theater but at the Seventh Regiment and the city for killing so many people.

The Astor Place Riot, as it came to be known, was not the worst in the city's history—that would come during the Civil War [67]—nor was it the first. Not only had nativists burned St. Mary's Church [43], there had been an election riot in 1834, anti-abolitionist riots in 1834 and 1835, and a food riot during a financial panic in 1837. As a result, the State of New York began work in 1847 on a new uptown arsenal that was to stand at Fifth Avenue and 64th Street—beyond the northern outskirts of town—and house munitions. That way, militia companies could have ready access to firearms if they needed them, but the building would be remote enough that if it exploded in the middle of the night, no lives would be lost.

The arsenal was designed as a miniature medieval fortress, not only to convey to the viewer its solid construction but to serve as a warning of the danger inside. (To underscore this point, the exterior was further decorated in 1935–36 under the guidance of the WPA with a banister of white rifles and other military decoration like drums, cannon balls, and medieval pikes.) The arsenal was completed in 1851, but just two years later found itself annexed into the land for the new Central Park [55]. Today, the arsenal survives in part because its picturesque design intrigued the park's designers, Calvert Vaux and Frederick Law Olmsted [61], and has become home to the New York City Parks Department.

The Astor Place Opera House, meanwhile, barely survived the riot. It passed through a succession of managers and eventually closed in 1853. In its last years, it opened its doors to all customers, including Five Pointers. But even though the riot gained them access to the theater, they did not patronize it enough to make it viable and it was sold to become a library; the building was replaced in 1892.

The front entrance of the arsenal in Central Park

53 Jenny Lind and P. T. Barnum: New York as Entertainment Capital

While the Astor Place Riot [52] made headlines for the Bowery Theater and the Astor Place Opera House, the most famous entertainment venue in the city by 1850 was Castle Garden in Battery Park, thanks to the showmanship of P. T. Barnum.

The structure, built for the War of 1812 and known for years as Castle Clinton [27], saw no action as a military fortification. It was used occasionally by the city for ceremonial purposes, such as hosting a gala for the Marquis de Lafayette in 1824 [**33**]. That same year, it was leased privately to become a concert venue and changed its name to Castle Garden, to better evoke its genteel atmosphere. The outdoor seating arranged around the top of the fort was soon replaced by an enclosed second story, and all of the original brownstone walls were enclosed in new wooden construction.

Jenny Lind onstage at Castle Garden

The most famous performer ever to grace the stage of Castle Garden was soprano Jenny Lind. Nicknamed "the Swedish Nightingale," she was brought to America in 1850 by Barnum, who was just hitting his stride as an impresario. In 1835, he took over the promotion of Joice Heth, a black woman who claimed both to be over 160 years old and to have been George Washington's nurse when he was a baby. She quickly was earning Barnum $1,500 a week (this in an era when many Five Pointers might not make that much in three years). By the 1840s, Barnum was running variety shows, and in 1841 he purchased a permanent home for his exploits at the corner of Broadway and Ann Street. Called simply the American Museum, it featured everything from minstrel shows to Charles Stratton, who was just 25 inches tall and nicknamed "Tom Thumb." It was here that Barnum could have—but probably did not—speak the oft-quoted words "There's a sucker born every minute but none of them ever die." (He definitely said the less quotable "The people like to be humbugged.")

Lind's sold-out run at Castle Garden is a great example of Barnum's deft public relations. Before Lind arrived in America, she was a star in Europe but virtually unknown in the United States. But the first performances (the proceeds of which were for charity) on September 11 and 14, 1850, netted $24,341—for just two nights!

By the time the run at Castle Garden was over, Lind was the most famous singer in America and Barnum was well on his way to becoming a household name.

However, the theater never got an opportunity to host another blockbuster event. In 1855, the building's lease returned to the city and it reopened as the Castle Garden Emigrant Landing Depot, America's first official immigrant processing station [**59**].

54 The Crystal Palace Exposition of 1853

*Around a palace, loftier, fairer, ampler
    than any yet,
Earth's modern wonder, history's
    seven outstripping,
High rising tier on tier with glass and
    iron facades,
Gladdening the sun and sky, enhued
    in cheerfulest hues,
Bronze, lilac, robin's-egg, marine and
    crimson,
Over whose golden roof shall flaunt,
    beneath thy banner Freedom,
The banners of the States and flags of
    every land,
A brood of lofty, fair, but lesser palaces
    shall cluster.*

—Walt Whitman, "Song of the
    Exposition"

London's Crystal Palace Exposition, the first World's Fair, opened in Hyde Park in 1851. Its gigantic iron-and-glass structure (it showcased over a million feet of glass) featured exhibitors from 28 countries demonstrating European technological innovation and, in particular, Britain's dominance in the burgeoning Industrial Revolution. Over 6 million people visited the exhibit in just six months; indeed, it was such a great success that it was later rebuilt in nearby Bromley as the Winter Park and Garden, the world's first theme park.

America, now 75 years old, was ready to step out of the shadow of its European rivals and show that it, too, was a progressive and inventive nation. New York, birthplace of such wonders as Robert Fulton's steamboat [24], seemed the perfect place to host the event, and in 1853, a Crystal Palace Exposition opened in its own iron-and-glass palace in Reservoir Square at 42nd Street and Sixth Avenue. Today called Bryant Park, the square stood beside the distributing reservoir for the Croton water system [46].

The Crystal Palace in Reservoir Square (today's Bryant Park)

The exposition was a tremendous success, drawing both American and European visitors. The greatest piece of showmanship at the fair—and, perhaps, the most important technological advance—was the first public demonstration by Elisha Otis of his new elevator safety brake.

The idea of the elevator was not new; since antiquity, hoists and pulleys had moved cargo. But ropes frayed and pulleys malfunctioned, which meant that there had never been a viable passenger elevator. Without elevators, commercial buildings were limited to six or seven stories, and rents diminished the farther one had to climb from the street. Otis's invention was a mechanism to automatically stop an elevator in the event of a fall. And to show the world how much he trusted it, he used himself as the test subject.

One block north of the Crystal Palace grounds stood the Latting Observatory, with a steam-powered elevator that could take visitors up two levels. They would then, however, have to climb stairs to the top of the observatory, as no one trusted an elevator to take them higher. For his demonstration Otis got inside the elevator cab, which was suspended from the top of the observatory, and called down to his assistant, who—with a dramatic flourish—severed the elevator cable. The cab lurched, dropped an inch, and then shook to a halt, held in place by Otis's new brake.

The hundreds of people in the audience witnessed a fundamental revolution in architecture. It would take a generation for it to be fully realized, but the Crystal Palace had given birth to the skyscraper. (The first building to use Otis's technology, E. V. Haughwout's china store, which still stands on Broadway, opened just four years later [60].)

Alas, the Crystal Palace did not last much longer. The exposition closed in November 1854, though the buildings were used for other events. In 1858, a fire swept through Reservoir Square. The 2,000 people inside the palace were evacuated, but despite the fact that the building had been touted as being made out of fireproof iron, it burned down completely in less than an hour.

55 The City Seizes the Land for Central Park

When William Cullen Bryant first proposed a city park [49], he had his sights set on Jones Woods on what is today the Upper East Side. Despite objections to this site by America's chief landscape designer, Andrew Jackson Downing, the state legislature moved forward with a bill to give the city the right of eminent domain to acquire the Jones Woods site for a park.

However, by 1851 the Jones Woods bill had stalled and Downing, seizing the moment, convinced the legislature that his plan for a larger, centrally located park of at least 500 acres was viable. The area he wanted ranged north of 59th Street and was some of the most inhospitable land in the city, with tremendous amounts of raw Manhattan schist rising up from the ground [1]. Most was owned by land speculators, but relatively little was being used. A few areas had been rented to pig farmers, bone boilers, or other so-called nuisance industries; there was a small village near 86th Street called Seneca that was home to over 250 Irish as well as black people emancipated in 1827 [**36**]; and in the center of it all was the massive limestone receiving reservoir for the city's water system [**46**]. Downing persuasively argued that the amount of work the city would have to do to prepare this area for sustained commercial or residential growth wasn't worth the investment. However, in the right hands, it could be turned into not just a park, but the most impressive park ever built.

On July 21, 1853, the legislature agreed and gave the city of New York right of eminent domain over an area bounded by Fifth and Eighth avenues (about half a mile across) running from 59th Street to 106th Street (just shy of 2.5 miles). To solve some engineering problems, the park expanded to its present northern border, 110th Street, in 1859, to occupy a full 843 acres.

The first task the city faced was removing the residents. The city estimated what it thought the land was worth and compensated the landowners, but that didn't mollify the people who were working the land. Most disruptive was the fact that Seneca Village sat just inside the Eighth Avenue boundary of the park, so the entire developed area, including homes, shops, and three churches, would have to be torn down. In order to win its case in the press, the city began early on referring to the park's tenants as "squatters" even though almost all had the legal right to be there. But the city's campaign succeeded in turning public opinion against the mainly immigrant and black residents and soon they were forced off the land.*

The next step was to survey the land and begin the arduous task of removing some of the worst outcroppings of bedrock. For this, the city hired noted engineer Egbert Viele, the foremost expert on the city's schist deposits. (Viele's map of Manhattan is still used by architects and engineers today.) However, the park was without an architect due to the death of Andrew Jackson Downing. In July 1852, Downing was on the steamboat *Henry Clay* on the Hudson River when the boat's owner decided to race with the *Armenia*, a nearby vessel. The *Henry Clay*'s overtaxed boiler caught fire and Downing drowned while attempting to save other passengers. This was a crushing blow—not only had Central Park lost its most fervent supporter, America had lost its premier landscape designer. It would fall to one of Downing's assistants, Calvert Vaux, to move the project to its next stage [**61**].

56 Mixed Ale Alley: Rich and Poor in Greenwich Village

It has always been true that in densely populated Manhattan, rich and poor have rubbed shoulders and neighborhoods can shift from wealthy to working class over the course of just one street. No place is this more apparent than the "back houses" of the West Village called Grove Court.

Because of a curve in Grove Street—a holdover from older prop-

---

*One lone foundation stone on the park's west side, near 85th Street, is the only visible reminder of Seneca Village.

erty lines—there was a small, unused section behind the house lots near Hudson Street. Tiny back buildings, aimed at the city's working poor, were built by a local grocer, Samuel Cocks, who ran the store at the corner of Bedford Street and hoped to profit from additional residents in the neighborhood.

The six small houses were officially named Grove Court but soon came to be known as Mixed Ale Alley—that is, if you lived there, you were so poor that you couldn't afford a glass of beer. Instead you were forced to mix from the bottoms of nearly empty casks. (Beer gives us a number of similar derogatory metaphors for the poor, such as "bottom of the barrel" and "dregs of society.")

Today, the homes of Grove Court, tucked away behind a quiet garden and locked iron fence, are seen as the epitome of West Village charm. But when the homes were finished around 1854, contemporary observers would have immediately known they were for the working class.

First of all, the homes were too small. Even the smallest townhouse of the era was usually 2,000 square feet (and many were double that size); the Grove Court homes were barely 900 square feet. Second, the homes were too far removed from the street. Street frontage was of great significance, not just to New York's elite, but for any homeowner. It allowed passersby to assess the size of the lot (wider ones being more expensive) and to admire the quality and material of the workmanship. But most important, street frontage showcased the home's stoop.

Stoops in New York were a fundamental social marker. Because the Commissioners' Plan of 1811 [25] left no room for back alleys, houses typically had no rear entrances. This meant that both the people who lived in the house and the servants would have to enter from the front. To solve the dilemma of how to get both groups into the house without having them use the same door, New Yorkers settled on the steep front staircase, called a stoop (after the Dutch *stoep*, or porch, that graced the front of most New Amsterdam houses). The door at the top of the stoop became the formal entrance to the house; a small door under the stoop was used by tradesmen and servants.

If you look through the gate at Grove Court today, you will see that the homes have no stoops at all; this alone would have been an indication that the people who lived here were the poorest residents of the Village, for by the middle of the 19th century even the least wealthy members of the city's middle class could afford to have one servant.

Grove Court appears in O. Henry's 1907 story "The Last Leaf" about an ailing young artist named Johnsy dying of pneumonia in one of the back houses. She swears that when the last leaf falls from the tree it will be a sign and she will die, so her downstairs neighbor takes it upon himself to make sure that never happens. (We won't spoil the rest for you.)

57 McSorley's Old Ale House

In 1854, John McSorley opened a saloon on Seventh Street near the

Bowery. It was only a five-minute walk from the just-closed Astor Place Opera House [52], a sure sign that the Irish-immigrant Bowery was quickly growing to envelop the area that only 20 years earlier had been the elite northern outpost of the city. (In turn, the richest New Yorkers were now moving farther uptown to the areas of Fifth Avenue north of 23rd Street, like Murray Hill.)

Little is known about the earliest years of McSorley's; some historians contest the 1854 opening date, but it is certain that even if the bar did not open that year, it was running by the late 1850s, which makes it the oldest pub still operating in New York. Like many bars of its day, it did not admit women and for years McSorley's motto was "Good Ale, Raw Onions, and No Ladies." (The onions refer to the bowls of raw pearl onions left on the bar for patrons to snack on.)

When Abraham Lincoln spoke at Cooper Union [66], it is said that Peter Cooper brought Lincoln by for a drink afterward. If this story is true, the abstemious Lincoln must have had water, as McSorley's only served one kind of beer—its own, initially brewed on the premises—and nothing else. After Lincoln was assassinated, the bar quickly hung a wanted poster for John Wilkes Booth, which is still there—along with, it seems, almost everything else that has ever been stuck to the walls in the last 150 years. The bar still only serves one type of beer, in light and dark varieties, which must be ordered by the round (i.e., a minimum of two small glasses). The "no women" rule was struck down by a lawsuit in 1970.

58 Horace Greeley and the Republican Party

No city in America has ever had the depth of newspaper coverage of New York. At the peak of the newspaper era, in the years surrounding the Civil War, the city had a dozen daily papers in English, along with German-language papers, Irish papers, weeklies, monthlies, and special-interest publications. Of the papers of this era, only two, the *New-York Evening Post* (today just the *Post*) and the *New York Times* survive. The *Times*, founded in 1851 on a decidedly anti-immigrant platform, would not become the "paper of record" for years and wouldn't achieve any real prominence until its role in the downfall of William "Boss" Tweed in 1872 [70]. The greatest rival to Wil-

Horace Greeley

liam Cullen Bryant's *Evening Post* was Horace Greeley's *New York Tribune*, one of the most progressive papers of its day.

Greeley, born in 1811 in Amherst,

New Hampshire, is probably best remembered today for an editorial that appeared in the *Tribune* in 1865 entitled, "Go West, Young Man!" in which he encouraged civil servants to leave Washington, D.C., and settle the country.* Though the question of slavery had been resolved by this point, the editorial was an outgrowth of Greeley's support for the pre–Civil War Free-Soil movement [**see 51**], which had hoped to see abolitionist settlers head west to fill the territories. The movement encouraged Irish immigrants to make the westward move; Greeley and other Free Soilers thought they had a good chance of convincing the Irish because they saw Catholicism as incompatible with slavery. If the Irish were to move west, the territories there would grow populous enough to be admitted as states. Those states, in turn, would choose to be free states that would fill Congress with enough votes to legislate slavery out of existence. By encouraging the Irish to leave New York, the Free-Soilers hoped to serve other agendas as well. Had the Irish gone west, it would have lessened the city's population problems and averted some of the conflict between Catholics and nativists. (That this mass migration never happened was mostly due to economics: while some of the country's Irish immigrants headed to Pennsylvania and Ohio, most of those who settled in large urban areas like New York did so because they lacked the money to leave the cities in which they had first arrived.)

When the Free Soil movement faltered, Greeley and his allies decided to form a new party with the goal of ending slavery. It was Greeley who in 1854 popularized the name Republican:

> We should not care much whether those united were designated Whig, Free Soil Democrats or something else; though we think some simple name like *Republican* would more fitly designate those who had united to restore our Union to its true mission of champion and promulgator of Liberty rather than propagandist of Slavery.

Greeley laid out for all to see that this was the party of union—no matter what happened, its goal was the preservation of the republic. (Contrast this with the Confederate States of America, whose very name confers the looser affiliation to its members.)

After the war, Greeley grew disillusioned with the Republican Party, in particular with its standard-bearer, Ulysses S. Grant. In 1872, he attempted to mount a run for the presidency as a Liberal Republican. He lost to Grant and died a few weeks after the popular vote. (He still received three electoral votes, most likely as a posthumous honor.) The *Tribune* continued until 1924, when it merged with one of its longtime competitors, the *Herald*. The *Herald-Tribune* folded in 1967, though its name lives on in the *International Herald Tribune*.

The *Tribune*'s offices stood on "Newspaper Row," the section of Park Row that runs along the edge of City Hall Park, but the building was torn down to make room for the widen-

---

*Though universally associated with Greeley, the phrase was first used by John Soule in a similar editorial in the *Terre Haute Express*.

ing of the Brooklyn Bridge approach ramps [**88**].

Greeley's importance to the city, however, has not been forgotten. Two statues of him stand in Manhattan. One sits prominently in the middle of Greeley Square (which is the proper term for the lower half of Herald Square). The other, better work by J.Q.A. Ward now graces City Hall Park near where the *Tribune*'s office once stood.

59 Castle Garden Emigrant Landing Depot

In 1820, the federal government had mandated that port cities keep a record of incoming immigrant arrivals. This was done on a ship-by-ship

ficult time keeping up its federal census. To solve this problem, New York took back the lease on Castle Garden [**53**], a well-known concert venue, and converted it into America's first immigrant landing depot in 1855.

While the Statue of Liberty [**93**] and Ellis Island [**96**] have become international symbols of the American immigrant experience, Castle Garden Emigrant Landing Depot was as significant in its day. It operated for 34 years and in that time saw nearly 8 million people pass through its doors. (It was so crucial in the development of Yiddish-speaking New York that the word *kesselgarden* entered the language to describe a noisy, congested place.) Because the United States had few laws concerning immigration, the information gathered at Castle Garden was minimal: name, age, sex, occupation, and

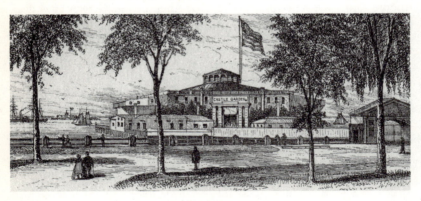

Castle Garden Emigrant Landing Depot

basis and, with the limited number of passengers arriving at the time, did not present too great a challenge. However, the end of the 1840s saw a steep rise in arrivals—mostly Irish fleeing the famine and Germans displaced by the revolutions in 1848—and the city was having a dif-

(if known) a destination. Because so many came with no plan and few prospects, this last often simply read "Unknown."

Another reason the city launched Castle Garden was to keep newly arrived immigrants from falling prey to unscrupulous touts who worked the piers promising—for a fee—to help the new arrivals find a job, a place to stay, and a hot meal. Too often the tout, and the money, would disappear into the crowded streets of Five Points. When Castle Garden opened, it featured job and housing assistance just outside its front door.

~ Though immigration dropped off in the years leading up to the Civil War, it rose again quickly during the postwar boom, and in 1889 the federal government stepped in to handle immigration directly. Castle Garden was closed in favor of Ellis Island, and the building reopened six years later as the New York City Aquarium. The aquarium was the building's longest tenant, staying until 1941, when Robert Moses [see 157] attempted to tear down Castle Garden to make way for the world's longest bridge, which would connect Brooklyn and Battery Park. Even after that project became the Brooklyn-Battery Tunnel, Moses still hoped to destroy the structure, which he derided as historically irrelevant and an eyesore.

However, New York's preservationists waged a tough, drawn-out battle, eventually getting the castle switched to the control of the National Park Service. By that point, most of the layers added by the aquarium, immigration center, and theater had been stripped away, leaving it much as it would have originally looked. The National Park Service, unsure of what to do with its castle, eventually turned it into the ticketing office for the Statue of Liberty and Ellis Island, which it remains to this day.

While there are no interior traces of the building's incarnation as an immigration depot, the statue outside, *The Immigrants* by Luis Sanguino, was dedicated in 1983 to serve as a reminder of the millions of people who first stepped onto American soil at this spot.

60 The Skyscraper Is Born on Broadway

The success of A. T. Stewart's Marble Palace [50] soon led to other department and specialty stores lining Broadway north of Chambers Street. However, few merchants could afford the luxury of using expensive marble and instead turned to the new architectural innovation that was sweeping New York: cast iron.*

The cast-iron process had been perfected in the late 18th century in England, but it was only in New York in the 1840s that foundries on the East River began to advertise their ability to take a plain masonry building and turn it instantly into a neoclassical palace with the addition of a simple iron frame. The advantages of cast iron were numerous: because it was cast in molds, it didn't require numerous skilled craftsmen to laboriously carve stone, just one talented mold maker. Because it was infinitely reproducible, a client needed only to specify the size of his building and the number of window bays; the pieces of the façade could be cast to match. And because of the tensile strength of the iron, larger panes of glass could be installed, letting much-needed light onto the showroom floor. As

---

*As tastes rapidly changed, Stewart would build his own Cast Iron Palace in 1862 on Broadway between 9th and 10th streets.

cast-iron buildings sprang up along Broadway, many of them became all-in-one establishments where customers would buy products on the ground floor that had been manufactured upstairs. (The large panes of glass also increased the number of working hours in these sweatshops, which drove down prices.)

While the first cast-iron building in the city, the 1848 Milhau Phar-

The Haughwout Building

macy by James Bogardus, is long gone, SoHo is still filled with excellent examples of the form. One of them, E. V. Haughwout's store at the corner of Grand Street and Broadway, is the most important cast-iron structure ever built.

Erected in 1857 for Haughwout, a china merchant, the building was designed by architect John P. Gaynor and fabricated by iron maker Daniel Badger. With symmetrical colonnades, arched window frames, and in-

tense attention to detail throughout, it was the most Palladian of all the neoclassical cast-iron buildings. However, where most buildings could get away with iron simply as a false front, Haughwout's store sat on a corner lot and would need cast iron on two sides, adding weight to the structure. To counteract this, Gaynor and Badger convinced Haughwout to allow them to incorporate the iron into the framework of the structure itself (and not merely hang the metal façade from the brickwork). That way, they could use the cast iron's weight to help support the building, not drag it down.

This innovative structural stability was necessary because of the other great innovation that Haughwout had decided to include: a passenger elevator. Having been impressed by Elisha Otis's safety brake demonstration at the Crystal Palace Exposition in 1853 [54], Haughwout engaged Otis to build him an elevator for the store. (At only five stories tall, the store wouldn't actually need an elevator, but Haughwout knew the value of good publicity.) A steam engine was installed in the basement (since commercial electricity was still years in the future) and when the store opened it was a great delight for New Yorkers to be able to come and ride up and down in Otis's contraption. As Haughwout had predicted, the fame of the store soon spread. When Mary Todd Lincoln moved into the White House in 1861, she found the place in great disrepair and immediately set out by train to New York to visit Haughwout to have official White House china made.

∽ With its structural frame and elevator, the Haughwout Building satisfies the two most important criteria for a skyscraper. While it would be a few years before the first steel-frame skyscraper was built, this cast-iron marvel—probably the most significant building still standing from the city's first 250 years—showed the world what lay ahead. And though its elaborate colonnades ape European styles, as the first skyscraper it can also be seen as the birth of an indigenous American architectural form.

In the 20th century, the city came perilously close to pulling the Haughwout Building down to build the Lower Manhattan Expressway [**167**]. It is a sign of just how rapidly the city changes that what in the 1850s was the technical innovation of its day was, by the 1960s, simply in the way.

61 Calvert Vaux and Frederick Law Olmsted's Greensward Plan

Throughout his life, landscape architect Frederick Law Olmsted was so prolific—and such a tireless self-promoter—that it is very common to find people who know that Central Park was designed by Olmsted but who have never heard of Calvert Vaux.

This is unfortunate, for while Olmsted's contributions to the park cannot be overlooked, there would be no Central Park as we know it without Vaux. Indeed, Vaux designed a remarkable number of parks and buildings that helped shape the fabric of the city, including Central Park, Morningside and Riverside parks on the Upper West Side [**73**], Prospect Park in Brooklyn, the Jefferson Market Courthouse [**79**], the Metropolitan Museum of Art and the American Museum of Natural History [**80**], the Samuel Tilden mansion on Gramercy Park [**76**], and Columbus Park in Chinatown [**105**].

Born in London in 1824, Vaux trained as an architect and was steeped in the Gothic Revival. He immigrated to the United States in 1850 to work with Andrew Jackson Downing, who had gone to London specifically to find an assistant. (While a noted theorist and America's leading proponent of landscape architecture, Downing couldn't draw.) Vaux probably hoped the job would give him the opportunity to work with Downing on the new Central Park. However, when Downing drowned in a steamboat accident on the Hudson, it fell to Vaux to get the work for himself.

In 1857, Vaux approached the Central Park Commission with a proposal. It should invite submissions for the park's design and choose the best one in a juried competition. The suggestion served two purposes: first, it gave Vaux a way to get his designs for the park into the hands of its board; second, it undercut Egbert Viele, the engineer who was hard at work clearing and surveying the land. Vaux was afraid that without intervention, the board would simply pick Viele to design the park because he was already there.

The board thought it was a great idea and announced the rules for the contest. Submissions would come in anonymously and would have to adhere to certain guidelines, including providing playgrounds (which, in the terminology of the day, meant ball fields), a parade ground for the military, a minimum of four roads through the park, a new reservoir to supplement the one already inside the park's boundaries, and an observatory.

Vaux, now faced with having to come up with 843 acres of landscape design, enlisted the aid of Frederick Law Olmsted, whom he had met only once before. Olmsted was the author of *Walks and Talks of an American Farmer in England*, a treatise on his travels in Europe. (Before Central Park, Olmsted was a bit of a dilettante. He was best known as a writer, having also published two volumes about his travels in the American South— *A Journey in the Seaboard Slave States* and *A Journey Through Texas*—that helped drum up abolitionist support just prior to the Civil War.)

In *Walks and Talks*, Olmsted expressed admiration for parks like Birkenhead (outside Liverpool), Eaton, and Windsor that would greatly influence the shape of Central Park. His description of Birkenhead sounds like the prototype for almost all future Olmsted designs:

> Walking a short distance up an avenue, we passed through another light iron gate into a thick, luxuriant, and diversified garden. Five minutes of admiration, and a few more spent in studying the manner in which art had been employed to obtain from nature so much beauty, and I was ready to admit that in democratic America

there was nothing to be thought of as comparable with this People's Garden. Indeed, gardening had here reached a perfection that I had never before dreamed of. I cannot undertake to describe the effect of so much taste and skill as had evidently been employed; I will only tell you, that we passed by winding paths, over acres and acres, with a constant varying surface, where on all sides were growing every variety, of shrubs and flowers, with more than natural grace, all set in borders of greenest, closest turf, and all kept with most consummate neatness. At a distance of a quarter of a mile from the gate, we came to an open field of clean, bright, green-sward, closely mown, on which a large tent was pitched, and a party of boys in one part, and a party of gentlemen in another, were playing cricket. Beyond this was a large meadow with groups of young trees, under which a flock of sheep were reposing, and girls and women with children, were playing. While watching the cricketers, we were threatened with a shower, and hastened to look for shelter, which we found in a pagoda, on an island approached by a Chinese bridge....

I was glad to observe that the privileges of the garden were enjoyed about equally by all classes. There were some who were attended by servants, and sent at once for their carriages, but a large proportion were of the common ranks, and a few women with children, or suffering from ill health, were evidently the wives of very humble laborers.

Together, Vaux and Olmsted sketched out their vision for Central Park, which they called "the Greensward Plan" after the English term for a sweeping green lawn. The hallmark of the plan was its constant change. Though each part of the park would flow seamlessly into the next, each would be clearly different. No section would be planted with exactly the same trees. Architectural elements would be kept to a minimum, but those that were built would not repeat. As people walked through the park, the landscape would unfold in front of them like a series of paintings, with every vista offering something new.

To make their presentation, Vaux and Olmsted included the required map, but they also attached a series of presentation boards that showed views of the park "before" (in rather soulless black-and-white photographs) and "after" (in lovely miniature paintings by Vaux's brother-in-law, Hudson River School artist Jervis McEntee). Unlike any of the other entrants, they spelled out how they would solve the problem of traffic in the park by building four sunken transverse roads that would allow city traffic to get across the island without disturbing the park's users. It was this innovation—and the fact the contest was Vaux's idea in the first place—that won them the commission.*

The pair's greatest champion on the Central Park Commission was Andrew Haswell Green, who would go on to extend Central Park's influence on the entire city and, ultimately, would work to unify the city's five boroughs in 1898 [107]. While Green would come to have a fractious relationship with Vaux and Olmsted over the next 20 years, he saw immediately that the Greensward Plan outshone all the other entries.

However, that did not mean that the board accepted Vaux and Olmsted's proposal at face value. In announcing that it had chosen the Greensward Plan, the board also immediately issued a list of 17 amendments to the plan that Vaux and Olmsted would need to incorporate. The most important of these was to take this idea of separating traffic and apply it to the paths inside the park as well. This is the reason that Central Park has so many bridges—to keep different types of park users separate. Thus, the bridle path never touched the pedestrian path and the six-mile carriage loop was never interrupted by a walking path. Any time two types of traffic reached each other, one was taken over and the other under. It is easy today, in the era of the superhighway, to forget what an innovation this was: the first, self-contained series of roads featuring traffic interchanges ever built in the world.

(So many paths have been added and rerouted over the last 150 years that Vaux and Olmsted's paths are no longer always separate. However, careful pedestrians, if they know what they're doing, can walk throughout the park and always be taken underneath the carriage road.)

---

*Though supposedly an anonymous competition, not only did Vaux have a personal connection to the judges, all the runners-up did as well.

62 Greenwich Village and the Arts: Richard Morris Hunt's Tenth Street Studio Building

Until the 1850s, architects in America had always been classified simply as "builders," and they received no formal training—they simply apprenticed with other architects. This changed in 1858, when Richard Morris Hunt returned to the United States from L'Ecole des Beaux-Arts in Paris with an actual diploma. Hunt would go on to be an acclaimed architect, building such well-known landmarks as the Fifth Avenue façade of the Metropolitan Museum of Art [80] and the pedestal of the Statue of Liberty [93]. But before Hunt achieved this success, he built perhaps his most important New York City structure, the now-demolished Tenth Street Studio Building, which stood between Fifth and Sixth avenues in Greenwich Village.

Opened in 1858, the Tenth Street Studio was an attempt to create a place for visual artists and architects to live together, to have affordable studio space, and to sell their works. Throughout most of the 19th century, the market for American art was abysmal. Whatever qualms Americans had about being dependent on Europe, they certainly depended on it culturally, from theater* to novels to art. (When Charles Dickens toured America in 1842 [45], he was this country's most popular writer—in part because American publishers didn't have to pay him any royalties, thus making more money from his works. A central theme of his 1842 lecture tour was convincing Americans to pay for their European art.)

American painters, including those of New York's Hudson River School, had been creating fantastic landscapes for some time. But the only market for American paintings was in portraiture; customers who wanted scenic works turned to the Paris salon to set their tastes. Hunt's Tenth Street Studio Building was supposed to counter this. By working together, the artists would be able to share ideas and thus encourage a greater flowering of American artistic expression. As there was no gallery system in the 19th century, art was either sold by brokers or by the artists themselves. By opening their studios to buyers on Sunday afternoons, they would be providing a single stop for those interested in purchasing their work.

The Tenth Street Studio was immediately popular with artists. Over the next century it was home not only to Hunt's own studio, but to painters and sculptors such as Frederick Church, Worthington Whittredge, William Merritt Chase, Alexander Calder, and Emanuel Leutze. The building was so popular that James Renwick [44] constructed Renwick Terrace, a rival set of apartments across the street, which over time housed such diverse talents as Marcel Duchamp, Dashiell Hammett, Kahlil Gibran, and Leonard Bernstein. And for those artists who didn't opt to live on Tenth Street, a small private club

---

*Note that when the riot broke out at the Astor Place Opera House [52] both it and the downtown Bowery Theater were performing *Macbeth*. American-penned drama was rare and, indeed, the only American form of theater really popular at the time was the minstrel show.

opened behind the house at 58 West 10th. Called the Tile Club, it lasted just a decade, but counted among its members Augustus Saint-Gaudens, Winslow Homer, and Stanford White [121].

The importance of the Tile Club, the Tenth Street Studio Building, and Renwick Terrace cannot be overestimated in the later development of Greenwich Village. When young artists started to flood into the Village in the early 20th century [136], it was already well established as a creative hub; without these buildings, that would never have happened.

While Hunt did draw attention to the Tenth Street Studio's artists (over 12,000 people lined up to pay 25 cents apiece to view Frederick Church's *Heart of the Andes*), it was not enough to refocus American taste on domestically produced art. For example, Americans John Singer Sargent and James McNeill Whistler only found acceptance because they had the imprimatur of living and working in Europe.

63 Theodore Roosevelt: Manhattan's Only President

Theodore Roosevelt is the only U.S. president (1901–1909) to be born and raised in New York City. He was born on October 27, 1858, in the family's brownstone townhouse at 28 East 20th Street. Often in poor health as a child, much of Teddy's later bullying and bravado was the result of the exercise he undertook in and around Gramercy Park[40], Madison

Square, and Union Square—where his grandfather lived—to boost his physique. The Roosevelt family moved out of the 20th Street house in 1872, and in 1916, the building was demolished to make way for a restaurant and retail shops.

The construction of the Theodore Roosevelt Birthplace is a good example of how a person's stock can rise after death—especially a former president. In 1916, when the original home was torn down, T.R. was still a polarizing figure in American politics. Having run unsuccessfully as the third-party candidate for president in 1912—which split the vote and ensured the election of Democrat Woodrow Wilson—Roosevelt chose in 1916 to throw his support behind Republican Charles Evans Hughes in an effort to thwart Wilson's reelection. But he did so only after the Republican Party made it clear that Roosevelt would not be given the nomination himself.

Three years later, he was dead and within weeks he was being lionized. The New York State legislature chartered the Woman's Roosevelt Memorial Association a mere 23 days after Roosevelt's death. By mid-March, the organization had purchased the building that had gone up in place of T.R.'s boyhood home as well as the property next door, which had been owned by Roosevelt's uncle, Robert. Their plan was to "restore" the houses as they would have looked in 1865, based on the "description written by Colonel Roosevelt in his autobiography." What this meant, in practice, was tearing the buildings down and starting from scratch.* In 1923, the

---

*Compare this to Fraunces Tavern [17], which is also a historical re-creation of an important presidential site.

newly built home was opened to the public and was praised as a "shrine to American patriotism." But nice as the reconstructed home may have been, it was no match for Gutzon Borglum's ultimate tribute to T.R.: Mount Rushmore.

64 The Church of the Transfiguration

In the years following the potato famine, the Irish population of New York grew so quickly that by 1860 it was the second-largest Irish city in the world—only Dublin was larger.

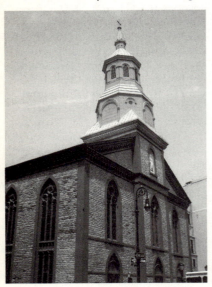

The Church of the Transfiguration

The census figures for the city are staggering: in 1830 the city had only 202,000 residents; in just 30 years, that figure had quadrupled to more than 813,000, a huge number of them Irish Catholics. In all, over 650,000 Irish arrived in New York because of the famine and nowhere was this growth better seen than in the city's parishes. In 1853, the diocese had purchased an old Lutheran church on Mott Street and rechristened it the Church of the Transfiguration.

Built in 1801, Transfiguration is the third-oldest church building in the city (the older ones being St. Paul's Chapel [14] and St. Mark's in the Bowery [10]). When it was constructed, the Collect Pond hadn't yet been drained [22], but the area surrounding the church would have been rife with slaughterhouses. Indeed, the namesake of Mott Street was butcher Joseph Mott. The congregants here were English-speaking Lutherans who had left their main church downtown due to its insistence on having Sunday sermons preached in German. Within six years, these breakaway parishioners on Mott Street had left the Lutheran fold altogether and had become Episcopalians.

As the Five Points became more populous, the Episcopalians ultimately sold the building to the Catholic archdiocese. In 1846, the membership of Transfiguration had already grown to 10,000 people; by 1860, the figure may have been closer to 20,000—which would have made it the single largest church in America, if not the world. (Of course, there is no possible way that 20,000 people received Communion each Sunday, even with back-to-back masses. But in order to receive the other sacraments—baptism, marriage, and last rites chief among them—it was necessary to be a member of the parish.)

Within another generation, the parish would begin to change its ethnic makeup, adding Chinese and Italians to the membership rolls. A plaque on the front of the church commemorates the parishioners who died in World War I: three names are Irish, the rest are Italian; this is as sure a sign as any that while New York was still a heavily Irish city, this neighborhood had inextricably changed.

65 Henry Ward Beecher's Slave Auctions

Henry Ward Beecher's statue in Cadman Plaza, Brooklyn, by J.Q.A. Ward

By 1860, when Henry Ward Beecher's Plymouth Church hosted Abraham Lincoln at Cooper Union [66], Beecher's status as one of America's foremost abolitionist preachers was well established [51].

Beecher's most impressive—and theatrical—events were the mock slave auctions he held at the church. As early as 1848, he began bringing enslaved Africans to Brooklyn in order to have their freedom purchased by the congregation. (Beecher was such an object of respect that Southern slave owners and brokers were willing to send their slaves to Brooklyn, trusting Beecher to return them if they did not fetch the agreed-upon price.)

Not only did these slave auctions serve to dramatically depict how human beings were being bought and sold in America like chattel, but they drew ever-growing crowds to what had already become standing-room-only Sunday services.

The most famous of the slave auctions took place on Sunday, February 5, 1860, when a nine-year-old mixed-race girl named Pinky was brought to the church. Beecher exhorted the congregation to save this girl who was "too fair and beautiful a child for

her own good." When the plate was passed around, $900 was collected along with an impressive ring from writer Rose Terry. Beecher took the ring, placed it on Pinky's finger, and supposedly declared, "With this ring I wed thee to freedom!" (In his own account of the tale, Beecher claims he said the less quotable, "Now remember that this is your freedom-ring.") Beecher, feeling that Pinky wasn't a dignified enough name for the girl, christened her Rose Ward after Rose Terry and himself, though she was known in later years by her married name, Mrs. James Hunt. In 1927, Mrs. Hunt returned to the church on the anniversary of Henry Ward Beecher's first sermon 80 years earlier, and gave back the ring, which is now housed (along with Pinky's bill of sale) at the church.

⌁ Beecher is so integral to Brooklyn history that two statues of him stand a 10-minute walk apart from each other in Brooklyn Heights.

One, by Gutzon Borglum, stands in the churchyard of the Plymouth

Church of the Pilgrims and shows Beecher orating. At his feet sit two freed slaves, supposedly the first two ever freed by the congregation. A bas-relief of Abraham Lincoln sitting in his pew listening to Beecher's sermon is embedded in the rear wall. (Borglum, a sporadically active member of the Ku Klux Klan, obviously didn't hate Lincoln—he included him on Mount Rushmore and named his son after him. But one wonders what he thought of Beecher.)

The other statue stands in Cadman Plaza, near Brooklyn Borough Hall. Sculpted by J.Q.A. Ward, it shows Beecher clutching a sheaf of papers. On one side of him, holding a palm frond as a symbol of peace, is a freed slave. On the other, two children place a garland of flowers on the statue's base. In the era directly following the Civil War, Decoration Day (now called Memorial Day) emerged as a way to honor the war's fallen heroes. Each year, statues and gravesites would be decorated with flowers. Because Beecher was not a soldier and did not die in the war, it would not have been appropriate to include him in the Decoration Day festivities. In this composition, J.Q.A. Ward cleverly solves that problem by having the children frozen in the act of honoring him with flowers every day of the year, subtly elevating him to the role of Civil War combatant.

66 Peter Cooper and The Cooper Union

Peter Cooper was one of the first generation of self-made men in America. In his early career, he was an apprentice coach maker and hat maker before moving on to earn his first fortune in glue. As he later commented:

I have always tried to do the best I know how, and then people have wanted what I made. I determined to make the best glue, and found out every method and ingredient looking to that end, and so it has always been in demand.

In fact, Cooper was so determined to make the most out of his factory that he figured out how to take a byproduct of the glue-making process and turn it into edible gelatin. (A few years later, a pharmacist would add cough syrup to the gelatin and give the world Jell-O.)

The money Cooper made in the glue business allowed him to invest in an iron works (which later produced the first beams necessary for cast-iron architecture [**60**].) He was hired by the Baltimore & Ohio railroad to design and build the first American-made steam locomotive, the Tom Thumb, which debuted in 1830. By the 1840s, Cooper was one of New York's 25 millionaires, and he had done it all without the benefit of a formal education. Clearly it wasn't aptitude holding Cooper back from a good education—he simply hadn't been rich enough to attend Columbia [**101**], which in his youth was New York's only college.

In 1854, Cooper set out to provide future students with the opportunities he lacked. He endowed and built The Cooper Union for the Advancement of Science and Art, a free institution emphasizing engineering and prac-

The Cooper Union for the Advancement of Science and Art

tical arts. (It is notable that practical arts included painting and sculpture; the handsome sculpture of Cooper that sits in front of the building is by Augustus Saint-Gaudens, a Cooper Union graduate.) The building went up at the junction of Third Avenue and the Bowery and contained a round elevator shaft—even though Elisha Otis had not yet installed any elevators—because Cooper felt that a round elevator would be the most efficient design. (The elevator shaft still peeks above the building like a chimney.) Using his own strong iron for the interior columns, Cooper also designed the single largest lecture space in the city, the Great Hall, which could accommodate over 2,000 people. It was here on February 27, 1860, that Abraham Lincoln, at the invitation of the Plymouth Church [51], delivered the "Right Makes Might" speech that catapulted him to the presidency. That same day Lincoln had his

photo taken (and quietly retouched) by Mathew Brady; a pamphlet of the speech, with Brady's photo of Lincoln on the cover, brought Lincoln lasting national exposure.*

Today, the college continues Cooper's original mission of providing a completely tuition-free education to those who pass its rigorous entrance requirements. However, despite Cooper's initial bequest of $100,000 (and additional money in his will), the college faced a problem with its endowment early on. Providing free education was growing too expensive. Cooper had hoped that retail shops on the ground floor of the main Cooper Union building would underwrite expenses. When that didn't work, the school began acquiring real estate. Today, its most noteworthy piece of land stands beneath the Chrysler Building [145], the lease for which provides a significant portion of the school's income.

*Cooper himself later ran for president, as the Independent Greenback Party candidate in 1876.

67 The Civil War Draft Riots

Six weeks after Abraham Lincoln was elected president in 1860, South Carolina seceded from the Union, sparking four years of bloody civil war. New Yorkers of all stripes—Republicans, Democrats, nativists, and immigrants—rallied behind the cause of the Union. (There were a few notable exceptions. Antiwar Democrats, soon to be known as Copperheads, opposed the war. New York City mayor Fernando Wood went so far as to suggest the city secede—not to join the Confederacy but to become an independent city-state that could trade freely with both sides.) The Irish and German populations were early supporters of the war effort, and when the war officially began in April 1861, New York's Irish 69th Regiment of volunteers ("the Fighting 69th") was one of the first to head south.

However, the war also brought out long-standing anti-Irish animosities, in particular among those who feared that if the pope opposed the war, Irish-Americans would defer to their "Prince of Rome" instead of the president. The pope never told Irish-Americans not to fight, but it didn't stop nativists from fanning the flames of anti-Catholic prejudice. As the war dragged on and casualties mounted, the Union army was faced with depleted ranks and a waning treasury. To solve both these problems, Congress authorized a draft, which took place in July 1863—just 10 days after the remarkable Union victory at Gettysburg.

The problems with the draft were manifold, but the key issue boiled down to money. If your name was called, you could choose to serve or to purchase a substitute for $300. For the poorest Five Points residents, who struggled to make $6 a week, this was a year's wages. The common cause that the war had promoted quickly dissolved. Republicans—mostly rich, white, and living uptown—were the instant target of poor, immigrant Five Pointers. In addition, fears grew among the working class that if the Union was victorious, New York would be flooded by freed slaves who would take away what few jobs existed. Some further feared that Republicans would favor the black people they were fighting so hard to free over Irish Democrats.

However, the proximate cause of the Civil War Draft Riots, which raged from July 13 to July 16, 1863, was the draft board's unwillingness to exempt volunteer firefighters who felt that their domestic service outweighed the government's need for soldiers. (Fire brigades had been traditionally exempted from service.)

On Saturday, July 11, the first names were picked and a little more than half of New York's 2,000-man quota was filled without incident. But over the weekend Peter Masterson, leader of Fire Engine Company 33, decided the best way to make sure his men didn't get called was to burn down the draft office, thus destroying any record of who was in the draft census. Word spread throughout the city of a planned confrontation at the draft board's offices at the provost marshal's office on Third Avenue at 46th Street. (This location had originally been picked because it was on the fringes of the city and thus was supposed to attract less notice.)

When the draft resumed at 9:00

a.m. on Monday July 13, a crowd led by Engine Company 33 attacked the provost marshal's office, breaking the windows and setting the building on fire. As all of New York's militia companies were either at the front or stationed in forts in New York Harbor, it fell to New York's police to try to control the mob. Police Chief John Kennedy, who came to the scene out of uniform, was recognized by the crowd, beaten, and left for dead.

That afternoon, rioters turned their attention away from the draft itself and targeted what they saw as the two chief causes of their dilemma: black citizens and Republicans. The *New York Times* and Horace Greeley's *Tribune* [see 58] were each threatened. The *Times* staff had somehow cajoled the army into giving them Gatling guns; manning one of them from the upper stories of the *Times* headquarters on Park Row was Leonard Jerome, a co-owner of the paper and grandfather of future British prime minister Winston Churchill. At the *Tribune*, Greeley insisted that no guns be brought into his building; late in the day the *Tribune* was attacked by a stone-throwing mob that dispersed quickly, however, when the police arrived.

Uptown, the situation was bleaker. Arsonists attacked the Colored Orphan Asylum on Madison Avenue, burning it to the ground. (Fortunately, all 237 orphans managed to escape.) Black New Yorkers were hauled out of their homes and businesses; some survived with only their houses ransacked. Others, however, were brutally beaten and killed. Over the next few days, black people in the city would be shot, beaten with bricks, drowned, and—in at least one case—lynched and burned.

On Tuesday most commerce in the city ceased as people were either too afraid to go out or had joined the riot. That same day, antiwar Democratic governor Horatio Seymour arrived in the city and called for calm. Seymour had hoped all along that the draft would be deemed unconstitutional and called off. However, it was also Seymour who had earlier in the month declared that the "revolutionary doctrine of public necessity can be proclaimed by a mob as well as by a government."

The federal government, meanwhile, was unable to lend much support to the overtaxed police department. Because martial law had not been—and would not be—declared, the government could only protect federal or state property, such as the Custom House on Wall Street. Also, fearing the mob would get into the armaments, many troops were stationed to protect the city's arsenals, such as the one in Central Park [see 52], that had been built for the very purpose of putting down such a mob.

In the end, it was up to the elite Seventh Regiment and other militia corps—battle-weary from their victory at Gettysburg—to return to the city and restore order. However, by the time the militia companies had arrived in full force on Thursday, July 16, the riots had basically burned themselves out. There was a final clash between troops and rioters near Gramercy Park (where some of the militia were encamped [see 40]), before the violence ended.

⌁ No one is certain how many people died in the clash. At the time it was estimated to be 1,000 but the official death toll afterward was reduced to just 100 people. The true figure may never be known, but surely rests somewhere in between, making the Draft Riots the single worst civil disturbance in American history.

New York's City Council immediately voted to pay the $300 for any person whose name was called but did not wish to serve. Had it followed through, this surely would have bankrupted the city. Instead, Democrats, led by rising Tammany Hall power-broker William "Boss" Tweed [**70**], reached a compromise that allowed the draft to continue. Tweed would appoint a commission on behalf of the city to hear claims by those who felt they could neither serve nor pay the $300, and the city would decide to hire substitutes on a case-by-case basis. In the end, through a combination of city money, medical infirmity, and people simply not reporting for duty, only one person from Five Points served in the war because of the draft.

After the war, the riots forced the city to examine the lives of the Five Points residents who had rebelled. The city knew the riot had started because the draft created a "rich man's war and a poor man's fight," and it realized it simply could not afford another upheaval. City Hall also wanted to delve deeper to see how other aspects of the immigrants' lives could be improved. Ultimately, these investigations would lead to the destruction of the Five Points in the early 20th century [**see 105**]. But in the short term, the city made a much smaller change: it extended Worth Street from the Five Points intersection to the Bowery. By connecting the more affluent Chatham Square neighborhood directly to the

center of the Five Points, it hoped that some of Chatham Square's middle-class values would filter into the Sixth Ward. In fact, the reverse happened. Though the Chatham Square area had been losing its middle class for years, opening up Worth Street proved to be the last straw. Within a few years, the homes east of the Bowery were firmly part of the Five Points.

68 Central Park's Bethesda Terrace

As the Civil War raged, work on Central Park continued, with particular attention paid to the formal heart of the park, Bethesda Terrace. While the park was years away from completion, it was already being championed as a symbol of the Union's inclusiveness. Bethesda Terrace would be that symbol's centerpiece.

Calvert Vaux first proposed the plan for Bethesda Terrace in the early 1860s, but his assistant, Jacob Wrey Mould, designed most of the decorative carving. During the Civil War, Frederick Law Olmsted left the park to work on the Sanitary Commission, which helped to improve the care of wounded soldiers. Vaux kept working until the Board of Commissioners announced that they'd selected Richard Morris Hunt [**62**] to redesign the park's main Fifth Avenue entrance. Choosing a rival to work on his park was too much for Vaux, and he stormed off. Though both Vaux and Olmsted would return after the war, the park was left in the hands of Jacob Wrey Mould during the creation of Bethesda Terrace.

The terrace adheres to a fairly rigid

decorative scheme. Vaux's plan called for groups of allegorical sculptures, including the four ages of man, the four seasons, the four primary landscape elements, and—at the top of the terrace—the four times of day. However, due to lack of funds, the sculptural program was abandoned except for the central figure—originally designated as "Love" by Vaux, and later transformed into *The Angel of the Waters,* a lovely 1867–73 piece by Emma Stebbins [**72**].

Detail of the flying witch and jack-o'-lantern from Bethesda Terrace

However, the bases for the other statues still stand, and the most interesting are those at the top of the staircase that leads from the Mall to the arcade under the 72nd Street Transverse. These four pedestals presumably would have held the four times of day. The two that directly flank the staircase are carved with six scenes designed by Mould: three on the eastern side that represent morning and three on the western side that represent evening.

The morning side features a rising sun, a crowing rooster, and a wheat field at threshing time. The evening side presents a Bible (accompanied by an oil lamp and an hourglass), an owl and a bat, and—tucked on the least visible, western side of the pedestal—a delightful scene of a flying witch with a jack-o'-lantern. These six vignettes not only take the viewer through a day's journey from dawn to the darkest part of night, they serve as social commentary. On the evening side, the witch and jack-o'-lantern—unmistakable symbols of Halloween—are paired with the lamp and Bible. At its most innocu-

ous, these are simply early evening (when you light the lamp and read from the Bible) and late at night—the witching hour.

But there is something deeper at work. Halloween symbols were new in America when these carvings were made—they would not have been immediately recognizable as such to many viewers. Those who did understand them would have associated them with the Irish immigrants who had brought these customs to the United States. The question is: Did Mould include them as a compliment to the Irish-American workers who were laboring in the park? Or were his motivations less noble?

Anti-Catholics took no small delight in pointing out what they took to be pagan practices of the Roman Church. When the Irish came to New York with folk traditions that included Halloween witches and the burning of candles in carved vegetables, it was simply further evidence that Catholicism was itself little better than witchcraft. It seems likely that Mould, no matter what his own personal views, would have realized that Protestant New Yorkers would associate a witch and jack-o'-lantern with what they considered the wretched excesses of the Catholic Church.

Most of the park's laborers were newly arrived immigrants, which meant most of them would have been Irish. Did they take this decoration as a subtle jab? Did they take it simply at face value—as a small nod to "Irishness" in the midst of this grand park—or did they perhaps see it as fitting into a greater pattern that was at work throughout the city? The park was, at its roots, designed to be a place of moral uplift and public improvement. There is no doubt that immigrants in New York in the 1860s knew that when Protestants said "improvement," they meant conversion to a Protestant faith.

Little did these old-guard Protestants realize that Catholicism would soon become the single largest denomination in the city and that Halloween would become one of the most popular holidays in the country. It's an interesting side note that when Americans did begin to embrace Halloween customs, they made certain to emphasize the holiday's Scottish and English—and therefore Protestant—roots.

PART 4

The City in Transition, 1866–1897

New York City prospered after the Civil War. In truth, the city has always profited from postwar economies, but the era immediately following the Civil War was different. With the South in ruins—with some parts of it still smoldering because of soon-to-be New Yorker William T. Sherman's March to the Sea—Northern industrialists capitalized on their virtual lock on American commerce. This was the era that saw the rise of men like Cornelius Vanderbilt and Jay Gould, the so-called robber barons. By the end of the century, New York had entered what Mark Twain called a "Gilded Age" (more on that in Part 5), and the newly rich spent their money on things to improve New York culturally (the Metropolitan Museum of Art and the American Museum of Natural History), educationally (new homes for Columbia and New York University), and spiritually (cathedrals for the Catholic archdiocese and—surprisingly late—the Episcopal Church).

New York's economic boom had other effects. Rich New Yorkers have always had a philanthropic bent, but now money was flowing into a greater number of institutions to aid the working class. Nothing spurred this more than the huge influx of immigrants from southern Italy and Eastern Europe. The Italians came first to look for seasonal work—they were called "birds of passage"—but as America tightened its immigration policies with the opening of Ellis Island, many of them decided to stay, bringing over their family members one at a time. Eastern European Jews had no such luxuries. The assassination of Czar Alexander II saw a crackdown on Jews living in the areas of Poland, Ukraine, and Russia known as the Pale of Settlement. Anti-Jewish pogroms forced entire villages to pack up and head for the safety of America. By 1898, nearly one million of the city's residents were Jewish, making New York the largest Jewish city in the world.

But perhaps the most lasting and visible contributions of these postwar New Yorkers was their desire to build—and to build *big*. Some of this was spurred on by the avarice of William "Boss" Tweed and his notorious ring of corrupt city officials, who pillaged the city treasury at the same time they helped New York expand. But more than that, it was fueled by New York's realization that it was on the verge of not just being a great commercial city, but the country's leader in style, culture, and architecture. In 1883, the Brooklyn Bridge opened—at the time, the largest-span steel suspension bridge ever built. It was hailed as the Eighth Wonder of the World. Just three years later, the Statue of Liberty was completed in the harbor, the tallest structure in the city and the first to be taller than the spire of Trinity Church, Wall Street. In 1890, Joseph Pulitzer's *New York World* built the first skyscraper to ever claim the title of world's tallest; that same year the cornerstone for the grand Arch was laid in Washington Square, which would usher in the City Beautiful movement and forever change the look of New York. While the *World* headquarters is gone, as are many other milestones from this era (including almost all the remnants of the El, the city's first flirtation with good public transit), enough grand monuments, large and small, remain for us to get an excellent view into the world of New York as it recovered from the war and prepared to greet the 20th century with the most audacious move in its history: five-borough unification.

69 Cornelius Vanderbilt, Grand Central Depot, and the Creation of Park Avenue

Today, the stretch of Park Avenue along the Upper East Side ranks second only to Fifth Avenue in prestige. However, when the street got that name, it was among the least desirable in the city. The story of its change from a noisy, dangerous thoroughfare to a grand boulevard is intertwined with the story of one of New York's most prominent 19th-century figures, Cornelius Vanderbilt.

"Commodore" Cornelius Vanderbilt

Born on Staten Island in 1794, Vanderbilt began working on ferries in New York harbor by age 11 and in less than a decade was running his own ferry business. He began styling himself "Commodore" Vanderbilt (a term not then in use by the U.S. Navy) and he was forever after simply referred to as "the Commodore."

In 1818, Vanderbilt added steamships to his fleet, in direct violation of Robert Fulton and Robert "the Chancellor" Livingston's state-sanctioned monopoly on steamship passage on the Hudson River [24]. When Livingston sued (after having tried to hire Vanderbilt away), the Commodore fought back; ultimately, the Supreme Court ruled in Vanderbilt's favor, one of the first significant antitrust cases in the country.

Following the Civil War, Vanderbilt turned his attention to the burgeoning railroad industry. Realizing that railroads were fast replacing his steam business, Vanderbilt acquired controlling interests in the New York and Harlem Railroad, the Hudson River Railroad, and the New York Central Railroad, merging them into one entity in 1869.

〜 In 1831, the New York and Harlem Railroad had established its at-grade tracks along a mostly uninhabited stretch of Fourth Avenue. The first New York and Harlem trains were horse-drawn along the entire length of the line; however, this soon gave way to steam locomotion, which drew complaints from people living and working along the more densely populated stretch of Fourth Avenue near the train's depot on 27th Street. In 1854, the city passed an ordinance banning steam travel south of 42nd Street, which forced the railroad to unhook its steam locomotives at 42nd Street, and, one by one, haul passenger cars by horse to the depot farther downtown. These horse-drawn cars were shunted into a covered viaduct from 42nd to 32nd streets, which not only solved an elevation problem, but also kept the horses and the trains out of sight. When the area atop this covered viaduct was planted, it came to be known as Park Avenue.

〜 It was just at this moment that Cornelius Vanderbilt merged his railroad companies into one, called the New York Central and Hudson River Railroad. Vanderbilt immediately embraced a solution that the previous owners of the New York and Harlem Railroad had dismissed. Instead of using horses to haul passenger cars to the depot, he would move the depot to the place where steam engines were forced to terminate: 42nd Street. In 1871, construction began on a new terminal named Grand Central Depot, which would serve not only Vanderbilt's trains but also the separately owned New York and New Haven Railroad. As Vanderbilt's depot took shape, so did a movement to force the locomotive tracks on Fourth Avenue north of the station into a sunken tunnel. This would make Fourth Avenue a more acceptable street and a safer one. (One letter to the *New York Times* in 1871 called it "Death Avenue.")

Vanderbilt initially balked, but when the city began talking about rescinding his right-of-way, he paid for a tunnel to be cut from 96th Street to 42nd Street. In 1888, the term Park Avenue was first used to refer to the entire length of the street from 32nd Street northward. This left only the stretch from Astor Place to 31st Street still called Fourth Avenue. As Park Avenue gradually transformed

itself into one of the city's most fashionable addresses, businesses on Fourth Avenue lobbied the city to have their addresses changed too. In 1959, the City Council renamed the stretch of Fourth Avenue from 17th Street to 32nd Street: it became Park Avenue South, and has its own numbering scheme. Thus, today, only the six blocks from Astor Place to Union Square are still called Fourth Avenue.

70 The Downfall of William "Boss" Tweed

New York loves its scoundrels. While the names of most of its civic leaders have faded into the past (William L. Strong, anyone?), the name that looms largest from the 1860s and 1870s is Tammany Hall's William M. "Boss" Tweed,* who held a number of civic posts during that time.

For a man whose reputation and influence are still so strongly felt, he had a remarkably short period of real power: he was involved in New York City politics beginning in the 1850s, but his stranglehold on the city really only lasted from the Civil War Draft Riots of 1863 [**67**] until the implosion of the New York County Courthouse project in 1871.

Tweed, the son of Scottish immigrants, was born in New York in 1823. His rise to political power came through his work on the Americus "Big Six" volunteer fire company. For two centuries, the city's firefighting had been done by all-volunteer companies; these also served as fraternal

---

*You will often see him referred to as William Marcy Tweed; Marcy was an insult hurled at him by famed political cartoonist Thomas Nast, comparing Tweed to Governor William L. Marcy, the man who had coined the phrase "to the victor belong the spoils." Tweed's middle name was undoubtedly Magear (his son was named William Magear Tweed, Jr.) but we actually have no documents listing Tweed's full name.

organizations, sometime gangs, and political clubs. Indeed, our modern notion of a "political machine" to refer to the well-oiled workings of insider politics was originally attached to fire companies.

In the 1850s, Tweed rose through the ranks of the Big Six to become its foreman.* At the same time, he joined the Society of Tammany (aka Tammany Hall), one of the foremost Democratic political clubs in the city. By the time of the draft riots, Tweed had replaced former mayor Fernando Wood as Tammany's leading figure and was perfectly positioned to broker the deals that would calm the rioters and save the city.

In the era after the war, Tweed swiftly moved to consolidate his power. Having served one term in Congress in the 1850s,

Two of Thomas Nast's editorial cartoons indicting Tweed

he realized that being in New York would allow him to yield more power than he could in Washington. Tweed secured a post on the innocuous-sounding New York County Board of Supervisors, a perch from which he would rob the city of millions of dollars over the next decade. Until five-borough unification in 1898 [107], New York City and New York County were "coterminous"—that is, they were two different political entities occupying the exact same

boundaries, in this case the island of Manhattan. Some officials, like the mayor, had dual roles in both city and county government.

After a succession of successful Tammany Hall mayors (one of whom, John Hoffman, Tweed helped catapult into the governor's mansion in Albany), Tweed got his friend A. Oakey Hall installed in City Hall in 1869. The next year, he pulled off his real coup: getting the state legislature to approve a new city

---

*There's a great scene in Martin Scorsese's *Gangs of New York* showing Tweed in his fire regalia instructing the Big 6 to fight with a rival fire company over who gets to extinguish a house fire. This was based on a real clash in 1865.

charter. Ostensibly, this new "home rule" charter transferred oversight from a number of state-run agencies (such as police and parks) to newly created city equivalents. In practice this meant a direct transfer of power—and money—into Tweed's hands. Beginning in 1870, the so-called Tweed Ring (made up of Tweed, "Elegant" Oakey Hall, City Comptroller Richard "Slippery Dick" Connelly, and Chamberlain [i.e., Treasurer] Peter B. "Brains" Sweeny) dubbed themselves the official Board of Apportionment, which awarded contracts for public works, including road paving, plumbing, streetcar and tracks. Work went to those bidders who understood that a percentage of the city's fees would then be returned to the ring.

The Tweed Ring made money off projects large and small [see 46], but the most audacious of them was the New York County Courthouse, now known universally as the Tweed Courthouse. Work began in 1862 and over the next nine years an estimated $12 million came out of the city's coffers to pay for construction.* Perhaps $4 million actually ended up in the building—the other $8 million lined the pockets of the ring. (Keep in mind that during this same period, the U.S. government spent only $7.2 million to purchase the entire state of Alaska.) When the fraud was exposed, investigators discovered carpet-layers' bills for $300,000—even though most of the place remained uncarpeted. Another favorite fraud was hiring repairmen who charged more for their services than the original work had cost. This became such a part of the system that some repairmen were hired before the work they were being brought in to "fix" had even begun.

With his ill-gotten gains Tweed led the good life. He bought an estate in Greenwich, Connecticut, a pair of yachts, and amassed Manhattan real estate. By some estimates, he was the single largest individual landholder the city had seen since John Jacob Astor [33]. Perhaps most ostentatiously, Tweed sported a diamond pin valued at $15,000.

In 1871, it all began to unravel. The problem with a scheme like Tweed's was that it required the complicity of dozens of lower-level bureaucrats. One such civil servant, Matthew O'Rourke, perhaps because he was honest or perhaps because he was annoyed that his share wasn't big enough, began quietly keeping a private set of accounting ledgers. And when he had amassed enough evidence, he took those ledgers to the newspapers.

The Tweed Ring thought they had successfully guarded against exposure by bribing journalists and editors. Also, at a time when a typical paper sold for a penny, the threat of the city pulling its advertising revenue was enough to keep most periodicals from exposing Tweed's corruption. *Harper's* magazine, through the famous editorial cartoons of Thomas Nast,** railed against the ring, as did the *New York Times*, but neither periodical had

---

*Though historian Leo Hershkowitz argues that the amount spent never got this high, other historians quote figures as high as $14 million.

**Thomas Nast's cartoons were full of vitriol; however, despite urban legends to the contrary, the word "nasty" did not come from his name.

the evidence to do much more than accuse. Lawyer Samuel J. Tilden—Tweed's biggest foe within the Democratic Party—had been looking for a way to prosecute Tweed since 1869. Suddenly, when O'Rourke brought his ledgers to the *Times*, he got what he was looking for. On July 8, 1871, the *Times* splashed "More Ring Villainy" across the front page, and outlined the Tweed Ring's scheme to defraud the city by paying exorbitant rent to an accomplice on unusable armory buildings and then diverting the money to themselves. Over the next few weeks, more and more fraudulent payment schemes were outlined in the paper; Tilden pored over the material, dissecting every payment and chit, building a case against the ring. However, despite all of Tilden's work, Tweed was ultimately never charged with a felony. Instead, he faced 220 misdemeanor counts, which related to his not exercising proper oversight of his fiscal responsibilities. After a first trial ended in a hung jury, a second jury in November 1873 found him guilty on 204 counts. He was sentenced to 12 years in prison by Judge Noah Davis, an ally of Tilden's. As far as New York City knew, this was the end of the mighty "Boss"; he had flown too close to the sun and plummeted back down to earth.

However, little did Samuel Tilden or New York know that the exploits of Boss Tweed were far from over [74].

71 Central Park's Mall and William Shakespeare

As Calvert Vaux and Frederick Law Olmsted's work progressed on Central Park [61], it made sense to concentrate their early efforts on the southern end for the simple reason that they knew that the bulk of the park's visitors would be entering at 59th Street.

One of the first park features to open was the Mall, a straight corridor linking the carriage road near 59th Street and Fifth Avenue to Bethesda Terrace, the formal heart of the park [68]. In the middle of what was to be a "naturalistic" experience, the Mall is a purposeful break from the rambling paths, thickly wooded areas, and general "unplanned" look of the rest of the park. When the Mall opened in 1858, it featured four rows of semi-mature American elm trees, planted in straight lines to evoke a formal Parisian *allée*. (The elms you see today are, for the most part, not the originals.* They are, however, the largest stand of elms in North America; Dutch elm disease decimated the rest of the country's population.)

The formalism of the Mall led many park supporters to see it as the ideal spot for commemorative statuary. However, except for a series of sculptures on Bethesda Terrace (represented today solely by *The Angel of the Waters* [72]), Vaux and Olmsted had not planned on stat-

---

*The original elms were planted by a contractor in 1858 with the proviso that he would only be paid if the trees lasted three years; almost all were dead within a year, the victim of the park's poor soil. A second set of trees lived from the early 1860s to the 1920s; the trees you see today are mostly 1920s replacements.

ues in the park. So, when a bust of Friedrich von Schiller was installed in the Ramble in 1859,* they and the Central Park commissioners decided to draw up a series of principles to guide future statues and their placement. First, they asked for advance approval of all designs; second, they wanted to choose where each statue would go (thus ensuring that the Mall would not become the park's de facto sculpture gallery); third, they requested that any commemorated individual be dead a minimum of five years. This last rule was to guard against "instant fame" and to stop New Yorkers from honoring every mayor, president, or robber baron industrialist who would quickly be forgotten. This was a wise move and, indeed, with the possible exception of Fitz-Greene Halleck [**78**], no obscure 19th-century New Yorkers are honored in the park (neither are any presidents). Only one mayor is honored: John Purroy Mitchel, who resigned his post to enlist when the United States entered World War I and died falling out of an airplane.

William Shakespeare by J.Q.A. Ward

~ One of the first statues to grace the southern end of the Mall—now called Literary or Poets' Walk—was William Shakespeare. There was a major fund-raising effort in 1864 (Shakespeare's 300th birthday) when Edwin Booth, New York's most beloved Shakespearean actor, teamed up with his brothers Junius and John Wilkes to stage a benefit performance of *Julius Caesar*.** The statue itself, by J.Q.A. Ward, was installed in 1872 and unveiled by William Cullen Bryant, the first champion of the park [**49**], who gave a long speech extolling Shakespeare's virtues. As Central Park historian Sara Cedar Miller has discovered, Bryant was an advocate of phrenology, the pseudoscience then in vogue that argued that intelligence was dictated by the size and shape of a person's head; in his speech he pointed out that you could tell how smart Shakespeare was simply by looking at his great, protruding brow. This contrasted nicely with another nearby statue by J.Q.A. Ward, the *Indian Hunter*—a noble savage, to be

---

*This bust now stands at the northern end of the Mall. It was donated by the German-American community and began a long tradition of ethnic groups promoting their civic and national pride through statuary. (See also the two Christopher Columbus statues in the park [98].)

**After the Civil War ended—and John Wilkes Booth had killed the president—Edwin Booth withdrew from the public eye for a couple of years; however, he was back onstage by the time this statue was unveiled.

sure, but still a savage; his tiny fore-head gave him away. Though phre-nology has all but disappeared, it was this same thinking that gave rise to our modern notions of "highbrow" and "lowbrow" culture.

New York's—and Central Park's—love of Shakespeare is not limited to this statue. Eight years after its un-veiling, Eugene Schieffelin released 80 starlings in the park, chagrined that Americans did not have the op-portunity to see these birds that were mentioned by the Bard. However, it's not as if the starling is a common Shakespearean trope: he mentions them exactly once, in *Henry IV, Part I*, when Hotspur says:

> I'll have a starling shall be taught to speak
>
> Nothing but "Mortimer," and give it him
>
> To keep his anger still in motion.

Indeed, this wasn't Schieffelin's first attempt to import Shakespear-ean birds, and he may have been getting desperate. Earlier efforts to release nightingales, thrushes, and skylarks had all been failures. Unfor-tunately for many endemic species who suffered as a result, the starling was a success, spreading across the continent from Central Park in the early years of the 20th century.

Elsewhere in the park there is a Shakespeare theater, the Delacorte, which is home to the Public Theater's annual Shakespeare festival [**see 165**], as well as a Shakespeare study garden.

72 *The Angel of the Waters*

During the planning of Central Park's Bethesda Terrace, Calvert Vaux sketched out a series of 17 allegorical statues to ring the upper and lower levels of the plaza, focused on themes such as the times of day and the ages of man. A central figure in the plaza was labeled by Vaux simply "Love."

By the time the terrace was com-pleted, plans for most of the statues were abandoned (though their ped-estals remained [**68**]). The central "Love" figure became instead *The Angel of the Waters* by Emma Steb-bins.

This is the first work of public art in New York City by a female artist (and one of the very first in Amer-ica). Stebbins's brother, Henry, was the chairman of the Central Park Commission and first suggested his sister for the work. Female sculptors in America were virtually nonexis-tent, since most male teachers were unwilling to accept female students. Emma Stebbins instead had to look to Europe, moving to Rome in 1857 to study under John Gibson. It was here that she met poet Charlotte Cushman, who would become her lifelong companion, and became part of a circle of expatriate female artists in Rome that Henry James dubbed "the White Marmorean Flock." It was also here that Stebbins did her work for *The Angel of the Waters*, which was completed in 1867 though not installed until May 31, 1873.

The terrace is named for the Bethesda pool outside Jerusalem, mentioned in the Gospel of John, pieces in the park, though at its opening reception, at least one reviewer was sorely disappointed. The anonymous voice in the *New York Times* complained that when the cloth was pulled back to reveal the statue

> there was a positive thrill of disappointment. All had expected something great, something of angelic power and beauty, and when a feebly-pretty idealess thing of bronze was revealed the revulsion of feeling was painful.

The Angel of the Waters
by Emma Stebbins

The angel stands in line with the Mall, which is not only the park's sole straight promenade, but also runs due north, drawing park visitors from the southern entrances of the park to the terrace. When the trees in the Ramble behind the angel were younger and more pruned back, Vista Rock—where Belvedere Castle stands—would have risen above her head, proudly displaying an American flag.

which was known for its rejuvenating powers. The angel's placement here seemed fitting: New York had only been benefiting from clean Croton water since 1842 [**46**] and the chief reservoir for that system took up the bulk of the center of the park [**see 151**]. The small cherublike figures around the statue's lower register symbolize aspects of water's importance, including health, purity, and temperance. The angel was also dedicated to those who had died serving in the Union navy. Today, the name Navy Terrace is sometimes used for the area, though this appellation was not officially added until after World War II.

Stebbins's statue is one of the most recognizable and beloved

73 The Making of the West Side 1: Riverside and Morningside Parks

With work on Central Park coming to a close in the early 1870s, the city and the park's designers turned their attention elsewhere. While Calvert Vaux and Frederick Law Olmsted formally dissolved their partnership in 1872, this did not actually stop them from collaborating on two other New York City parks: Riverside

Park, which runs along the west side of Manhattan north of 72nd Street, and Morningside Park, which occupies the area below the rocky cliffs that sit between 110th and 120th streets and what is now called Morningside Drive.*

What made these parks possible was the vision of Andrew Haswell Green [see 107], the most influential board member of the Central Park Commission. It was Green who pushed the state legislature to grant his board oversight for parks built on any land north of 59th Street.

In 1865, real estate developer William R. Martin, who also sat on the Central Park Commission, suggested that the rocky, undulating coastline on the city's west side be developed into a park (which would no doubt boost the price of his nearby land holdings). In 1872, the state legislature granted the city the right of eminent domain and Vaux was asked to prepare a survey for the new park. Vaux handed off the job to Olmsted, who in 1875 presented his plan for building a narrow Riverside Park and an accompanying Riverside Drive that would follow the natural contours of the land. The tree-lined park would serve as a shield between the future homes on the drive (which would later be touted as the "Fifth Avenue" of the West Side) and the Hudson River Railroad, which operated tracks down the steep cliffs at the water's edge.

Around the same time that Riverside Park was being planned, Olmsted and Vaux were engaged to create a landscape for Morningside Park. (The city had already rejected a plan by the Parks Department's new engineer-in-chief, M. A. Kellogg.**) However, it wasn't until 1880 that any work on Morningside Park began, with Jacob Wrey Mould [see 68] in charge of bringing Vaux and Olmsted's vision to life. Mould's work, from 1883 until his death in 1886, concentrated mainly on the upper portion of the park along Morningside Drive, including the massive retaining wall and the staircase access down to the lower level. After Mould died, Vaux returned to the park and continued work—with some input from Olmsted—over the next decade, until his own death in 1895.

Meanwhile, construction on Riverside Park (delayed because the city's treasury was feeling the drain of the Tweed Ring's massive plundering of funds [70]) also began in 1880, with Vaux in charge of bringing Olmsted's plan to fruition. Only the upper level of the park, which hews to—and is occasionally bisected by—Riverside Drive, is Olmsted and Vaux's creation. Most of what people experience today is the lower level of the park, which was the work of Robert Moses [see 151] in the 1930s. Extending the park toward the Hudson River shoreline not only gave the city the excuse to cover over the old railroad tracks, but also to create the West Side Highway.

---

*Their other great New York project, Prospect Park, in Brooklyn, was built concurrently with the last phase of Central Park.

**As part of Boss Tweed's consolidation of power into a "home rule" charter [see 70], he was able to dissolve the state-appointed Central Park Commission and replace it with a New York City Parks Department. M. A. Kellogg was put in charge in place of Vaux and Olmsted.

74 Boss Tweed on the Lam

Attorney and State Assemblyman Samuel J. Tilden skyrocketed to fame as the man who brought down William "Boss" Tweed in 1873 [70]. He parlayed his position as Tweed's nemesis and a political rival of Tweed's Tammany machine into the

"WHAT ARE YOU LAUGHING AT? TO THE VICTOR BELONG THE SPOILS."

Thomas Nast depicts Tweed's downfall.

1874 nomination for New York's governor. Less than two years later, he was tapped to run as the Democratic nominee for president [76].

But Tilden had a problem: Boss Tweed wouldn't go away. He had been sentenced to 12 years in prison for his misdemeanors. However, the

sentence was utterly illegal because New York law stipulated that the longest a person could be held for one misdemeanor indictment was one year—no matter how many separate counts were under the umbrella of that indictment. It took Tweed and his attorneys a year and a half, but in June 1875, he was released from prison.

As the man who'd risen to prominence by sending Tweed to jail, Governor Tilden could not afford to allow New York's most notorious scoundrel to be a free man. What if Tweed started campaigning against him? So Tilden had already taken precautions, filing a $6.3 million civil suit against Tweed on behalf of New York, and the moment Tweed was freed from prison he was thrown into the Ludlow Street jail. With bail set at $3 million—then a record—Tweed had little hope of buying his way out. As far as Tilden was concerned, Tweed could simply remain there until he died.

Tweed's jailer was sympathetic to the old Boss, who was clearly ill and had been forsaken by many of his former cronies. The jailer would let Tweed out for supervised carriage rides in Central Park or for Sunday dinners at home with his wife. During one of those dinners in December 1875, while his guard napped on the front stoop, Tweed donned a wig and one of his wife's dresses and snuck out of the house and into a waiting carriage. He managed to get to New Jersey, where he hid out for a few weeks* and eagerly followed

---

*There is a story that Tweed's mother died during this time and that he arranged to have her funeral at St. Augustine's Church [36] so that he could watch, undetected, from the slaves' gallery. However, the timing of his mother's death doesn't align correctly with his period on the lam, so the story is clearly just an urban myth.

the press coverage of the manhunt for him. The city distributed handbills, offering $10,000 for information leading to his capture, but to no avail.

Tweed soon left New Jersey for points south. He eventually arrived in Cuba, which was in the midst of its Ten Years' War, and then decamped for Spain, where he thought he would be safe because Spain had no treaty of extradition with the United States at the time. However, the Spanish government, eager to curry favor with President Grant (and, perhaps, with potential incoming president Tilden), turned Tweed over to the U.S. Navy immediately upon his arrival.

Tweed was returned to the Ludlow Street jail on the eve of the 1876 presidential election. He was now a broken man. To get out of his predicament, he offered to go into court and provide information about how he and the Tweed Ring had stolen so much money from the city. In eleven days of testimony, Tweed detailed exactly how the ring had functioned, but when it was over, he was simply

returned to Ludlow Street. Tilden's attorney general was still unwilling to let Tweed go free.

Tweed died on April 12, 1878, and while Tammany Hall would remain a potent force in New York politics for generations, the city would never again be run by a "Boss" quite like him.

75 Fleischmann's Vienna Bakery and America's First Breadline

In Cincinnati in 1868, Austrian immigrants Charles and Max Fleischmann perfected the process for packaging and selling compressed yeast. This was a revolution for home bakers, who'd been forced up to that point to keep yeast alive themselves in their kitchens. In 1875, Louis Fleischmann joined his brothers and hit on the idea of expanding their market by setting up a "model" Vienna bak-

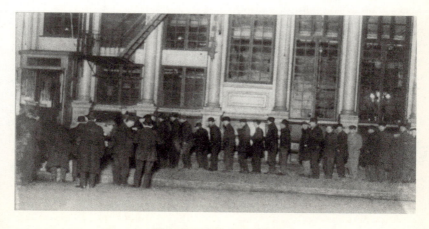

Fleischmann's breadline

ery at the upcoming 1876 Centennial Exposition in Philadelphia. People would be drawn in by the aromas of fresh-baked pastries and would leave having sampled their revolutionary product.

The bakery at the fair was such a success that later that same year, Louis Fleischmann moved to New York and set up a permanent Vienna Bakery at the corner of Tenth Street and Broadway. By 1876, this area had become the high-end shopping district, supplanting the blocks south of Houston Street [see 60]. Fleischmann figured that a café here would introduce his family's product not just to New York's savvy shoppers, but to the thousands of people who flocked to the city every year to buy the latest fashions.

But perhaps what became best known about the bakery was not its daytime clientele, but the line that stretched around the corner every night at midnight—the first breadline. According to Fleischmann's *New York Times* obituary in 1904:

When the bakery was first started at Tenth Street and Broadway, a few hungry tramps, attracted by the smell of the hot loaves, hovered about the grating in the pavement. Finally one of the men plucked up courage enough to ask for something to eat. Mr. Fleischmann was there at the time, and he gave the man a loaf of bread and a loaf as well to the hungry men who stood near by. He bade them come again when they were hungry, and the next night they were there. The men told others,

and it was taken for granted that the feeding would continue.

Fleischmann's charity served another purpose, however, beyond simply feeding the hungry. By giving away his unsold bread at the end of the day, he was publicly advertising that all the products purchased there the next day would be freshly baked.

In 1905, a year after Fleischmann's death, the bakery's next-door neighbor, Grace Church [44], purchased the land and three years later, the bakery was demolished for a lawn. However, the breadline had permanently embedded itself into American culture.

76 The Stolen Election of 1876: Tilden vs. Hayes

In the history of American politics, there is no presidential election as contentious as the 1876 contest between New York governor Samuel J. Tilden and Ohio governor Rutherford B. Hayes.*

Tilden, famous for his prosecution of William "Boss" Tweed [70; 74], was billed as the reform-minded outsider Democrat who could combat the corruption that had flowered in Washington under President Ulysses S. Grant [106]. The party hoped that Tilden, despite his basically chilly demeanor, could appeal to Northerners and Southerners alike.

Though it is often stated that the outcome of the election was the

---

*New York also put forward a third-party candidate—Peter Cooper [66]—who ran on the Independent Greenback ticket.

Samuel Jones Tilden

would usher America into its next hundred years.

The night of the election, November 7, most newspapers reported that Tilden had won. However, the *New York Times*, sensing that the election would be close in Louisiana, South Carolina, Oregon, and Florida, prepared an editorial that ran the next day entitled "A Doubtful Election," laying out the scenario that the election still hung in the balance. After meeting with Republican leaders, the *Times* managing editor, John Reid, sent telegrams to Republican governors in the disputed states:

> Hayes is elected if we have carried South Carolina, Florida, and Louisiana. Can you hold your state? Answer immediately.

result of the Compromise of 1877, which ended Reconstruction in the South, in fact both candidates ran on platforms that would have ended the federal military presence in Southern states. The Republicans—as they had of every Democratic presidential candidate since the end of the Civil War—tried to paint Tilden as an implicit supporter of slavery. (As the saying went at the time: "Not all Democrats were Rebels, but all Rebels were Democrats.") They argued that by paying off Southern war debts, Tilden would bankrupt the country or destroy its credit. The Democrats, in turn, accused the Republicans— as they had in all elections since the end of the Civil War—of "waving the bloody shirt" (that is, making the election about the war and not about the issues). As the campaign unfolded, it took on disproportionate historical importance because it was being waged in 1876, the country's centennial—the winner would not just be the next president, he

When the governors replied that they *could* try to "hold" their states— despite election returns tilting in Tilden's favor—the most fractious post-election period in American history began. Not even the Gore/ Bush imbroglio in 2000 can match the months that followed November 1876. In canvasses roiled by partisanship, the three Southern states in dispute* certified two sets of returns and sent them to Washington—one for Hayes and one for Tilden. With the votes from those states thus rendered void, neither candidate had a majority, which constitutionally was supposed to send the election into the House of Representatives. However, since it was not simply a case of one candidate not having received the sufficient number of votes to win, Congress took a different tack. Instead of letting the House decide, a 15-member Electoral Com-

---

*In Oregon, the problem lay with the eligibility of one elector.

mission was formed to figure out who had won. The commission had five Republican congressmen and five Democrats. The remaining five members were to be drawn from the Supreme Court: two Republicans, two Democrats, and the fifth member to be chosen for his impartiality by the first four. However, the final member initially chosen, Justice David Davis, was simultaneously appointed by the Illinois legislature to serve in the Senate, and he resigned from the Supreme Court. This caused the final seat on the commission to go to Republican justice Joseph Bradley. Along completely partisan lines, the commission voted 8–7 in favor of Hayes in each disputed case, giving him the electoral votes he needed to secure the presidency. The commission's final decision came on March 2, 1877—only three days before Inauguration Day!

While all this was happening, Samuel Tilden waited patiently in his elegant double townhouse on Gramercy Park. The two buildings, once separate homes, had been purchased by Tilden in 1863 and 1874. In the 1880s, Tilden hired Calvert Vaux to remodel the homes in high Victorian Gothic style, with red sandstone banding and delicate carved vignettes. Inset into the façade are the faces of great thinkers and writers: Goethe, Shakespeare, Dante, Milton—and one American, Benjamin Franklin.*

Tilden had clearly won the popular vote by over 200,000 votes. It may never be known if he would have carried the Southern states—there was so much voter irregularity and suppression that an accurate count probably could never have been made. But it seems likely that Tilden did, in fact, carry enough states to have won the election outright. How or when he would have ended Reconstruction is also unknowable. What is certain is that the election of Hayes brought about the end of Republican-dominated politics in the South, caused the end of federal troop deployments, and ushered in a new wave of violence against and disenfranchisement of black citizens, and the Jim Crow era of nearly a century of lawful segregation.

Tilden, not surprisingly, grew increasingly bitter as the years went on. His paranoia supposedly led him to have a tunnel constructed from his home on Gramercy Park to 19th Street so that he could escape if the city rioted. His greatest contribution to the city came upon his death, when he donated the bulk of his fortune and his immense private book collection to found the New York Public Library [128]. (He held back $50,000, however, to have a statue of himself erected—fearing, perhaps, that if he didn't pay for it, no one else would. Originally slated for the median in Park Avenue, it now stands at Riverside Drive and 112th Street.)

77 Alexander Graham Bell's First Telephone

The fashionable section of Broadway in the 1870s was the area between Houston Street and Union Square. Here were the trendiest department stores, such as A. T. Stewart's Cast

---

*Franklin is also the only American to grace the front of the similarly designed Brooklyn Historical Society [86].

Iron Palace [**see 82**], cafés such as Fleischmann's Vienna Bakery [**75**], elegant Grace Episcopal Church [**44**], and one of the city's nicest hotels, the St. Denis.

The St. Denis, built by Grace Church architect James Renwick in 1853, still stands on Broadway at 10th Street, though it has been converted into an office building. The St. Denis's most historic moment occurred on May 11, 1877, when Alexander Graham Bell demonstrated the telephone to a New York audience for the first time. Though he had already patented the device and made public demonstrations of its efficacy—a week earlier in Boston, he'd made a connection to Providence, Rhode Island, 43 miles away—he hadn't yet found a market for it. At the St. Denis a crowd of about 50 filled the drawing room on the second floor where Bell made telephone calls to the A&P Telegraph office in Brooklyn, using wire strung across the not-yet-completed Brooklyn Bridge [**88**]. In the audience were potential financial backers, such as Cyrus Field, the president of the company that 11 years earlier had successfully laid the first transatlantic telegraph cable.

At least one observer at the St. Denis, telegraph pioneer Walter P. Phillips,* derided the invention as "a toy, if not an absolute humbug." But it is clear that others were impressed. Later that year, the first telephone was installed—connecting J. Lloyd Haigh's home on John Street to his factory in Brooklyn. By 1878, the first telephone directory was published:

it contained 252 listings: 235 businesses and 17 people who had telephones installed at home.

78 Fitz-Greene Halleck and Poets' Walk

Fitz-Greene Halleck

Save for one odd man out, the statues on the southern end of Central Park's Mall are all poets—Shakespeare (installed in 1872) [**71**]; Sir Walter Scott and Robert Burns (installed in 1872 and 1880, respectively); and American poet Fitz-Greene Halleck. (The odd man is Christopher Columbus, added in 1894 as part of the Columbus Quadricentennial [**98**].)

But the real odd man out on Literary Walk is Halleck, one of the most obscure American poets of his age. Reading the official park sign accompanying the statue, one might think

---

*Walter Phillips created Phillips Code, a method of shorthand for telegraph operators; it lives on today in the acronym he coined, POTUS, which stands for "President of the United States." It is used by the Secret Service and, perhaps more popularly, by author Tom Clancy.

that Halleck is the great lost poet of the 19th century. He is perhaps best described as a one-hit wonder. He and his best friend (and boyfriend?) Joseph Rodman Drake penned a series of poems in 1819 that were published in New York newspapers under the pseudonyms "Croaker" and "Croaker, Jr." The poems, which satirized New York society, were eagerly anticipated, but in the end were little more than a pleasant diversion. After Drake died in 1820, Halleck went on to write a few other mildly successful works and to become part of the "Knickerbocker" circle of New York writers that included William Cullen Bryant, James Fenimore Cooper, and the original Knickerbocker, Washington Irving. However, even as a part of this esteemed group—and there is no doubt that Halleck *was* esteemed by them—he was the least famous of the writers.

Since writing poetry didn't pay Halleck's bills, he spent most of his adult life as personal secretary to John Jacob Astor [33]. When Astor died in 1848, Halleck retired to Guilford, Connecticut, where he spent the next 20 years nursing his legacy. He died in 1867, and almost immediately his good friend James Grant Wilson began to work on getting Halleck a statue in Central Park.

Wilson—a decorated Civil War general, New York City historian, and general man about town—had no trouble convincing Astor's friends to come up with the money; reading the list of contributors to the Halleck monument is like reading a *Who's Who* of postbellum New York: Secretary of State Hamilton Fish, Samuel F. B. Morse, William Cullen Bryant, and financier J. P. Morgan. Some of these contributors were familiar with Halleck's verse; others, however, probably only knew him because he worked for Astor. Also on the statue's fund-raising committee was Andrew Haswell Green [107], the most prominent member of the Central Park Commission; this alone virtually guaranteed the statue would get prominent placement.

The statue was unveiled on May 15, 1877. In a real coup, James Grant Wilson persuaded newly inaugurated president Rutherford B. Hayes to do the honors. This was a piece of political theater for Hayes, who had just been appointed president after the disastrous election of 1876 [76]. Even many who didn't support his rival, Samuel J. Tilden, still distrusted Hayes and didn't consider his presidency legitimate. In coming to New York, Hayes saw an opportunity to prove his detractors wrong and to show support for the things that New Yorkers seemed to hold dear: Central Park, poetry, and—even though he'd likely never heard of him—Fitz-Greene Halleck.

Somewhere between 10,000 and 50,000 people showed up to see the new president—so many people that the city immediately declared the Mall off-limits to large gatherings. And from that moment forward, people began to wonder why they'd never heard of Fitz-Greene Halleck. After all, he has a statue in Central Park that was unveiled by the president of the United States, and paid for by people like J. P. Morgan—he must be a "somebody."

Alas, while it would be unfair to characterize Halleck as a "nobody," his rightful place as a "somebody" is pretty tentative as well.

79 Victorian Splendor: Jefferson Market Courthouse

At the very center of Greenwich Village, at the corner of Sixth Avenue and 10th Street, stood the neighborhood's fire tower, an 1832 structure built above the Jefferson Market, the local produce market. When the city decided in the early 1870s that it wanted to build a courthouse in the Village, it tore down the market, fire tower, and other buildings that had agglomerated over time to replace them with a modern structure.

The architectural commission went to the firm of Vaux and Withers. Calvert Vaux was busy at the time putting the finishing touches on Central Park, in particular the Metropolitan Museum of Art and the American Museum of Natural History [80], so the design of the building fell to Frederick Clarke Withers.

Withers came from the same background as Vaux and his work on the Jefferson Market Courthouse gave him the opportunity to create a full-blown Victorian Gothic structure that looked, for all intents, like a church. Withers reasoned that an ornate structure with a bell tower was going to look like a church no matter what he did; rather than fight that inevitability, he added a host of ecclesiastical touches, including a prominent tympanum above the main entrance.

On a church, the tympanum usually features Christ in the center, often on a throne, surrounded by apostles, angels, or other assorted saints. For his courthouse, Withers instead chose the most famous courtroom scene in literature—the culmination of Shakespeare's *Merchant of Venice*. Seated in the center is

The tympanum above the doorway to the Jefferson Market Courthouse

the judge, preparing to render a verdict. To the right is Shylock, a pair of scales in one hand and a dagger in the other. To the left is Portia, dressed as a man, pointing with her index finger to the line in the contract where it says "pound of flesh."

The Jefferson Market Courthouse became so busy that the city had to institute a night court—the first in the nation—to handle the overflow arraignments. This was in part due to the fact that the court was used to arrest people in the nearby theater district (which was then located in the area near Madison Square), so having a Shakespeare play featured over the front door was doubly appropriate.

The most famous arraignment at Jefferson Market was that of Harry K. Thaw, who in June 1906 murdered celebrity architect Stanford White at the old Madison Square Garden [121].

By the 1950s, the courthouse was closed and a successful preservation effort was launched to keep the city from selling the property to developers. In 1967, the building reopened as the Jefferson Market Library—keeping the scene from the *Merchant of Venice* as relevant as ever.

80 The American Museum of Natural History and the Metropolitan Museum of Art

By 1877, the principal work on Central Park was drawing to a close. Frederick Law Olmsted would soon be removed from his superintendent's position and Vaux had ceased his association with the park except for two final projects: the building of the American Museum of Natural History and the Metropolitan Museum of Art.

Conceived as twin structures—and initially intertwined in their state and city funding—both buildings were to stand inside the park's boundaries so that they became an integral part of one's Central Park experience.

~ The Natural History museum was the brainchild of Albert S. Bickmore, a Harvard-trained naturalist, who convinced eminent New Yorkers to help him create a museum that would showcase all of the natural sciences. Original backers included Central Park commissioner Andrew Haswell Green [107], J. P. Morgan, and Theodore Roosevelt, Sr., whose son would become the most famous champion of the museum. Organized in 1869, the museum moved into temporary quarters in the old Arsenal [52] in 1871.

(A quick aside: Subsequent to being decommissioned as a state military outpost, the Arsenal had become home to the first Central Park Zoo—a stopgap measure the park adopted when people began presenting the city with animals. Olmsted and Vaux had never planned a zoo as part of their park, but the donations forced them to move the animals into the Arsenal. Plans were then drawn up to move the zoo to an area called Manhattan Square, which ran from 77th Street to 81st Street on Eighth Avenue* and to that end, the park acquired the square in 1864. However, by 1871, the zoo had moved instead into terrible Victorian quarters just behind the Arsenal—the current zoo has replaced that dreary place—and the Manhattan Square land was instead given to the Natural History museum.)

The Museum of Natural History's original building was designed by Calvert Vaux and his Central Park assistant, Jacob Wrey Mould [see 68]. The resulting Victorian Gothic structure—similar in style not only

*Manhattan Square was one of the few original squares on the Commissioners' Plan of 1811 [25].

The original Metropolitan Museum of Art as designed by Calvert Vaux and Jacob Wrey Mould

to its partner, the Metropolitan Museum of Art, but also to the Jefferson Market Courthouse [79]—is now almost completely buried from sight beneath layers of subsequent additions.* From 1892 to 1898, Josiah C. Cady added a Romanesque Revival wing facing 77th Street. In 1924, Trowbridge & Livingston built a Central Park West façade and that same year, Governor Alfred E. Smith [144] announced a competition to further enhance the Central Park West entrance by creating a grand memorial for President Theodore Roosevelt. Completed in 1936, the memorial features an equestrian statue of Roosevelt facing into the park (as well as a bas-relief frieze around the entrance extolling the former president's virtues). Had plans been carried forward, the Roosevelt statue would have been facing toward a grand boulevard through the park, connecting this museum directly to the Met.

Today, busy traffic on Central Park West cuts off the museum from Central Park, making it easy to forget that this was once considered part and parcel of the park. When the museum moved to this space from the Arsenal, however, its biggest problem was that it was simply too far away. Street cars didn't travel this far north and there was nothing else of note on the West Side. (It also didn't help that the rather elite curatorial staff only labeled the exhibits in Latin.) More important, it was no longer located next door to the zoo—it would take years for the museum to see anything like the number of visitors it had welcomed in its few years at the Arsenal.

∿ The building of the Metropolitan Museum, on the east side of the park, followed a similar trajectory. In 1869, a group of 50 prominent citizens were selected to draft plans for an art museum in the city; from the beginning, Andrew Haswell Green promoted the idea that it be located

*To catch a glimpse of the original building today, visitors need to enter Theodore Roosevelt Park at 79th Street and Columbus Avenue.

in Central Park, and Vaux and Mould drew up plans for a Victorian Gothic museum. The Met acquired its first art in 1870—174 paintings from three private collections and one Roman sarcophagus—and opened in temporary quarters on Fifth Avenue. The museum soon moved downtown to an old mansion on 14th Street, where it remained until Vaux and Mould's building was ready for occupancy in 1880.

As at the Museum of Natural History, the Met soon found its headquarters too small and commissioned additional wings. In 1888, Thomas Weston's Italianate expansion opened, and in the first decades of the 20th century, the museum saw a major overhaul—including moving the entrance from Central Park to Fifth Avenue. This grand new entrance was the work of Richard Morris Hunt [62], one of the leading proponents of Beaux-Arts architecture in the city. McKim, Mead, and White later added wings to Hunt's Fifth Avenue pavilion and a flurry of activity in the 1970s and '80s added modern wings, including the Lehman Collection and the Sackler Wing, which houses the Temple of Dendur. The Metropolitan Museum is now the largest art museum in America and, in terms of its holdings, rivals the Louvre and the Hermitage as one of the greatest museums in the world.

Seeing Vaux and Mould's original Victorian Gothic structure is a little more difficult here than at the Museum of Natural History and requires going inside. Though bits and pieces peek through at various places in the museum, the largest section of their structure was revealed during the construction of the Lehman wing in 1975.

81 The Elevated Railway

As the city laid out its street grid north, following the Commissioners' Plan of 1811 [25], two ongoing problems emerged: the lack of open space in the city* and the desperate need for public transportation. The problem of space was solved by the creation of Central Park [49; 61], though early use of the park was hampered by the lack of decent transportation.

The first attempts at regular public conveyances were horse-drawn railroads and omnibuses; by the Civil War, these clogged every Manhattan avenue, bringing traffic to a virtual standstill. The horse-drawn railroads alone carried over 100,000 passengers a day, but transportation was going to have to improve if people living on the new Upper East Side and Upper West Side were ever to hope to get down to jobs in the financial district.

In 1869, New Yorkers got their first taste of the radical changes that lay ahead when the city's first subway opened. It was only 295 feet long; it ran underneath Broadway between Warren and Murray streets; and it had been built on the sly by inventor Alfred Ely Beach. There had been long-standing opposition to any public transit on Broadway—merchants

---

*The grid did provide some open space, including Hamilton Square, later home of the Seventh Regiment Armory [85], and Manhattan Square, which now hosts the American Museum of Natural History [80].

The Eighth Avenue El

like A. T. Stewart [50] feared it would diminish the value of the storefronts. Rather than suffer defeat before he'd even started, Beach instead got the state legislature to grant him the right to build a pneumatic tube system for ferrying mail. Once construction began, he had the charter quietly amended, and instead built a passenger conveyance that, when it opened, became the toast of the town. Beach appealed to the state for the right to extend his pneumatic subway (which was propelled by a giant fan) farther up Broadway, but by the time he was given the approval in 1873, New York was undergoing an economic downturn and he simply couldn't find the financial backing necessary to continue. (Beach blamed Tammany Hall for his failures, but the Tweed Ring [70] didn't stonewall the project as much as Beach claimed it did.)

Around the same time that Beach was building his pneumatic subway, engineer Charles T. Harvey was constructing a rival public transit scheme in the air, the city's first elevated railway. In July 1868, Harvey demonstrated a one-car elevated locomotive on a length of track he'd erected along Greenwich Street north from Battery Park to Dey Street. Based on the success of that test, he was granted the right to extend the track up to 30th Street. Harvey's Greenwich Street "El" opened June 11, 1870. However, he was beset by engineering problems—his cars ran on a complicated cable system—and though over 50,000 people rode the El in its first three months of service, it soon shut down. Harvey was bought out by the New York Elevated Company, which convinced the state legislature to authorize a solution: steam locomotion. The Greenwich Street (later Ninth Avenue) Elevated rapidly expanded northward and by 1875 was serving stations up to 59th Street. Soon, the rival Metropolitan Elevated got into the act, securing the rights to lines along Sixth and Second avenues. The Sixth Avenue El opened in 1878, the New York Elevated Company's Third Avenue line in 1878, and the Second Avenue El in 1879.

Alfred Ely Beach, who—when he wasn't inventing subways was editor of *Scientific American*—condemned the new elevated lines:

> Perhaps in the future, after people have become habituated to trains thundering over them, to thoroughfares blocked with great iron columns, to the impartial distribution of ashes, oil, and sparks upon the heads of pedestrians and on awnings (a couple of the latter were set on fire this way the other day), to the diffusion of dirt into upper windows, to the increased danger of life from runaway horses and the breaking of vehicles against the iron columns, to the darkening of lower stories and shading of the streets so that the same are kept damp long after wet weather has ceased, and to the numerous other accidents and annoyances inherent to this mode of transit, more such bridges will be erected, and we shall have two storied streets. . . . The business population on some thoroughfares will be troglodytes—dwellers in dark and shaded caverns—and the other portion will be aerial.

Beach was not the only one concerned about the constant soot and ash deposited by the El's locomotives; in 1902 the Second Avenue El began the conversion to an all-electric system. Soon, all the Els would be electric, but it would be too late to save them from obsolescence: just

two years later the first line of the IRT subway would open [119] and the elevated railroad would rapidly fall out of favor. It took decades for the lines to come down, but the last piece of the Third Avenue El in Manhattan closed in 1955.*

Very little of the El remains. However, on Allen Street at Division Street, its sign decrepit and falling apart, is a "station" of the Manhattan Railway Company's Second Avenue El. This is not a passenger terminal; rather, it was one of the many substations along the line that provided electrical power for the trains.

82 The Strange Case of A. T. Stewart's Corpse

When A. T. Stewart died in 1876, he was one of the richest men in America—worth an estimated $40 million—and still at the forefront of New York's retail industry. He had decided, in 1862, that his original Marble Palace [50] was too far downtown to be fashionable and constructed the Cast Iron Palace on Broadway between 9th and 10th streets. He also started a mail-order business for his goods, paving the way for famed catalogue merchants like Sears, Roebuck. He was nominated by Ulysses S. Grant to serve as secretary of commerce, but conflicts of interest—and a close personal friendship with Judge Henry Hilton, who'd been a pal of William "Boss" Tweed and was damaged by fallout from the prosecution of the Tweed Ring [70]—forced him to turn down the post.

---

*The IRT continued to operate the Third Avenue El in the Bronx as the No. 8 train until 1973.

Stewart's success, however, earned him few admirers. In *The Gangs of New York*, Herbert Asbury wrote that

> at the height of [Stewart's] commercial power many of his clerks were merchants whom he had driven out of business. . . . [H]e had few if any friends, although because of his wealth and position he possessed great influence. His attitude toward everyone was suspicious and forbidding, and he is said to have made it his rule never to trust either man or woman.

Thus, it shouldn't have been all that surprising when, on October 8, 1878, grave robbers attempted to steal his body from the family crypt at St. Mark's in the Bowery [10]. That evening they were unsuccessful; they broke into the graveyard but were probably interrupted before they could lift the slab guarding the vault. However, they returned on the evening of November 7, successfully opened the grave, removed the body and pieces of the coffin, and disappeared.

The next day, Judge Hilton offered a $25,000 reward for the return of the body, and while the police and the newspapers followed the case relentlessly, nothing turned up. There was no ransom demand until two months later, when the grave robbers finally contacted the family asking for $250,000. Over the next few months, negotiations went nowhere. Judge Hilton wasn't willing to pay more than his original $25,000 reward and the thieves were unwilling to accept so little. It wasn't until a year later that Stewart's widow took it upon herself to contact the thieves and offer $20,000. The thieves—likely tired of storing Stewart's remains—agreed. They set up a rendezvous in Westchester County; two carriages met in the dead of night and a sack of money was exchanged for a sack of Stewart's mortal remains.

Instead of being returned to St. Mark's, Stewart was taken to the still-under-construction Episcopal Cathedral in Garden City, Long Island. One of Stewart's lasting contributions was the creation of Garden City, a planned community in what had once been called Hempstead Plains. Stewart bought the land, built the houses, and even paid for a railroad to run out from New York City, which still operates today as part of the Long Island Railroad.

Stewart's remains were interred in the vault at the new cathedral; allegedly, the door to the vault was rigged with a latch that would ring the cathedral's bells if the vault was broken open, thus foiling any future ghoulish heist.

83 St. Patrick's (New) Cathedral

On July 19, 1850, Pope Pius IX elevated the diocese of New York to the rank of archdiocese; almost immediately Archbishop Joseph Hughes announced plans to create a new, grander cathedral to match the diocese's new status. Back when construction had started on the original cathedral on Mott Street in 1809 [28], the diocese had also purchased some land in the countryside for a boys' school. Hughes selected this land, at 50th Street and Fifth Avenue, for his new cathedral. To design it, he turned to James Renwick, whose Grace Church [44] had only recently

St. Patrick's Cathedral

work continued on the church for the next thirty years. The towers—which, at 330 feet, were the tallest spires in the city and for decades soared over everything else in Midtown—were not completed until 1888; the Lady Chapel, an addition by Charles T. Matthews, opened in 1906.**

Among the saints on the massive front entrance doors are notable New Yorkers, including St. Isaac Jogues, the first Catholic missionary in the city (he was the person who reported in 1647 that 18 languages could be heard on Manhattan's streets); St. Elizabeth Ann Seton [23]; St. Frances Xavier Cabrini, the first American saint; and the Blessed Kateri Tekakwitha ("Lily of the Mohawks"), a Native American convert to Catholicism.

opened on Broadway and was quickly becoming one of the best known Protestant churches in the city. As he had done at Grace, Renwick did not hew too closely to any particular Gothic style for the new cathedral, combining instead both English and Continental elements in the overall design. He submitted plans in 1853 and work began in 1858 on what was to be the largest cathedral in America* and the first truly to rival the churches of Europe.

Construction on St. Patrick's halted during the Civil War but was restarted in 1865 and the building was dedicated on May 25, 1879. (The former cathedral on Mott Street became a parish church.) However,

84 Tenement House Laws

As the Civil War drew to a close, prominent residents formed the Citizens' Association of New York, which sought to improve living conditions in the city's poorest areas. In part this was due to rampant disease, but it was also an attempt to better understand—and thus control—those citizens who had destroyed so much city property during the Civil War Draft Riots [67]. The Citizens' Association issued its report in 1865 and it was an eye-opener. Everyone knew that New York's immigrants often lived in bad conditions, but they were shocked to

---

*With the opening of the nave at the Cathedral of St. John the Divine in 1941 [100], St. Patrick's lost its title as America's largest cathedral.

**To build the Lady Chapel, a portion of Renwick's original apse of the church had to be dismantled. It was moved to Harlem and serves as the main portion of the sanctuary of Our Lady of Lourdes, on West 142nd Street.

discover that over two-thirds of the city's population lived in tenements [32] that would be deemed substandard—if, indeed, the city had any standards to live up to.

As a result, the state legislature passed the Tenement House Act in 1867, which mandated improvements such as mandatory fire escapes. This gave every apartment two exits: one through the front door and one down the fire escape.* The law also mandated water closets for every 20 residents, but these did not have to be indoors.

Seeking to give the law more backbone, the state augmented it in 1879 with a Second Tenement House Act, which came to be known as the Old Law. The law dictated that a tenement could occupy only 65 percent of its lot and mandated improved toilets.** Most important, it called for access to ventilation in every room. To help builders—and, ideally, to provide more jobs for plumbers—a magazine called *Plumber and Sanitary Engineer* organized a contest to design an ideal tenement that would adhere to the new laws. The winner, James Ware, created what would come to be the most prolific style of housing in the city, the dumbbell tenement (so-called because, viewed from above, it appears to shaped like, well, a dumbbell).

Not only did Ware's prizewinning tenement design provide for two toilets on every floor of the building (in hallway water closets shared by the four apartments), it created air shafts between the buildings so that there would be a window in every room. Often this air shaft was only a few feet deep, but if a tenant opened both the side and the front windows, air could theoretically circulate through the apartment. This, in turn, was supposed to reduce the prevalence of diseases like cholera and tuberculosis. These air shafts, however, cut down on the available floor space and many tenement apartments, though three rooms deep, were less than 400 square feet.

From 1879 to 1901 almost all new buildings in immigrant neighborhoods were dumbbell Old Law tenements. For some of the new Italian and Eastern European immigrants who would begin to enter the city in the next few years, these apartments would become the center of their lives, serving for many as home, work place, and social center. In the poorest families, the apartment's three rooms would be split between two families: one that paid the rent and lived in the front and another that lodged in the back rooms and paid the actual tenant.

In 1901, the city sought to further improve living conditions by creating a "New Law," which mandated enlarged air shafts, running water, and bathrooms *in* every apartment. Though some post-1901 tenements adhered to a quasi-dumbbell plan, the provisions of the New Law were too strict to allow Ware's design to persist much in the 20th century. In 1929, a further strengthening of the tenement laws essentially outlawed dumbbells, and their construction

---

*The fire escape law was more honored in the breach than the observance; today, fire escapes are one of the features of a "classic" New York streetscape, but for over 30 years after the law was passed, building owners basically ignored this provision.

**In 1888, the toilets would be improved again to have "an ostensible means of flushing."

was replaced from the 1930s onward with the city's new preferred mode of low-cost housing: housing projects. Though many tenements fell into disrepair during the Depression, a remarkable number of them still stand today, not only in immigrant neighborhoods like the Lower East Side, but throughout the city.

85 The Seventh Regiment Armory

Around the same time that Commodore Vanderbilt built the first Grand Central Depot [69], New York's Seventh Regiment began petitioning the city for space to build a new drill hall and headquarters to replace its outmoded one near Tompkins Square.*

The Seventh, or "Silk Stocking," Regiment—so-called because it drew its membership from the sons of New York's first families—was the outgrowth of the state militia movement popular in the years prior to the War of 1812. (For most of the 19th century the United States relied on citizen militias, not a large standing army, for national defense.) First known as the Eleventh Regiment, it guarded New York harbor during that war [27]. During the Marquis de Lafayette's farewell tour of America [33], the regiment acted as his honor guard and gave itself the name National Guard after Lafayette's *Garde Nationale* in Paris. When militia companies were reorganized later in the 19th century, this idea of having a National Guard stuck. In 1826,

Mayor Philip Hone inaugurated the Washington Memorial Parade Ground (now known as Washington Square) [35] for the use of the regiment. Over the next few years its name changed again twice; it finally became the Seventh Regiment in 1847. The regiment was called in to quell the Astor Place Riot [52] and was instrumental in the military's role in ending the Civil War Draft Riots in 1863 [67].

The city responded to the Seventh Regiment's request for more land by ceding it a block on Fourth Avenue between 66th and 67th streets. Originally, this had been part

The Veterans' Room of the Seventh Regiment Armory, designed by Louis Comfort Tiffany's Associated Artists

of Hamilton Square, one of the few public plazas that had appeared on

---

*The biggest problem with the Tompkins Square site was that it sat above a meat market.

the original Commissioners' Plan of 1811 [25] but had never been built, in part because it lay along the awful stretch of Fourth Avenue that was the New York and Harlem Railroad's right-of-way.

While the city was happy to rent the land to the Seventh Regiment for a nominal fee, neither it nor the state had any funds available for construction, so the regiment was forced to raise its own funds. It turned first to its wealthy members, who contributed $200,000, before holding events to raise more. From that point forward, the regiment and its new headquarters would be associated with large events, from fairs and grand balls to sporting events and antique shows.

The regiment picked one of its own veterans, Charles Clinton, to design the building. The massive structure, opened in 1880, takes up the entire block between Park and Lexington avenues. The rear section was a drill hall—at the time, the largest interior drilling space ever created, spanned by a tremendous 300-foot barrel vault—and the front was three stories of meeting rooms for the various regimental companies. These rooms are some of the most lavishly appointed in the city; of particular note are the Veterans' Room and Library on the main floor, which were done by Louis Comfort Tiffany's Associated Artists, and remain today the most complete Tiffany interiors. These rooms—and the others in the Seventh Regiment—are considered some of the finest extant 19th-century examples of interior design. The materials in the rooms are an eclectic assortment, from aluminum foil in the coffered ceiling to recycled wallpaper rollers reused as

column capitals. A gorgeous Tiffany fireplace with turquoise tiles stands against one wall of the Veterans' Room and the walls are capped by an elaborate frieze depicting 20 great battles from the dawn of history to the modern era.

86 The Brooklyn Historical Society

The creation of the Brooklyn Historical Society underscores what made Brooklyn feel so different from Manhattan in the 19th century. Founded in 1864, during the height of the Civil War, it did not receive its charter from the New-York Historical Society across the river, which had been founded in 1801 and is today New York's oldest museum. Instead, the charter came from the New England Historical Society in Boston, thus reinforcing Brooklyn's stance as a solid Puritan, abolitionist city—the southernmost outpost of New England. Also, the society was at the time of its founding called the Long Island Historical Society, reflecting Brooklyn's identification as part of the island's history, not New York City's.

Erected in 1881 at the corner of Clinton and Pierrepont streets, the society's home was one of the first buildings designed by George B. Post, who would go on to build the New York Stock Exchange [114] and City College in Harlem [125]. The building has some Gothic elements in common with buildings by Calvert Vaux, such as the Metropolitan Museum [80] or Samuel Tilden's Gramercy Park townhouse [see 76], but is much more in keeping with the emerging Beaux-Arts style advo-

The main entrance to the Brooklyn Historical Society

cated by Post's mentor, Richard Morris Hunt, with whom Post trained at the Tenth Street Studio Building [**62**].

Above the foundations, the building is made almost entirely of red materials, a style in vogue in the 1880s when terra-cotta ornamentation was first being widely used. The wonderful portrait busts, by Olin Levi Warner, are early examples of monumental terra-cotta on a city building. The four carvings of faces along the building's Clinton Street side show four Europeans associated with the values of the society: Michelangelo (art), Beethoven (music), Gutenberg (publishing), and Shakespeare (writing). Above the main Pierrepont Street entrances are four faces that represent the founding of America. Over the original entrance are a Native American and a Viking, representing the synthesis of European and Native American cultures. At a higher level are Christopher Columbus and Benjamin Franklin, the latter depicted here (as he is on Vaux's Tilden mansion) because he was the Founding Father with the broadest range of interests—he was a scientist, diplomat, writer, inventor, and patriot all rolled into one.

Today, the society continues to function as a library and research center, but also houses exhibitions about Brooklyn's history.

87 The Chinese Exclusion Act

In discussing New York's immigrant populations of the 19th century, it is easy to overlook the Chinese. Today, New York's Chinatown is the largest and fastest growing in North America,* but when the first Chinese settled along Mott Street—still today

*Unless it isn't. Verifiable population statistics are hard to come by, and San Francisco, Toronto, and Vancouver also lay claim to having the largest and/or the fastest-growing Chinatown.

the heart of Chinatown—it was the center of a thriving Irish community [see 64].

In the mid-1860s, there were fewer than 200 Chinese men living in Five Points. Not surprisingly, most of the country's Chinese population until that time was located on the West Coast. Chinese laborers and farmers had arrived during the gold rush, but as gold became scarce, rising anti-Chinese sentiment kept them from finding other work. Many Chinese settled in San Francisco and took whatever jobs they could get, often as day laborers, in restaurants, or running laundries. The next wave of Chinese immigrants was imported by the Central Pacific Railroad to do the grueling work of getting the tracks laid over the Sierra Nevada. It was the completion of this railroad in 1869 that sparked a Chinese migration from the west to New York. European immigrants from the East Coast suddenly had access to California, where they arrived during an economic downturn and were forced to compete with the Chinese for jobs. This situation, in turn, caused those Chinese who'd saved enough for the fare to head east, arriving in New York in ever-increasing numbers between 1870 and 1882.

At the same time, the U.S. government was crafting legislation to curb Chinese immigration. Despite higher courts having overturned a number of racist California laws limiting Chinese employment (the preferred racial slur of the time was to label Asians "the yellow peril"), in 1882, Congress passed the Chinese Exclusion Act. It was the first time America had restricted immigration on such a large scale and the only time in its history that it would single out a particular ethnic group. The law not only forbade any Chinese people from coming to America—except for occasional merchants with special hard-to-acquire visas—it also put pressure on the Chinese living in America to return to China. Those who stayed were required to have spe-

An early 20th-century view of Chinatown

cial identification papers—without which they could be arrested—and were forbidden from naturalizing and becoming U.S. citizens.

In 1882, New York's Chinese population had risen to between 2,000 and 5,000 people* who now faced a terrible dilemma: they were not welcome, but if they *did* want to stay in America they could never leave—if they went to China to visit

---

*Some scholars think the number was even larger, estimating that more than 10,000 Chinese were living in New York at the time of the Chinese Exclusion Act.

family, they wouldn't be allowed to return to the United States. It was at this moment that modern Chinatown came to be, with the Chinese coalescing for economic and physical protection in one small stretch of the Five Points. In 1882, the Chinese community took up no more than the three blocks of Mott Street south of Canal, the two short blocks of Pell Street, and tiny Doyers Street [141].

During the first years of the Chinese Exclusion Act, as the population struggled to find gainful employment, the notion of selling "Chinese-ness" to Americans came to the forefront. Restaurants that had once only catered to the male Chinese population began selling Americanized fare such as moo goo gai pan and chop suey—watered-down Cantonese cuisine aimed at the Western palate.

Shops began selling real and fake chinoiserie. The oldest of these shops, at 32 Mott Street, features a magnificent tin ceiling and a gorgeous carved arch designed to keep evil spirits at bay. Alas, the economic downturn Chinatown suffered in the wake of the World Trade Center attack [180] forced the Lee family, who had run the store since 1891, to close up shop; a new owner—keeping some of the original décor intact—began operating out of the space in 2004.

The Chinese Exclusion Act was set to expire after ten years. However, it was renewed for an additional decade in 1892, and then made permanent in 1902. The law was not repealed until 1943, when it seemed politically expedient to reward China, America's ally in World War II. Congress knew it could revoke the law with impunity because in 1924 a quota system had gone into effect, based on the census of 1890. Each country with an immigrant population in the United States was allowed to send another 2 percent of the number of people who had been in this country in 1890. The Chinese were further restricted—only 105 people per year could enter the country. Real Chinese immigration to New York did not begin until the 1924 laws were superseded in 1965 by the Immigration and Nationality Act.

88 The Opening of the Brooklyn Bridge

It is so easy to condemn William "Boss" Tweed for his brazen corruption that it's also easy to overlook his many contributions to the city. (To paraphrase Tweed biographer Kenneth Ackerman: If Tweed hadn't been a crook, he'd be remembered as one of the greatest New Yorkers of his age; unfortunately, being a crook was his only motivation.) It was Tweed, for example, who secured funding for the Metropolitan Museum of Art and the American Museum of Natural History; it was also Tweed who, as commissioner of public works, was behind such mundane necessities as street paving and sewer laying. And Tweed was responsible for some of the most charming parts of Central Park, such as the carousel and the sheepfold that later became Tavern on the Green [see 151]. But perhaps most important, it was Tweed who helped secure for New York City the greatest engineering project of its age: the Brooklyn Bridge.

The Brooklyn Bridge was the

brainchild of John A. Roebling, the leading expert on suspension bridge design in the 19th century. Contrary to popular belief, the Brooklyn Bridge was not the first steel suspension bridge—Roebling had already built others, including the Roebling Bridge, connecting Ohio and Kentucky at Cincinnati. However, the Brooklyn Bridge was the culmination of Roebling's earlier work, and since it connected the largest city in America (New York) to the third-

The job of constructing the bridge then fell to Roebling's son and partner, Washington. To build the massive towers, workers had to dig far below the bottom of the East River. (They were looking for bedrock, which—at least on the Manhattan side—they never found.) To reach the river bottom, gigantic pressurized caissons were constructed, allowing workmen to dig in air-filled chambers far below the water's surface. Unfortunately, no one yet knew

A late-19th-century view of the Brooklyn Bridge

largest (Brooklyn), it was the one that captured the world's attention. Every suspension bridge from this point forward has the Brooklyn Bridge in its DNA.

Sadly, Roebling did not live to see construction begin. He and his team were scouting for locations for the bridge's Brooklyn tower in 1869 when his foot caught on the dock and was crushed by an incoming ferry. While this injury didn't need to be life-threatening, Roebling believed in a 19th-century pseudo-medicine called hydropathy ("water therapy") and insisted that his wounds be treated solely with water. Within three weeks he'd contracted tetanus and was dead.

about the bends (still known as "caisson disease") and dozens of workers were incapacitated by nitrogen expanding in their blood because they surfaced too fast. This included Washington Roebling, who was crippled by the bends in 1879 and had to spend the rest of the bridge's construction watching through a spyglass from his Brooklyn Heights home; he sent notes via his wife, Emily, to the construction foreman.

Because the Roeblings knew the public's innate distrust of crossing such a large span (the bridge is over a mile end-to-end), the bridge was engineered to be much stronger than necessary. This turned out to be a good precaution, as the bridge was built of substandard material. After the wire from the factory was inspected, supplier J. Lloyd Haigh [see 77] secretly inserted material back into the inventory that had failed inspection. By the time this was discovered, the thick bridge ropes had been spun and there was no going back. Because the Roeblings were such conservative engineers, the bridge was still more than sturdy enough.

The bridge opened with dramatic flair on May 24, 1883. Mayor Franklin Edson of New York and Mayor Seth Low of Brooklyn [see 101] led President Chester Arthur and Governor Grover Cleveland across the bridge from New York to Brooklyn, where they ended up at Washington Roebling's home for a reception. They were followed by over 150,000 pedestrians who had paid a penny apiece to cross the bridge. For the first few days the bridge was open there were no problems, but on May 30, a nervous pedestrian heard a noise and cried out that the bridge was collapsing. In the stampede to get to dry land, a dozen people were trampled to death.

Despite this initial tragedy, the bridge soon became indispensable and, just as John Roebling had hoped, it created a surge of bridge building around the country. More important for New York, it linked the hearts of Manhattan and Brooklyn together. For the first time, weather, ferry schedules, and capacity were no longer an obstacle for moving people and goods between the two cities. Though talk of uniting the two into one city had been raised before, it was the Brooklyn Bridge that inexorably led, 15 years after its opening, to the modern city of New York [107].

89 The Hotel Chelsea and the Birth of Cooperative Apartments

Today's Hotel Chelsea, which opened in 1883, was part of a rapidly developing trend in the early 1880s: the apartment building. The very idea that wealthy New Yorkers would choose to dwell in shared living space was a radical shift. Up to this point everyone who could afford it owned a private home. Certainly, there were tenements for poor immigrants [84], as well as boardinghouses and the anomalous artists' residences, like the Tenth Street Studio Building [62]. However, respectable families lived in private homes. If you had only a small amount of money, it might be a small wooden home in a less desirable neighborhood; if you had a lot of money, it would be a mansion on Fifth Avenue.

In 1883, the *New York Times* surveyed residential construction in the city and presciently declared:

> If [apartments] are readily taken there is little doubt that the building of apartment houses on a comprehensive scale will receive a decided stimulus, and the influence of such a trend on the future of the City cannot be over-estimated.

Indeed, in 1869 there had only been one rental apartment building in the entire city; by 1885, there would be 300.

What made the Chelsea truly unusual was that it was *not* a rental building; instead, the apartments would be owned cooperatively by the tenants as part of a "Hubert Home Club," named after the building's designer, Philip Hubert. Hubert and his partner, James Pirsson, created the first home club in 1880 to solve the financing problem for the Rembrandt, a six-story artists' residence they were building on 57th Street. Hubert and Pirsson built large apartments for the building's shareholders along with rental units, the income from which went to lessen each shareholder's annual costs. But the advantages of club membership were more than just economic: the co-op took care of those petty annoyances like water bills and property tax payments. And by having a building staff, even bachelors or small families could have the luxury of on-call servants.

The success of the Rembrandt led to more Hubert Home Clubs, the most famous of which was the Chelsea on 23rd Street, which at 11 stories and 90 apartments dwarfed its neighbors. As in many of Hubert's buildings, a number of apartments were duplexes, with parlors and public rooms on the lower floor and private rooms and bedrooms above. Though the Chelsea was initially a success, the blossoming of the elevated railroads [81] allowed the city to rapidly expand north and the middle class—still ultimately suspicious of the idea of apartments as suitable habitations—preferred the rows of brownstones going up on the Upper West Side, Upper East Side, and Harlem. Hubert was soon bankrupt and by 1903, the neighborhood around

the Chelsea had changed so significantly that the building was sold to become a hotel.*

It is as a hotel that the Chelsea has achieved its greatest fame, drawing a diverse group of creative residents over the years. It was here that Arthur C. Clarke wrote *2001: A Space Odyssey* and Bob Dylan composed "Sad-Eyed Lady of the Lowlands." More notoriously, it was where Dylan Thomas collapsed from alcohol poisoning. (After bingeing at the White Horse Tavern in Greenwich Village, Thomas's famous last words were, "I've had eighteen straight whiskeys. I think that's the record.") And, in 1979, Nancy Spungen's body was discovered in Room 100, a hunting knife protruding from her belly. Her boyfriend, Sex Pistols bassist Sid Vicious, was the prime suspect, but he died of a heroin overdose before the case could move forward.

90 The Making of the West Side 2: The Dakota

There's a great story that when developer Edward Clark announced that he was going to build a luxury apartment building at the corner of Eighth Avenue and 72nd Street, someone told him that if he was planning to build that far out of town, he "might as well build it in the Dakotas," and the name stuck.

In truth, Clark's choice of the term was a pointed attempt to lure people to the "wilds" of the Upper

---

*Today, the oldest existing co-op is the building at 34 Gramercy Park, which also opened in 1883.

New Yorkers skating on the lake in Central Park. The Dakota stands in the background.

West Side. Why, Clark reasoned, be a pioneer by moving out west when you could be a pioneer without ever leaving New York? Clark also championed a plan to rename Upper West Side streets "after such of the States as have well-sounding names." His suggestions: for Eleventh Avenue, Idaho Place; for Tenth, Arizona Place; for Ninth, Wyoming Place; and for Eighth Avenue—the street that runs along the side of the Dakota—Montana Place. While Clark never got his wish, within a decade Eighth Avenue had become the now-familiar Central Park West, and the nearby avenues had changed to Columbus and Amsterdam.

The Dakota, designed by Henry Hardenbergh, who would go on to build the famous Plaza Hotel, laid its cornerstone in 1881. (It's high above the 72nd Street entrance and shows the profile of a Dakota chief.) The apartments welcomed their first ten-

ants in 1884. Unlike Philip Hubert's experimental cooperative buildings [89], the Dakota was strictly a rental. But what it lacked in the cachet of ownership, it more than made up for in amenities, including its own electric plant, central heating, and hundreds of miles of pipe to bring water from tanks on the roof to every apartment. The apartments themselves ranged from four-room "bachelor" flats to 20-room mansions in the sky, some of which had formal parlors 45 feet deep. Because the building was constructed around a central courtyard, it was airier than most large buildings of its time. And because it kept a large staff—in addition to whatever private servants tenants employed—it must have seemed like a palace. Indeed, composer Peter Tchaikovsky visited music publisher Gustav Schirmer at the Dakota and mistook the building for Schirmer's private residence ("bigger than the czar's!" he wrote in his diary) and Central Park for his front garden.

The Dakota hoped to simultaneously prove that the rich could benefit from apartment living and that the Upper West Side was not a backwater. It succeeded so well on the first count that within 50 years it was rare to find new single-family homes being constructed in the most expensive parts of the city. If you were rich, you had to live in a fashionable apartment. However, it never quite succeeded as well on the second count. While the Upper West Side is today filled with expensive apartments that cater to the rich and famous and wouldn't be considered by anyone a "backwater," it still struggles to match the property values (and cachet) of Fifth Avenue on the opposite side of the park.

91 Kleindeutschland: The Ottendorfer Bequest

Nineteenth-century German-Americans don't get discussed nearly as often as the Irish who immigrated to New York at roughly the same time. In part, this is 20th-century anti-German sentiment at work [see 123]. But it is also because the Germans faced, on the whole, fewer barriers in New York. There had been German immigrants since the 18th century—such as John Jacob Astor [33]—so the Germans already had a greater foothold by the time massive numbers of people began to arrive after 1848. But more significantly, while some Germans were Catholics, many were Protestants and Jews, which made them altogether more acceptable to the average New York citizen.

By the 1880s, the German community had split into two recognizable groups. Some Germans had fully assimilated and were an integral part of the city's mercantile elite, including sewing machine pioneer Isaac Singer and Central Park commissioner August Belmont, the horse-fancier who later created the Belmont Stakes (and financed the first New York City subway [119]). But most Germans had settled in the area of the Lower East Side between Houston Street and 23rd Street—centered on St. Mark's Place and Tompkins Square Park—that came to be known as Kleindeutschland: "Little Germany."

Two of the most prominent buildings in the area opened in 1884 on Second Avenue, just north of St. Mark's Place. Built as a pair, they housed the Freie Bibliothek und Lesehall, New York City's first free lending library, and the German Dispensary, a free clinic in the tradition of the Northern Dispensary [38]. The buildings were the gift of newspaper editor Oswald Ottendorfer and his wife, Ann. Ottendorfer's paper, the *Staats-Zeitung*, was one of the largest circulating dailies in New York and, Ottendorfer claimed, had the largest circulation of any German-language paper in the world.

The buildings were designed as a pair by William Schickel in an early Beaux-Arts (sometimes referred to as Queen Anne) style, similar in execution to George B. Post's Brooklyn Historical Society [86]. The German Dispensary features wonderful terra-cotta busts of scientists such as Hippocrates and Celsius. Though the clinic no longer functions, the library next door continues today as a part of the New York Public Library

[128], making it the oldest branch in the modern system.

Nearby, other remnants of Kleindeutschland peek through the layers of later neighborhood development, including the German-American Shooting Club at 12 St. Mark's Place; the former Arlington Hall at 19–25 St. Mark's (later home of Andy Warhol's Exploding Plastic Inevitable [164]) and testaments to the event that destroyed Little Germany, the sinking of the *General Slocum* in 1904 [118].

92 Little Italy: Banca Stabile

Though Italian immigration to America began as early as the 17th century, by the Civil War, New York's Italian population still numbered only a few thousand people. (Perhaps the two most famous pre–Civil War Italians in New York were Lorenzo Da Ponte, Mozart's librettist, and—many years later—Giuseppe Garibaldi, who lived with his friend Antonio Meucci on Staten Island from 1850 to 1854, working in the latter's candle factory.)

Immigration began to pick up in the years after the Civil War, with most arrivals coming from southern Italy, particularly Sicily. These new arrivals, predominantly single men, mainly clustered in boardinghouses in two areas, East Harlem (the first part of the city to gain the appellation "Little Italy") and the area of Five Points around Mott and Mulberry streets called Mulberry Bend [105]. These men were known as "birds of passage"—seasonal workers who would live in New York for six months to a year, earn money

to support their families, and then return to Italy.

In response to all these laborers saving their paychecks, Little Italy was soon awash with banks. (The *New York Times* noted in 1890 that "Italian signs, Italian shops, and Italian bankers abound.") In the early 1880s, Francesco Stabile founded a bank on Mulberry Street. In addition to being eponymous, the name also had the advantage of promoting the bank's solidity: Banca Stabile literally means "stable bank." In 1885, the bank moved into larger headquarters on the corner of Grand and Mulberry streets, where it prospered during the largest wave of Italian immigration to the United States. Between 1890 and 1910, the Italian population grew from 40,000 to 500,000 people—faster than any ethnic group in the city's history.

Over the years, the bank added services, including a telegraph office and passenger ship ticketing. In the 1930s, the bank merged with Banca Commerciale Italiana, but the building remains intact. In 2007, the Italian American Museum acquired the building from the Stabile family and moved there in 2008, to provide a destination in Little Italy that showcases the depth of Italian contributions to American society.

93 The Statue of Liberty Opens

Because the Statue of Liberty was a gift marking America's centennial in 1876, it is little remembered today that the statue was originally intended to show support for the Union cause in the Civil War. French jurist Edouard René Lefèvre de Laboulaye conceived a gift to the United States as a symbol of the triumph of Republicanism. As France's Third Republic teetered toward monarchism (and ultimately, the Franco-Prussian War of 1870 and the ill-fated Paris Commune), de Laboulaye saw a gift to America as way of reminding the French—and the world—of the shared democratic values of these two longtime allies. As the idea took shape, it seemed appropriate to give a present to America in 1876 that would also serve to remind Americans of France's invaluable role in winning the Revolution [see 33].

Meanwhile, de Laboulaye's friend Frédéric Auguste Bartholdi was at work on a plan for a massive

The Statue of Liberty

statue to stand at the entrance to the Suez Canal, one of France's greatest triumphs of the 19th century. His statue was to combine elements of two of the Seven Wonders of the World: the Colossus of Rhodes and the lighthouse at Alexandria. However, lacking any real financial backing from Egypt or France, Bartholdi's statue languished until he found out about de Laboulaye's plan to honor America. Bartholdi made a few rough changes to his Suez statue and— voilà!—it was "Liberty Enlightening the World."*

The engineering problems for Bartholdi were numerous. No one had built a freestanding statue of this giant size since antiquity—and never out of thin sheets of copper. (The "skin" of the statue is only three millimeters thick, roughly the same as two pennies held together.) For help Bartholdi turned to Gustave Eiffel,** who constructed an innovative system of puddled-iron struts to hold together the 350 pieces of the statue.

⌒While the people of France agreed to pay for the construction of the statue, it was up to the Americans to pay for its erection, including the costs of a massive stone pedestal designed by Richard Morris Hunt [62]. Meanwhile, work in Paris was progressing slower than Bartholdi had expected and by

*This is still its actual name; the Statue of Liberty is a nickname.

**In 1889, Eiffel's name would be forever linked to the centerpiece he built for the World's Fair in Paris, the Eiffel Tower.

1876, only the torch and a portion of the right arm were finished. The torch and hand were shipped to Philadelphia, where they were on display at the 1876 Centennial Exposition. Visitors to the fair could pay 50 cents to climb to the top of the torch. The torch later moved to Madison Square in New York, where it remained until the statue could be erected.

Though fund-raising in America was initially strong, by 1882 it was flagging, with only half the needed money in the bank. That same year, Joseph Pulitzer [115] purchased the *New York World* from financier Jay Gould and, looking for something to invigorate its moribund circulation, announced that he was going to champion the fund-raising for the statue. In six months, he raised as much as the official committee had done in seven years.

Pulitzer was not the only fund-raiser for the statue. Songs, poems, and souvenirs were all sold to generate revenue. The most famous of these was the poem "The New Colossus" by Emma Lazarus, a young writer from Greenwich Village. (The poem is known more famously by the lines "Give me your tired, your poor,/Your huddled masses yearning to breathe free.") In 1903, the poem was cast in bronze and added to the interior of the statue's pedestal.

↷ The statue arrived, disassembled, in June 1885, and sat in its crates for a year as Hunt's pedestal was completed. It then took four months to erect the statue, which was officially unveiled by President Grover Cleveland on October 28, 1886.

(At the subsequent parade up Broadway, an enterprising office worker in one of the brokerage houses lining the road decided to open up his window and toss out used stock ticker tape as streamers. By the time the parade was well under way, Broadway was a blizzard of paper and the ticker tape parade [**see 169**] had been born.)

There was one glaring omission among the hundreds of people who'd been invited to the dedication: women. Indeed, the flotilla of boats surrounding the statue for its grand opening held only men. So, taking matters into their own hands, the New York State Woman Suffrage Association chartered a steamboat and crashed the party.

94 The Eldridge Street Synagogue

On March 13, 1881, Czar Alexander II was assassinated in St. Petersburg, which not only set back the progress of political reform in Russia by decades, but had a disastrous effect on the Russian Empire's Jewish population. The new czar, Alexander III, was an anti-Semite, and many blamed the Jews for the assassination. As a result, wholesale pogroms were unleashed against Jewish cities in Russia, Ukraine, and Poland.

Fleeing this persecution, huge numbers of Eastern European, Yiddish-speaking Jews ended up in New York in the mid-1880s. These new arrivals transformed the Lower East Side into a vibrant Jewish community, making New York by the end of the 19th century the largest Jewish city in the world, which it remains to this day.*

The most spectacularly preserved work of art from this new Jewish population is also the first major synagogue built by Eastern European Jews in America, Congregation Kahal Adath Jeshurun Anshe Ludz, more popularly known as the Eldridge Street Synagogue.

Opened in 1887, the synagogue was an offshoot of the first Russian-Polish congregation in New York, Beth Hamedrash ("house of study"), which was founded in 1848. By the 1880s, the congregation had split in two: the name Beth Hamedrash continued for the branch that purchased the old Norfolk Street Baptist Church [112], while Kahal Adath Jeshurun (the "community of the people of Israel") built the new temple on Eldridge Street. The congregation hired the Herter Brothers to build the structure, which they designed as a sort of neo-Gothic/Moorish hybrid. This commission made the Herters the preferred architects of the neighborhood, and over the next eight years they would build hundreds of buildings—mostly tenements—but never another synagogue.

Though on its face the building reveals a Christian architectural heritage—in particular in the large rose window—it has a tremendous amount of encoded Jewish meaning on its façade. For example, that rose window is made up of 12 rosettes, which represent the 12 tribes of Israel. Below that stand five windows that

are the five books of the Torah and the four entrances represent the four matriarchs.

At its peak, the congregation numbered in the thousands. However, with the decline of the Jewish population on the Lower East Side, the synagogue was no longer able to afford to heat or cool the building and moved services into the study

The Eldridge Street Synagogue

room in the basement (where they are still held to this day). By the mid-1950s, the sanctuary was completely shut and for the next 30 years, broken windows, a leaking roof, and

---

*New York's Jewish population is between one and two million (depending on who you ask). This is smaller than metropolitan Tel Aviv, which has close to 3 million people. However, the actual city of Tel Aviv only has a population of just under 350,000 people, making New York a larger Jewish city.

general neglect wreaked havoc on the inside. In the 1980s, a nonprofit organization, the Eldridge Street Project, was founded to restore the building to its former glory and open it as a museum dedicated both to the Eastern European experience in New York and more generally to the history of the Lower East Side as an immigrant enclave. Substantial work was completed in 2007.

95 The Educational Alliance

Founded in 1889, the Educational Alliance aimed to help immigrants adapt to New York City and to serve as a secular counterpoint to the Lower East Side's large synagogues, such as the one that had recently opened on Eldridge Street [94].

Headquartered at the corner of East Broadway and Jefferson Street, the Alliance—originally called the Hebrew Institute—was created by a group of prominent merchants led by Isidor Straus. Born in 1845 in Germany, Straus had arrived in New York with his family after the Civil War. With his father, Lazarus, and brother, Nathan, he sold china and crockery in the basement of R. H. Macy's;* by 1896, the Straus brothers owned the entire store.

The main goal of the Educational Alliance was, in Straus's words, "to help immigrants understand American ideas" and—perhaps revealing his own distrust of these new immigrants—"to appreciate an American atmosphere of obedience to law." In 1905, the Alliance reaffirmed these aims, noting its desire to "Americanize the recently arrived immigrant and to socialize him in the sense of making him better able to do his share in the work of society."

The Alliance's main way of Americanizing the Yiddish-speaking Lower East Side was to teach English. Classes were offered from early in the morning until late at night in order to accommodate just about any schedule. But the Alliance also added art exhibitions, cultural classes, singing lessons (Eddie Cantor was one pupil) and dance instruction (Arthur Murray took his first classes here) to the mix.

The Alliance was not without controversy. Though many who sat on its board were neither German nor Jewish, the organization came to be seen as an attempt by earlier Jewish immigrants, who were sometimes derogatorily known as Uptown Jews, to unduly influence the lives of the Yiddish-speaking population. German Jews not only spoke a different language, they were—more important—members of Reform congregations, which many Orthodox saw as an affront to their traditional mode of worship. The critique leveled at Straus was that he wasn't just trying to Americanize the population culturally, he was trying to Americanize their religion too.

The building today carries the name of David Sarnoff, the pioneer at RCA who promoted the early use of radio, became the head of the NBC network, and shepherded television onto the national stage. Born in Belarus in 1891, Sarnoff immigrated to New York in 1900 and learned

---

*Macy's Cellar, its housewares department, keeps this tradition alive.

English at the Educational Alliance, to which he later donated significant sums of money.

Across East Broadway from the Educational Alliance's front door is one of the original Carnegie Free Libraries in New York [**see 109**]. Until World War II, it was the most popular library in the city, staying open 19 hours a day. This was mostly due to its large collection of Yiddish books; it was not unusual to see children leave their Educational Alliance English lessons and head across the street to the library to keep up their Yiddish skills.

96 Ellis Island

In the 1880s, as the number of Italian and Eastern European immigrants rose from a few thousand a year to a few thousand a month, the U.S. government grappled with ways to better process and limit new arrivals.

Some of the first laws were aimed at denying access to specific "unde-sirables." The Immigration Act of 1882 levied a 50-cent tax on all arriving immigrants as well as excluding the mentally ill, convicts, and the indigent. That same year also saw the passage of the Chinese Exclusion Act [**87**], which effectively barred the arrival of the Chinese until 1943.

During this time, the actual processing of immigrants was the duty of each individual port, and New York handled its arrivals at Castle Garden in Battery Park [**59**]. After 1882, Castle Garden continued to operate under joint state-federal oversight, but in 1890 the federal government announced that it would run the immigrant depot itself. So, New York promptly kicked the government out of Castle Garden.

The first federal facility was a former barge office at the foot of Whitehall Street, but in 1892, facilities were transferred to Ellis Island in the harbor. The original Ellis Island buildings were much smaller than the ones you can visit today. The first federal facility burned down in

Ellis Island

1897; the current main waiting hall, designed by the firm of Boring & Tilton, opened in 1900. It was through the Great Hall of this building that the vast majority of Ellis Island's 12 million immigrants passed over the next 50 years. It is estimated that 40 percent of the American population has at least one ancestor who was processed at Ellis Island. And while there were many other ports of entry into the country, including Baltimore, New Orleans, Galveston, and Angel Island in California, Ellis Island processed more immigrants than all the others combined. (However, one thing to remember is that only 70 percent of New York's arriving passengers went through Ellis Island; the other 30 percent who could afford first- or second-class tickets were processed aboard ship and allowed to disembark at the passenger ship piers.)

For most immigrants, their stay on the island averaged a day and a half. They were subjected to a brief medical exam, questioned about their sponsorship, and had their papers checked and rechecked. An average of 4,000 people were sent back each year, mostly due to illness—this was less than 2 percent of the more than 200,000 people who arrived at Ellis Island annually. Stories have circulated for years of names being changed at Ellis Island, but in fact that rarely happened. (When it did, it was through clerical error.) Because Ellis Island immigrants traveled with documents proving their identity and the government hired translators to help people work their way through the island's bureaucracy, the records at Ellis Island show remarkable fidelity to people's actual names. When people did change their names,

it was later, either to try to fit in better in American society or due to misunderstandings with employers or local government officials.

The island saw a dramatic downturn in arrivals after 1924, when the National Origins Act limited new entrants to 2 percent of any country's immigrant population in the United States in 1890. Choosing a date over 30 years earlier had the intended effect of reducing the number of Italian and Eastern European arrivals. Ellis Island remained in operation until 1954, when it was shuttered due to lack of activity. Parts of it reopened as a museum in 1991 and plans are under way to restore some of the medical facilities on the island and open them to visitors.

97 The Club Scene: J. P. Morgan's Metropolitan Club

At the end of the 19th century, private membership clubs became the backbone of many business and social relationships in the city. These clubs ranged widely in their goals and membership criteria. Some, like the Players and the National Arts Club—next-door neighbors on Gramercy Park [**40**]—appealed to artists and their patrons. Others, like the University Club, only admitted people with particular credentials. Almost from its founding in 1836, the most important of these organizations was the Union Club, then located on Fifth Avenue at 21st Street. (Today it stands at the corner of Park Avenue and 69th Street.) The club acted as a social arbiter, and membership conveyed the same sort of social standing as being on Ward McAllister's list of the "First Four Hundred." (According to McAllister, Caroline Schermerhorn Astor's ballroom on 34th Street held 400 people; thus, only 400 could be on her invitation list, and if you weren't invited to Mrs. Astor's parties, you might as well not exist [**see 44**].)

The Metropolitan Club

However, over the years the Union Club's membership choices were not without controversy. The Knickerbocker Club was founded in 1871 as a result of the Union Club's supposedly lax membership standards. While you did not have to be an actual Knickerbocker to join,* you certainly needed to be well established. Evidently, too much new money was getting into the Union Club.

One of those upstart members was banker J. Pierpont Morgan. But while Morgan had been accepted into the Union Club, many of his friends were blackballed by the membership committee. In response, Morgan founded his own club, the Metropolitan, in 1891. Architect Stanford White (who specialized in club buildings, often bartering membership for his services) designed the grand marble building at the corner of 60th Street and Fifth Avenue,

strategically placed at the corner of Central Park. To maximize the effect of the Fifth Avenue façade, the entrance was placed around the corner on 60th Street, with a grand carriage drive. On the ground floor, the windows were placed high enough so that the members could see out but passersby could not peer in. On the second-floor balconies, White placed a large "M," which ostensibly stood for "Metropolitan" but could equally have stood for Morgan. Interior amenities included a grand ballroom, dining room, billiard room, and bowling alley for the exclusive use of members.

While club membership would wane in the 20th century, many of New York's 19th-century clubs—including the Metropolitan, Knickerbocker, and Union—all continue to operate to this day.

---

*The "Knickerbocracy" was made up of those who could trace their ancestry back to the Dutch colonial period and was named after Washington Irving's Dutch character, Diedrich Knickerbocker. The city's current basketball team is named for the same term.

98 The Christopher Columbus Quadricentennial

Of all the people honored in Central Park, only one person gets two statues: Christopher Columbus. Both were erected as part of the celebrations surrounding the 400th anniversary of his voyage of discovery, but for essentially opposite reasons. The better-known of the two stands just outside the park atop a giant

Gaetano Russo's statue of Christopher Columbus in the center of Columbus Circle

marble pillar in what is now known as Columbus Circle (which, before 1892, was simply "the Circle" or "the Great Circle"). The other statue faces Shakespeare on the park's Mall and

was largely built as a middle-class Protestant reaction to the Great Circle's very pro-Italian statue.

In the years leading up to 1892, Carlo Barsotti, the publisher of the Italian-language paper *Il Progresso Italo Americano*, diligently promoted the idea that Columbus be honored in New York, which was fast becoming one of the largest centers of Italians in the world. Through public subscription, *Il Progresso* raised the money for a statue to be erected at the Great Circle, and hired Sicilian artist Gaetano Russo to create a monument to be ready for October 12, 1892. It was unveiled in the newly named Columbus Circle as part of the celebrations for Columbus Day.

At the same time, New York historian and Civil War general James Grant Wilson (promoter of the statue of Fitz-Greene Halleck [**78**]) rallied the New York Genealogical and Biographical Society to erect its own statue of the famous explorer. Whereas Russo's sculpture would symbolize Italian heritage, the statue on the Mall would—at least on its face—emphasize the Spanish contribution to discovery. Designed by Gerónimo Suñol (who had sculpted a similar piece in Madrid), it shows the explorer, a globe at his feet, holding the Spanish flag and turning his eyes to heaven. The flag also bears a cross at its top, a reminder of Spain's missionary impulses in the New World.

In its review of the Suñol statue, the *New York Times** derided both the aesthetic ("rolling his eyes up . . . like a duck in a thunderstorm") and the tacit approval of the Spanish:

---

*The *Times* seems to have had it in for Central Park sculptures [see 72].

It is bad enough to have the foreign colonies in this city present the city with wretched specimens of sculpture like the Bolivar, Garibaldi, Robert Burns, and Sir Walter Scott, but worse when New-Yorkers, who have enough apparent interest in their city and its past to run a Genealogical Society, seem unable to grasp any higher idea of their duty to native art.

However, the erection of Suñol's Spanish explorer was actually *not* a particularly pro-Spanish gesture. The New York Genealogical and Biographical Society was, from its inception, more inclusive than other heritage organizations, but there's no denying that these societies were purveyors of nativism. As one genealogist noted in 1894, "the descendants of those who founded this country deserve to run it." While Italians and Spaniards were both invited to the opening ceremonies, it was the Knickerbocker New Yorkers, like the Vanderbilts, who paid for the statue; it was *their* New World it was glorifying.

At the same time that Barsotti's and Suñol's statues were being proposed and funded, a third Columbus for Central Park—this one by and for the Spaniards—was also put forward. Designed by Fernando Miranda, it was to have sat at the main Fifth Avenue entrance to the park. However, disagreements between the statue's supporters and the Parks Department (which offered other, less prominent locations) scuttled the project. A statue of William Tecumseh Sherman [117] now stands at Fifth Avenue and 59th Street.

An additional Columbus, by Emma Stebbins, was given to the park in 1869 by Marshall O. Roberts. Lacking a decent place to put it, the statue sat in the basement of the Arsenal [52] for a number of years and then was erected in the park—where, precisely, is unclear—before it was deemed to be suffering from the elements. Around 1892, just as America was celebrating the Columbus Quadricentennial, the Stebbins statue was moved indoors to the McGown's Pass Tavern, which stood at 102nd Street, just inside the park. In 1912, the statue was "discovered" there and the Italian Knights of Columbus petitioned to move it to Columbus Park [105], but no action was taken. It then seems that the statue was lost again. In 1934, it turned up in a Central Park storage facility and was immediately moved to Columbus Park. In 1971, it was sent to Brooklyn's Cadman Plaza to adorn the tiny Christopher Columbus area of that park, where it can be seen today.

99 The Kletzker Brotherly Aid Association

Arriving at Ellis Island [96] was an overwhelming experience for new immigrants. In 1893, *Harper's Weekly* reported:

The place is singularly suggestive of a prison in many of its aspects. Uniformed guards are everywhere—in all the passageways and at every door—to restrain the inquisitive roamer ... On either side [of the Great Hall] are ... great cages:

one with a motley crowd of immigrants, eating, walking, sleeping, sitting listlessly with folded hands, or soothing their children's fretfulness; these are awaiting remittances or friends to take them on their journey, or else are suspects to be more closely inquired into by-and-by. The smaller company opposite are no more miserable in appearance, though more wretched in their state. They are the rejected, to be sent home again on the next sailing of the steamer which brought them.

In fact, many of those "awaiting remittances or friends" had no one to collect them. Instead, agencies like the Hebrew Immigrant Aid Society established an office at Ellis Island, discovering where people were from and connecting them to their town's *landsmanschaft* (mutual aid society). This guaranteed that Eastern European Jews arriving in New York had someone waiting for them from their own hometown.

Two institutions were central to every Jewish immigrant: the synagogue and the aid society. One took care of spiritual needs and the other, secular, but both were intimately tied to a particular place. For large cities, like Bialystock, Poland, there were large synagogues.* Most, however, were tiny *shteiblach*—"storefront" synagogues run out of shop fronts or tenement parlors—that catered exclusively to the people from one village. If only a dozen people had come from that place, only those dozen worshipped together.

Landsmanschaften were the same: they almost exclusively served people from one city or town. A *landsmanschaft* not only sent volunteers to claim people from Ellis Island, it also guided people toward better tenements, acted as a job procurement agency, and provided a sense of identity and belonging—a connection back to the Old World. Aid associations also frequently served as banks, as people trusted having their money held by someone from their own hometown rather than loaned out by a larger, impersonal bank.

Most *landsmanschaften* were run from tenements, but one grand structure remains near the corner of Ludlow and Canal streets. At the top of the cornice it reads "Est. 1892" (though this building dates from 1910) and below that is spelled out "IN[dependent] KLETZKER BR[o]THERLY AID ASSN." This was the *landsmanschaft* for people from Kletzk, a town in what is today Belarus. If you look at the façade, you can still see the faint outline between the top windows of a Jewish star. The star is there not just to indicate Jewishness, but to show that this building once served as both the synagogue and the aid association.

The building had a succession of owners after the *landsmanschaft* moved out, including a bank, which added the beehives to the façade. Today, it serves as the Boe Fook Funeral Parlor, but for many years it was a joint Italian-Chinese funeral home, with separate Canal and Ludlow Street entrances for each ethnicity even though they were ultimately provided services in the same space.

---

*The Bialystoker Synagogue on Willett Place is the largest and most active synagogue in operation on the Lower East Side today.

While there is no longer an Italian element at Boe Fook, an Italian band still works at a nearby Chinese funeral parlor, making for the incongruous sight of Chinese flowers, incense, and white mourning clothes paired with a button-down Italian brass band.

100 The Cathedral of St. John the Divine

Considering the wealth, influence, and social status of the Episcopal Church in New York, it's somewhat surprising that the diocese didn't get around to seriously contemplating a cathedral until 1873, when Bishop Horatio Potter received a charter for St. John the Divine from the state legislature. In part, Potter was egged on by the existence of the Catholic St. Patrick's, which was then in the final stages of construction on Fifth Avenue [83]. However, the city's eco-nomic downturn in 1873 put plans for the cathedral on hold until Potter's nephew, Henry Codman Potter, was elected bishop in 1887 and immediately began rallying support for an uptown cathedral.

Henry Potter's choice of Morningside Heights was both symbolically and economically shrewd. By selecting land in an area of the city still relatively undeveloped, the church could guarantee itself a substantial plot for a reasonable price. The land it ended up purchasing between 110th and 113th streets had been occupied by the Leake and Watts Orphan House [47]. By building on one of Manhattan's tallest hills, the cathedral would tower over the rest of the city—reminding people that no matter how other religions might prosper, the Episcopalians were still, quite literally, on top.

But Morningside Heights had other value, as well. Two Episcopal institutions, St. Luke's Hospital and

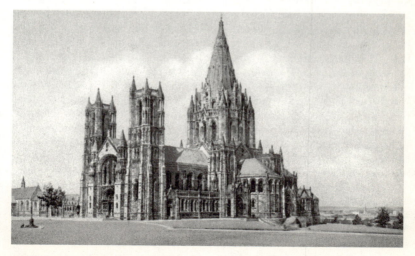

This early postcard shows what the Cathedral of St. John the Divine would have looked like if Heins & La Farge's plans had been carried to fruition.

Columbia University [101], were also contemplating moves to the neighborhood, which would give the church dominance over the spiritual needs, bodily health, and educational welfare from this "American Acropolis."

In 1888, the diocese held a contest to design the church and immediately ran into problems. First, more ecclesiastically conservative members of the diocese successfully lobbied to have the cathedral's orientation pivoted 45 degrees so that the apse would face east—the direction from which, tradition dictates, Christ will rise again. This dashed Potter's original hope to have the church's front entrance on 110th Street, opening onto the city, with the cathedral rising up the hill to the north. Then, once the contestants' architectural plans had been submitted, Bishop Potter requested that the judges remove from consideration one of their top picks, designed by the firm Potter & Robinson, because William Potter was Bishop Potter's half-brother and it would smack of back-door dealing. At least publicly, the selection committee refused, saying that Potter & Robinson had qualified on their merits. However, when it came to picking a winner, they ultimately settled on a neo-Byzantine design by the firm of Heins & La Farge, which, as architectural historian Andrew Dolkart has noted, was everyone's second choice.

The cornerstone for the cathedral was laid on December 27, 1892—the feast of St. John the Divine—but work proceeded slowly. The sheer size of the project was daunting, and despite the rocky nature of the heights, it took workers a full two years—and 72 feet—to hit solid bedrock. Once construction began, the architects' grandiose plans were difficult to execute, in particular Heins & La Farge's apse, which called for the world's largest granite columns. A lathe had to be custom-built and only one granite quarry in the nation—in remote Vinalhaven, Maine—was deep enough for the excavations. However, the columns kept breaking under their own massive weight, and ultimately the plan had to be abandoned. (The columns, which surround the choir, are still massive; however, if you look closely you can see the seams where pieces of stone have been connected together.)

In 1907, before even the apse and choir were finished, George Heins died, which freed the cathedral from its contract with the firm. Once the apse was completed in 1911, the cathedral fired La Farge and hired Gothic aficionado Ralph Adams Cram to finish the church. Cram promised he could build the church faster and bigger. He also jettisoned any of Heins & La Farge's Byzantine touches for a completely Gothic building. Cram's work began at the crossing in 1916 and over the next 25 years his team completed the massive nave. On November 30, 1941, the church kicked off an eight-day festival to celebrate the nave's completion. On the final day of the festivities, December 7, the Japanese bombed Pearl Harbor and, for all intents, work on the cathedral stopped.* Even unfinished, it is the largest cathedral ever built: 146 feet wide, 601 feet long, and over 124 feet to the top of the rafters. (To give you

---

*Work on the towers and decorative carvings commenced after the war, but the cathedral has done no major expansion since Cram's nave was completed.

a sense of comparison, St. Patrick's is only 306 feet long.)

The best place to see the difference between Cram's nave and Heins & La Farge's apse is at the crossing, where a "temporary" dome by Rafael Guastavino soars over the center of the building. If the cathedral were to ever build the transepts (the arms of the cross), it would need to tear down or move the Leake and Watts orphanage—today owned by the cathedral—which stands in the way of the south arm of the cross.

101 Columbia: Seth Low's University

Seth Low, who was the mayor of Brooklyn when the Brooklyn Bridge opened and second mayor of the unified city of New York [107], is today best remembered for the job he held between those two posts—president of Columbia University.

When Low accepted the position in 1890, Columbia College was located on Madison Avenue between 49th and 50th streets, in space it had occupied since 1856 but had outgrown. Columbia was New York's oldest college; founded by royal charter in 1754, it was known as King's College until the Revolution began and it was forced to close. It reopened after the war, reborn as Columbia, and for the next 60 years continued to be headquartered in Lower Manhattan, near St. Paul's Chapel, before moving to the Madison Avenue campus.

It was Low's chief task as president to find the college a new home; at the same time, he added schools

and graduate programs, transforming it into a genuine university. After contemplating a move to the countryside, the school instead acquired the property owned by the Bloomingdale Insane Asylum [47] in 1892 and solicited the city's best architecture firms for plans for a new campus. However, rather than have a design competition, Richard Morris Hunt [62], Charles McKim (partner of Stanford White [see 102]), and Charles Haight (designer of the new buildings at the General Theological Seminary [see 29]) were invited to collaborate on a master plan. In the end, though the three men presented some ideas jointly, it was ultimately McKim that Columbia selected to create a Beaux-Arts campus for the school. At its center would be a grand temple—based on the Pantheon in Rome—that would serve as the university's library. Facing incessant fund-raising problems, the wealthy Low paid for the library himself,

Low Memorial Library at Columbia University

naming it after his father, shipping magnate Abiel Abbot Low.

The remainder of the campus was designed in symmetrical groupings of red-brick classroom buildings (there were to be no dormitories), with monumental limestone entrances. Originally, McKim only planned a campus north of 116th Street. However, within 20 years, Columbia had purchased the blocks south to 113th Street and McKim reconfigured his master plan to include this new area. It was here that Columbia built its journalism school—the first of its kind in the country—with funds donated by Joseph Pulitzer [115] in 1912, and in the 1930s a new library opened to replace the beautiful, but inadequate, Low Memorial Library.

Columbia's move to Morningside Heights not only allowed the school to expand its own offerings, but also helped solidify its relationships with other schools. Seth Low's predecessor, Frederick A. P. Barnard, had started a women's college in 1888. It, too, moved to Morningside Heights, building a campus across Broadway on the spot where the Battle of Harlem Heights had taken place during the Revolution [see 16]. Teachers College came into the Columbia family in 1893, building a campus north of 120th Street. Over the next 25 years, The Juilliard School (now at Lincoln Center), Union Theological Seminary, and Jewish Theological Seminary all built campuses along Broadway, making Morningside Heights the most intensely academic neighborhood in the city.

102 The Washington Arch and the City Beautiful Movement

As New York neared the end of the 19th century, two distinct architectural trends were born that would remake the city. One was the sky-scraper, which would come to its fruition in the 20th century with buildings as diverse as the Flatiron [111] and the Empire State Building [148]. The other was much more short-lived but no less influential—the City Beautiful movement.

In part, the City Beautiful era was the natural result of having a generation of architects who had trained at L'Ecole des Beaux-Arts in Paris. (The terms "City Beautiful" and "Beaux Arts" are often used interchangeably.) Not only did the country now have a cadre of well-schooled, professional builders, it had a group of men who had lived and studied in Europe, absorbing both historical architecture and contemporary European trends. But the movement was also about putting America forward as not just a follower of European fashion, but as a rival. If New York was to be taken seriously as a great American city, it would need the architecture to match. Moreover, the City Beautiful planners saw their ideals—which included reworking entire cities—as a way to combat the growing tide of poverty and the proliferation of cheap housing in places like New York.

Chicago architect Daniel Burnham (who had *not*, in fact, studied at L'Ecole des Beaux-Arts, but instead apprenticed with William Le Baron Jenney, who had perfected the steel-frame skyscraper) is usually credited as the "father" of the City Beautiful movement through his work at the 1893 World's Columbian Exposition. However, the cornerstone for New York's first Beaux-Arts monument was laid in 1890—Stanford White's Washington Memorial Arch, which ushered in City Beautiful architecture to New York.

Stanford White (who also, by the way, didn't study at L'Ecole des Beaux-Arts) actually built the Washington Arch twice. The first, constructed in April 1889 and made of wood, plaster, and papier-mâché, was intended only to be temporary. It was erected for the centennial of George Washington's inauguration on Wall Street [18], which was celebrated on April 29, 1889. By the time the arch was dismantled a few days later, fund-raising had already begun for a permanent replacement. At first, plans called for a limestone arch, but that was soon upgraded to marble.

White's design for the marble arch —which would flank the Fifth Avenue cut-through of Washington Square [see 104]—was directly modeled on the Arc de Triomphe in Paris, Napoleon's grand monument to the French imperial armies. Scaled down to fit the context of Fifth Avenue, White's earliest drawings for the arch included large allegorical figures in front of each pier, similar to *La Marseillaise* and *The Triumph of 1810* on the Arc de Triomphe. By the time the arch was formally dedicated in 1895, White's plans had been altered to include statues of Washington, but lacking the necessary funds, the installation of the statues was delayed for over 20 years. During that time, White was murdered [121], and so never got to see his work completed. In 1916, Hermon A. MacNeil's *Washington at War*, showing Washington

The Washington Memorial Arch

as commander in chief of the Continental Army, was added to the right pier (the viewer's left). Two years later, A. Stirling Calder added *Washington at Peace*, depicting Washington as president of the United States.

White's allegorical figures do make cameo appearances. The general is flanked by bas-relief figures of Fame and Valor and the president by Wisdom and Justice, who hold a book inscribed with Washington's motto: *Exitus acta probat* (or, roughly translated, "The end justifies the means.")

The arch badly deteriorated due to the endless stream of traffic through it until Village resident Shirley Hayes successfully lobbied to remove the Fifth Avenue cut-through in 1959. Modern Washington Square was born at that point, though construction launched in 2007 is—as of this writing—transforming the square into more what it was like when it first opened as a park in 1828 [35].

103 Lillian Wald and the Settlement House Movement

In the years before the Civil War, philanthropic New Yorkers turned their attention to helping the city's poorest citizens in the Five Points [see 45]. This work was often religiously based—and often decidedly anti-Catholic. For example, in 1852, the old brewery—the most notorious squatters tenement—was torn down so that the Five Points Mission, a Protestant organization that sought to feed, clothe, and convert the Irish Catholics in the neighborhood, could be built in its place.

After the Civil War, there was a shift away from religious-based charity and an embrace of the new settlement house movement (imported to the United States from Great Britain in 1886), which advocated that trained professionals "settle" in the neighborhoods they were serving. The first settlement house in America was the University Settlement—still in existence on Eldridge Street—whose full-time staff all had university degrees. This was followed in 1894 by Lillian Wald's Nurses' Settlement on Henry Street, which was located in the midst of some the city's most crowded tenement blocks. Wald's original offices, a pair of once-elegant 1830s townhouses, were purchased for her by banker Jacob Schiff, and served as offices, clinic, and sleeping quarters. (In warm weather, the nurses would often camp out on the back porch.)

As the Nurses' Settlement grew, it took on more roles in the community, providing day-care services and schooling. Eventually, the professional nursing component was spun off into its own organization—the Visiting Nurse Service of New York—and the original organization was renamed the Henry Street Settlement. Like the Educational Alliance [95], the Henry Street Settlement is still extremely active in the neighborhood—though no one sleeps on the porch anymore.

104 Renaming New York: Laurens Street, South Fifth Avenue, and West Broadway

New York has a long history of renaming its streets and neighborhoods in an ongoing attempt to prop up property values, memorialize its heroes, distance itself from its own past, or simply head off in a new direction. This can be seen throughout the city's history, from changing Crown Street to Liberty Street after the Revolution to the creation of scores of new honorary street names in the wake of the World Trade Center attack [180].*

Few streets have as convoluted a history as West Broadway. Originally named Laurens Street, it was—like all the streets near it in Greenwich Village and SoHo—named for a prominent figure in the Revolutionary War. However, by the 1870s, few remembered Continental Congress president Henry Laurens. Moreover, real estate values south of Washington Square Park were beginning to sag—in part, it was thought, due to the fact that the park stood in the way of the free flow of traffic up and down Fifth Avenue. So, in 1870, William "Boss" Tweed, as commissioner of public works, backed a plan to ram Fifth Avenue through the park and connect it to Laurens Street. To better benefit from Fifth Avenue's cachet,

*For other examples, see the Five Points [37] and the creation of Park Avenue [69].

A detail of the façade of 130 South Fifth Avenue (now 422 West Broadway)

Broadway, perhaps hoping this new appellation would make it a shopping street like Broadway. (Another plan, floated around the same time, suggested that the Bowery become Central Broadway, but it went nowhere.)*

No physical trace of the Laurens Street name remains, and there are only a few subtle reminders of South Fifth Avenue. On the façade of 422 West Broadway, cast into the iron columns of the building, is the address 130—this is the building's South Fifth Avenue address, preserved in its metal façade as a relic of its earlier incarnation.

the street would also be renamed South Fifth Avenue, and get a new numbering scheme, beginning with No. 1 South Fifth Avenue just below Washington Square and counting south to the Financial District.

The new name and the new connection through Washington Square did little to improve the street's fortunes. In a city where almost every street counts south to north, South Fifth Avenue was confusing. Then, in 1877, the Sixth Avenue Elevated Railroad built tracks on portions of the street, pushing property values down even further.

When reform-minded mayor William L. Strong was elected in 1894, he did away with South Fifth Avenue and the city renamed it West

105 Mulberry Bend, Columbus Park, and *How the Other Half Lives*

A member of the first generation of what President Theodore Roosevelt [63] would later call "muckraking" journalists, Danish-born immigrant Jacob Riis had a profound influence on New York City's poorest neighborhoods, proving the old adage that sometimes a picture can be worth a thousand words.

Riis first came to America in 1870 and did a variety of jobs before finding himself out of work and essentially homeless. In 1873, he began his career as a police reporter, moving through a succession of city newspapers until landing at the *New York Sun*

---

*The Bowery, in this period, was famous as "skid row." But in another example of how quickly things change, 50 years later, when the Third Avenue El was torn down [see 81], some civic boosters put forward the idea that Third Avenue—which has *never* been part of the Bowery—could have its fortunes improved if it was renamed the Bouwerie. (Note the archaic spelling, lending it an air of ancient respectability.)

in 1888. Though all of his work centered on alerting the reading public to the problems confronting New York's poor, it was his embrace of flash photography that earned him world renown. Riis's photos were published first in the *Sun* as "Flashes from the

Mulberry Bend Park soon after its opening. The park was renamed for Christopher Columbus in 1911.

Slums: Pictures Taken in Dark Places by the Lightning Process." In his autobiography, *The Making of an American*, Riis explained his method:

It is not too much to say that our party carried terror wherever it went. The flashlight of those days was contained in cartridges fired from a revolver. The spectacle of half a dozen strange men invading a house in the midnight hour armed with big pistols which they shot off recklessly was hardly reassuring, however sugary our speech, and it was not to be wondered at if the tenants bolted through windows and down fire-escapes wherever we went.

Riis's photos of tenement life soon gained him a following. They were

published in an exposé in *Scribner's Monthly* and then in 1890 in his landmark book *How the Other Half Lives*.

Riis focused his attention on the area he knew best, the part of the Five Points [45] that centered on Mulberry Bend—a crook in Mulberry Street just north of Worth Street—that was a locus of poverty and crime, or, in Riis's words, the "foul core of New York's slums." In Riis's estimation this area did not simply need help—it needed to be condemned.

To that end, Riis became active in convincing the state legislature to pass the Small Parks Act of 1887, which granted the city the right of eminent domain over any land it wanted to take to create a playground or small public park. The first test of the law came when the blocks of Mulberry Bend (Worth to Bayard between Baxter and Mulberry) were condemned—dispossessing over 2,500 people (many of whom likely relocated to Hell's Kitchen in Midtown). Calvert Vaux was brought in to turn the area into a park, which opened in 1897, not simply to provide respite from its densely crowded environs but also to act as a positive influence, deterring local youth from crime and idleness.

According to Riis, it worked. He later wrote:

I do not believe that there was a week in all the twenty years … as a police reporter, in which I was not called to record there a stabbing or shooting affair, some act of violence. It is now five years since the Bend became a Park, and the police reporter has not had business there once during that time; not once has a shot been fired or a knife been drawn. That is what it means to let the sunlight in and give the boys their rights in a slum like that.

In 1911, the name of the park was changed from Mulberry Bend Park to Columbus Park in recognition of the dominance of Italian immigrants in the neighborhood. In 1934, Emma Stebbins's statue of Columbus was installed; it remained in the park until 1971 [**see 98**]. Today, the park is a vital part of Chinatown.

106 Who's Buried in Grant's Tomb?

If you are older than a certain age, you've likely heard the riddle "Who's buried in Grant's Tomb?" It was a consolation question on Groucho Marx's quiz show, *You Bet Your Life*. Like other consolation questions—"What color is an orange?" "What year did the War of 1812 start?"—it was designed to have such an obvious answer that no one could get it wrong. Most people answered, "Grant, of course!" and won $25, though a few poor souls thought it was a trick question.

But while Groucho would accept that answer, it isn't correct. Technically, no one is buried in Grant's Tomb: both the former president, Ulysses S. Grant, and his wife, Julia Dent Grant, are entombed there, *above-ground*, in marvelously monumental stone sarcophagi. So those *You Bet Your Life* contestants who thought it was a trick question were correct. It was a trick question—no one is buried in the building.

Grant died in 1885, having lived the last four years of his life in New York. His tomb sits at 122nd Street and Riverside Drive, at one of the highest points in Riverside Park [**73**], and is the largest mausoleum in North America. It is also a remarkable testament to the high esteem in which Grant was held after his death (despite two terms as president marked by scandal and perceived mediocrity) as well as to New York's growing obsession in the 1890s with becoming the premier American city. First, New York beat out other places

A typical Sunday afternoon at Grant's Tomb in the late 19th century

Grant had lived—including Galena, Illinois, and St. Louis, Missouri—for the right to bury the president. Then, the Grant Memorial Association held two contests to determine who would design the structure, the second contest being held because none of the entries the first time around were deemed grand enough. The tomb, by John Duncan, is modeled on the Mausoleum at Halicarnassus, one of the Seven Wonders of the World. In 1897, the tomb was officially opened, and it fast became the leading tourist attraction in the city. Indeed, more people visited Grant's Tomb in the early years of the 20th century than went to the Statue of Liberty [**93**].

PART 5

The New "City Beautiful," 1898–1919

"How do I get to Broadway? . . . I want to get to the center of things."
"Walk east a block and turn down Broadway and you'll find the center of things if you walk far enough."

—JOHN DOS PASSOS, *Manhattan Transfer*

The City Beautiful era, led by architects like Richard Morris Hunt and Charles Follen McKim of New York and Chicago's Daniel Burnham, burst on the scene with the "White City" World's Fair—the 1893 Columbian Exposition in Chicago. But while the fair was temporary—and its buildings reduced to ashes by a pair of fires just seven months after its closing—it was in New York City that Beaux Arts architecture took hold. In part, this was due to New York's ongoing rivalry with Chicago. (It was New Yorkers, after all, who dubbed it the "Windy City"—because people talked too much—and the "Second City," just to make sure Chicagoans knew their place.) But it was also because New York suddenly found itself in a unique position at the beginning of the 20th century.

The unification of Manhattan, the Bronx, Staten Island, Queens, and Brooklyn into the "Greater City of New York" on January 1, 1898, instantly doubled the city's population and took its geographical reach from the 23 square miles of Manhattan to over 300 square miles, all unified under one municipal government. This tremendous growth encouraged the city to build big. Over the next 20 years, the face of the city was transformed with the addition of grand civic buildings, such as the U.S. Custom House on Bowling Green, the Municipal Building, and the Police Headquarters; transportation hubs (Grand Central Terminal and the original Pennsylvania Station, now gone); cultural venues, including new additions to the Metropolitan Museum of Art and the American Museum of Natural History, along with a score of new Broadway theaters; grand mansions for the country's wealthiest citizens, including Andrew Carnegie and J. P. Morgan; and commercial buildings—many of them the first world-famous skyscrapers, such as Daniel Burnham's Flatiron and Cass Gilbert's triumphant Woolworth Building.

And below it all ran the biggest and most lasting change of the era: the IRT, New York's first subway.

Many of the following chapters look at the era through these edifices; the best way to understand the City Beautiful era is to enjoy the buildings themselves. This is the first time that New York put itself forward not just as a great American city, but as the greatest city in the world.

With so much monumental architecture going up at such a fast rate, it can be easy to overlook the other side of the story: the second great wave of immigrants—predominantly Italians and Eastern European Jews—who were coming through Ellis Island in ever-greater numbers in the first two decades of the 20th century. But these immigrants and their contributions to the city are not mutually exclusive from the City Beautiful ethos. It was, after all, immigrant labor that built the grand buildings, from the ironworkers to the highly skilled sculptors who carved the massive statuary that adorns so much of the city from this time. Moreover, one aspect of the City Beautiful movement was to directly address urban planning in order to improve city services for immigrants, and in these years the tenement house laws were strengthened, new municipal playgrounds—like Seward Park on the Lower East Side—were built, and convenient, reliable public transport was finally made available, which allowed immigrant families to move out of the densely populated Lower East Side without sacrificing their ability to earn a living.

It is often too easy to talk about Andrew Carnegie in his Upper East Side mansion and a newly arrived Jewish immigrant in his Lower East Side tenement as living in separate worlds. One of the hallmarks of the City Beautiful era was the breakdown of those barriers. While the immigrant and millionaire may not have traveled in the same circles, it was very apparent by the 1920s that the lines between those separate worlds had been forever blurred.

107 The "New" New York: Unifying the Five Boroughs

Though every New Yorker knows the city has five boroughs—the Bronx, Queens, Brooklyn, Staten Island, and Manhattan—very few know how this came to be and that much of the credit goes to one of the most important late-19th-century New Yorkers (historian Thomas Kessner called him "New York's Napoleon") whose name has all but disappeared: Andrew Haswell Green.

Born in Worcester, Massachusetts, in 1820, Green arrived in New York at the age of 15. He trained as a lawyer and when he was in his twenties became a protégé of Samuel Tilden, future governor and presidential candidate [76]. Green's life was one of service to the city. He was president of the fledgling Board of Education in the 1850s; he was a charter member of the Central Park Commission [61] and, as its head, led the move to expand city parkland throughout northern Manhattan [73] as well as to fund cultural institutions such as the American Museum of Natural History and the Metropolitan Museum of Art [80].

In the 1860s, Manhattan's workforce began to move out of the city to the Bronx, but since there was no central authority to pave roads or build bridges, there was no decent transportation or infrastructure there. To help rectify this problem, Green was a part of the movement in 1868 to extend the Manhattan street grid into the Bronx, the first step toward annexation. As Kessner explains, Green's goal was to create in New York "a central place for organizing the regional economy, fostering national wealth, molding a refined civic culture, and setting a standard for municipal grandeur." In 1870, William "Boss" Tweed managed to wrest control of many city functions away from the state legislature in Albany, giving New York what was known as home rule. While this created a short-term setback for Green, who was ousted from all his positions of power, it would ultimately set the course for five-borough unification, handing New York much greater control over its own affairs.

After the fall of the Tweed Ring in the early 1870s [70], Samuel Tilden encouraged the city to appoint Green as the new comptroller. Soon thereafter, parts of the Bronx were annexed into New York City, but no further action would take place for nearly 20 years. In those two decades, two crucial things happened: the Brooklyn Bridge opened in 1883 [88], thus linking New York and Brooklyn for the first time via a reliable conduit, and Manhattan's population topped one million people. But as Green pushed harder for a larger city, upstate Republicans began to worry that a giant, consolidated Democratic stronghold like New York City would have undue influence on state politics. In 1894, Green managed to get a referendum on the ballot asking the citizens of Manhattan and the surrounding suburbs to vote on consolidation. The vote in most places was overwhelmingly in favor of joining New York City. A few areas like Flushing, in Queens, and the oldest parts of Brooklyn voted against the measure, but in general the citizens of what were about to become the new boroughs were in favor of becoming part of New York City.*

Green's vote showed that people were ready for a Greater New York, but it was not a legally binding measure. Only when Republican Party

The Hall of Records (aka Surrogate's Court)

boss Thomas Platt backed the idea (for his own reasons, which remain obscure) did the state legislature create an act of consolidation to take effect January 1, 1898. On that day, New Yorkers woke up to find themselves citizens of the second-largest city in the world, with over 3 million people.** (What a contrast this was from a century earlier, when New Yorkers had rung in the New Year in a city that stopped at Chambers Street and was home to fewer than 60,000 people.)

~ Andrew Haswell Green did not live to enjoy the fruits of his labors. As he was leaving his house one night

in 1903, a man approached and shot him to death. It turned out to be a case of mistaken identity.

Green is memorialized in only one place: the most obscure spot imaginable in Central Park, a small hill near the 102nd Street transverse road. There sits a memorial bench, dedicated in 1929, surrounded by five elm trees representing the five boroughs.

Perhaps a more fitting, albeit unofficial, tribute is a pair of buildings in the city's Civic Center: City Hall [26] and the Hall of Records. As the city was preparing for consolidation, the Municipal Building Commission hosted a contest to design a replacement for the antiquated 1811 structure. The winner was John Rochester Thomas, who created the most thoroughly French-inspired design the city had yet seen. City Hall, meanwhile, was offered to the cash-strapped trustees of the New York Public Library [128], who planned to move it to 42nd Street and re-erect it.

All of this was too much for Andrew Haswell Green. Proud as he was of his efforts to see New York grow, he did not want to do it at the expense of its treasured monuments or its sense of its own history. In 1895, he founded the American Scenic & Historic Preservation Soci-

---

*Because the citizens of Mount Vernon and Yonkers in Westchester Country voted so overwhelmingly against consolidation, the Bronx County line was drawn to exclude them from the city. This was a blow to Green, who had been very interested in having both communities as part of New York. Today, they remain separate municipalities.

**London, the world's largest city, had a population of about 4.5 million.

ety, the cornerstone of the modern preservation movement. As a trustee of the library, he convinced his colleagues to abandon plans to relocate City Hall; in turn, he prevailed on the city not to get rid of its historic civic home. (Instead, the 40-story Municipal Building on Centre Street was built to handle the new, larger city bureaucracy.)

Meanwhile, John Rochester Thomas's ornate plans did not go to waste. In 1889, he modified his winning City Hall design to house the Hall of Records (and since 1962, the Surrogate's Court). The fact that it was once to have been City Hall may explain the row of male figures standing above the Chambers Street cornice, all of whom are either mayors or other municipal figures. They are, from the viewer's left, David Pietersen De Vries, Caleb Heathcote, DeWitt Clinton [25], Abram Hewitt, Philip Hone [35; 39], Peter Stuyvesant [4; 10], Cadwallader Colden,* and James Duane. Sculptural figures by Philip Martiny flank the entrance and depict *New York in Its Infancy* (on the viewer's left) and *New York in Revolutionary Times* (on the right). Two other Martiny pieces were removed from the Centre Street side and relocated to the rear entrance of the nearby Supreme Court building.

Inside, two allegorical sculptures hint at the building's connection to the city's history. Both are by Albert Weinert. The group above the west door supposedly commemorates the purchase of Manhattan in 1626 [3] and that above the east door the unification of the five boroughs.

However, only the most astute reader of allegorical statuary would be able to fathom that meaning from these rather dimly lit and uninspired carvings.

108 Missionary Work at Home: The Church of San Salvatore

A great example of the growth of the City Beautiful movement [102] is one of the most ornate churches in Little Italy, the Church of San Salvatore, erected on Broome Street in 1901. It is also the most unusual: an Italian Protestant parish in the heart of New York's most Catholic district.

Protestants building in Catholic neighborhoods was not a new tactic. There was a constant tug-of-war between Catholic immigrants and the Protestant New York establishment, not only in terms of houses of worship, but also via hospitals, schools, and charitable institutions. Beginning in 1822, the Catholic diocese began erecting private schools for immigrant children to counter the fact that New York's public schools often featured little more than Protestant indoctrination. The city fought against these parochial schools, denying them funding and often setting up competing institutions. St. Patrick's Cathedral—when it was still on Mott Street [28]—ran a parish school next door; the Protestants countered this in 1888 by moving the Fourteenth Ward Industrial School of the Children's Aid Society to a spot directly facing the church.

---

*Grandson of the Cadwallader Colden who was burned in effigy at Bowling Green in 1765 [13].

However, the Church of San Salvatore was something new: an Episcopal parish in the middle of Little Italy where immigrants could worship in their own language. Ostensibly, this was to serve the small preexisting Italo-Anglican community. The church would also provide an alternative for Italians who sometimes felt they were facing as much discrimination from within the Catholic Church as from outside it.

When Italians began arriving in New York in large numbers in the 1890s, every parish was dominated by the Irish, which gave rise to cultural differences in the church. In Italy, the feast of a town's patron saint was one of the most important days on the liturgical calendar, with elaborate celebrations that often included a parade. With hundreds of villages across southern Italy coming together in the few streets of Little Italy, the Irish-run church saw this never-ending stream of festivals as a threat to what it considered a more orthodox approach. Moreover, the festivals often garnered a lot of money, much of which didn't make it back into the parish coffers.

One way the Irish church segregated Italian parishioners was through the collection of pew rents. While seats were not sold to the highest bidder as happened at some of the tonier Episcopal churches, Irish Catholic parishes still collected a fee at the door for church attendance. As many newly arrived Italians could not (or would not) pay this fee, they were relegated to separate free services. At the Church of the Transfiguration on Mott Street [**64**], these were in the basement.

It was into this tense atmosphere that the Episcopal Church inserted itself as a new ingredient. Using money donated by philanthropist Catharine Lorillard Wolfe, the diocese built the Church of San Salvatore. It hired an Italian-born pastor, who conducted Sunday services in the Italian language. Of all the Protestant denominations, the Episcopal Church was the most Catholic in its rites and rituals, making this an easy choice for many Italians feeling left out of the nearby Irish churches.*

Eventually, the conflict between the Irish and Italians was solved by the building of "national" parishes. Traditional New York parishes were geographically based—people attended the church closest to where they lived. But as soon as St. Anthony of Padua and Our Lady of Pompeii were established in the Italian section of Greenwich Village, the Irish parishes in Little Italy saw a drop-off in attendance. This shift—along with the overwhelming number of Italians now entering New York—forced the Irish parishes to fully integrate and by World War I, churches like Transfiguration were almost completely Italian.

This shift toward national parishes also undercut the Church of San Salvatore's success. After a number of years of dwindling attendance, the Episcopal diocese ultimately sold the church. It is today the Ukrainian Orthodox Cathedral.

---

*Not only were the parishes Irish run, but the mass was still, of course, being said in Latin.

109 Andrew Carnegie's "Roomy" Mansion

For many Americans of the 19th century, Andrew Carnegie epitomized the self-made tycoon. He had come to America from Scotland in 1848 and his first job, at age 13, earned him $1.20 per week. By the time he sold the Carnegie Steel Corporation to J. P. Morgan in 1901, he was worth over $480 million.

Carnegie had begun to contemplate retirement after the disastrous Homestead Strike of 1892, when Carnegie's crony Henry Clay Frick ordered the lockout of 1,100 workers at the steel mill in Homestead, Pennsylvania [see 134]. In 1898, Carnegie acquired the lots on Fifth Avenue between 90th and 91st streets—at that point much farther north than polite society deemed fashionable—so that he could build a large mansion in relatively isolated splendor. (In the rapidly growing city, the Carnegies were always concerned with light. When Carnegie's widow, Louise, sold the lot next door to the Church of the Heavenly Rest in 1926, it was with the proviso that the Gothic towers have no north-facing windows and they be clipped so that no shadows would fall on her lawn.)

Carnegie reputedly told his architects, Babb, Cook & Willard, that he wanted his retirement home to be modest, plain, and "roomy"; upon completion in 1901, the 64-room structure certainly had plenty of space. A grand first floor showcased the public rooms, including a conservatory and a music room featuring Carnegie's gargantuan Aeolian organ. Above were the Carnegies' private quarters on the second floor, guest rooms on the third, and servants' quarters in the attic. Amenities

Andrew Carnegie's mansion (today the Cooper-Hewitt National Design Museum)

included a passenger elevator (one of the first in a private home) and a prototype of central air conditioning.

It was from this building that Carnegie spent his fortune. Perhaps his greatest contribution to American life was the establishment of more than 2,500 Carnegie Free Libraries across the United States (as well as in such far-flung places as Fiji and Serbia). In New York, many Carnegie libraries were built by Babb, Cook & Willard, including the Seward Park branch [see 95], which was the most popular library in the city before World War II.

Carnegie died in 1919 and his wife, Louise, continued to live in the home until her death in 1946. It later housed the Columbia University School of Social Work before being sold to the Smithsonian to become the home of the Cooper-Hewitt National Design Museum. The museum has restored much of the mansion back to its former glory. Today, it is one of only two full-block mansions left on Fifth Avenue; the other is Henry Clay Frick's home at 70th Street.

110 The Great White Way

In 1895, Oscar Hammerstein opened the Olympia Theater on 45th Street, just around the corner from what was still called Longacre Square. Hammerstein, a cigar manufacturer (and sometime writer of short theatrical comedies) was a great devotee of the opera.* He built his first theater, the Harlem Opera House, in 1889 in the heart of what was then an up-and-coming German neighborhood. Hammerstein wanted the average workingman to enjoy opera as much as he did and to that end, he constructed the Manhattan Opera House on 34th Street in 1892–93. When it failed, he turned his attention to Longacre Square.**

Though most theaters centered on Union and Madison squares, the new Metropolitan Opera House had opened in 1883 at Broadway and 39th Street and a cluster of other theaters soon joined it. However, no one before Hammerstein wanted to build farther north. Longacre Square was known for livery stables and—much more important for theatergoers—

its lack of electric lights, leading some to call it the "thieves' lair." Hammerstein, however, needed lots of space for his next venture, and land north of 42nd Street was cheap. The Olympia promised something for everyone: restaurants, opera, comedies—even a Turkish bath. Most of these features never came to fruition, but the theater itself was a success, proving that audiences would travel to 42nd Street to see a show.

In 1900, Hammerstein opened the Republic on 42nd Street. Three years later, the New Amsterdam had opened across the street, the Lyric a few doors down, and the Lyceum on 45th Street; by the end of the first decade of the 20th century, serious theatergoers had abandoned Union Square and were happily coming to the new Broadway theater district. In 1902, the area received a new appellation, "the Great White Way." However, contrary to later stories, the phrase had nothing to do with glitz, glamour, or neon lights. It referred to snow.

As linguistic historian Barry Popik has discovered, the name derives from a 1901 novel entitled *The Great White Way*, which was set in Antarctica. A popular columnist in the *New York Evening Telegram*, Shep Friedman, often titled his articles about Broadway happenings after current novels; on November 23, 1901, his column came out under the heading "Found on the Great White Way." By sheer coincidence, when people woke up that morning to read the *Telegram*, the

---

*His grandson, Oscar Hammerstein II, and composer Richard Rogers, wrote Broadway musicals including *Oklahoma!* and *The Sound of Music*.

**Hammerstein reopened the Manhattan Opera House in 1906. It lives on today as the performance venue called the Hammerstein Ballroom.

city had been blanketed by snow and Broadway was, indeed, a "great white way."

At the same time, the pioneer of outdoor electric advertising, O. J. Gude, was having success selling lighted sign space to the buildings being built around the new Times Square [124]. Soon, Gude had picked up the phrase "Great White Way" and ran with it, giving the term its present-day meaning.

111 Daniel Burnham and the Flatiron Building

In the wake of the popular Columbian Exposition in Chicago in 1893, the fair's chief architect, Daniel Burnham, took on the role of America's leading proponent of the City Beautiful movement [see 102]. He had a far-reaching influence on Beaux-Arts architecture—Louis Sullivan later complained he had set American architecture back 50 years—and his projects ranged from the ambitious Plan of Chicago of 1909 to Washington, D.C.'s monumental Union Station. Burnham's most lasting maxim, quoted by generations of architects since, was "Make no little plans. They have no magic to stir men's blood and probably will not themselves be realized."

For all his fame and influence, however, Burnham's work in New York is limited to one building, the spectacular Flatiron skyscraper at the junction of Broadway and Fifth Avenue at 23rd Street.

North of 14th Street, Broadway had been eliminated from the Commissioners' Plan of 1811 [25]. However, as the city developed northward

following the new grid, Broadway was never removed and this meant that every place Broadway crossed one of the new, numbered avenues, a pair of orphaned triangles of land were created. At 23rd Street, where Broadway intersects Fifth Avenue, one of these small triangles was dubbed "the flatiron" due to its resemblance to a typical 19th-century iron. In 1901, the Chicago-based Fuller Construction Company purchased the flatiron lot and hired Burnham to design a skyscraper to fit the land. At the turn of the 20th century, the area around Madison Square Park was a burgeoning retail and entertainment district:

The Flatiron Building

the shops that comprised "Ladies' Mile" extended down Broadway from 23rd Street and Stanford White's Madison Square Garden [see 121] sat on the opposite corner of the park. Many companies—including the Metropolitan Life Insurance Company, which would build the tallest building in the world on Madison Square in 1909—hoped that the area would soon become a bustling business district, as well.

Burnham embraced Fuller's odd parcel of land, designing a building that took full advantage of its triangular shape. Because the building was surrounded by roads on all three sides and the expanse of Madison Square Park across the street, offices were guaranteed plenty of access to light and air—then the two key factors in deciding commercial rents. The premium offices at the 23rd Street point of the building had windows on three sides (the point of the building was wide enough for one window, facing north), flooding them with natural light throughout the day. Part of the building's ongoing popularity stems from its placement. Too often, older skyscrapers are jockeyed out of position by newer, taller towers that compete for space and attention. The Flatiron, by contrast, sits alone. It is visible from all sides, but seen best from Madison Square Park, where the view makes it look like a ship sailing up Fifth Avenue. The building was a favorite of photographer Alfred Stieglitz, who called it "a monster ocean steamer."

On the Flatiron's exterior, Burnham covered the steel frame in limestone and terra-cotta detail; every possible surface is textured, from the rough-hewn limestone panels of the base to the terra-cotta insets and fleurs-de-lis. Like many early skyscrapers, it follows the form of a classical column with separately designed base, shaft, and capital. However, where many architects put little ornamentation on the shaft—saving the best work for the street-level base or the soaring capital—Burnham created Beaux-Arts flourishes throughout. As architect Buckminster Fuller (presumably no relation to the founders of the Fuller Company) later noted, Burnham and his Beaux-Arts compatriots "were pretending there was no steel."* Never again would New York see a skyscraper quite this elaborate.

Though the Flatiron has gone down in history as one of New York's quintessential skyscrapers, the Fuller Company wasn't necessarily all that happy. The dawn of the 20th century also saw skyscrapers built as publicity tools; had people referred to it as "the Fuller Building" when praising it, everything might have been fine. But even in Burnham's preparatory sketches it was being called the Flatiron. Thus, while in its earliest days it was sometimes referred to as "the Flatiron (Fuller) Building," the potential for a branding opportunity (as we might say in modern parlance) largely passed them by.

However, the building did receive a lot of publicity for another reason: its odd shape created strange—and sometimes deadly—wind currents. In 1903, a boy was blown by a gust of wind into the street, where he was run over. Less seriously, the wind wreaked havoc with men's hats and women's skirts; police stationed at the intersection popularized the

---

*In their book *History Preserved*, preservationists Harmon H. Goldstone and Martha Dalrymple also point out that the Flatiron was one of Buckminster Fuller's favorite buildings.

term "23 skidoo" to tell ogling men not to linger on 23rd Street waiting for a well-timed gust of air.

112 Rabbi Jacob Joseph and Beth Hamedrash Hagadol

In 1885, the oldest Russian-speaking Jewish congregation in New York split into two groups. Half went to construct the first purpose-built Eastern European synagogue in the city on Eldridge Street [94]; the others bought a church on Norfolk Street, which they renamed Beth Hamedrash Hagadol ("house of great study").

The building on Norfolk Street had been built in 1850 to house the Norfolk Street Baptist Church at a time when the neighborhood was becoming extremely Irish Catholic [see 43]. Within ten years, the middle-class Baptists had moved uptown* and the building became a Methodist Episcopal parish church before being sold to Beth Hamedrash in 1885. The new owners added a Jewish star to the roof and reconfigured the altar area as a bima, but otherwise left the plain Gothic church intact.

The congregation's controversial rabbi, Abraham Ash, died a couple of years after the move, prompting the search not only for a replacement, but for a man who might serve as chief rabbi for the Orthodox in New York. A Union of Congregations was formed to search for someone who could oversee kosher supervi-

sion, help enforce stricter observation of the Sabbath, and—perhaps most important—help organize a more permanent *beth din* (rabbinical court) to adjudicate in religious matters. In 1888, the congregation hired Rabbi Jacob Joseph of Vilnius, Lithuania—apparently the only candidate who was interested in the job. Thousands showed up for his first sermon at Beth Hamedrash Hagadol, only to be disappointed when it was preached in Lithuanian, which many of them could not understand. Things only grew worse when the Union of Congregations agreed to a one-cent tax on kosher meat. (It turns out this was because the union had promised to pay off the rabbi's outstanding debts in Vilnius.) As various congregations began to disagree with Joseph's teachings and his *beth din*'s oversight, they withdrew their financial support. Within two years, Joseph had so thoroughly disappointed people that a handful of congregations independently selected a competing chief rabbi. Soon after, Rabbi Joseph had a stroke, and while he was still able to perform his duties at Beth Hamedrash Hagadol, he withdrew from public view.

However, when Rabbi Joseph died in July 1902, thousands of mourners poured into the streets to lament his passing and a heated argument broke out as to which congregation would have the honor of burying him. Ultimately, Beth Hamedrash Hagadol prevailed, and his funeral procession was followed by as many as 30,000 mourners. (Finding so many Eastern European Jews in one place was too tempting for some hotheaded Irish

---

*This Baptist congregation still exists as Riverside Church [147].

New Yorkers, causing riots to break out along the route.)

As the number of congregants at Beth Hamedrash decreased in the mid-20th century, the building fell into disrepair. Though the synagogue is listed on the National Register of Historic Places, it is also considered one of the most endangered landmarks in New York City. Meanwhile, though the main sanctuary is closed, the congregation continues to meet; however, it now numbers only about 15 people.

113 Seward Park, the City's First Municipal Playground

A key component of the City Beautiful movement was its emphasis not just on grand civic monuments like railway stations and triumphal arches [see 131 and 102], but also on smaller-scale projects aimed at revitalizing the city's poorest neighborhoods. One of the earliest examples in New York is Columbus Park, a pet project of reformer Jacob Riis [105] and the Society for Parks and Playgrounds. But perhaps even more significant was the creation in 1899 of Seward Park at the junction of Canal Street and East Broadway.

The park was the brainchild of the Outdoor Recreation League, an offshoot of the settlement house movement and supported by both Lillian Wald [103] and the University Settlement. In 1897, they convinced the city to condemn the rundown tenements in the parcel of land bounded by Straus Square and Essex, Jefferson, and Grand streets. Though the city cleared the land, it was up to the Out-

door Recreation League to maintain it. The league planted and laid paths and also funded and maintained the area for the next four years.

However, in 1903, the city took over the park and added all-new playground equipment, thus making it the first city-run playground anywhere in America. In an era when enforcement of mandatory schooling laws was lax and many children worked from a very young age, the city's acknowledgment of the need for abundant open space in one of its most crowded precincts was a real victory for progressive reformers. (Not all parents agreed, however, citing the playground as an example of idle hands being the devil's playthings.) That same year, the state's Tenement House Commission deemed Seward Park a success, adding that anyone who visited it would "appreciate what this opportunity for natural play means to the anaemic, underfed, and mentally overdeveloped young people of the East Side."

The park was named for William H. Seward, who was both a New York senator and governor, but is best remembered today for "Seward's Folly"—the purchase of Alaska—which he did as secretary of state. In his own lifetime, Seward was famous for having survived a separate assassination attempt by one of John Wilkes Booth's co-conspirators the same night that Abraham Lincoln was killed. Booth had planned to kill Lincoln, Vice President Johnson, and Secretary of State Seward and thus destroy the three top men in the Union government so that Robert E. Lee could march unhindered into Washington. Though Seward suffered severe stab wounds, he survived and became an influential member of Johnson's cabinet. He is also commemorated in a handsome statue in Madison Square Park.

114 The New York Stock Exchange

The New York Stock Exchange, founded under a buttonwood tree on Wall Street in 1792 [19], had a series of temporary homes until its first permanent trading floor was built on Broad Street in 1865. Despite setbacks brought on by the Panic of 1873 and the Panic of 1893 (when many banks and western railroads failed), the volume and value of the stock exchange continued to rise and in 1901, it moved out of its headquarters so that a new, grander edifice could be built on the same spot.

Designed by George B. Post (who also built the Brooklyn Historical Society [86] and City College's Harlem campus [125]), the 1903 building is a soaring neoclassical temple, a style that was not only popular with Beaux-Arts architects for civic and commercial buildings, but which also mimicked the old treasury building across Wall Street [see 18]. The massive five-story trading floor ran the entire length of the building between Broad and New streets; behind the Corinthian colonnade on each side were walls of glass to let abundant natural light onto the trading floor.

(Today, the Broad Street colonnade is usually blocked by a giant American flag, a conspicuous post-9/11 addition. However, if you look behind the flag, you can see that the windows are also blacked out. The invention of fluorescent lighting and the need to see computer monitors did away with Post's innovative lighting scheme.)

In the Broad Street pediment, artist J.Q.A. Ward built his most massive work, a tribute to the power of the exchange known as *Integrity Protecting the Works of Man*. The 16-foot-tall Integrity stands at the center, her powerful fists extended. (And just so you know she represents financial integrity, she wears the winged cap of Mercury, god of commerce.) The

The New York Stock Exchange

figures to the viewer's right represent mining and agriculture (including a young woman in a kerchief holding a ram). The figures on the other side—featuring young naked men handling heavy equipment—represent industry. Thus, the two great strains of the American economy are brought together under the New York Stock Exchange's watchful eye.

The figures, originally carved from Georgia marble, weighed 90 tons. This weight, combined with the effects of automobile and coal exhaust, began to eat away at the marble, and by the time of the Great Crash in 1929 [146], Integrity was literally collapsing. Worried about the effect that a physically crumbling stock exchange would have on an already skittish investing populace, the statues were replaced in 1936 by a 10-ton copper and lead replica.

In 1954, Pulitzer Prize–winning *New York Times* columnist Meyer Berger wrote a lengthy article discussing how the pediment had been replaced in secret. He detailed the covert operation, which included taking photographs of the sculptures from the roof of the Morgan bank across the street [see 137] and destroying the original marble so that no one would ever find out. What is fascinating about this tale is that it is completely false. The work was done in full view of the public—indeed, it was a lunchtime spectacle for Wall Streeters to watch workers replacing Ward's originals with the copper copies. The only real mystery is why Berger didn't verify his sources.

The adjacent building at 11 Wall Street—which people today often mistake for the main trading floor—was built in the 1920s by Trowbridge & Livingston to add more office space and enlarge the trading floor (this annex is called the Garage).

115 Joseph Pulitzer and the Silent Bedroom

Hungarian-born publisher Joseph Pulitzer was one of the key figures in New York journalism after his purchase of the *New York World* in 1882. He has been praised for his contributions to the city, such as spearheading the campaign to raise funds for the Statue of Liberty's pedestal [93] and the creation of the Columbia University School of Journalism [see 101], but he has also been vilified for his rivalry with William Randolph Hearst, which led to the sensationalistic yellow journalism surrounding the Spanish-American War [133].

The stress of his job wreaked havoc with Pulitzer's nerves. Moreover, by the turn of the 20th century his always poor eyesight was all but completely gone. As his eyesight failed, he became increasingly sensitive to noise—it was rumored, for example, that he would not accept a dinner invitation unless he knew he would be seated between two very soft-spoken ladies. In 1900, Pulitzer's mansion on 55th Street burned down; that same year, he purchased a lot at 11 East 73rd Street and hired Stanford White to build him a Beaux-Arts home that would please his failing eyesight and his sensitive hearing. The house, based on two 17th-century Venetian *palazzi*, is stripped of much of the exterior decoration common in City Beautiful homes; as architectural historian Andrew Alpern has pointed out, this would have appealed to Pulitzer's "sightless fingers." Inside, the bedroom was built with thick walls and extra insulation to protect Pulitzer from outside noise.

Pulitzer moved into the house in 1903 and almost immediately hired the architectural firm of Foster, Gade & Graham to build him a new, even more soundproof bedroom. The new bedroom was in the garden and attached to the main house by (in the words of Alleyne Ireland, one of his many secretaries) "some ingenious device which isolated it from all vibrations originating there." (This may, in fact, have been a foundation of sound-absorbing ball bearings.) The new bedroom had only one window, which Ireland noted was

> a very large affair, consisting of three casements set one inside the other and provided with heavy plate glass panels. This triple window was never opened when Mr. Pulitzer was in the room, the ventilation being secured by means of fans situated in a long masonry shaft, whose interior opening was in the chimney and whose exterior opening was far enough away to forbid the passage of any sound from the street. At intervals inside this shaft were placed frames with silk threads drawn across them, for the purpose of absorbing any faint vibrations which might find their way in. In this bedroom, with its triple window and its heavy double-door closed, J.P. enjoyed as near an approach to perfect quietness as it was possible to attain in New York.

Pulitzer died in 1911 aboard his yacht and in 1934 his home was converted into apartments. The back bedroom and study became a private apartment with an entrance through the garden. Today, the bedroom is visible through the gate to the left of the building's main entrance.

116 The Ansonia

The Ansonia, opened at 74th Street and Broadway in 1903, was one of the grandest and most lavishly appointed apartment buildings of its day. Its location was chosen to take advantage of the express station for the new IRT subway, which was slated to open only a few months later [119] and it offered unparalleled amenities for its residents, including telephone service built into each apartment, maid service three times daily, a restaurant with a live orchestra, and—in the ornate lobby fountain—live seals.

Early advertisements for the building call it "the largest and most completely appointed apartment hotel in the world." Among the enumerated features:

- "A1" restaurant and café
- Game parlors
- Meals served à la carte in apartments
- Ice boxes chilled by artificial refrigeration
- An attendant stationed on each landing
- Milk depot

What the advertisement didn't mention was that the milk depot was in fact a menagerie on the roof—including goats and chickens—that provided fresh eggs and dairy for the tenants. There was also a caged bear for parties. However, not long after the building opened, the health department made the Ansonia get rid of its rooftop barnyard and the animals were transferred to the Central Park Zoo. Presumably, the seals from the fountain left at the same time, but there is no record of this.

Some of the luxury services offered to tenants of the Ansonia were outlandish, like the seals, but others were cutting-edge. How many people had refrigerators in 1903? The Ansonia needed every bell and whistle—competition was stiff. Twenty years earlier, when the Dakota was being marketed [90], the idea of a luxury apartment hotel was radical. By the time the Ansonia opened, apartment buildings had to clamor to capture the public's attention.

Thus, the Warrington on Madison Avenue at 32nd Street tongue-twistingly boasted that "every convenience skilled thought could suggest has been incorporated" and that "the situation speaks for itself." Both the Wellington on Seventh Avenue and the Normandie on Broadway emphasized in their ads, in capital letters, "ABSOLUTELY FIREPROOF," and the Arlington, near Madison Square, provided both a "chef and cuisine of superior order."

Augustus Saint-Gaudens' equestrian statue of William Tecumseh Sherman

But our favorite is probably the Hotel Carlton, which promised "SOMETHING NEW. The only hotel apartments in the city having a BUTLER'S PANTRY, with refrigerator, china closets, and chafing dish conveniences, without which it is impossible to enjoy APARTMENT HOTEL LIFE."

Those were the days.

117 The Gilded Warrior: William Tecumseh Sherman

Civil War hero (or villain, depending on your perspective) William Tecumseh Sherman arrived in New York City in 1886 to reenter civilian life after retiring from the army. (He served as commander of the army until 1883. In 1884, the Republican Party tried to convince him to run for president, to which he famously replied, "If drafted, I will not run; if nominated, I will not accept; if elected, I will not serve.")

Sherman lived in a townhouse on West 71st Street, near the present-day Sherman Square (the southernmost of the two small triangles of land where Broadway and Amsterdam Avenue meet). He was an avid theatergoer and a charter member of Edwin Booth's Players club on Gramercy Park [see 97]. He was also a gifted after-dinner speaker and spent many nights out on the town being feted for his wartime accomplishments.

In February 1891, Sherman died in New York and immediately the chamber of commerce began fundraising for an equestrian statue to honor the city's adopted son. The chamber's members were the mercantile elite and in many ways they were the people who had most benefited from Sherman's famed March to the Sea. By utterly subduing the South through a campaign of total war, Sherman had guaranteed that Northern industrialists, merchants, and bankers would reap the benefits of the postbellum economy.

The commission went to Augustus Saint-Gaudens (whose other work in the city includes statues of Admiral David Farragut in Madison Square and Peter Cooper at the Cooper Union [66]). Saint-Gaudens created a monumental figure of the general astride his horse; he positioned the horse's rear hooves so they would trample over Georgia pine. The horse and its rider are led forward by an allegorical figure of Victory. (Saint-Gaudens, often harshly critical of his own work, was pleased with the results. He later wrote, "It's the greatest 'Victory' anybody ever made. Hooraah!") Because Saint-Gaudens disliked the ugly, industrial patina of most metal sculpture, he gilded the general in two layers of gold leaf; when it was erected, it was the only gilded statue in the entire city.

The city's original plan for the statue was to place it in Riverside Park, near Grant's Tomb [106]. However, when Sherman's family objected, the chamber of commerce suggested moving it to the plaza— now called Grand Army Plaza—at the Fifth Avenue entrance to Central Park, thus giving the general one of the most prominent spots in New York. The statue was unveiled on Decoration Day* 1903, with prominent national and local dignitaries in attendance. There is an oft-repeated (and certainly apocryphal) tale that one Southern woman in the audience, seeing Sherman on his horse and Victory leading him forward, remarked: "Well, isn't that just like a Yankee to make the woman walk!"

(An aside: people often stand at this statue trying to determine whether or not the position of the horse's legs indicates that Sherman died in battle. There is an urban myth that posits that one hoof raised means the person died of wounds sustained in battle; two hooves raised means he died in battle; and all four hooves on the ground means he died in peace. If this were true, Saint-Gaudens's statue—which shows the horse walking forward, two hooves raised—would indicate Sherman died in battle, not at home on West 71st Street.)

118 The *General Slocum* Disaster

Before the terrorist attacks of September 11, 2001 [180], the single largest one-day loss of life in New York City's history was the sinking of the pleasure boat *General Slocum*, which set out on June 15, 1904, to take families from St. Mark's Evangelical Lutheran Church on a picnic excursion. The event not only decimated the parish, it destroyed Kleindeutschland [91], and marked the beginning of the end of the central German-American community in New York.

The trip was an annual event for the St. Mark's Sunday school, and the boat carried families from just about every block of the area surrounding Tompkins Square Park, the heart of the German neighbor-

---

*One of the hallmarks of the holiday, now called Memorial Day, was unveiling statuary of fallen soldiers or decorating the ones that had already been erected.

hood. The boat left from the pier at East Third Street around 9:30 in the morning, and trouble developed almost immediately. A spark, probably from a stove, set the stern on fire; as the ship steamed up the East River, observers on either bank could see smoke and flames billowing from the vessel. Captain William Van Shaick could have headed for Manhattan, the Bronx, or Queens.

Detail of the *General Slocum* memorial

Instead, he decided to make for North Brother Island, which lies in the East River near the entrance to Long Island Sound. Captain Van Schaick, who survived the tragedy, later said that he'd hoped in doing this to keep the fire from spreading, but in fact he was piloting into a steady wind and the blaze quickly got out of control, enveloping the ship's three decks, which then collapsed. Van Schaick may have also picked North Brother Island because of the hospital there (where Mary Mallon,

the infamous Typhoid Mary, would later spend the last two decades of her life). However, by the time the ship ran aground, the hospital staff could do little to help: most of the passengers had already drowned or burned to death.

Compounding the tragedy was the ship's utter disregard for safety standards. Life preservers that were shoddily constructed in the first place had not been replaced in years. Mothers, hoping to save their children, bundled them into life preservers and threw them over the side only to watch them drown as the defective flotation devices became instantly water-logged and sank. The ship's lifeboats could not be detached from the vessel and the crew had no instruction on how to handle a fire. Indeed, one of the only things Captain Van Schaick was ever punished for was lack of safety preparedness. (The jury refused to find him guilty of manslaughter.)

The loss of life—the official death toll was 1,021, many of them children—crushed Kleindeutschland. Within a decade, the German-American community left the East Village. Some settled in the Yorkville section of the Upper East Side, which already had a strong German influence. Others left for the outer boroughs or beyond. By the time World War I was drawing to a close and anti-German sentiment was running high, Kleindeutschland was fading from memory—and so was the *General Slocum* disaster.

Many of the victims are buried in the Lutheran cemetery in Queens, where a monument erected on June 15, 1905, commemorates the event. In Kleindeutschland itself, however, there is only one small memorial—a small marble stele (a type of ancient funerary monument) in a playground in Tompkins Square Park. It depicts in stark profile a young girl and a young boy holding a stick and hoop. The inscription reads "They were the Earth's purest, Children Young and Fair." Below it is a water fountain, a symbol of purity. However, beyond this statue and a small explanatory plaque affixed to the former home of St. Mark's church (now the Community Synagogue) on Sixth Street, the *General Slocum*'s most profound effect on this area is that, as a German neighborhood, it has all but disappeared.

119 The Opening of the IRT

On October 27, 1904, Mayor George "Max" McClellan took the controls of a northbound passenger train at the City Hall station, revolutionizing New York's public transportation. While the unification of the five boroughs in 1898 [107] is rightly seen as a seismic change in New York's political landscape, the opening of the first subway had the most far-reaching effect on the city's development since the institution of the street grid nearly a century earlier [25].

The first working subway in the city, Alfred Ely Beach's one-block "secret" pneumatic tube, opened in 1870 and was popular enough to lead to calls for an underground railway along Broadway. Competing subway proposals were formulated, but none happened. This was due, in part, to

the success of the elevated railroad [81], but it was also because powerful business interests along Broadway, led by A. T. Stewart [50; 82], were worried about its interrupting their traffic and scaring clientele away from their stores.

However, by 1894, there was enough support for a metropolitan subway that the state legislature authorized a Board of Rapid Transit Railroad Commissioners. The board was to determine the best route for a subway and then either supervise construction or hire out the contract to a private firm. It considered two routes: along Elm Street (today's Lafayette) or along Broadway. Again, a coalition of business owners scuttled the Broadway plans, so instead a route was drawn up from City Hall to 42nd Street along Lafayette Place and Lexington Avenue. At 42nd Street, the track would take a sharp turn and run across the island westward to Longacre Square, where it would turn again and head north to Harlem. Construction, led by engineer William Barclay Parsons and paid for by financier August Belmont, began in 1900. Two years later, with construction half completed, Belmont incorporated the Interborough Rapid Transit Company, or IRT, to have a 50-year lease to run the trains.

Construction was difficult. The majority of the IRT's right-of-way lay along streets that already had sewer, electric, and telegraph wires buried beneath them.* Once those were cleared out of the way, workers faced the task of tunneling through mostly solid schist, the bedrock that makes

---

*Following a colossal blizzard in 1888 that paralyzed the city, New York City began enforcing a law that it had passed a few years earlier requiring that all public utilities be buried beneath the street; this policy is still in force today.

up the entire island of Manhattan [1]. To simplify work, the system was built using a technique called "cut and cover": workers would tear up the street, dig down one story below-ground, lay the track, and then cover over the top with an iron-and-steel roof that could be paved over. This not only saved the IRT from laborious deep tunneling, but also meant that passengers would usually only have to walk down one flight of stairs to reach the track. (Parsons was afraid that if they had to walk any farther, they'd opt for surface transit.)

To distinguish themselves from the more utilitarian elevated railroads (parts of which Belmont bought for the IRT), the company hired architects Heins & La Farge, original architects of the Cathedral of St. John the Divine [100], to design 28 stations for the system. Each station used a unique three-color tiled mosaic pattern, and many featured wonderful terra-cotta artwork, including beavers in the Astor Place station (to remind people of the original source of John Jacob Astor's wealth [see 33]), the City College logo at its station on 137th Street [125], and tulips at 96th Street, the former site of the Dutch village of Bloomingdale (literally, "vale of flowers"). The best of Heins & La Farge's work, however, was reserved for the first station of the line, City Hall, which looped around to allow the trains to switch direction. The ceilings here were of graceful terra-cotta by Rafael Guastavino; the walls were decorated in interlocking, multicolored tile, and the entire place was lit by the warm glow of chandeliers.

The IRT proved to be such a great success that the system expanded quickly, and by the 1930s, it followed the basic layout that New Yorkers know today. (It was not, however, a municipally run system until 1940, when the city finally took over all the competing, independent lines.) One of the major changes during the system's expansion was the switch from five-car to ten-car trains. Most stations were expanded to accommodate the new length, but the City Hall station, as it was built on such a tight curve, could not be expanded and was taken out of service.

The southbound No. 6 trains still use the City Hall station to loop around and begin their trek back uptown. For years, the city asked passengers to get off the train, but as of this writing, it is acceptable to stay on the train as it passes through the City Hall station. Most of the time it is too dark to see anything, but every once in a while the lights are left on, thus providing a spectacular view into a bygone era.

120 Lombardi's: America's First Pizzeria

There is probably not an American alive today who has not eaten pizza; indeed, it and the hamburger now fight it out for the title of America's favorite food. But even as recently as 1956, the *New York Times* was still helpfully defining the pizza for neophyte readers as "a circular mixture of dough, cheese, sauce, and Italian lore."* And if you wanted to experience authentic Italian pizza, you had

---

*This, despite the fact that the same article reveals that as early as 1956 the dreaded pizza bagel was already in existence.

to travel to Little Italy, where one restaurant stood out from the others: Lombardi's, the first full-service pizzeria in America.

In 1897, Gennaro Lombardi opened a grocery store at 53 ½ Spring Street. Within walking distance of the factories along Broadway and the western section of Greenwich Village [see 126], workers could pick up lunch at Lombardi's in the morning as they walked to work. Soon Lombardi was selling individual pizzas tied up with string, and in 1905 he received a business license to operate a full-time pizzeria. Now open for dinner as well, he sold entire pizzas for those who could afford them (celebrities like Enrico Caruso were fans), but also continued to sell pizza by the slice for those who could not, thus starting a venerable New York tradition.

The business passed from Gennaro to his son George and they continued to operate out of their original location until 1984. At that point, with Little Italy shrinking and property values in the area on the decline, Lombardi's closed. However, this proved to be temporary, and a few years later, one of Gennaro's grandsons reopened Lombardi's, with much of the original equipment, in a space just down the block.

Photograph of Evelyn Nesbit, ca. 1900, by Gertrude Käsebier

121 The Crime of the Century: The Murder of Stanford White

Stanford White is remembered today as much for the way he died as for the architectural legacy he left behind. As one-third of the firm McKim, Mead & White,* his contributions to New York in the Beaux Arts period included the Washington Arch [102], Judson Memorial Church, Madison Square Garden (now demolished), the Pulitzer Mansion [115], and the Metropolitan Club [97], along with many others. But White's architectural prowess was often overshadowed by his over-the-top personal life. He had a predilection for young women—much to the chagrin of his wife—and for spending his nights

---

*Partner Charles Follen McKim, who created Columbia University's home on Morningside Heights [101] and the Morgan Library [122], was the other lead architect. William Rutherford Mead served as the firm's chief engineer, its office manager, and as the person who kept, in his own words, the other two "from making damn fools of themselves."

at one of his many private clubs (he often bartered membership in lieu of design fees) or at the theater.

It was at a performance of the musical *Florodora* in 1902 that White first spied Evelyn Nesbit, who had been cast as one of the six Florodora Girls, the show's main attraction. Nesbit had moved to New York a year earlier to pursue modeling. She modeled for Charles Dana Gibson's *The Eternal Question* and became the most famous of the Gibson Girls. Her move to the stage was a calculated effort to keep herself in the limelight; when Stanford White began showing his attention, Evelyn's mother did nothing to discourage the architect's affection, which she (perhaps too naively) took to be more fatherly than romantic.

White had a series of hideaways in various Manhattan buildings where he could take young women; one, on West 24th Street, contained a red velvet swing, on which he liked to watch girls like Evelyn dangle. After a couple of relatively chaste encounters, White took Evelyn to one of his hideaways when her mother was out of town, got her drunk, and—depending on which version of the story you believe—they had consensual sex or he raped her.

Over the next few years, White and Nesbit continued to see each other, but Evelyn had other lovers, including the young John Barrymore. Twice she was rushed out of town to have emergency appendectomies (a nice trick, considering the fact that no one has two appendixes), which were presumably abortions. She soon met and fell in love with Pittsburgh millionaire Harry K. Thaw, who—like many delusional and violent lovers—often showed his adoration

Stanford White's
Madison Square Garden

through mental and physical abuse. What drove Thaw to distraction was Nesbit's clear affection for Stanford White, though White by this point had moved on. In 1905, Thaw and Nesbit were married and moved to Pittsburgh, but this did little to cool Thaw's anger at White.

On June 25, 1906, Thaw and Nesbit were in New York and had tickets to the opening of *Mam'zelle Champagne*, a musical debuting that evening at the roof garden theater of Madison Square Garden (which was then still on Madison Square). The building was one of Stanford White's favorites among his designs. They dined at Martin's, a nearby restaurant, where White happened to be dining as well. For Thaw, seeing his rival was evidently the final straw. He and Evelyn continued on to the theater, but Thaw—who seemed to always carry a pistol with him—was ready. During the song "I Could Love a Million Girls," Thaw walked up to White's table, shot him three times at close range, and cried out, "You've ruined my wife!" (Or, perhaps, "You've ruined my life!").

Thaw was immediately hustled to the Jefferson Market Courthouse [79] to await arraignment and from there was taken to the Tombs, the main prison downtown. Thaw's mother pledged a million dollars to save her son and she spent almost the full amount, hiring defense attorneys, allegedly suborning witnesses, and—in perhaps the most novel twist—mounting a play featuring characters named Harold Daw and Stanford Black that told the story in a way wholly sympathetic to her son.

Thaw's first trial ended in a hung jury. A second jury found him not guilty by reason of insanity* and he was shipped off to the State Hospital for the Criminally Insane in Matteawan, where security was so lax that he walked out one day to a waiting taxi and hightailed it to the Canadian border. He was later caught and sent back, but evidently his behavior was exemplary enough to warrant a full release in 1915.

∿Very little physical evidence of the Thaw/White/Nesbit scandal remains. White's old Madison Square Garden, which had never made money, was torn down in 1924, and the venue moved to 50th Street and Eighth Avenue, where it remained until the construction of its current home atop Penn Station. White's

own home, near Gramercy Park [40], is long gone, and the building where he kept the infamous red velvet swing collapsed in 2007. New York still has a prison called the Tombs, but the current one was built in 1941, partially demolished, and then expanded in the 1990s.

However, one intriguing building stands on the Upper West Side. The Evelyn, an apartment building, was erected in the early 1880s just as the Dakota [90] and the American Museum of Natural History [80] were being built nearby. It was owned by the Thaw family, who presumably built it as an investment property or a pied à terre for business trips to Manhattan. During Harry Thaw's incarceration and trials, it is said that Nesbit stayed here, and many have often assumed that the building was later named for her. However, evidence suggests that the building was called the Evelyn from its inception, long before Thaw met his wife.

122 The Panic of 1907 and the Morgan Library

By the time J. P. Morgan began constructing his library on East 36th Street in 1900, he was the most famous financier in New York, if not America. His "House of Morgan" sat at the corner of Wall and Broad streets [137], directly across from the New York Stock Exchange [114], and was quite rightly seen by many as the real central bank of the United States. (During the Panic of 1893, President Grover Cleveland turned to Morgan

---

*The Thaw trial popularized the word "brainstorm." Thaw's attorneys used it to convey the rampant insanity coursing through his head; only in the 1920s did it take on a positive connotation.

to help organize a bailout of the federal treasury.)

The most conspicuous trapping of Morgan's wealth was his love of collecting fine art, inspired by a five-year sojourn in Europe when he was a teenager. After Morgan helped the Vanderbilts recapitalize the New York Central Railroad in 1879, the bank netted $3 million and Morgan bought a steam yacht, the *Corsair*, which he would sail to Europe on art-buying expeditions. His collection included everything from old master paintings to gemstones to rare illuminated manuscripts. In 1900, he hired McKim, Mead & White to build an elegant Renaissance Revival library to hold these treasures. Charles Follen McKim's palazzo featured an entrance flanked by twin lions by sculptor Edward Clark Potter, who would go on to design the mammoth lions guarding the entrance of the New York Public Library [128]. Inside, the polychrome rotunda led visitors into Morgan's study or the elaborate library itself. (A third room, in the rear, was for Morgan's librarian.)

The library took seven years to construct and on November 2, 1907, it played host to a remarkable meeting of the leaders of New York's biggest banks and trust companies. Nearly two weeks earlier, on the news of the Knickerbocker Trust Company's insolvency after an ill-fated attempt to corner the copper market, Morgan had saved the day. In just 15 minutes, he had extracted promises of $25 million to help prop up the stock market. However, there

remained the issue of a number of failing trust companies. So, Morgan gathered New York's financiers at the library. According to historian Ron Chernow, the commercial bankers were locked in the library, "beneath signs of the zodiac and a tapestry of the seven deadly sins" and the trust company men were put in the study, "beneath the gaze of saints and Madonnas." Morgan sat in the librarian's office playing solitaire.

At five o'clock in the morning, the incarcerated bankers finally agreed to a $25 million bailout of the weaker trusts and were allowed to go home. This was the end of the panic, though it would have far-reaching implications. Most important, the U.S. government realized it could not keep turning to Morgan in times of crisis and in 1913 the Federal Reserve Act was passed, establishing a central bank for the United States for the first time since Andrew Jackson's presidency.

J. P. Morgan died six years later on a trip to Italy and his son Jack took over the business and the library. The Morgan Library and Museum opened to the public in 1924, in accordance with J. P. Morgan's wish (as expressed in his will) that his collection be "permanently available for the instruction and pleasure of the American people." In the 1920s, Morgan's original brownstone at the corner of Madison Avenue was torn down and Benjamin Wistar Morris built a library annex on the site. In 2006, a modernist expansion by Italian architect Renzo Piano greatly expanded the museum's floor space.

123 Imperial America: The Alexander Hamilton U.S. Custom House

New York was America's premier port, and it's chief source of income until well into the 20th century was through shipping. This meant, in turn, that the U.S. Customs Department was also indelibly linked to the city, and the fortunes of New York politicians often could not be separated from the collection of tariffs. (The most famous New York politicians connected to the Customs Department were Senator Roscoe Conkling and his protégé, Customs Inspector Chester A. Arthur, who ultimately rode Conkling's patronage all the way to the White House. Statues of Arthur and Conkling—who had a tremendous falling-out during Arthur's presidency— face off against each other in Madison Square Park.)

A number of buildings that still stand in Lower Manhattan served as the Custom House, including Federal Hall National Memorial (site of Washington's inauguration [18]) and the old Merchants' Exchange at 55 Wall Street. But the grandest of them is the former Alexander Hamilton U.S. Custom House on Bowling Green. Designed by Cass Gilbert (who later built the Woolworth Building [132]), and opened in 1907, the Custom House rivals Grand Central Terminal [131] and the New York Public Library [128] as the greatest Beaux-Arts building in

New York. It is also remarkable for its sculptural program, which conveys America's role at the beginning of the 20th century as an emerging global superpower.

Across the front of the building are four seated female figures sculpted by Daniel Chester French, who, in 1922, created the seated Abraham Lincoln for the Lincoln Memorial. They represent (from the viewer's left when facing the building's grand staircase) Asia, North America, Europe, and Africa, and create a fascinating political commentary. Asia sits on her throne, eyes closed in meditation. She holds a lotus flower in her right hand, and a

Seated figure of North America by Daniel Chester French on the front of the Alexander Hamilton U.S. Custom House

small statue of Buddha rests on her lap. However, her throne sits on a base of human skulls and she is flanked by three men who are bound together. These are typical of America's dim view of Asian religions at the time: the skulls indicate ancestor worship and the bound men convey the idea that Asians were enslaved by their faith. At the same time this building was being constructed, America won the Spanish-American War [133], gaining control of the Philippines from Spain. Among the many reasons the United States decided not to hand the country over to the Filipinos was President McKinley's desire to see them saved by Christianity.* If you look over the figure's right shoulder, you can see a gleaming cross rising up behind her, signaling the arrival of Western, Christianizing civilization.

Just to the left of the grand staircase sits North America. She carries the torch of liberty in her hand, a Native American brave stands stoically behind her, and an American eagle perches next to her throne. Underneath her cloak crouches a virile young man pushing forward a wheel with wings as an allegory of progress.** Beneath North America's foot is a toothed Mayan serpent—a reminder that South America, in the era of "big stick" diplomacy, was firmly under North America's boot.

The figure to the immediate right of the staircase is Europe, sitting on a throne carved with scenes from the Parthenon. She wears a crown, a breastplate (like Athena), and has the crests of Europe's royal families subtly sewn into the hem of her skirt. He left arm rests on a book (knowledge) and the book rests on a globe (discovery). If you look behind the statue, you can see a second figure, shrouded in a cloak, staring at a laurel-ringed skull. This man—the opposite of North America's young figure of

progress—is Europe contemplating its own demise.

The last statue, Africa, is naked from the waist up and sound asleep. The nakedness indicates savagery; the fact that she is asleep is likely a commentary on America's lack of direct trade with Africa. In an era when tremendous amounts of raw materials, like rubber, were coming into the United States from Africa, it was galling that we had to deal with European colonial powers to extract what we needed. Perhaps if we'd had our own colony, Africa would have been awake.

Above the projecting cornice stand a dozen statues that represent a history of maritime trade. From the viewer's left, they are:

- Athens (represented by Athena)
- Rome (as a centurion)
- Phoenicia
- Genoa (birthplace of Columbus)
- a Venetian doge
- Spain's Queen Isabella
- the Netherlands (here shown as Peter Stuyvesant)
- Portuguese hero Henry the Navigator
- Denmark
- Germany
- France
- Great Britain (represented by Queen Victoria)

Notice the copper statue being held out by France—that's a miniature Statue of Liberty [93]. (Actually, if you look through binoculars, you can see that it is a generic figure

---

*Of course, since the Philippines had been a Spanish possession for centuries, most Filipinos were already Catholics. But, as has been amply demonstrated in earlier chapters, this was akin to heathenism in the eyes of many American Protestants.

**The same wheel can be seen in the column capitals on this building as well as above the windows that surround the Main Concourse at Grand Central Terminal [131].

of *Liberté* and not a replica of the woman standing in the harbor.)

The oddest statue is that of Germany. When you stand at a certain angle (a good place is in front of 1 Broadway), you can clearly see the word BELGIUM in large letters across Germany's shield. Just after the end of World War I, when anti-German sentiment was at its highest, the Treasury Department decided that its Custom House should not have a depiction of our enemy, but that Belgium—where so many U.S. servicemen had died—deserved a place, despite its tentative claim to being one of the great historical maritime powers. Over the objections of sculptor Albert Jaegers, the shield was reconfigured and the word was carved on the statue ca. 1920.

124 Times Square and the Ball Drop

As August Belmont's Interborough Rapid Transit Company was hard at work on the city's first subway line [**119**], Belmont was lobbying his friend Adolph Ochs, the publisher of the *New York Times*, to relocate his paper's headquarters to Longacre Square.

In theory, it was enough that the new subway connected the growing residential neighborhoods on the Upper West Side and Harlem to the city's business district below City Hall. However, Belmont realized that to make the subway indispensable, he needed to develop real estate along the 42nd Street corridor as its own, independent business district. So he turned to Ochs and encouraged him to consider building the *Times* a new all-in-one

editorial and printing plant along the path of the IRT.

Ochs had purchased a controlling interest in the *Times* in 1896 and quickly boosted the paper's circulation (by dropping the price to a penny) while raising the standard of its journalism. Belmont had long held a financial stake in the paper and saw the marriage of the newspaper and his new subway as a mutually beneficial enterprise. By printing the paper on 42nd Street—in a new building with a subway station right inside it—the *Times* would get a jump on the competition: papers could

The Times Tower in the first decade of the 20th century

be whisked by newsboys uptown to be sold on street corners on the Upper West Side; or people would start getting off the train at Longacre Square, and buy the *Times* right there in front of its offices, as they now did from other newspapers lining Park Row below City Hall.

To sweeten the deal, Belmont persuaded Mayor McClellan to rename Longacre Square after its new tenant. One of the *Times*'s chief rivals, James Gordon Bennett Jr.'s *New York Herald*, had moved to 34th Street in 1894, and its new location was soon renamed Herald Square. Belmont argued that the *Times* deserved the same courtesy; on April 8, 1904, Mayor McClellan presided over the opening of Times Square.*

The new headquarters for the *Times* was the second-tallest skyscraper in the city in 1904, and the paper boasted that it could be seen from 12 miles away. To celebrate its opening—and to further bolster the paper's influence—the *Times* played host to a New Year's Eve party in 1904 and throngs of people gathered in Times Square to watch a fireworks display from the top of the building. By New Year's Eve 1907, so many new buildings had gone up in Times Square that the city banned fireworks and the *Times* had to find a new way to usher in the New Year. It decided to borrow the idea of a dropping ball from the Western Union Company. Every day at noon, a metallic ball dropped from a spire at the top of the Western Union headquarters on Lower Broadway. Visible from the harbor and many spots downtown, it allowed people to synchronize

their watches and keep more accurate time. (The telegraph company also sent out the noon time signal to railway stations, which allowed trains to keep to a proper schedule.) Thus, by 1907, a dropping ball had long been associated with timekeeping and the *Times* merely extended the metaphor to make it a resetting of one's watch for the entire year.

The Times Tower still plays host to the dropping ball, but the newspaper moved out years ago, finding the building inadequate for its continued growth. Like all buildings on Times Square, it hosts a series of illuminated signs (there's actually a law requiring them as part of the square's zoning), which are some of the most visible pieces of advertising on the planet. The building also features a news "zipper" that displays headlines in a constant crawl around the building. The first zipper was installed in 1928 to report election returns in the contest between hometown favorite Alfred E. Smith [144] and Herbert Hoover.

125 City College Moves to Harlem

In 1847, New York chartered a Free Academy "for the purpose of extending the benefits of education gratuitously to persons who have been pupils in the common schools of the said City and County of New York." As founder Townsend Harris proclaimed:

---

*Technically, Times Square is only the bottom portion of the X formed by the intersection of Broadway and Seventh Avenue. The northern triangle of land is Duffy Square, today most famous for hosting the TKTS ticket booth. The same is true of Herald Square at 34th Street; it is the northernmost of the two triangles; the southern one is Greeley Square, named for *New York Tribune* editor Horace Greeley [58], a statue of whom stands there.

Open the doors to all—Let the children of the rich and the poor take their seats together and know of no distinction save that of industry, good conduct and intellect.

Originally, the school combined elements of secondary school and college, but by 1866, when its name was changed to the City College of New York, it was a four-year program, though it continued to maintain a large "sub-freshman" class of younger students preparing themselves for higher education. For its first 50 years, City College occupied the Free Academy Building on 23rd Street, designed by James Renwick. Though enrollment increased dramatically in the years following the Civil War, the city did not approve a move by the college until 1895, when a tract of land in Harlem, along Convent Avenue, was purchased and George B. Post (who would soon begin work on the New York Stock Exchange [114]) was commissioned to create a new campus.

The resulting structures are the city's best example of collegiate Gothic architecture. Though there are entrance gates on all four sides, the tall walls of schist make the college an imposing, protective fortress—a true medieval walled city. Post chose Manhattan schist as his main material not only because of its aesthetic qualities, but because it was the right price: much of the bedrock came from the tunneling for the nearby IRT [119], which also provided a convenient station just a block away from campus.*

The grandest of Post's five original 1908 campus buildings was the Main Hall (today's Shepard Hall), a soaring cathedral-like space that was the primary classroom building. Other buildings housed academic offices and the college's power plant,

City College's Main Hall (today called Shepard Hall)

complete with a tall battlement-studded smokestack. (The smokestack still towers over Compton Hall, but is inoperable.)

At the same time the new campus was moving to Harlem, the college was undergoing a radical shift in its demographics. Seventy-five percent of the student body was now Jewish, and the college's move to Harlem also sparked a mass exodus of Jewish families from the Lower East Side to the college's environs. In an era when many colleges, particularly the

*Today, as the city builds the Second Avenue Subway—its first major addition in 50 years—the same schist is selling for $100 a square foot, making it a potentially great money-maker for the Metropolitan Transit Authority.

Ivy League, were trying to limit Jewish attendance, City College became known as "the Harvard of the Proletariat" and in the years between the two world wars was a particularly strong bastion of Marxist intellectualism.

Since 1961, City College has been a part of the larger City University of New York. The college remained free until the city's growing fiscal crisis [see 172] forced it to begin charging tuition in 1975.

126 The Triangle Shirtwaist Factory Fire

By the beginning of the 20th century, the traditional "Ladies' Mile" shopping districts of Sixth Avenue and Lower Broadway had given way almost entirely to light manufacturing, the cast-iron department stores converted into garment factories.

The most dramatic change was in the area east of Washington Square, where once-elegant streets like Bond, Great Jones, and Lafayette [33] had become a large-scale garment district. It was here, on the corner of Washington and Mercer streets on March 25, 1911, that the city suffered its worst-ever workplace fire at the notorious Triangle Shirtwaist sweatshop ("shirtwaist" is an old-fashioned word for blouse), which occupied the eighth, ninth, and tenth floors of the Asch Building.

Long before the fire broke out, the factory was infamous for its poor labor practices. In 1909, New York's largest job action, known as "the Uprising of the 20,000," began

when workers walked off the job at the Triangle Shirtwaist Factory. For months, the majority of the city's shirtwaist factories were crippled by the strike, but the factory owners refused to budge. Though the International Ladies Garment Workers Union brokered a settlement in 1910 that stopped short of forcing the recognition of its union, the owners of the Triangle Shirtwaist Factory, Max Blanck and Isaac Harris, refused to agree to it. The factory's workers went back to work having gained few concessions.

On the day of the fire, a Saturday, only about half of the factory's 500 employees had come to work. Just as the afternoon shift was ending, a fire broke out on the eighth floor. Typical of garment centers of the day, the factory floor was a virtual tinderbox, with clothes, scraps of cloth, and unswept trimmings everywhere. When the fire started, the majority of the workers on the eighth and tenth floors were able to escape,* but those on the ninth floor had been locked in. This was done, some speculated, to cut down on unauthorized breaks, though it is also likely that it kept union organizers off the factory floor. Soon the elevators stopped working, which meant that the only remaining exit was the fire escape. Tragically, the fire escape had been poorly installed and maintained, and when too many young women began to climb down, it collapsed beneath their weight, sending them plunging to their death. The rest of the women on the ninth floor were then faced with jumping out of windows or waiting to burn to death. Many

---

*Blanck and Harris, the owners, were able to get up to the roof and escape from there.

chose the former, raining down on the assembled crowd from above. The fire department did arrive, but as their ladders reached no higher than the sixth floor, it did little to save the women. In the end, 148 women died, most of them at the scene. Almost entirely immigrants from Little Italy and the Lower East Side, some were only 13 years old.

Max Blanck and Isaac Harris were brought up on criminal charges but acquitted of any wrongdoing; under another name, the Triangle factory soon reopened nearby. However, the fire brought on a tremendous revolution both in unionization and the establishment of worker safety protocols. Much of this was led by New York politicians Robert F. Wagner and Alfred E. Smith, who was beginning his rise as a Tammany Hall powerhouse [see 144]. Hundreds of people watched in horror as the women fell to their death that day; one passerby was Frances Perkins. She was already a supporter of the garment workers, and the Triangle fire galvanized her career path. In 1933 she became the first woman ever appointed to a presidential cabinet when Franklin Delano Roosevelt made her secretary of labor.

The Asch Building was refurbished after the fire. Now known as the Brown Building, it houses classrooms for New York University.

127 St. Philip's Episcopal Church, Strivers' Row, and the Creation of Black Harlem

The history of Harlem—like the history of much of New York City—is tied to real estate and transportation. For New York's black population, transportation destroyed one neighborhood and created another.

In 1901, the Pennsylvania Railroad Company was given the right-of-way to build under the Hudson River, thus bringing its trains into Manhattan for the first time [see 131]. To give the railroad space for its terminal and rail yards, the city exercised its right of eminent domain in the West Side neighborhood commonly known as the Tenderloin, which was at that time the city's largest black district. This sudden pressure on the black community to find a new place to live resulted in two important real estate transactions

Victims of the Triangle Shirtwaist Factory fire

in Harlem: the purchase of a row of tenements by St. Philip's Episcopal Church—then the largest sale to black buyers in the city's history—and the opening up of two prime streets of townhouses to black renters. This townhouse development, officially known as the King Model Houses, soon came to be known as Strivers' Row.

∼ At the end of the 19th century, David H. King was the most prominent building contractor in New York, having worked on well-known projects such as the Washington Arch [102] and the pedestal of the Statue of Liberty [93]. In the early 1890s, he decided to branch out into real estate development and began planning a high-end townhouse community along blocks of West 138th and West 139th streets in Harlem. The elevated railroad [81], which ran along Eighth Avenue, and the promise of a new subway that might extend to Harlem [119] made speculators realize that what had so recently still been the countryside was on the verge of becoming Manhattan's next fashionable district.

King hired three celebrated architects to help him create the King Model Houses. James Brown Lord (whose works included Delmonico's Restaurant and the New York Supreme Court building on Madison Square) designed a row of matching homes on the south side of 138th Street. Bruce Price, probably America's best-known townhouse architect, built the bulk of the development, designing everything on the north side of 138th Street and the south side of 139th Street. The most elegant homes were designed by King's friend Stanford White [121],

who built a row of Italianate structures along the north side of 139th Street.

A common problem with townhouses in New York was the lack of back alleys (which had been purposely left off the Commissioners' Plan of 1811 [25]). Not only did this mean no rear entrances for servants and tradesmen, it meant no carriage houses. Thus, King advertised that one of the greatest advantages of his development would be rear alleys. (On 138th Street, you can still see "Walk Your Horses" posted on some of the carriageway gates.) Stanford White even went so far as to eliminate the front entrance stoop from most of his row on 139th Street, reasoning that the main purpose of the front staircase was to hide a servants' entrance. With proper alleys, the servants would have back doors and stoops would be unnecessary.

While the houses themselves were beautiful, King immediately ran into problems. Harlem was not developing as rapidly as he had hoped, and the people who moved in weren't wealthy enough to afford carriages, thus rendering his back alleys and carriage houses an expensive waste of space. The Panic of 1893 sent real estate into a depression and when, two years later, King's mortgager foreclosed, he'd been able to sell only 9 of the 146 homes in the development.

His mortgage was held by the Equitable Life Assurance Company, which immediately began renting out the properties. Some were rented as single-family homes; some were converted into apartment houses; and some were run as boardinghouses, where meals were included in the rent. Most significantly, the insurance company was willing to rent to black families moving up from the Tenderloin, though they had to pay a much higher rate than whites. By the 1920s, so many black people had moved in that people began to call the area Strivers' Row in honor of its residents' quest to live as middle-class citizens. (Some used the term pejoratively, but for the most part it was seen as a positive moniker.)

Among the prominent black residents of Strivers' Row were musician W. C. Handy, known as the Father of the Blues; Fletcher Henderson; Eubie Blake; surgeon Louis Wright; and Vertner Tandy, the first black architect to gain membership into the American Institute of Architects.

~ In 1909, Vertner Tandy's firm received the commission to build St. Philip's Episcopal Church on 134th Street. St. Philip's, the oldest black Episcopal church in the city, had been founded in 1809 in the Five Points neighborhood [37; 45]. As the black community moved, the church moved with it, eventually building its headquarters on West 25th Street in the Tenderloin. As the building of Penn Station began to destroy the neighborhood, St. Philip's pastor, Hutchens Bishop, went to Harlem and purchased five and a half lots on 133rd and 134th streets to relocate the church. In 1911, Vertner Tandy and his partner, George W. Foster, Jr., finished the new church, an excellent example of brick-faced neo-Gothic. That same year, St. Philip's sold some property in the Tenderloin to the Pennsylvania Railroad and used the proceeds to acquire a row of tenement apartments from 107 to 145 West 135th Street, thus ensuring that not only was the church itself mov-

ing to Harlem but the parishioners could afford to do so as well.

These tenements—which had once sported a sign in the window that read "We guarantee that these houses will be rented to white tenants only"—made the public aware of the changing face of Harlem. Not only were black tenants arriving in ever greater numbers, they could afford to buy entire block fronts of property. Just six years later, the *New York Times* could announce that Harlem was "The Wealthiest Negro Colony in the World" (while, at the same time, perniciously commenting that Harlem had been, a decade earlier "one of the city's best residential districts"). By the 1920s, Harlem was so thoroughly the center of New York's black population that the name of the neighborhood itself—which less than a generation earlier would have conjured up images of German or Jewish New York—was shorthand for African-American culture and a destination all its own [see 153].

128 The New York Public Library

When former governor (and one-time presidential candidate) Samuel J. Tilden [76] died in 1886, he left his estate—valued at approximately $6 million—to "maintain a free library and reading room in the city of New York."

New York at this point had a number of private libraries, some of which were free, but most of which required an annual subscription. (Some lending libraries worked on a system remarkably similar to Netflix: at the beginning of each year, patrons marked down on a list what books they wanted to read. Titles would be sent out by mail one at a time; when you returned one book, the next would be mailed to you.) The two largest libraries in the city were the Astor Library on Lafayette Place [**see 33 and 165**] and the Lenox Library, a collection of rare books, on Fifth Avenue.

Tilden's will was immediately challenged by his nieces and nephews, who ultimately got their hands on over half the money. While the

The New York Public Library

dations themselves were left for the library building.)

The library was designed by the firm of Carrère & Hastings, which had to come up with a plan that would integrate Tilden's desire that the library be free and open to the public and the Lenox Library's need to preserve its treasure trove of rare books. The result was a combination of open and closed stacks; about 30,000 common reference works lined the shelves around the main reading room on the third floor (which, at two city blocks long, is about the size of a football field). Specialized collections like maps and rare manuscripts were stored in their own departments on the first and second floors, but the bulk of the books were shelved behind

case was wending its way through the courts, the trustees of the new library realized they would have to get creative if they wanted Tilden's vision to survive. Trustee John Bigelow approached the Lenox and Astor libraries and proposed a merger; in 1895, the New York Public Library, Astor, Lenox and Tilden Foundations was formed and soon work began on building the library's new home on Fifth Avenue at 42nd Street. (Before actual construction could start, however, the site's previous occupant, the distributing reservoir of the Croton Aqueduct system [**46**] had to be torn down to its foundations; the foun-

the scenes. The building's engineers created a system of pneumatic tubes and dumbwaiters. Call slips were whisked by pneumatic tube to librarians in the deep recesses of the building who would find the books and send them by dumbwaiter up to the third-floor reading room. The library was very proud that on opening day the first book requested, N. I. Grot's *Ethical Ideas of Our Time*, made it up in just six minutes. (The system still works today exactly as it did when the building opened in 1911; however, wait times now generally exceed six minutes.)

The library's main entrance sits

approximately 90 feet back from Fifth Avenue, creating an outdoor plaza. Architect Thomas Hastings had encouraged the city to acquire 90 feet of land on the opposite side of Fifth Avenue to create an even more monumental entryway, but the city was unwilling to lose tax revenue on those desirable blocks. The approach to the building is guarded by two majestic lions by Edward Clark Potter. Originally known as "Leo Astor" and "Leo Lenox," they were later nicknamed "Patience" and "Fortitude"—after the traits that would carry New Yorkers through the Depression—by Mayor Fiorello La Guardia. Above the entryway, dedications to James Lenox, John Jacob Astor, and Samuel Tilden are inscribed between allegorical statues representing the works enshrined in the library, including religion, poetry, and drama. Fountains on either side of the entrance, inspired by Italian Renaissance designs, depict Truth and Beauty, the two most important qualities found in the library's collection.

129 The Birth of the Oreo

The year 1898 saw two mergers that shaped the rest of the 20th century: the unification of the five boroughs of New York City [107], and the merger of the American Biscuit & Manufacturing Company and the New York Biscuit Company into the National Biscuit Company—Nabisco. In 1906, the company moved its national headquarters to the New York Biscuit Company's factory between Ninth and Tenth avenues in West Chelsea, having recently introduced two bestsellers: the Uneeda Biscuit and Barnum's Animal Crackers (which were not endorsed or authorized by the circus). In 1912, the factory created its most famous confection, a disc-shaped, cream-filled cookie dubbed the Oreo. No one at Nabisco knows where the name came from, though etymologists have suggested everything from *or* (French for gold, and perhaps a reference to the fact that the cookie originally also came in a lemon meringue flavor) to the Greek *oros* for mountain (because early cookies had a mound of filling). Some have even suggested that the "re" in the middle is the cREam and the "o" on either side is the chOcolate, but that seems like wishful thinking. Perhaps the simplest explanation is correct: Oreo just sounded like a good name for a cookie. To date, close to 500 million Oreos have been sold, making them the most popular cookies in the United States.

Hot on the heels of the Oreo's introduction, Nabisco expanded across Tenth Avenue and became the dominant landowner near the river; its buildings were among the many there to be altered in the 1930s to accept the elevated freight railroad known as the High Line. However, with most industry moving out of New York in the years following World War II, it did not take long for Nabisco to follow suit, and the Chelsea buildings were sold in 1959 after the company decamped for New Jersey.

The main building, between Ninth and Tenth avenues, was completely revamped in the 1990s to be office space (a number of television studios are located here) and a gourmet shopping arcade, known as Chelsea Market.

130 Abraham Cahan and the *Forward*

In the early years of the 20th century, New York boasted a tremendous number of Yiddish-language newspapers, including the *Algemeiner Journal*, the *Morning Freiheit*, and the most famous of them all, the *Jewish Daily Forward*, which by the 1930s

The *Forward* building on Straus Square

had achieved a national circulation of over 275,000 copies a day.

The driving force behind the *Forward* was longtime editor Abraham Cahan, a devout Socialist who used the paper to further union and labor causes while at the same time appealing to the needs of uprooted immigrants who were having trouble adjusting to American culture and the frenetic pace of life in New York. By far the most popular column in the paper was the "Bintel Brief" (Yiddish for "bundle of letters"), an advice column normally penned by Cahan himself. As Cahan later wrote: "People often need the opportunity to be able to pour out their heavy-laden hearts. Among our immigrant masses this need was very marked." Questions ranged from religious practice to assimilation [see 95] to economics and socialism. (One mother wrote in forlornly that her son "doesn't want to get married [because] he is a socialist and he is too busy.") Cahan always wrote back with great care, steering a middle path between old-world traditions on the one hand and his own socialist views on the other.

To get a sense of Cahan's politics, you need look no further than the front door of the *Forward*'s headquarters building on Straus Square on the Lower East Side. At the time the tallest building ever to grace the neighborhood, the 1912 structure housed editorial offices and presses for the paper. Right above the front entrance, "Forward Building" is carved in English, and to either side are terra-cotta portrait busts of Marx, Engels, Liebknecht, and LaSalle, the founders of modern socialism and Cahan's heroes. The year the building opened was the high point of American Socialism, with Socialist Party candidate Eugene V. Debs garnering nearly one million votes in that year's presidential election.

The paper was also known for the quality of its writing. Cahan was himself a well-regarded novelist, and his book *The Rise of David Levinsky* is considered a classic depiction of the Lower East Side. Other writers on the *Forward*'s staff have included future Nobel Prize winners Isaac Bashevis Singer and Elie Wiesel.

The paper's circulation dropped after World War II; an English edition was added in the 1960s to broaden the paper's appeal, and in the 1970s it finally left the Lower East Side for offices in Midtown. The building, owned for years by a Chinese religious society, has recently been converted into high-end condominium apartments (which, undoubtedly, has Abraham Cahan spinning in his grave).

131 Grand Central Terminal and the Great Age of Rail

gave birth to the short-lived Grand Central Station.*

In 1902, the New York Central Railroad suffered a terrible accident. A train was waiting outside the station for clearance when a second locomotive came up from behind. Because the tunnel was so filled with soot and steam exhaust, the engineer of the second train could not see that he had a red signal holding him and he collided at full speed with the other train. Seventeen people were killed and countless others were trapped in the tunnel for hours. Immediately following the accident,

Grand Central Terminal

When Cornelius Vanderbilt's Grand Central Depot was built in the early 1870s [69], the tracks along Park Avenue were sunk to put the steam locomotives below grade. However, this did little to improve the avenue, as the steam exhaust continued to billow from the open median down its center. As traffic increased throughout the 1890s, the depot outgrew its home on 42nd Street and a series of internal and external renovations

politicians and the press clamored for the railroad, now run by William Henry Vanderbilt, to do something to prevent future mishaps. The city began crafting a law to make steam locomotion illegal within New York's borders.

At the same time, Vanderbilt was feeling a threat from a second front. His archrivals at the Pennsylvania Railroad had received the right-of-way from the state legislature to

*There's an old riddle: How long does it take a train traveling from Chicago to reach Grand Central Station? The answer is that a train can *never* reach Grand Central Station—it no longer exists; Grand Central Terminal is the only proper designation for today's railroad station.

build a railroad tunnel under the Hudson River and to construct a Penn Station on the West Side. Up to this point, Grand Central was the only station in town—customers for the Pennsylvania's routes had to take a ferry to New Jersey to begin their trip. Not only was the construction of Penn Station going to provide an easier alternative for travelers, the building was designed by Charles Follen McKim, whose fame from the Chicago World's Fair and Columbia University's new campus [101] made him one of the most sought-after architects in the city. McKim's plans for Penn Station would make it the grandest City Beautiful structure in town—and the fourth-largest building on the planet.

Confronted with the bad publicity from the accident and the mounting competition from the Pennsylvania Railroad, Vanderbilt decided on a radical course of action. One of the New York Central's mechanical engineers, William Wilgus, had been experimenting for two years with electrifying the rolling stock. Going electric now became the railroad's highest priority, allowing it to finally cover over Park Avenue and also giving it the excuse to create a gorgeous new Grand Central Terminal to be both the crown jewel in Vanderbilt's empire and to outdo McKim's Penn Station.

(Penn Station's demolition in 1963–64—and its replacement with the banal Madison Square Garden—has long been considered one of the greatest crimes against architecture in New York's history. The positive benefit it produced, however, was the creation of New York's Landmarks Preservation Commission, which now oversees the legal protection of many of New York's most important historical and architectural treasures. A large number of the sites in this book are official New York City landmarks.)

∿ A handful of architects were invited to submit proposals for the new Grand Central Terminal, and the commission went to Reed & Stem, a firm from Minnesota. However, New York architect Whitney Warren was a cousin of William Henry Vanderbilt and he used his family connections to get the railroad to consider his firm's proposal too—*after* Reed & Stem had been selected. As a result, his firm, Warren & Wetmore, were also hired. Officially, the terminal was designed by Warren & Wetmore and Reed & Stem Associated Architects. However, the guiding hand was Whitney Warren, and many consider the terminal—completed in 1913—to be the grandest Beaux-Arts structure in the city.

Many of the engineering decisions had already been made by William Wilgus, including the idea that the now-electrified trains could be completely covered, not merely along the length of Park Avenue, but also in the train yards just north of 42nd Street. This, in turn, would allow the terminal to lease what had heretofore been unusable land. The area became known as Terminal City. (One tenant is the Waldof-Astoria Hotel [150].) Wilgus also suggested such innovations as having long-distance and commuter trains come in at different levels and of building the Park Avenue viaduct, which brings automobile traffic around the station.

But what Grand Central is exalted for is not its engineering but its brilliant interior space, exemplified by the soaring Main Concourse (which is approximately the height of a 13-story building), one of the most striking public spaces ever built. Across the vaulted ceiling, artist Paul César Helleu painted the night sky, complete with the constellations and hundreds of twinkling stars lit by incandescent bulbs [see 173]. (The constellations are backward, likely the result of Helleu relying on a celestial globe as his model. If you look today at the windows surrounding the ceiling, notice terra-cotta decorations above each window. Above some of the windows is a depiction of a celestial globe, which shows a "God's-eye view" of the heavens.)

Passageways lead out from the main concourse to the streets, the subway station, and—on the lower level—an extensive dining concourse. The most famous and longest-serving eatery is the Oyster Bar, which includes one of the best Guastavino tile ceilings in the city. If you take the Graybar Passage (so-called because it connects to the Graybar Building on Lexington Avenue) from the Main Concourse, you can see a well-preserved example of what the terminal looked like during the Depression, when WPA artists were assigned to paint murals. This one, covering one of the vaulted sections of the ceiling about halfway down the passage, shows the progress of transportation, including a wagon train, an old-fashioned steam railroad, and—an unintentional sign of what would ultimately be Grand Central's undoing—a series of planes taking flight.

Out front, the 42nd Street entrance is capped by Jules-Félix Coutan's sculptural group *Transportation*, in which Minerva and Hercules (wisdom and strength) hold up a standing figure of Mercury (commerce). The statue is a staggering 48 feet tall—the clock alone is 13 feet and is, in fact, the largest example of Tiffany glass ever produced. Just below the group, greeting passing motorists, is a statue of Commodore Vanderbilt in his fur coat; the sculpture was rescued from a Vanderbilt-owned warehouse when it was torn down.

132 "The Cathedral of Commerce": The Woolworth Building

It is difficult to pinpoint the end of the Gilded Age. Some see it as the coming of World War I; others suggest the sinking of the *Titanic* on April 15, 1912. Some, thinking purely in terms of economics, look to the passage of the 16th Amendment, which allowed for a federal income tax, thus radically readjusting how America's elite spent their money. But in terms of the Beaux-Arts/City Beautiful architecture that characterized the era, the best way to examine the period's decline is by focusing on the greatest architectural innovation of the time: the skyscraper.

Between 1890, when Joseph Pulitzer's 309-foot *World* building became the first self-consciously "tallest building in the world" and 1916, when new zoning laws went into effect, the skyscraper in New York underwent tremendous upheaval. Despite a couple of excellent examples from the Chicago School (including Louis Sullivan's Bayard-Condict Building on Bleecker Street and Daniel Burnham's Flatiron [111]), New York's skyscrapers struggled to find a style of their own. The best example of a Beaux-Arts skyscraper is Cass Gilbert's 1913 Woolworth Building, the most dazzling high-rise of its era and still one of the most beloved buildings in New York.

Frank W. Woolworth, the inventor of the dime store in 1878 and

The Woolworth Building

the most revolutionary retailer in America since A. T. Stewart [50], had become rich off a simple notion: low prices and high volume. Not only was everything at Woolworth's priced at either five or ten cents, all the merchandise was on display. In an era when store clerks normally had to

fetch items from the back, the ability to browse store shelves gave buyers greater power over their selections. And, as Woolworth soon realized, it made them purchase more. In 1910, he added a lunch counter to a store in Manhattan—another tool to keep shoppers in the store longer—and by 1911, when the Woolworth Corporation was founded, Frank Woolworth was worth millions.

That same year, the company hired Cass Gilbert to build its new corporate headquarters on Broadway. Gilbert, who had just six years earlier finished his Beaux-Arts masterpiece, the U.S. Custom House [123], gracefully transitioned into high-rise construction. He was one of the first New York architects to embrace the idea that tall buildings should actually *look* tall, and he used a variety of techniques to draw the viewer's eye from the decorated street-level entrances to the soaring tower. The window bays are separated by vertical piers that rise, almost uninterrupted, from the base to the spire. The building is faced in terracotta that lightens toward the top of the building, emphasizing its height. Gilbert had been asked to create the tallest building in the world (thus topping the 700-foot Metropolitan Life Insurance tower on Madison Square), but he didn't want to simply build a massive slab facing City Hall Park. Instead, he took his cue from the building opposite the Woolworth plot on the Park Row side of the park, R. H. Robertson's 30-story Park Row Building, which had been the tallest building in the world when it opened in 1899.* To put the Wool-

---

*The Park Row Building has two small cupolas; one of these featured the building's observation deck.

worth Tower in context, Gilbert built his base to be the same basic height as the Park Row Building and then affixed a slender tower on top of that, rising to a copper, peaked roof and a final height of 793 feet.*

Gilbert's use of neo-Gothic tracery (sometimes referred to as "wedding cake" Gothic) gives the building a medieval feel and, indeed, led Brooklyn minister S. Parkes Cadman to dub it "the Cathedral of Commerce" at its opening gala. Cadman was not only making a commentary on its architectural style but on the fact that in the battle between God and Mammon, Mammon appeared to be winning.

Inside the lobby—which has been closed to the public since the World Trade Center attack [180]—Gilbert created a fantastically ornate space that looked like the crossing of a small church. He carved images into the ceiling in the style of medieval grotesques, including one of himself cradling an architectural model of the building and another of Woolworth counting out his dimes.

In the end, Woolworth paid about $13.5 million to build the tower out of his own deep pockets. It is often remarked with awe that Woolworth paid for it in cash, conjuring up an image of the five-and-dime king arriving at the end of construction with wheelbarrows full of $100 bills (or nickels). In truth, Woolworth's financial advisers were afraid the company's stock value would plunge if shareholders found out how much he was paying for the tower, and he was forced to use his own money.

Indeed, despite the fact that over 90 percent of the building was rented out to commercial tenants, many felt the building would never earn back Woolworth's investment. But Woolworth had other plans. He was one of the first to realize the sheer publicity value of building a noteworthy skyscraper, from using its image in advertising to having postcards sent around the world showing off his creation. As with all skyscrapers claiming the title of tallest in the world, the Woolworth tower had an observation deck that drew in over a quarter million people a year until it was displaced by the Chrysler Building in 1930. (The observation deck finally closed to the public during World War II [see 155].)

133 "Remember the Maine!"

The Spanish-American War lasted only four months in 1898, but it had remarkable long-term effects on American history. In the peace treaty, Spain ceded Cuba, Puerto Rico, the Philippines, and Wake Island to the United States. (This, along with the official annexation of Hawaii that same year, gave America a remarkable reach across the Pacific.) The war also earned New Yorker Teddy Roosevelt [63]—who resigned as assistant secretary of the navy to lead the Rough Riders up San Juan Hill— a spot as William McKinley's running mate in 1900. (When McKinley was assassinated on September 6, 1901, this made T.R. the first and only

---

*Though the roof still has the beautiful verdigris patina of copper, it is now painted on. During World War II, the original copper was stripped and melted down. To maintain the classic look of the building, it has been painted green ever since.

native-born Manhattanite to occupy the Oval Office.)

But the aspect of the war that has probably had the strongest influence on popular culture is the yellow journalism undertaken by the tabloid papers, particularly William Randolph Hearst's *Journal* and Joseph

The goddess Columbia atop the USS *Maine* monument

Pulitzer's *World*, which used sensationalized coverage of the war to sell more newspapers.*

As Cuban citizens struggled for their independence from Spain, the United States sent the battleship *Maine* to Havana to patrol and protect American commercial interests. On the night of February 15, 1898, the *Maine*'s forward ammunition magazines exploded and the ship sank. Two days later, Pulitzer's *World* asked, "Maine Explosion Caused by Bomb or Torpedo?" Hearst's *Journal*

didn't bother to frame it as a question, merely stating that the "Destruction of the War Ship Maine Was the Work of an Enemy." (A hurried investigation by a U.S. naval board of inquiry determined that the *Maine* had been felled by a Spanish mine; in truth, the cause of explosion will likely never be known, but may have been caused by a spontaneous explosion in the coal boiler.)

Two days later, Hearst upped the ante by announcing a National Maine Monument Committee to raise funds to commemorate the 258 men who'd died in the explosion. With the rallying cry "Remember the *Maine*!" on everyone's lips, the United States officially called on Spain to leave Cuba. A month later, Spain declared war on the United States.

The most famous example of yellow journalism is also probably apocryphal. As tensions in Cuba were mounting, Hearst sent artist Frederic Remington to create illustrations for the *Journal*. Bored at the lack of action, Remington is said to have telegraphed, "There is no trouble here. There will be no war. I wish to return." Hearst allegedly blasted back, "You furnish the pictures and

---

*The term "yellow journalism" comes from a comic called *Hogan's Alley*, which starred a character named the Yellow Kid. Originally, the strip appeared only in Pulitzer's *World*, but when Hearst hired the cartoonist away, Pulitzer brought someone else to draw his own version of *Hogan's Alley*. The two papers battled it out, each claiming to have the real Yellow Kid. Those who condemned tactics the papers used to boost circulation derided Hearst and Pulitzer as yellow journalists.

I'll furnish the war." Though this story was reported as early as 1901, the telegrams in question no longer exist and many scholars believe the incident was fabricated.

Though the war only lasted a few months, it would take 15 years for Hearst's *Maine* monument to find a home. Hearst favored a spot "at the mouth of the Narrows, looking out over the ocean." Not only would it make the monument a beacon for arriving steamship passengers, they would see it before getting a glimpse of the Statue of Liberty—a statue still strongly associated with Joseph Pulitzer's fund-raising campaign [**93**]. The spot eventually chosen was Duffy Square (the lesser-known half of the Times Square interchange [**see 124**]), but between the time of the site's selection and the monument's groundbreaking, a public restroom had gone up on the site (oops!) and the city quickly arranged for the Columbus Circle entrance to Central Park to be rebuilt to accommodate the massive statue and fountain.

The long gap between the war and the statue's completion had another beneficial side effect. In 1911, the *Maine* was raised from the bottom of Havana harbor to facilitate further investigations into its sinking. While most of the ship was later dumped back into the ocean, the bronze guns were melted down for the primary statue on the *Maine* monument, a gilded figure of the goddess Columbia rising in a chariot from the sea.

When Joseph Pulitzer [**115**] died in 1911, he left $50,000 in his will to build a fountain; the design was awarded to Karl Bitter and Thomas Hastings, and in 1914 the Pulitzer Fountain, topped by Bitter's statue of the Roman goddess Pomona, opened in front of the Plaza Hotel. One can't help but wonder if this placement—down 59th Street from Hearst's monument—wasn't one final piece of one-upmanship by Pulitzer, even from beyond the grave.

134 Henry Clay Frick's Mansion

By the time Henry Clay Frick moved to New York from Pittsburgh in 1905, he was infamous for his role in the Homestead Strike of 1892. As Andrew Carnegie's partner,* Frick was the person who called in Pinkerton detectives to break the strike. After a fierce gun battle, 12 people (some from each side) lay dead, but the strike continued. Less than three weeks later anarchist Alexander Berkman walked into Frick's office and shot him twice at point-blank range. Frick survived, but the strike was broken and the events set back the union movement, especially in the steel industry, for decades.

Like Carnegie before him, Frick left Pittsburgh for New York; allegedly, one of the deciding factors for Frick was how polluted Pittsburgh had become due to his own coal furnaces. Also like Carnegie, the second act of Frick's life was to spend his money. In addition to supporting some cultural and scientific institutions, Frick used his fortune to acquire art. To house his collection, he decided to purchase the Lenox Library on Fifth Avenue at 70th Street, tear it down, and build a mansion in its place. (The collection in the

---

*Frick's syndicate produced the coal that fueled the steel furnaces.

Lenox Library was being transferred to the newly built New York Public Library [128].) From the beginning, Frick had an eye toward building a home where he could enjoy his art (and have a private gallery to show off his collection to friends), but which after his death would be open to the public.

Frick's announcement of his plans for the Lenox Library was greeted by indignation from architects and preservationists, who claimed the building was one of the late Richard Morris Hunt's greatest works. (Hunt's supporters had even erected a statue of him on the edge of Central Park, where he gazed lovingly across Fifth Avenue at the Lenox Library.) Frick agreed to preserve the Lenox Library by carefully dismantling it and paying to have it re-erected in Central Park—but only if the city would agree to tear down the Arsenal [52] in order to make room for it. When the city refused, Frick simply tore the Hunt building down.

The mansion, finished in 1914, was designed by Thomas Hastings, who had just put the finishing touches on the New York Public Library. Frick may have hired Hastings because of his library connection, but he may also have been impressed by his work at the Knoedler & Company Gallery, the home of Frick's principal art buyer. Eager to outdo former boss Andrew Carnegie's "roomy" home farther up Fifth Avenue [109], Frick evidently instructed Hastings to make Carnegie's mansion "look like a miner's shack."

Much of the interior work on the house was designed by Joseph Allom and Elsie de Wolfe, as Frick didn't think Hastings would cre-

ate an interior that showcased his artwork in proper style. (Perhaps Frick hadn't been that impressed with the Knoedler Gallery, after all.) Just as the house was being completed, financier J. P. Morgan died. Though much of Morgan's collection remained at his library [see 122] or was donated to the Metropolitan Museum of Art, Morgan's son, Jack, did sell some pieces, in particular the work from his father's London residence, which had been purchased for Morgan by art dealer Joseph Duveen. When Duveen found out that Frick was considering purchasing some of the paintings—including an entire room of paintings by Jean-Honoré Fragonard—he swooped in to handle the sale, effectively making himself Frick's new buyer. Until Frick's death in 1919, Duveen helped him enlarge and shape his collection and, upon the death of Frick's widow, Adelaide, in 1931, Duveen helped open the home as the Frick Collection, considered by many to be the finest small museum in New York.

135 The Equitable Building and the 1916 Zoning Resolution

As skyscrapers began to dominate the skyline in Lower Manhattan in the first decade of the 20th century, engineers and architects had to devise ways to ensure that the offices in their high-rises would have ample access to light and air. In the era before air conditioning and fluorescent lighting, these two factors had the greatest impact on commercial rents.

In 1907, architect Francis Kimball

built a pair of skyscrapers facing each other across tiny Thames Street—the U.S. Realty Building to the north and the Trinity Building to the south. Because the Trinity Building faced the graveyard of Trinity Church [44], those offices would have plenty of light. And the north side of the U.S. Realty offices, along Cedar Street, faced a row of short buildings, which made them safe—for the time being. However, the space between the two buildings was so narrow that no light could penetrate, thus making the offices facing Thames Street virtually unrentable. Kimball solved this problem by putting supply closets and elevator banks in this unusable space, but as more buildings were being planned, it was only a matter of time until the only way to guarantee a light-filled office would be to build taller than your surroundings. (There are pointed editorial cartoons from this period wondering what would happen once the buildings got too high—would they build ski slopes on the top of office towers?)

But New York City didn't really begin to deal with the problem of height and bulk until plans were announced in 1913 for the new headquarters of the Equitable Assurance Company, whose previous headquarters had burned down the year before. Standing on a narrow plot across Broadway from Thames Street, the Equitable would rise only 36 stories but would be so bulky that it would have the largest volume of office space ever constructed. (Indeed, there was so much floor space in the Equitable that its volume was not exceeded until the Empire State Building [148] opened in 1931.)

The completed building would be so large that it would cast a seven-acre shadow, diminishing real estate values in the entire surrounding area.

As the Equitable was rising, New York's commercial real estate community began to put together a plan to block future bulky office towers. While part of the resulting 1916 Zoning Resolution created zoning districts, most of the ordinance dealt specifically with height and bulk and gave birth to what is known as setback zoning. (It's also sometimes referred to as "stacked box" or "wedding cake" zoning.)

Depending on the neighborhood, a building would be allowed to rise between 1 and 2.5 times the width of its street before the next level was set back from the lot line. Many commercial neighborhoods in New York have 100-foot-wide avenues and therefore allow buildings to go up 2.5 times that amount—or 250 feet—before the first setback. As the building continued to rise, the setbacks would come more frequently. Once the building's bulk was trimmed back to only 25 percent of its lot size, it could go up as tall as it wanted without interference.

What this meant in practical terms was that the 1916 law mandated buildings that were wide at the base and narrow at the top, creating the classic New York skyscraper style embodied by the Chrysler [145] and Empire State buildings. With only a few modifications, this law would remain in effect until 1961, when it was replaced with what is known as "tower in a plaza" zoning that encouraged greater use of public space in commercial projects.

136 Bohemian Greenwich Village

Few neighborhoods changed as quickly or as radically as Greenwich Village at the beginning of the 20th century. When Mark Twain moved into a rented house at 14 West 10th Street, the neighborhood was still relatively genteel. By the end of World War I, the words "Greenwich Village" were so firmly a synonym for bohemian radicalism and creative expression that the idea that anyone in polite society would build a house there was absurd.

This rapid change was the result of a confluence of factors. Richard Morris Hunt had already paved the way with his Tenth Street Studio Building [62] and over the years some noted writers had called the Village home, beginning with radical pamphleteer Thomas Paine. (Paine, hounded in his latter years for being an atheist, died on Grove Street.) Edgar Allan Poe lived on Waverly and Amity streets [see 38] and just after the Civil War, Louisa May Alcott wrote *Little Women* from her uncle's home on MacDougal Street. But writers did not begin arriving en masse until after 1900, lured by cheap rents. The Panic of 1893 had softened the real estate market and the subsequent Panic of 1907 [122] had caused Greenwich Village property owners to convert large numbers of former single-family residences into apartments and boardinghouses.

Among the first generation of Village writers and activists (who were often one and the same) were Willa Cather, Eugene O'Neill, Max Eastman, Upton Sinclair, Emma Goldman, John Dos Passos, and John Reed. Many of the places associated with these writers no longer exist. Cather and her partner, Edith Lewis, lived for years at 5 Bank Street, which is gone; earlier, Cather had lived at the so-called House of Genius, a boardinghouse on Washington Square, which was also at various times allegedly home to Stephen Crane, Theodore Dreiser, and O. Henry. It, too, is long gone (on its spot sits NYU's student center).

John Reed's last home, however, still stands on tiny Patchin Place, an alleyway near Sixth Avenue. A series of small apartments were built here in the mid-1800s and by the early 20th century, they were still some of the cheapest accommodations in the neighborhood. (As at nearby Grove Court [56], the lack of street entrances automatically downgraded them in the eyes of the establishment.) It was here that Reed lived the last years of his life with his wife, Louise Bryant, while he worked on his 1919 chronicle of the Russian Revolution, *Ten Days That Shook the World*. Reed, a leading figure in New York's Communist scene, was in Russia when the Bolsheviks took power and his book remains the best eyewitness account of the events. (Most people know Reed and the book much better today as the subject of Warren Beatty's epic film *Reds*.)

Other residents of Patchin Place over the years included poet e.e. cummings, modernist novelist Djuna Barnes, and Marlon Brando. Today, it houses a lot of therapists' offices and, at the very back of the alley, the city's last remaining original gas lamp, though it has, unfortunately, been electrified.

PART 6

Boom and Bust, 1920–1945

It's tempting—perhaps *too* tempting—to neatly divide the 1920s, '30s, and '40s into three distinct eras: the Roaring Twenties, the Depression, and the War. And it's hard to dispute the fact that when the value of the stock market sank 95 percent in three years, times had gone pretty quickly from good to bad.

However, what's also worth remembering is how much New York continued to boom even during the worst depths of the Depression. One example is sports. The Yankees' golden age began in 1920, when owner Jacob Ruppert acquired Babe Ruth from the Boston Red Sox, leading not only to the 86-year "Curse of the Bambino," but also laying the cornerstone for one of the greatest Yankee teams in history. By the mid-1920s, the "Murderers' Row" Yankees were in place, making for one of the most awesome displays of power on the baseball field then or since. (In 1927, four players—Ruth, Lou Gehrig, Bob Meusel, and Tony Lazzeri—combined for 544 RBIs, and Ruth hit 60 home runs.)

Ten years later, Ruth was gone (back to Boston), but Joe DiMaggio was on board and the Yankees headed to the World Series against cross-town rivals the Giants (the Yankees won).* It was easy to forget, when looking through the narrow lens of sports and with bleacher seats costing only 55 cents, that things were bad.

The same was true for art and culture. Though the 1920s were more successful on Broadway, the 1930s and 1940s brought forth more lasting works, from *Strike Up the Band* and *Porgy and Bess* in the 1930s to *Oklahoma!, Carousel, Annie Get Your Gun*, and *Kiss Me, Kate* in the 1940s. (And though a live show was more expensive than a movie, the top price for a play was still less than $5 and cheap seats for a musical could be had for less than half that amount.) The Museum of Modern Art, founded in 1929, didn't really hit its stride until it moved into its permanent home in 1939. Moreover, projects sponsored by the Works Progress Administration meant that more public art was being created than in any previous era in American history. Between the WPA (and its cousin, the Civilian

---

*New York had a third team, the Dodgers, during this time, but their later defection to Los Angeles is still a sore subject, so we will draw a veil over it.

Conservation Corps) and the final grand skyscrapers—the Empire State Building and Rockefeller Center—jobs in New York didn't disappear quite as quickly as they might have in other places.

This isn't to say that times weren't tough. The city passed strict new tenement house regulations in 1929, only to see them ignored by landlords who couldn't afford to make upgrades. By 1939, the city's aging housing stock was in terrible shape, which led to two measures that still help define New York today: the large-scale construction of public housing projects and the creation of rent regulations, today enshrined as rent stabilization and rent control.

In the end, the biggest difference between New York in 1920 and in 1945—having survived Prohibition, the worst economic slump in American history, and World War II—was that it had actually become the world city it had been pretending to be at the turn of the century. When the Alexander Hamilton U.S. Custom House on Bowling Green opened in 1907, it said in bold artistic strokes "We're No. 1!"—perhaps too loudly, the bravado only drawing attention to the insecurity underlying it. By 1945, New York really was No. 1. (In the last section of the book we'll look at how the city came perilously close to losing that status.)

137 September 16, 1920: The Morgan Bank Bombing

At 12:01 p.m. on Thursday, September 16, 1920, the church bells of Trinity Church, Wall Street [44], finished pealing and were suddenly replaced by another noise—the horrible sound of 500 pounds of lead sash weights exploding from a horse-drawn wagon on Wall Street. In an instant, 30 people were dead and between 300 and 400 injured from the strength of the blast. It was the worst terrorist attack in American history (and would remain so until the Oklahoma City bombing in 1995).

As the smoke cleared and people began to pick themselves up from the street (including Joseph P. Kennedy, JFK's father, who was then a stockbroker), they were faced with a scene of carnage and devastation. Approximately 100 pounds of dynamite had expelled the sash weights into the air, shattering windows and tearing through nearby pedestrians. The most gruesome sight was the north wall of the House of Morgan. Amid the gouges in the marble from the shrapnel there was also a woman's head—severed from its body but still wearing a proper hat. Police, fire, and Red Cross workers descended on the area. Some eyewitnesses claimed they'd seen an Italian fleeing the scene; others called him a more generic "peddler." Soon, a leaflet was found in a nearby mailbox that read, in crudely stamped letters:

Remember
We will not tolerate
any longer
Free the political
prisoners or it will be
sure death for all of you

American Anarchist Fighters.

The previous day, anarchists Sacco and Vanzetti had been indicted for the murder of two payroll guards in South Braintree, Massachusetts. To many people, the connection between the Wall Street attack and the two Italians became immediately apparent.

However, the leaflet was never tracked to its source and other leads came back empty; to this day, the bombing remains one of the great unsolved crimes of the 20th century. Not only was no one ever apprehended, but investigators weren't even certain what the target was. The wagon was

The Wall Street façade of the House of Morgan showing the gouges from the bombing on September 16, 1920.

parked near "the Corner," the most prominent spot on Wall Street. At the southeast intersection of Wall and Broad streets stood the Morgan bank, surely the most influential financial institution in the city. J. P. Morgan had not only averted the Panic of 1907 [**122**], he had organized investors to buy Andrew Carnegie's steel mills [**see 109**] and was a stakeholder in the shipping monopoly International Mercantile Marine (whose holdings included, among other ships, the *Titanic*). Morgan had died in 1913, and his son Jack had taken over the business and made himself the focus of anticapitalist sentiment. Not only did Jack Morgan receive a constant stream of death threats, but he was also the target of direct attacks. In April 1920, Thomas Simpkin, a self-described anarchist (and lunatic asylum escapee) showed up at Jack Morgan's church and shot physician James Markoe, mistaking him for Morgan, who was, in fact, out of town. When asked why he'd done it, Simpkin replied that he heard Morgan was against the International Workers of the World (the "Wobblies").

In fact, Morgan may not have been the object of the blast. Across Wall Street from the bank stood the U.S. Assay Office, which tested the purity of precious metals and housed over $900 million in gold. Next door, the U.S. Subtreasury building (today's Federal Hall National Memorial [**18**]) stored the bulk of the country's gold supply. (By the end of the decade, this would transfer up the street to the Federal Reserve.) At the corner of Broad Street and Exchange Place, the open-air Curb Market was in session [**138**], and directly across Broad Street from Morgan's front door stood the New York Stock Exchange [**114**], the most potent symbol of American capitalism.

The next morning, business proceeded as normal. The stock exchange—which had suspended trading after the attack—opened as usual, as did the Morgan bank, its north wall shrouded in temporary scaffolding. When the repair work to the bank was finished, Jack Morgan had them leave the shrapnel marks on the wall, a reminder then and today of both the force of the blast and the sheer strength of the bank's fortress-like marble walls.

138 The Curb Market

Until 1921, the New York Stock Exchange [**114**]—the largest trading floor in the city—was accompanied on Broad Street by the Curb Market, where outdoor brokers gathered around lampposts and mailboxes to transact business. In many ways, this was the outgrowth of the fact that some traders had not signed the Buttonwood Agreement in 1792 [**19**], and thus had not been invited into the circle of brokers who moved into Tontine's Coffee House as part of the official exchange. After the California gold rush brought more capital into New York, the Curb Market expanded to handle more transactions, often for companies deemed too small or too new to gain entrance to the New York Stock Exchange. (Many of these companies—like General Motors—did eventually graduate indoors.) In boom years, the Curb Market was sometimes trading 10 times the number of shares that were being sold on the Stock Exchange's floor.

To better transact business amid the bustle of the street, curb brokers

Curb Market, Broad Street, New York City.

Curb Market brokers gather on Broad Street.

desks at the far side of the room. As volume increased in the late 1920s, the Curb Market decided to expand its building by making it taller and by eliminating a small front lawn on Trinity Place to enlarge the trading floor. The original architects' more Italianate design (still visible on the rear of the building) gave way to popular Art Deco motifs of commerce and industry. In 1953, having finally divested itself of its long history on the street, the exchange dropped the word "curb" from its title and became the American Stock Exchange.

139 Prohibition and Speakeasy Culture

It is easy to forget in America today, where alcohol flows so freely, that Prohibition—the so-called noble experiment—lasted a full 14 years, and had actually started even earlier, with the wartime restrictions dating back to 1917.

The 18th Amendment, passed by Congress in December 1917 and ratified by the majority of the states in January 1919, was the outgrowth of years of temperance crusading in America. While there was always a moralistic tone to the temperance movement, there was also a genuine desire to improve public health. In no era did Americans drink as much as they did in the late 19th century. Alcohol was cheap, it was served at saloons that acted as de facto community centers, and it was considered by most immigrant New Yorkers to be safer than water. In Tompkins Square Park, in the middle of Kleindeutschland [see 91

came up with a series of elaborate hand signals to communicate with each other. Soon, clerks in windows overlooking the market adopted these signals to initiate trades. By the early 1920s, the Curb Market was handling more trades than could be easily accommodated on the street, and business moved into a building on nearby Trinity Place. However, it did not immediately abandon its way of doing business. Inside the floor of the exchange, 16 symbolic lampposts were installed for brokers to gather around. They still used hand signals to negotiate trades and the clerks who had once signaled from Wall Street windows instead sat at long

and 118] Henry Cogswell, a crusading dentist from San Francisco, set up a temperance fountain in 1888 to provide clean drinking water and convince the Germans there to stop drinking beer—and stop feeding it to their children. Similarly, a working dairy was planned for Central Park directly next to the German children's playground (called the Kinderberg), where children would be provided with free, uncontaminated milk. (The rustic Dairy was built, but no cows were ever brought to the park and it ended up as a restaurant. Today it's the park's gift shop and visitor center.)

By 1919, enough Americans were convinced of the perils of drinking to give Prohibition a try. However, as soon as the law took effect in 1920, it was thwarted at every turn, and as the Roaring Twenties progressed, the speakeasy culture that flowered in New York completely altered its cultural landscape. Many people who had never been drinkers started consuming because it was socially expected. Women, who in Victorian America would never have entered a men's club, now found themselves on more equal social footing in the relaxed atmosphere of the speakeasies. And in Harlem [**153**], where whites went in droves to hear jazz and to give themselves a sense that they were doing something exotic and transgressive, white and black people drank together as equals for the first time.

At first, some bars and restaurants tried to get around the Volstead Act, the law passed in 1919 to enforce the 18th Amendment. When these attempts failed, some of the city's most eminent eateries, such as Delmonico's, finally went out of business, brought down by their inability to go "underground." Soon, places to drink fell into two categories: cabarets, which offered legitimate entertainment and served alcohol on the sly, and speakeasies, which, because they only served alcohol, were hidden from view. Though linguists argue about the origins of the term, "speakeasy" likely comes from 19th-century London, where "speak softly shops" were established to get around Victorian liquor licensing laws.

In New York, speakeasies multiplied rapidly; every time the state or federal government tried to step up enforcement, more illegal bars opened. Within a decade the number of places to drink had doubled, from 16,000 before the passage of the Volstead Act to 32,000. Some were in the cellars of old homes; some were former bars that masked themselves as legitimate businesses while still serving alcohol. (Pete's Tavern on Irving Place became a flower shop. Savvy patrons knew to walk past the counter, through the refrigerator, and into the bar beyond.) And McSorley's Old Ale House [**57**] didn't even go through that pretense; it moved its brewery into the basement and stayed open, pretending to serve "near beer."

However, the most famous speakeasy in the city—and the only one still operating as if it were still the 1920s—is Chumley's on Bedford Street.* Like most speakeasies, the

---

*A 2007 partial wall collapse shuttered Chumley's. As of this writing, reconstruction is under way for reopening in the near future.

nondescript door at 86 Bedford Street has no sign; it looks like the entrance to any West Village townhouse, albeit one that's a bit less kept-up than its neighbors. Those who know what to do realize they can open that door, climb up and down a set of small stairs (put in to thwart Prohibition inspectors) and find themselves in a charming old bar. The bar has a second entrance, through a door and courtyard at 58 Barrow Street, which is even more hidden.

The bar was named for its owner, Leland Chumley, who founded it sometime after 1922 (as with many illegal places, its origins are obscure). Chumley was an activist writer and a member of the International Workers of the World (the "Wobblies"), who occasionally met there, but what the bar became famous for early on were its literary patrons. These included not only local talent like Willa Cather [see 136] and Edna St. Vincent Millay (who lived just up the street at 75½ Bedford Street [140]), but such luminaries as F. Scott and Zelda Fitzgerald, who had a regular table, Eugene O'Neill, and—in a later era—Norman Mailer, Jack Kerouac, and Allen Ginsberg.

There's a persistent story that the bar's address, 86 Bedford Street, gave rise to the slang term "eighty-six it," which means to get rid of something. When Chumley's was raided, the barkeep supposedly yelled out "Eighty-six it!" to the patrons, and they would clamber out the door. However, the phrase predates Chumley's founding and, at best, they might be credited for moving it from restaurant parlance (it originally meant to take something off the menu) into more common use.

140 Edna St. Vincent Millay and the Cherry Lane Theatre

In 1923, poet and playwright Edna St. Vincent Millay and some of her friends from the Provincetown Playhouse leased land from the descendants of coppersmith Harmon Hendricks along Bedford and Commerce streets. They converted the former brewery at 38 Commerce Street into a theater and planned to rent the rest of the property for profit.

The theater opened the next year and soon became known for its adventurous programming, featuring works by Pirandello, Gertrude Stein, Samuel Beckett (whose play *Happy Days* premiered there)—it even dared stage F. Scott Fitzgerald's only play, *The Vegetable*, which was evidently so bad that Scott and Zelda walked out of its premiere in Atlantic City.

Harmon Hendricks's original home, at 77 Bedford Street, was built in 1799 and remains the oldest home in the Village (though it has been much altered over time). Just to the east of the house's front door would have stood a 9½-foot-wide carriage drive leading to the stables in the rear. At some point perhaps as early as the 1850s, but no later than 1873—that carriage drive was filled in by a tiny four-room house, only 8½ feet wide on the inside and approximately 30 feet deep. It was here Millay moved in 1924, renting the house from the theater, having just received the Pulitzer Prize for Poetry for her collection *The Harp Weaver*. She and her new husband, Eugen Boissevain, remodeled the home, adding a skylight for

Millay's studio and Dutch gabling on the front, perhaps as a nod to Boissevain's heritage. However, they only stayed in Greenwich Village another year, preferring to move to the countryside in 1925.

The Cherry Lane Theatre continued on, providing early work for notable actors such as Jerry Stiller

The Cherry Lane Theatre

(who painted scenery), Beatrice Arthur, who made her stage debut here, Barbra Streisand (who was an understudy and assistant stage manager for Sean O'Casey's *Purple Dust* in 1956), and John Malkovich. In the 1950s, the theater was also the home of Judith Malina and Julian Beck's Living Theater. When the fire department tried to shut down their production of *Ubu Roi* (allegedly

because Beck's sets were a firetrap, but perhaps because the Living Theater was simply too weird), Malina chased the fire inspector down the street with a bamboo spear.

If you stand today at the corner of Bedford and Commerce streets, you'll see an official plaque that tells the story of Commerce Street, noting that it was originally lined with cherry trees before the 1822 yellow fever quarantine [31] sent commerce north from the city, altering the street's use and name. This is a nice story, but there never was a Cherry Lane. When theater co-founder William Rainey was asked for the new theater's name, he—probably thinking of London's Drury Lane— said, "Cherry Lane." Then, to cover his tracks, he concocted the story of Dutch colonial cherry trees. Today, there's even an official street sign at the corner of Commerce Street and Seventh Avenue South marking it as Cherry Lane;* perhaps it's only a matter of time before the story replaces the truth and the street truly becomes Cherry Lane.

141 Chinatown's "Bloody Angle": The Most Dangerous Place in America

By the mid-1920s, the Chinese Exclusion Act [87] was taking a considerable toll on New York's Chinese population; the lack of immigration and the natural attrition of the

---

*The city claims this is an honorary street sign. However, the sign has white lettering on a green background—the colors used for official signs—not white on blue, which is reserved for unofficial designations.

area through death and relocation meant that Chinatown was gradually shrinking away.

However, it wasn't shrinking fast enough for those who considered Chinatown a bad idea in the first place. In 1910, New York police began a campaign to clean up the area. They shut down joss parlors* and "fraudulent 'opium joints.'" They also discouraged white women from dining in groups in chop suey restaurants, figuring that any group of women out on the town in the company of Asian men were prostitutes. They asked the five tour companies that took groups on late-night Chinatown excursions to stop offering those outings, arguing that the streets were becoming too dangerous. As the *New York Times* reported, "the Chinaman is a mysterious being, and there is no telling when he may start a rumpus."

But Chinatown continued to be a draw, despite the real dangers that did exist during periodic outbursts of violence between the Hip Sing and On Leong tongs. Tongs were, in general, mutual benefit associations, similar in makeup to the Jewish *landsmanschaften* [99]. However, feuds between the two tongs often ended in bloodshed and the favorite place for this gang violence was the so-called "Bloody Angle" of Doyers Street, where rivals could easily ambush their prey. The police declared that more murders happened on Doyers Street than anywhere else in America, despite the lack of any empirical evidence to back up their assertion. This also did little to dampen enthusiasm for tourism to Chinatown, and—with the revocation of the Chinese Exclusion Act in 1943—the neighborhood finally began to grow again.

Today, Doyers Street is lined with barbershops. It is also home to Nom Wah Tea Parlor, Chinatown's oldest dim sum parlor, which opened

The "Bloody Angle" of Doyers Street

in 1920. Walking the street, which sees almost no vehicular traffic, gives a sense of old Chinatown. While some of the buildings that line the street are of more recent vintage, the atmosphere that permeates the street is that of an earlier era. The present Chinese community likes Doyers Street because it exemplifies good feng shui: the curve in the road confuses evil spirits.

---

*These Chinese temples—like the ones that still exist in Chinatown today—were a mixture of worship space, clubhouse, and mutual aid association. It is likely that to Western eyes, a group of men sitting around playing cards in a joss parlor made the place seem more like a gambling den than a house of worship.

142 "Gentleman" Jimmy Walker

Perhaps the greatest symbol of the Roaring Twenties was the election of playboy James J. "Jimmy" Walker to the mayor's office in November 1925. Walker, the son of a Greenwich Village alderman, grew up in the environment of Irish-dominated Tammany Hall, and it seemed natural that he would eventually go into politics himself.

However, as a young man his loves were vaudeville and songwriting. Walker wrote a handful of popular songs and in 1905 scored a hit with "Will You Love Me in December as You Do in May?" According to historian James Trager, Walker, always a dandy, used the $500 advance from that song to buy "three custom-made suits . . . , a dozen silk shirts, four pairs of shoes with sharply pointed toes, three fedora hats, a new walking stick, and gifts for his mother and girlfriend."

However, "Will You Love Me?" also marked the end of Walker's success as a songwriter and he soon shifted careers. In 1909, he was elected to the New York State Assembly and in 1914 to the state senate, where he worked to protect the rights of working-class New Yorkers. Always focused on entertainment, Walker strove to eliminate the state's blue laws, which forbade baseball games or prizefighting on Sundays. Perhaps most significantly, he was a fierce opponent of Prohibition [**139**]; in 1925, Tammany Hall picked him to run as the "wet" candidate for mayor. He won by a landslide and spent the next four years as New York's "nightclub" mayor. In addition to his impeccable taste in clothes (which allegedly included over 150 pairs of silk pajamas), the mayor drove an exorbitantly expensive Duesenberg and was a fixture in New York's cabaret circuit. Because he seldom arrived at City Hall before noon, he earned the sobriquet "the late mayor of New York."

One of Walker's favorite hangouts was the Casino in Central Park [**see 151**], where he was often seen with his mistress, Ziegfeld Girl Betty Compton. Compton lived at 12 Gay Street—not far from the mayor's own house on St. Luke's Place—on a block filled with artists and writers. Not long after, *New Yorker* writer Ruth McKenney (who wrote *My Sister Eileen*) moved into 14 Gay Street; nearby at No. 18 was author and critic Mary McCarthy.

Walker's high style fit with the mood of the city and he handily won reelection in 1929. However, a growing scandal about his inability to account for how he was spending the city's money forced him to resign in 1932. He and Compton fled to Europe to await his divorce and to see if anyone was planning to prosecute him. When it appeared the coast was clear, Walker and Compton—now married—returned to New York to a hero's welcome. It seemed all was forgiven: even his nemesis, Mayor Fiorello La Guardia, eventually gave Walker an appointment. But by this time the Depression and the coming world war had taken their toll on Walker's beloved nightclub scene and he found himself increasingly irrelevant. "Gentleman" Jimmy died in 1946, and thousands of people turned out for his funeral, as much to mourn the era he represented as the man himself.

143 The Knights of Pythias and the Shriners

In many ways, the history of New York could be told through its fraternal organizations. The first Masonic lodge was established in the city in 1730, and numerous early residents, including George Washington, were Freemasons; the Bible on which he swore the oath of office in 1789 [18] is still owned by the Masons.

In the 19th century, a host of other fraternal organizations were established: some were veterans' organizations, like the Society of Cincinnati; others were philanthropic bodies, like the Manumission Society; and some were simply gentlemen's social clubs [97].

The era after World War I saw a growing interest in secret societies. Some of this was likely the result of the decade's penchant for secrecy brought on by Prohibition [139]. But in two cases—the Knights of Pythias and the Ancient Arabic Order of the Nobles of the Mystic Shrine (aka the Shriners)—their soaring membership ranks rode a wave of interest in the Middle East that followed Howard Carter's discovery of King Tut's tomb.

The Knights of Pythias were founded in 1864 as a fraternal organization dedicated to healing the deep wounds of the Civil War. Founder Justus H. Rathbone, who was both a Mason and a member of the Improved Order of Red Men (a tangential outgrowth of the Revolutionary War's Sons of Liberty) came up with the requisite secret rituals and started the first lodge in Washington, D.C. (He wrote to Abraham Lincoln about

Near Eastern figures adorn the façade of the Knights of Pythias headquarters.

the order and received warm encouragement.)

The order's motto, "If fraternal love held all men bound, how beautiful this world would be," summed up their appeal. Pythianism grew rapidly, especially in New York, where many members were Jews who felt excluded from the Masons or Catholic fraternities like the Knights of Columbus or the Ancient Order of Hibernians [43]. By the 1920s, the boom in real estate and the appeal of all things vaguely Oriental led the Pythians to hire theatrical architect Thomas Lamb to build them a grand New York lodge on West 70th Street. The façade of the building, finished in 1926, reveals a hodgepodge of Egyptian and other Middle Eastern motifs, including bearded column capitals, winged Babylonian lions, and—at the upper level—giant seated Pharaonic figures lifted, it seemed, from a Hollywood set. What it didn't have was windows. Instead, it presented a blank façade—the better to preserve the secret rituals inside.

~ The Ancient Arabic Order of the Nobles of the Mystic Shrine was founded in New York in 1872 by a group of Master Masons who met regularly for lunch at a restaurant called the Knickerbocker Cottage on Sixth Avenue. Hoping to found a fraternity within the Masons that emphasized camaraderie over ritual practice, two members of the lunch club, William Florence and Walter Fleming, created the Shriners. Florence, an actor, had recently toured the Middle East and brought back with him ideas for organizing their group around Islamic and Oriental imagery. Fleming took Florence's ideas and crafted them into the order's rituals and symbols. Today, the most recognizable of these symbols is the Moroccan fez, the order's preferred headgear, still worn by Shriners at public events, such as parades. (The tiny cars are, undoubtedly, a later addition.)

Like the Knights of Pythias, the Shriners found themselves with a growing membership in the Roaring Twenties and had to rent Carnegie Hall and Madison Square Garden for their larger events. To build an auditorium of their own they hired Shriner Harry P. Knowles, and work began on the grand Mecca Temple on West 55th Street in 1922. Designed in a Moorish Revival style, the façade features gorgeous polychrome tile work, and the building is capped by a giant dome covered in 28,000 individual terra-cotta tiles. The auditorium accommodated over 2,700 people, who sat facing a giant proscenium arch inscribed with the Shri-

ners' greeting *"Es salaam eleikum"* ("Peace be with you" in Arabic).

~ The Depression took its toll on both organizations. By 1943, the Shriners had accumulated so much tax debt that the city took the building. However, Mayor Fiorello La Guardia and City Council President Newbold Morris had long championed the idea of the city running a performing arts center, and rather than tearing it down reopened the temple in 1943 as the City Center for the Performing Arts, which it remains to this day.

The Knights of Pythias held on to their headquarters until the 1950s. After that point, the building housed a number of tenants, including a recording studio—it is where Bill Haley and His Comets recorded "Rock Around the Clock" and altered music history. It was also for many years a branch of Manhattan Community College before being converted into a luxury apartment building in the early 1980s.

144 Alfred E. Smith: The Tammany President

In 1928, ninety-nine years after the *New-York Evening Post* christened the slum behind City Hall the "Five Points" [**37**], the neighborhood had its proudest moment when one of its own, Alfred E. Smith, received the nomination to be the Democratic candidate for president. This was a remarkable step forward: no Catholic had ever been nominated for the nation's highest office.

Smith was also the most successful product of Tammany Hall,

Alfred E. Smith

In one of the most lopsided victories of the era, Hoover beat Smith by nearly 20 percent. (Smith carried only eight states—not even taking New York.) Journalist Frederick Wile blamed Smith's loss on the three P's: Prohibition, prejudice and prosperity. Smith later blamed prosperity—he could not counter the robust economy of the 1920s and Hoover's promise of "a chicken in every pot and a car in every garage." However, to many observers, Prohibition was the foremost factor and, as historian Michael A. Lerner persuasively argues in *Dry Manhattan*, the "dry" Republicans essentially conflated Prohibition and anti-Catholic prejudice into one movement. Some took to calling the candidate "Al-cohol Smith." And, worried that Smith would owe greater allegiance to Rome than to America, Methodist bishop Adna Leonard summed up a widespread attitude that "no Governor can kiss the papal ring and get within a gunshot of the White House." A pastor in Oklahoma was even more blunt: "If you vote for Smith, you're voting against Christ and you'll all be damned."

In the end, however, Smith might have just been too New York for the job. To his supporters, his campaign theme song, "The Sidewalks of New York," conjured up images of the electric hustle and bustle of the city. It spoke to the same idea, later popularized in Kander and Ebb's "New York, New York," that if someone like Smith could "make it" in New York, he could "make it anywhere."

By contrast, to many Americans, "sidewalks of New York" represented everything to be feared in the nation's largest city. Anti–Saloon League member James Cannon, Jr.—another

the Democratic Party machine with a history that stretched all the way back to Aaron Burr [see 21] and included as its most famous leader William "Boss" Tweed [70]. By the time of Smith's first elected position—a seat in the New York State Assembly in 1903—Tammany Hall, headed by "Silent" Charlie Murphy, was an Irish-run institution and the Irish hold on politics in New York was solid.

In the state assembly, Smith quickly rose to prominence for his progressive views and his tough stance. When Franklin Delano Roosevelt later nominated Smith for president, he dubbed him "the Happy Warrior." In the assembly, Smith was instrumental in toughening workplace standards following the disastrous Triangle Shirtwaist Factory fire in 1911 [126]. He later became sheriff of New York County—a job that in those days afforded a lot of political exposure—and from there became governor of New York. By 1928, he was the acknowledged leader of the Democratic Party and easily won the nomination to face Republican Herbert Hoover.

Methodist bishop—cautioned that Smith "wants the kind of people [running the country] that you find today on the sidewalks of New York" such as "the Italians ..., the Poles, and Russian Jews. That kind has given us a stomach-ache." And Smith was not alone as a target of this prejudice. As a different detractor had written a year earlier about Fiorello La Guardia: "He's from New York, where there are few real Americans."

The sidewalks of New York in Smith's old Five Points neighborhood still reflect this same electricity—and the same jumble of ethnic groups, old and new, struggling to find their way in the city. His house at 25 Oliver Street, now on the National Register of Historic Places, sits just a block from his old church, St. James [see 43], which draws its congregation largely from the Hispanic residents of the nearby Alfred E. Smith housing project. The deli on the corner is Chinese but serves Southern fried chicken. Just up the street is the Mariner's Temple, the oldest Baptist church still standing in New York, and just beyond that Chatham Square, the gateway to the new, Fujianese Chinatown [179]. As the song says:

Things have changed since those times,
  some are up in "G"
Others they are wanderers but they all
  feel just like me
They'd part with all they've got, could
  they once more walk
With their best girl and have a twirl on
  the sidewalks of New York.

(In 1945, after Smith's death, he was memorialized in the naval vessel USS *Alfred E. Smith*; fitted into the ship's binnacle was a piece of New York City sidewalk.)

145 The Race to the Top: The Chrysler Building vs. the Manhattan Company

In 1929, the Chrysler Building was racing against the Manhattan Company on 40 Wall Street to best the height of the 792-foot Woolworth Building [132], which had since 1913 been the tallest building in the world.

New York has always looked to its skyline as a unique expression of its lofty place in the world. (Today, the 1,776-foot Freedom Tower being erected at the World Trade Center site brings new meaning to the idea of height alone as a symbol [182].)

But the race to make the Chrysler Building the tallest in the world was also a question of personal ego. In fact, two egos: those of Walter Chrysler, the automobile magnate and owner of the building, and his architect, William Van Alen. The building they were racing to beat, the Manhattan Company, was being designed by Van Alen's former partner and now bitter rival, H. Craig Severance.

The rivalry played out in the press. In March 1929, the announced height of the Chrysler Building was 809 feet, to be topped with a dome. The Manhattan Company rejoined by announcing it was to be 840 feet. By October, Chrysler's estimated final height had risen to 905 feet and—after a few last-minute drafting sessions by Severance and partner Yasuo Matsui—the Manhattan Company was revised upward to 925 feet.

But no one knew of the "vertex," a secret spire that Van Alen's crew had been assembling inside the steel

The Chrysler Building

the topping out of its 925-foot skyscraper, hailed as the world's tallest. Van Alen only let that sit for four days before revealing the truth—his vertex had not only catapulted the Chrysler Building 121 feet taller than his rival, but it was also 60 feet taller than the Eiffel Tower—and thus the tallest man-made structure ever built.

It was a short-lived victory. Within a year of the Chrysler Building's opening, the Empire State Building was completed [**148**], towering over the Chrysler Building by more than 200 feet. More important, the Empire State Building's 86th-floor observatory—the only part of a skyscraper most people would ever experience—far outstripped the Chrysler Building's 71st-floor deck, which closed after only 15 years in operation.

As for the poor Manhattan Company building, it does appear on lists of the tallest buildings in the world, but really only as a consolation prize. As a finished building it was never higher than Chrysler. It did, however, open for business one day ahead of Chrysler.

So, technically, for one day, it was the tallest building in the world.

dome since September. On October 23, 1929, it was set in place. No newspapers carried the story the next day; no newsreel cameras were on hand to record the momentous occasion. Chrysler and Van Alen were happy to keep their secret—if you can call a 185-foot spire crowning a 1,046-foot building a secret—until the time was right.

As Van Alen succinctly put it: "We'll lift the thing up and we won't tell 'em anything about it. And when it's up we'll just be higher, that's all."

Their timing couldn't have been worse. The next day, October 24, the Wall Street crash began, culminating five days later on Black Tuesday [**146**]. The race to be the tallest in the world had suddenly taken a backseat to more pressing matters. On November 12, the Manhattan Company held a media event to showcase

146 The Great Crash

The New York Stock Exchange [**114**], which had surged throughout the 1920s to a new high, lost close to 18 percent of its value in September 1929, but this had not been enough to truly shake investors' confidence. Financial prognosticator Irving Fisher, who believed the market was still on its way up, shrugged off the market's volatility as simply its way of "shaking out of the lunatic fringe."

The first sign of trouble came on Thursday, October 24—later called "Black Thursday"—when 12.9 million shares traded hands. (A normal trading day in the 1920s saw about 3 million shares traded.) The stock ticker, unable to keep up with the volume, fell 90 minutes behind and panic set in. A group of bankers hurriedly assembled at the Morgan bank and pooled $130 million to bail out the market (in a move similar to Morgan's intervention during the Panic of 1907 [**122**]). The market settled down when Stock Exchange vice president Richard Whitney strode onto the trading floor in the afternoon and placed an order for 10,000 shares of U.S. Steel. He proceeded to use the $130 million to prop up other stocks and the market closed on a note of confidence. Trading was mixed over the next two days (there was still Saturday morning trading in those days), allaying some fears, but on Monday the slide began. Nervous investors began selling at the start of the trading day and by the close, the market had lost 13 percent of its value—the worst one-day decline in the market's history and a record that would not be beaten until the 1987 crash [**176**], which was also on a "Black Monday."

On "Black Tuesday" the bottom fell out. A record 16.4 million shares traded that day and the market declined an additional 12 percent—the total losses for the week surpassed the annual federal budget. No pool of investors stepped in to prop up the market this time. By the end of the day, the Roaring Twenties were over, and though the country wouldn't realize it yet, it had been plunged into the worst economic downturn in its history, the Great Depression.

The stock market would continue to fall until November 13, when it hit a "false" bottom. General Electric, which had been trading at 396¼ in September, was now trading at 168⅛. However, despite a temporary recovery over the next few months, the market soon began to decline again and by the time it hit its real bottom in 1932, GE was trading at just 8½, a staggering loss of 98 percent of its value. It would take the Dow Jones Industrial Average 22 years to climb back to its September 1929 levels.

147 John D. Rockefeller's Riverside Church

One goal during the construction of the Cathedral of St. John the Divine [**100**] was that the church would have an ecumenical focus. One of New York's richest men, John D. Rockefeller, Jr., was intrigued. Rockefeller, the son and heir of the head of Standard Oil, was in charge of the family's wide-ranging philanthropic efforts and was particularly interested in forging strong interfaith bonds. He wrote a check to the cathedral for $500,000—which the church graciously accepted—and then asked for a role in determining how the money was spent. The cathedral demurred; Rockefeller was a Baptist and while it welcomed his cash, the church would always be run by Episcopalians.

Rebuffed, Rockefeller began working on plans with his own pastor, Harry Emerson Fosdick, to create a new ecumenical parish of their own. Fosdick was one of the most progressive clergymen of his day; his 1922 sermon "Shall the Fundamentalists Win?" excoriated conservative, evangelical churches and promoted his own liberal viewpoints. The sermon cost him his job at First Presbyterian Church, but earned him a fan in Rockefeller. Soon, ground was broken to move Rockefeller's Park Avenue Baptist Church* to Morningside Heights with Fosdick at the helm.

Riverside Church (right) and Grant's Tomb (left)

Initially, Rockefeller turned to St. John the Divine's architect, Ralph Adams Cram, for ideas, but ultimately chose a design by the firm of Allen & Collens drawn up in collaboration with Henry C. Pelton, whose work on the Park Avenue church Rockefeller admired. Unlike

the Episcopal cathedral, which still seemed barely started in 1926, Riverside Church would be built as a steel-frame skyscraper. Not only would a steel tower be necessary to support a massive carillon, which would include the world's largest tuned bell, the tower's 22 stories could be occupied by offices and meeting rooms. And, building as a skyscraper, the church could be completed in just four years.

From its site on Riverside Drive at 122nd Street, just next to Grant's Tomb [**106**], the church soared above the neighborhood and was visible for miles (unlike St. John the Divine, which couldn't really be seen from anywhere). The church opened in 1930, but Rockefeller continued to invest in the neighborhood, paying for nearby Claremont (now Sakura) Park to be relandscaped, helping the Union Theological Seminary with its new dormitory, creating a parish house, and—in 1954—funding the Interchurch Center (aka "the God Box") just south of the church on Riverside Drive.

The church is an eclectic mix of Gothic styles. Rockefeller had paid for Collens and Pelton to go on a fact-finding trip to Europe, and the church combines many of their favorite elements from French, Italian, and Spanish design. The church reflected Rockefeller's and Fosdick's humanist leanings, including representations of Kepler, Einstein—who was still very much alive—Darwin, and Galileo among the scientists carved above the west door. Inside, the glass was copied from Chartres—except for four priceless early 16th-century

---

*This was the outgrowth of the Norfolk Street Baptist Church [112].

Flemish windows that Rockefeller donated.

At the time of its opening, it was praised for its theology but damned for its looks, with critics complaining that one shouldn't simply slap Gothic details onto a modern building. While that criticism has softened over the years, it remains true that Riverside Church was one of the last conspicuous examples of revival architecture in the city. By the time the church was finished, Rockefeller was deep in the planning for his next project, the monumental—and staggeringly modern—Rockefeller Center [**149**].

148 The Empire State Building

When Alfred E. Smith [**144**] lost the presidential election of 1928, he found himself out of work for the first time in years and was immediately tapped by his campaign manager, John Jakob Raskob, to head the syndicate that was planning to build the world's tallest skyscraper.

Raskob had started his career as secretary to Pierre du Pont and had worked his way up to being vice president of both DuPont and General Motors. He had initially conceived the skyscraper as a GM Building to rival the Chrysler Building [**145**]. However, by the time Smith announced the project in August 1929, it had been christened the Empire State Building, which honored New York's nickname* and cashed in on Smith's own popular-

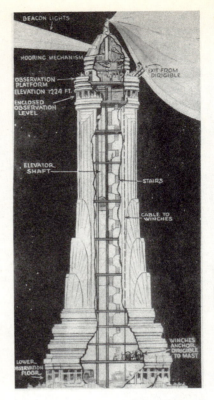

An early publicity drawing shows the Empire State Building's spire used as a dirigible mooring mast.

ity as governor. With Smith in place as the public face of the Empire State Corporation, Raskob hired architects Shreve, Lamb & Harmon to design the building. According to the oft-told story, Raskob met with William Lamb, set a No. 2 pencil on end to give him a general idea of what the building should look like, and said, "Bill, how high can you make it so that it won't fall down?"

The story of the Empire State

---

*New York has long called itself the Empire State because of its vast natural resources—and its overinflated sense of self-worth. Some claim it was George Washington, crossing into Manhattan in 1783 [17], who proclaimed the area "the seat of empire."

Building is often told in statistics—and they are stunning. After the demolition of the Waldorf-Astoria Hotel [see 150] in October 1929 and the laying of the foundations, construction took just a record-setting 410 days, during which time 10 million bricks and 60,000 tons of steel were set. The steel was shipped from the mills in Pennsylvania by train, then loaded into trucks and delivered in an ongoing procession to 34th Street. It was often being riveted into place less than eight hours after it had left the mill. Keeping to this tight schedule, the building rose at an average rate of a floor per day. As the Depression worsened, labor became both cheap and replaceable, and construction came in far below its $50 million budget.

Even before the Chrysler Building or the Manhattan Company were completed, Smith and Raskob had announced that the Empire State Building would be the world's tallest, coming in at "at least 1,000 feet." After William Van Alen revealed the Chrysler Building's vertex, it became imperative to make the Empire State Building taller without adding a "useless" spire. To that end, Smith announced in December 1929 that the top of the Empire State would house a mooring mast, 1,300 feet from the ground, for transatlantic dirigibles.

This was utter folly. Not only does a dirigible need to be anchored by both the nose and the tail (which is why they landed at airfields in New Jersey in the first place), the updrafts in Midtown were so strong that a zeppelin the length of two city blocks would have whipped around in the wind like a child's toy. More to the point, a dirigible's gondola was in the ship's center; people would never have been able to

(as pictured on the previous page in an early publicity drawing) exit from the helium-filled balloon straight into the 102nd-story waiting room.

In late September 1931, the *New York Evening Journal* completed the only successful dirigible mooring. At great danger to life and limb, it delivered a package of newspapers from the Financial District to the Empire State Building's roof. It looked great on the newsreel cameras, but would be the closest the mooring mast ever saw to real use.

When the building opened on May 1, 1931 (at a final height of 1,252 feet), it was prepared to house 25,000 tenants. It was not simply the tallest building the world: with over 2.1 million square feet of rentable floor space, all of the offices of the Chrysler Building *and* the Manhattan Company could fit inside with room left over. However, those tenants failed to materialize. Unlike the Chrysler Building, conveniently located next to the city's main commuter rail terminal, the Empire State Building was on a line with Penn Station, which in those days only served long-distance trains. People took to calling it "the Empty State Building," and Raskob, in a vain effort to dispel that notion, paid the custodial staff to go around and flip on the lights at night in vacant offices. The only part of the building that was profitable was the 86th-floor observatory; in its first year, the observatory brought in $1 million, almost as much as the combined rent rolls for the rest of the building.

The observatory—along with the building's starring role in *King Kong*, released in 1933—cemented its place not just as a tall building but as an exciting one. Even when the

World Trade Center's taller observatory opened in 1975 [170], many preferred the romance of the Empire State to the stark modernity of the Twin Towers. As Deborah Kerr said to Cary Grant in *An Affair to Remember*, "It's the closest thing to heaven we have in New York City!"

149 Rockefeller Center and the Making of Modern Midtown

It is easy to forget that opulent Rockefeller Center, New York's greatest skyscraper complex—and perhaps the greatest urban building project of the 20th century—was constructed during the depths of the Depression. To many, this symbolized just how rich John D. Rockefeller, Jr., was; in truth, Rockefeller had to keep a close eye on the project's finances and more than once he was afraid that the center would be his undoing.

What grew to be America's first multi-use business, retail, dining, and entertainment complex started as a plan to move the Metropolitan Opera from its old home on 39th Street to a newly constructed opera house. The old opera house was considered a great place to be seen by others in polite society, but an inadequate space to actually perform opera. Rockefeller, a longtime champion of the opera company, began negotiations with Columbia University to take over the lease on a tract of land in Midtown known as the Upper Estate.* By the time Rock-

Rockefeller Center

efeller had negotiated the lease and had bought out the various tenants already occupying the land, the stock market had crashed [146] and the Metropolitan Opera had backed out of the deal. This left Rockefeller with two choices: abandon the project, or seek to turn the area into a profit-making venture on his own.

The resulting complex was constructed between 1930 and 1939 and designed by a team known as Associated Architects, led by Raymond Hood (and including Wallace K. Harrison, Harvey Wiley Corbett, and J. André Fouilhoux). It was Hood who promoted the Radio Corporation of America (RCA) as an anchor tenant

---

*At one point, Columbia had considered the Upper Estate for its new campus before moving instead to Morningside Heights [101].

to replace the Metropolitan Opera, and the main building of the complex, 30 Rockefeller Center, became its headquarters;* this in turn lent the entire complex the nickname "Radio City," which today still exists in the title of the famous Radio City Music Hall. (The name Rockefeller Center was eventually adopted—over John D. Rockefeller's initial objections—in order to lure more high-paying tenants.)

The RCA Building (today called the GE Building), was set back from the center's main Fifth Avenue entrance by a sloping promenade and offset by a grand plaza. Its innovative setbacks were fashioned not only to comply with the 1916 Zoning Resolution [**135**], but to take maximum advantage of light and air, with no interior wall more than 30 feet from a window. On top, the observatory was reminiscent of the deck of a steamship, with Adirondack chairs facing the view. RCA's most famous tenant in the building was its broadcasting arm, NBC, which still has studios in the building for the *Nightly News, Saturday Night Live,* and—in a separate glassed-in studio just south of 30 Rockefeller Plaza—the *Today* show.

In front of the RCA Building, the three-level plaza (called by I. M. Pei the "most successful urban space in America") connects the 14 buildings of the complex and revolves around the two most famous parts of the center: the spot on the upper plaza where the annual Christmas tree is erected each November; and the sunken section of the plaza, which features the world-famous skating rink.

Plans called for the sunken plaza to lead to the Sixth Avenue subway (which wouldn't be completed until 1940) and the innovative underground concourse of shops and restaurants, which was, for all intents, America's first enclosed indoor shopping mall, and which was initially a flop.

By 1935 (with the buildings not even finished yet) over 60,000 people were visiting the plaza every day—yet only a few thousand ventured downstairs into the "catacombs," and the retailers there were having a hard time paying their rents. To solve this problem, Rockefeller Center inaugurated the skating rink on Christmas Day 1936, and soon the rink became one of the center's top attractions. In 1940, a roller rink was added in warm weather; today, a restaurant occupies the space when it is too hot to ice skate.

Presiding over the rink is Paul Manship's statue of Prometheus stealing fire from the gods. Derided in its day as garish and out-of-place, it has become so famous that in his history of the center, *Great Fortune*, Daniel Okrent supposes it is the fourth-most-famous statue in America.** Considering its location above the rink and below the Christmas tree, it certainly has to be among the most photographed pieces of American art.

---

*It was in its Rockefeller Center era that RCA was run by David Sarnoff, one of the best-known success stories of New York's Lower East Side [see 95].

**The top three are the Statue of Liberty [93], Mount Rushmore, and Abraham Lincoln at the Lincoln Memorial.

Paul Manship's statue of Prometheus at Rockefeller Center

The skating rink and plaza are reached from Fifth Avenue via a promenade cut between two low-slung buildings on Fifth—the British Empire Building and La Maison Française. These were part of Rockefeller's plan to make the center more than just a commercial project. Instead, he hoped that by bringing together the international business community in one place, he would foster mutual understanding and promote a common cause—that Rockefeller Center would succeed on a commercial and cultural level where the League of Nations had failed. Thus, in addition to the French and British buildings, there was an Italian building, and— had Hitler's rise to power not prevented it—there would have been a German building. (In fact, the Italian building had to undergo a major face-lift after Mussolini, who had personally approved the plans for it, became America's enemy. In 1940, Attilio Piccirilli's glass sculpture *Advance Forever, Eternal Youth* was deemed too Fascist and removed from the entrance to the Palazzo d'Italia.)

Rockefeller did not want these buildings to merely have vague associations with their home countries: he hoped to lure a mix of commercial tenants and government offices, creating a miniature European complex along Fifth Avenue. The buildings had varied success; only France moved its consular offices to La Maison Française and though the consulate later moved, the building is still the most committed to its original intention.

~ The Sixth Avenue side of the center was given over to entertainment. Originally, the complex had two theaters: the RKO Roxy Theatre for movies and Radio City Music Hall for live shows.

Both were the brainchild of showman S. L. "Roxy" Rothafel and, at first, neither was a success. Radio City famously opened on December 27, 1932, with Roxy's overblown, everything-but-the-kitchen-sink extravaganza. It began with *Symphony of the Curtains*, which showcased—you guessed it—the curtains, included among its many acts Martha Graham's cutting-edge *Choric Dance for an Antique Greek Tragedy,* and ended, five hours after it began, with the vaudeville duo Weber and Fields, who had not been cutting-edge since about 1895. The most famous opening-night act was the Rockettes. Originally a St. Louis dance ensemble called the Rockets, they were discovered by Roxy Rothafel and moved to New York under the name the Roxyettes. They became the most popular draw at the theater and, in honor of their new home, they became the Rockettes in 1934.

To keep the theater from being a laughingstock—and from losing money—Radio City began a policy of combining live shows with film, a tradition that continued into the late 1970s. This seriously undercut the RKO Roxy, which was to have been the center's sole film venue. The Roxy struggled to find an audience and was sold to NBC in 1950; it was demolished in 1954.

⁓ Perhaps what is most alluring about Rockefeller Center is the scope of its public art. From the famous statues, like *Prometheus,* to the more obscure detailed reliefs atop the cornices of the international buildings, it is the most completely realized Art Deco/Art Moderne building complex ever designed.

Few remember today that the decorative scheme revolved around a theme called "New Frontiers," which itself was an outgrowth of an idea by master epigram-maker Hartley Burr Alexander that the center focus on *Homo Faber*: "Man the Builder." The variety of art—both in style and quality—led many to decry the center's aesthetics. Cur-

mudgeonly architecture critic Lewis Mumford of *The New Yorker* opened his first piece for that magazine in 1931 lambasting Rockefeller Center's "hit-or-miss, helter-skelter," "Cloudcuckooland" architecture. And, indeed, one would be hard-pressed to understand the deep meaning in some of the pieces.

For example, the entrance to 1250 Avenue of the Americas features a mosaic by Barry Faulkner with Thought (via the written and spoken word) banishing Poverty and Ignorance by the use of Hygiene and Publicity. It is a sign of the influence of Rockefeller's PR guru, Ivy Lee, that the main conduit of the written word is Publicity.

The most discussed work of art in the entire complex is the one that no longer exists. At the urging of John D. Rockefeller's wife, Abby—a founder of the Museum of Modern Art—and his son, Nelson (later governor of New York and Gerald Ford's vice president), the mural for the lobby of 30 Rockefeller Plaza was entrusted to Diego Rivera. His theme, lifted straight from Hartley Burr Alexander's *Homo Faber*, was "Man at the Crossroads Looking with Uncertainty but with Hope and High Vision to the Choosing of a Course Heading to a New and Better Future." Work began in March 1933; by April, observers could see that Rivera's fresco contained a portrait bust of Vladimir Lenin. When asked to remove it, Rivera demurred, offering instead to add Abraham Lincoln as a counterbalance. A month later, Rivera was dismissed from his job and the still unfinished mural covered over. José Maria Sert, who had already been hired to do other decorative work in the building, replaced

Rivera's fresco with *American Progress, the Triumph of Man's Accomplishments Through Physical and Mental Labor.* Perhaps taking his cue from Rivera, the composition—which shows industrial laborers working with heavy machinery—prominently features Abraham Lincoln, stovepipe hat and all.

Other notable artwork at the center includes the roundels representing Music, Drama, and Dance on the side of Radio City Music Hall by Hildreth Maier; Isamu Noguchi's *News* on the Associated Press Building; and Lee Lawrie's massive statue of Atlas, which stands on Fifth Avenue opposite St. Patrick's Cathedral [**83**].

∼ In the end, Rockefeller Center is important both for what it is and what it created: a true Midtown business district. While the opening of the IRT subway [**119**] and the Times Tower [**124**] had made business in Midtown a possibility, it was the triumvirate of the Empire State Building on 34th Street [**148**], the Chrysler Building on 42nd Street [**145**], and Rockefeller Center that cemented Midtown as the place for companies to be in the center of things. As New York entered its post–World War II era, Midtown would finally surpass the Financial District as the true business center of the city.

150 The Waldorf-Astoria Hotel and FDR's Secret Elevator

One of the poshest hotels in New York, the Waldorf-Astoria (or, as it is officially styled, the "Waldorf=Astoria") began as two separate ventures spurred by family one-upmanship. The first of the two, the Waldorf, opened in 1893, on Fifth Avenue at 33rd Street. It was built by William Waldorf Astor next to the home of his aunt, Caroline Schermerhorn Astor, who was the doyenne of New York high society. (It was Caroline Astor's ballroom that held 400 people, thus lending the name "the Four Hundred" to New York's high society.) The story is often told that William Astor didn't care for his aunt and built the 13-story hotel out of spite, hoping the crowds of hotel guests would be a nuisance. However, Mrs. Astor was already contemplating a move to upper Fifth Avenue and, indeed, the area around 34th Street was no longer very fashionable. Soon Mrs. Astor's home had been replaced by the family-built Astoria Hotel and in 1897 the two were connected via Peacock Alley (that's what the "=" in the name stands for) to become the Waldorf-Astoria hotel.

The hotel was a great success and was soon a fixture of the New York social scene. However, by the late 1920s the economic advantages of skyscraper construction prompted the hotel to sell its land to the Empire State Building [**148**] and buy new property on Park Avenue; the papers were signed on October 29, 1929, the day of the Great Crash [**146**].

The new building, a 42-story skyscraper designed by Schultze & Weaver, took up an entire city block facing Park Avenue between 49th and 50th street. With 2,200 rooms, it was the largest hotel in the world—its massive four-story ballroom could accommodate 6,000 people. It was also one of the city's first Art Deco hotels, designed throughout in warm metallic tones, including elaborate nickeled bronze elevator grates, Louis Rigal's complex, 148,000-piece mosaic, *Wheel of Life* set into the lobby floor, and soaring bronze cupolas done in high Art Moderne style. Inside, the building showcased an odd mix of eras (*The New Yorker* critic Lewis Mumford called it, "Modernism, revivalism, eclecticism, and plain gimcrackery"), with some interior designs conspicuously echoing the old hotel on 34th Street. This included the immense eight-faced lobby clock from the 1893 Chicago World's Fair featuring portraits of American presidents and Queen Victoria.

The most famous tenants of the hotel were presidents of the United States. Beginning with Herbert Hoover, every U.S. president has stayed at the Waldorf, and this has given rise to one of the most persistent Waldorf myths: that there is an elevator going from a railroad track beneath the hotel directly to the Presidential Suite.

The story got started because there is, indeed, a railroad siding beneath the hotel. Built entirely on land owned by Grand Central Terminal [131], the hotel sits above a spur track, perhaps originally used for holding trains outside the station. In 1929, the *New York Times* reported that this track was being converted into a private siding for the hotel and that

Guests with private rail cars may have them routed directly to the hotel instead of to the Pennsylvania Station or the Grand Central Terminal, and may leave their cars at a special elevator which will take them directly to their suites or to the lobby.

Whether this was actually the plan or just the reporter's overindulgent imagination is unclear. By the time the hotel opened in 1931, no provisions had been made to connect the siding directly to the hotel. Instead, an elevator used by Grand Central employees led to 50th Street, next to the Waldorf's parking garage.

Over the decades, the story of the hotel's "secret" entrance became entrenched. The most popular retelling said that the siding was particularly used by Franklin Delano Roosevelt so that he could be whisked from his special rail car to the Presidential Suite without being seen—and thus without revealing his inability to walk, a tightly guarded secret.

However, the elevator led only to the street, not the suite, and transportation historian Joseph Brennan has thoroughly researched the issue and can find no examples of FDR even using the elevator to get to the street. In theory, the president's Pierce-Arrow touring car could have been offloaded from the siding and brought him to 50th Street, thus allowing him to privately get from the train to the car without anyone seeing him being lifted in. But evidence for this ever happening is close to nonexistent.

The siding was used for occasional photo ops for visiting dignitaries. When General Douglas MacArthur moved into the hotel in 1951, he exited his train on what by then was consistently referred to as the "presidential siding" and posed for pictures before heading up to the hotel. Presumably other VIPs, including presidents, could have used the siding, riding the elevator to the street and then sneaking in a side entrance to the hotel. Alas, because they would have done this to preserve their privacy, there is no evidence to prove it either way.

151 Robert Moses 1: Sheep Meadow and the Great Lawn

There is perhaps no figure in New York City's history more likely to set off a heated debate than Robert Moses. Everyone, it seems, has an opinion about "the Power Broker" (as biographer Robert Caro called him), and he is vilified and praised in equal measure—often in the same breath.

It is certainly true that no single figure influenced the shape of New York City in the 20th century as much as Moses did. As a protégé of Governor Alfred E. Smith [**144**], Moses created the New York State Council of Parks (today's State Parks Commission) and became president of the Long Island State Park Commission. When Fiorello La Guardia was elected the city's mayor in 1933, he asked Moses to run the city's Parks Department; Moses agreed, on the stipulation that he be able to keep his state jobs and that he be allowed to turn the Parks Department into the far-reaching bureaucracy that it is today.

First on Moses's list of projects was replacing Central Park's Casino, a fancy restaurant that had been built on a bluff overlooking the Mall [**71**]. La Guardia and Moses had two primary objections to the Casino: one was that it that it catered to the city's wealthy residents at the expense of the majority of park

users. (In an era when a cup of coffee at a Horn and Hardart Automat cost a nickel, the Casino charged 40 cents.) Secondly—and perhaps more important—the Casino had been a favorite haunt of disgraced mayor Jimmy Walker [**142**], who spent his evenings drinking there during Prohibition, his mistress on his arm. This irked Moses, who firmly believed that Walker had politically betrayed Governor Smith, and he wanted to see the "nightclub" mayor's hangout not just closed down but physically removed from the park.

To remove the Casino, Moses needed to find an alternative spot for an eatery. And, since public sentiment opposed building anything new in the park, he instead came up with a clever plan to convert the 1870 sheepfold at 66th Street into a restaurant. First, he needed to rid the park of its sheep, which were loaded in trucks in 1934 and sent to join their brethren in Prospect Park. This was more than just expedience: the ruins of the old Croton Receiving Reservoir [**46**]—today's Great Lawn—had become a notorious shantytown during the Depression and Moses may well have been concerned that the sheep were going to become someone's dinner. Rumors also abounded that the sheep were inbred. Whatever the real reason, the removal of the sheep meant that the sheepfold, constructed by Jacob Wrey Mould [**see 68**], could begin conversion into a "popular priced" restaurant; it opened October 20, 1934, as Tavern on the Green.

Immediately, the restaurant ran into trouble. The concessionaire running it was rumored to be a crony of Moses. The "dress rehearsal" the night before the opening was an invi-

Central Park's Sheep Meadow

tation-only $25-a-plate affair—not exactly indicative of a restaurant for the masses. After it opened, the confusing pricing scheme (where some items rose in price as the day went on and others fell) engendered suspicion. And while Moses was adamant that Tavern on the Green's menu was well within reach of the ordinary park user, a cup of coffee was a dime (a pot of coffee ran 25 cents) and the set menu was $1.50—a princely sum in the depths of the Depression.

⌁ In 1934, Moses also moved forward with a plan that had been formulated by the American Society of Landscape Architects a few years earlier to convert the remnants of the Croton Receiving Reservoir, or "lower" reservoir, into a lawn.* Even before the lower reservoir was drained in 1930, people had come up with ideas to fill the space. One scheme, put forth by Thomas Hastings around the same time he was building the New York Public Library [**128**], was to construct an elaborate homage to the 1893 Columbian Exposition, with Frederick MacMonnies's monumental fountain from the fair gracing a central lagoon. Others suggested a cross-park promenade connecting the Metropolitan Museum of Art and the American Museum of Natural History [**80**], perhaps lined with statuary of great Americans. And, after World War I,

*There is still a reservoir in the park—today called the Jacqueline Kennedy Onassis Reservoir—which was built by Frederick Law Olmsted and Calvert Vaux during the park's initial phase of construction. This was known as the "new" or "upper" reservoir. The original 1842 structure, which predated the park's construction, was generally called the "lower" reservoir.

a proposal was advanced to honor fallen American soldiers by re-creating Flanders Fields—complete with trenches.

However, Parks Commissioner Moses was facing a more immediate problem than aesthetics. Inside the empty reservoir, a giant "Hooverville" had sprung up, filled with some of the city's homeless men. While not the largest encampment in New York, the Hooverville in Central Park was a particular eyesore. In 1933, Moses evicted the men and began the two-year process of converting the reservoir into the Great Lawn. The original drainage area of the old reservoir was landscaped into Turtle Pond with the 13-acre lawn stretching north toward the upper reservoir. Originally the lawn and the upper reservoir would have been connected, but a planned promenade connecting the two was scrapped.

152 Abyssinian Baptist, the Largest Church in America

Today, the most recognized church in Harlem is Abyssinian Baptist, which is also the second-oldest black congregation in New York.* The church was founded in 1808, when black parishioners at First Baptist Church broke away in protest against the church's discriminatory policies. Like many churches of the day [see 36], First Baptist had a separate Negroes Gallery, where black parishioners—free and enslaved—sat segregated from the rest of the congregation.

A group of Ethiopian (then called Abyssinian) merchants visiting New York City deplored this situation and encouraged the black congregants to create their own house of worship. Initially in Five Points [37], the congregation later moved to Waverly Place in Greenwich Village and then to Midtown.

At the same time that Harlem was blossoming as a black neighborhood [127], Abyssinian's new pastor, Adam Clayton Powell, Sr., proposed that the church move to 138th Street; with the promised tithe of 10 percent of their income from 3,000 congregants, the church was able to break ground on a new building in 1922 and begin worshipping in Harlem in 1923. The new building was designed in a neo-Gothic style by Charles W. Bolton, one of the 20th century's most prolific ecclesiastical architects; by the time he died in 1942, he had designed over 500 churches across the country.

By 1935, Abyssinian had grown into the largest Protestant church in the world, with over 12,000 members. To accommodate such a large membership, *Time* magazine reported that the church

holds three or four services every Sunday, runs two Sunday schools with 1,000 members each. Also it maintains a Community House with gymnasium and roof garden, Home Economics and Health Education departments, a weekday Church School for children, the nation's largest Daily Vacation Bible School, an employment

---

*The oldest black congregation, AME Zion, was founded in 1801. Today, it is a block away from Abyssinian Baptist on 137th Street.

agency, a Music School, a Dramatic School and 53 clubs and auxiliaries.

The year after this article was published, Adam Clayton Powell, Sr., stepped down as pastor in favor of his son, Adam Clayton Powell, Jr., who was fast becoming a central political figure in New York City [171].

153 Music, *Macbeth*, and the Harlem Renaissance

The influx of black residents to Harlem in the first decades of the 20th century came not only from other areas of New York [127], but also from other American cities, from the Deep South during the Great Migration, and from the Caribbean, which has always been a significant source of the city's black population. By the mid-1920s, Harlem had established itself as a black cultural center, and the terms "Harlem Renaissance" and "New Negro Movement" were being applied to a flowering of not just music and literature, but also of political awareness among urban black New Yorkers.

In 1922, Jamaican-born poet and novelist Claude McKay published *Harlem Shadows*, one of the first collections of poetry by a black author to be released by a major publisher. Suddenly, great attention focused on Harlem's literary output. However, what garnered the most attention was a book by white author Carl Van Vechten, *Nigger Heaven*, which drew crowds of curious white tourists to Harlem, much as Charles Dickens's *American Notes* had done for Five Points nearly a century earlier [45].

The primary goal for white audiences was to hear black music. The Savoy Ballroom, the Cotton Club, Small's Paradise, Connie's Inn, the Renaissance Ballroom, and countless other clubs—large and small—drew crowds eager to hear jazz. In 1927, Duke Ellington's band became the house band at the Cotton Club, cementing both his career and the club's popularity. The Apollo Theater, originally a whites-only burlesque house, reopened in 1934 with "Jazz à la Carte" and soon inaugurated its famed Amateur Night. One early winner, Ella Fitzgerald, became a fixture on the Harlem music scene with a regular gig at the Savoy Ballroom. By the mid-1930s, every prominent black musician in America—including Eubie Blake, Louis Armstrong, Bessie Smith, Fletcher Henderson, and Dinah Washington—was performing in Harlem. Indeed, many of these musicians could perform nowhere else, as strict musicians' union codes kept them from downtown theaters because of their race.

On Seventh Avenue (now Adam Clayton Powell Jr. Boulevard) between 131st and 132nd streets was an old elm tree nicknamed "the Tree of Hope" that performers would visit before shows to rub for good luck. In 1934, the street was widened and the tree cut down, with pieces being sold off for souvenirs. One piece was taken to the Apollo Theater (where it remains to this day) and another was taken by Bill "Bojangles" Robinson to the nearby Lafayette Theatre. This piece was reinstalled in the boulevard's median circa 1941. It could not, however, withstand the elements and in 1972 a sculpture—*Tree of Hope III* by Algernon Miller—went up in its place. In 2007, a new Tree of Hope was planted in front of the Williams CME Church, once home to the Lafayette Theatre.

The Lafayette opened in 1912 and a year later became the first theater in New York to desegregate, selling orchestra seats at the same price to both black and white audience members. The theater became nationally famous in 1936 when 20-year-old Orson Welles directed an all-black cast in the WPA's Negro Theater production of *Macbeth*. Set in 19th-century Haiti, with the weird sisters recast as witch doctors, the play was soon dubbed "the Voodoo *Macbeth*." It played 10 sold-out weeks in Harlem before transferring to Broadway, and it opened up Harlem to an all-new audience. However, like every place in America, the Depression was taking its toll, and as World War II loomed, the size of the audiences in Harlem began to shrink. It also didn't help that the repeal of Prohibition [**139**] in 1933 meant that nightclubs and speakeasies were no longer the only reliable sources of alcohol. And, despite the success of Welles's *Macbeth*, a riot in Harlem in 1935, spurred by the racial discrimination of what were still largely white shopkeepers and landlords, marked the neighborhood as dangerous in some people's eyes.

Today, traces of the Harlem Renaissance can be hard to find. The Apollo Theater on 125th Street has been beautifully refurbished and is a hub along the neighborhood's busiest street. The Lafayette Theatre still stands, though it has been much altered by its current tenant. The great nightclubs are all gone, as well. A business trading under the name Cotton Club has set up shop on the west end of 125th Street, but it is not the place that Duke Ellington called home. And Small's Paradise on 135th Street, once famed for its dancing waiters who would do the Charleston on roller skates while delivering Chinese food and liquor to the tables, has become an International House of Pancakes.

154 The Art of the Works Progress Administration

During the Depression, thousands of artists and writers were put to work by the federal government as part of the Works Progress Administration, which ultimately provided millions of jobs to Americans across the country.

In New York, the Federal Writers Project embarked on numerous books—the city's municipal archives hold documentation for 41 manuscripts, finished and unfinished—including the *New York City Guide*, the first truly comprehensive, modern guide to the city, along with books as varied as *A Maritime History of New York* and *The Jewish Landsmanschaften* [**see 99**], written in Yiddish. The Federal Theater Project was famous for its all-black "Voodoo *Macbeth*" [**153**] and the controversial musical *The Cradle Will Rock*.

But the artists that best left their imprint on the city were painters, who created a host of murals—often in fast-drying and potentially impermanent fresco—in buildings old and new. Many of these were on government property and were overseen by the Treasury Department's Section of Fine Arts, a parallel body to the

WPA's Federal Artists Program. In New York, the grandest of these "Section" murals are those by Reginald Marsh in the rotunda of the Alexander Hamilton U.S. Custom House [**123**].

Marsh, born in Paris, where both his parents were working as artists, but raised in Nutley, New Jersey, was a keen chronicler of city life. His 16 Custom House murals depict the dominance of American shipping; the eight larger panels show the stages of a steamship's entrance into New York harbor, from its approach to the Narrows to its discharge of passengers and cargo. In one panel, the ship pauses to take on the press so that they can interview an arriving celebrity— Greta Garbo. Eight smaller panels depict famous explorers, such as Giovanni da Verrazzano and Henry Hudson [**2**].

Just before work was to begin in September 1937, Marsh received word that Joseph P. Kennedy, U.S. maritime commissioner, objected to the fact that two prominent ships in the panorama were foreign vessels— the *Queen Mary* and the *Normandie* [**see 51**]. Kennedy wrote that Marsh should instead depict "the new passenger liner which we will probably commence building"; Marsh, however, kept the ships intact. He allegedly "smudged" the word *Normandie* to make it harder to read, but didn't do a very good job, as it is still perfectly legible. The work—painted

almost entirely by Marsh himself during backbreaking 14-hour days— was finished by the end of December 1937.

Manhattan's other most famous extant WPA murals stand on the third-floor rotunda of the New York Public Library [**128**]. Here Edward Laning's *Story of the Recorded Word* tells the history of printed communication from a wild-eyed Moses bringing the Ten Commandments to a depiction of contemporary

The *Normandie* by Reginald Marsh from the interior of the Alexander Hamilton U.S. Custom House

New York. Of particular interest is this last panel, which shows Ottmar Mergenthaler, inventor of the modern Linotype machine, resting while a gentleman in evening attire (who may or may not be *New York Tribune* editor Whitelaw Reid) reads the paper. Behind them a newsboy hawks a copy of the paper on "Newspaper Row" at the foot of the Brooklyn Bridge.

At the very bottom right corner of the mural is Laning's dedication to his patron, I. N. Phelps Stokes, who helped him get the commission. The note rests on two drawings; one is a copy of the oldest extant depiction of Manhattan [see 4], which represents Stokes's great contribution to New York history, his magnificent six-volume history, *The Iconography of Manhattan Island*, still one of the most valuable reference works ever written about the city. Lurking beneath the map is a blueprint, which alludes to Stokes's earlier career as an architect. (His best-known work is St. Paul's Chapel at Columbia University, one of the few early buildings not part of Charles McKim's master plan [see 101].)

The largest WPA mural in the city was *Flight,* completed in 1940 by James Brooks at the Marine Air Terminal at LaGuardia Airport. Painted over in the 1950s—perhaps because of its supposed leftist bias—it was uncovered in 1980 and restored to its former glory. The Marine Air Terminal is the only working terminal in the country left from the grand early era of commercial flight.

155 The City and World War II

On December 7, 1941, the Japanese bombed Pearl Harbor and America entered the war; for New Yorkers, changes to daily life came suddenly in ways both large and small.

The Brooklyn Navy Yard at Wallabout Bay went into overtime production and lifted its ban on female workers. The yard had been producing naval vessels since 1820, including such famed vessels as the Civil War–era USS *Monitor,* the USS *Maine*—whose destruction in 1898 led to the

Spanish-American War [133]—and the USS *Arizona*, destroyed by the Japanese at Pearl Harbor. At the height of the war, nearly 70,000 men and women worked at the factory; in 1944, they finished the USS *Missouri*, the ship on which the final surrender would be signed between the Americans and the Japanese.

Immediately after the attack on Pearl Harbor, the government closed the observatory atop the Woolworth Building [132] for fear that the vantage it gave of New York Harbor was too strategically important. Later in the war, the copper cladding on the Woolworth's roof was removed and melted down for the war effort; today, the roof is painted green instead. Just seven months earlier, President Roosevelt had tapped Mayor La Guardia to be head of the Office of Civilian Defense; on December 9, La Guardia immediately issued pointers on what to do in the unlikely scenario that the Japanese attacked the city. (He also reprimanded "all persons who have been sneering and jeering at defense activities.") On December 11, Germany declared war on the United States, bringing the possibility of an attack on the city into sharper focus. An antiaircraft battery was set up on the Great Hill in Central Park, near the spot where Blockhouse No. 1, a battery from the War of 1812, still stands [27].

Windows of prominent buildings, such as the New York Public Library [128], Grand Central Terminal [131], and the neon signs of Times Square were blacked out in case of air raids. In 1942, the Rainbow Room atop 30 Rockefeller Plaza [149] closed as part of a move to curtail ambient light—not so much to guard against the Luftwaffe, but in an attempt to darken the harbor so that merchant vessels would be less easily targeted by German U-boats.

However, in other ways the city's lights didn't dim at all. Screaming girls stood in line for hours in December 1942 to get a ticket to see Frank Sinatra at the Paramount in Times Square. Rodgers and Hammerstein's *Oklahoma!* opened at the St. James Theater and became a smash hit, running for over 2,000 performances; in 1944, the Leonard Bernstein/Jerome Robbins collaboration *On the Town* depicted a madcap day in the life of three sailors on shore leave in New York. Indeed, the city was awash in military personnel—the public phone booths in Times Square recorded over 350,000 calls per day, mostly servicemen calling home. As a service to those on leave, the American Theatre Wing opened its first Stage Door Canteen in the basement of a theater on 44th Street in 1942.

Here, enlisted men—no officers allowed—could eat, see a show, and dance, often with celebrities. Lauren Bacall volunteered on Monday nights, often spending the entire evening dancing; Broadway stars Katharine Cornell and Helen Hayes bussed tables; Alfred Lunt even took out the garbage. Onstage, everyone from Benny Goodman to Ethel Merman performed, and on an average night over 2,000 GIs passed through the door. The Stage Door Canteen (later immortalized in a film of the same name) operated until October 1945, by which time the number of active servicemen in the city had dwindled to the point that the club was no longer necessary. Just a little over two months earlier, at 7:03 p.m. on August 14, 1945, the "zipper" on the Times Tower announced, "Official—Truman Announces Japanese Surrender," causing the thousands of people in Times Square to break out into a joyous celebration.

PART 7

The City Since World War II, 1946–present

The last six decades in New York's story (much of it not quite history yet) have been marked by tremendous cycles of what historian Max Page has called the city's "creative destruction"—a constant need to build, to change, to reinvent itself, even when that reinvention isn't always necessary or in the city's best interests.

What is perhaps most striking is that, with the advent of, first, television and then the Internet, what is happening in New York—which has long thought of itself as the center of the universe—is now instantly broadcast to the world, thus reaffirming the city's sense of its own self-worth.

(This became apparent to us a few years ago when there was a minor construction accident near our apartment—the sort of thing that once upon a time wouldn't have warranted even a paragraph in a 19th-century penny paper—and someone called to see if we were okay because they'd seen it on the BBC Web site.)

At no time was worldwide interest in New York more noticeable than on September 11, 2001, when hijacked airplanes rammed into the Twin Towers of the World Trade Center. This event has become an instant modern touchstone, our generation's Kennedy assassination. When we lead people on tours of Lower Manhattan, they inevitably ask, "Where were you when the World Trade Center was attacked?" While this question is asked out of genuine interest, it always leads those asking the question to tell us where *they* were—at home watching the television; on the way to work; awakened by a phone call; or, in the case of people in, say, Australia, already in bed for the night. In an instant, New York became the world's city and the shock and sorrow over that tragedy became a point of connection between us and people across the globe.

But the media spotlight doesn't always work in the city's favor. Back in the 1970s, when its finances were failing, a serial killer was stalking the streets, and a blackout plunged it into looting and arson, the city became the butt of one big, national joke. "Once More, With Looting," read *Time* magazine's cover story on the blackout.

As crime continued to spiral out of control, tourism declined; those who did come went only to circumscribed, tourist-friendly areas. Even today, with New York trumpeting its status as the safest big city in America, the stigma of those years is hard to shake—the media's imprint on people's minds is just too strong.

But times have not been all bad, as the chapters in this section show. (Even in the midst of the summer of 1977, contributors to the *New York Times*'s venerable "Metropolitan Diary" were good-naturedly submitting poems about the blackout, overheard bits of conversation between purse snatchers, and zingers about X-rated movies.)

New York in the 1950s became an incubator of innovative architecture and design, from groundbreaking Midtown skyscrapers to Frank Lloyd Wright's Guggenheim Museum. The arts have flourished in the city as never before, from big Broadway shows to readings at tiny Greenwich Village coffeehouses. In the 1960s, the city gave us Bob Dylan; in the 1970s, the Ramones and punk rock; in the 1980s, Madonna. Never in the city's history has it drawn a larger or more diverse group of artists, from singers to dancers to painters to multimedia performance artists. And despite the occasional sigh that New York "isn't what it used to be" creatively (a lament that has been heard going back at least a century, if not more), the city remains the undisputed creative center of the country. Yes, other cities have great theater, museums, flourishing art scenes, and top-notch music venues. But no city has quite the confluence of them that New York does.

156 The UN Secretariat and General Assembly

As World War II ended, the leading Allied powers—the United States, Great Britain, the Republic of China, the Soviet Union, and France—met to draft the provisions for the United Nations, a far-reaching global organization to help maintain prosperity and security in the postwar era. Fifty countries signed the UN charter in June 1945, and it was ratified just four months later. The United States formally requested that the United Nations make its home in America, and John D. Rockefeller, Jr., donated the cash necessary to buy the 18-acre site facing Turtle Bay on Manhattan's East Side. (Rockefeller's son Nelson had first proposed giving 1,000 acres from their family estate, Kykuit, in Westchester County, but this was deemed too remote from New York City.)

To reflect the spirit of the United Nations, the main buildings of the new complex were not chosen by juried competition, but were instead to be built by an international committee headed by Wallace K. Harrison, one of the architects of Rockefeller Center [**149**]. The biggest name on the panel was Swiss-French architect Le Corbusier, the world's leading proponent of International Style architecture. It was Le Corbusier's plan, "Project 23A," that ultimately provided the starting point for the two main buildings at the United Nations, the General Assembly and the Secretariat.

The Secretariat, a 39-story rectangle of glass, was the first starkly mod-

The United Nations General Assembly and Secretariat buildings

ernist building in the city as well as the first to have a sheer glass curtain wall. The dark green Thermopane glass was chosen to regulate heat; while Le Corbusier wanted windows that opened, Harrison overruled him, making the building entirely climate-controlled. (This idea would be followed and expanded on by Lever House and the Seagram Building [**158**].)

In contrast to the Secretariat building, the low-slung, bow-faced General Assembly inspired nothing—except perhaps derision then and nostalgia today. Lewis Mumford, writing in *The New Yorker,* called it the UN's "architectural anticlimax" and added: "The architects who created it would have a hard time defending its exterior even if they had been designing a modern motion-picture palace, which is the only thing it resembles."

Today's critics liken the experience of visiting the building to stepping into a time warp. Like Eero Saarinen's TWA terminal at Kennedy Airport, opened in 1962, the General Assembly building is a perfect symbol of its era, with protruding, curved balconies and art by Fernand Léger that looks completely and utterly of its time.

157 Robert Moses 2: The Brooklyn-Queens Expressway

Starting with his appointment as New York's parks commissioner in 1934 [see 151], Robert Moses's power in city government seemed to grow exponentially. By the end of World War II, he not only continued as head of the city and state parks departments, he also ran the Jones Beach Parkway Authority, the Bethpage State Park Authority, and the increasingly important Triborough Bridge and Tunnel Authority. In addition, he was New York City's construction coordinator, chairman of the Mayor's Committee on Slum Clearance, *and* the New York City planning commissioner. This meant (in the popular imagination, at least) that if you wanted something built, you had to go through Moses—and

if Moses wanted something built, he would go through you.

But despite his reputation for combativeness, not every Robert Moses project was greeted with anger. Indeed, in the years following the war, the building of the Brooklyn Heights section of the Brooklyn-Queens Expressway (BQE) was seen as a victory for the residents of Brooklyn Heights.

Construction on the BQE had begun in the 1930s with a section that included the Kosciuszko Bridge, which connects Brooklyn and Queens over the Newtown Creek. By the 1940s, Robert Moses was hard at work on plans for a Brooklyn-Battery Bridge, spanning New York Harbor from Lower Manhattan to Brooklyn;* extending the BQE south to the bridge's terminus seemed like a logical next step. However, the proposed path of the BQE through Brooklyn Heights—along congested Hicks Street—would have further divided a neighborhood that was already feeling hemmed in by Moses's other local neighborhood project, Cadman Plaza. (Built in stages in the 1940s and 1950s, Cadman Plaza was a dubious slum-clearance project designed to create a space that, in Moses's words, would be to Brooklyn as "the great cathedral and opera plazas are to European cities . . . as much the pride of Brooklyn as Piazza San Marco is the pride of Venice.")

To prevent the BQE from further disrupting their neighborhood, residents of Brooklyn Heights lobbied hard to move the path of the express-

---

*The Brooklyn-Battery Bridge was replaced by the Brooklyn-Battery Tunnel after Franklin Delano Roosevelt's secretary of war nixed the bridge for national security reasons. (There was evidently no love lost between FDR and Moses and that may have played a role in the decision too.)

way to the area just west of the bluff overlooking the more industrial riverfront. They developed a scheme, known as the Citizen Alternative Plan, that proposed stacking the levels of the BQE on top of each other and building on top of that a cantilevered promenade, giving Heights residents access to the spectacular view of Lower Manhattan. The idea of a promenade was not new; Hezekiah Pierrepont, the first booster of the area [see 42], had lobbied for public access, as had, later, Brooklyn resident Walt Whitman.

Moses—to the surprise of many —accepted the plan. The promenade (also known locally as the Esplanade) opened in 1954, providing eight blocks of public access in what had once been only the domain of the neighborhood's wealthiest residents.

Today, the promenade is notable not only for its view of the Manhattan skyline and the Brooklyn Bridge [88], but as the location of the "Four Chimneys House" (now long gone) from which George Washington oversaw the strategic retreat following the Battle of Brooklyn in 1776. It was Washington's ability to sneak 9,000 men across the river to Manhattan in the dead of night that allowed them to regroup and fight another day [see 16].

158 The New Midtown: Lever House and the Seagram Building

Sitting diagonally opposite each other on Park Avenue at 53rd Street, Lever House and the Seagram Building form the most significant postwar architectural statement in America. These two buildings, along with the United Nations Secretariat building [156], are the forerunners of New York's modern skyscraper design. After years of construction that was defined by the city's 1916 Zoning Resolution [135], these were the buildings that first broke free from the rigid setbacks that defined the shape of classic skyscrapers like the Chrysler Building [145] and the Empire State Building [148].

Lever House, completed in 1952, was designed by Gordon Bunshaft of Skidmore, Owings & Merrill, a firm that would become a dominant force in shaping the city's modern skyline. Lever, one of America's premier soap manufacturers, was looking to move to New York to be closer to the action. As a company executive noted at the time: "The price one pays for soap is 89 percent advertising . . . and the advertising agencies of American were there." Bunshaft's decision to

Lever House

build a gleaming, glass structure was in part dictated by Louis Sullivan's famous dictum that "form ever follows function." This was, after all, going to be a building that sold soap; how better to advertise the products than to build something that would constantly have to be cleaned!

More radically, Bunshaft abandoned the idea that the skyscraper needed to be built out to its lot line or be as tall as necessary to make money. In 1900, Cass Gilbert had prophetically dubbed the skyscraper a "machine that makes the land pay" and, in general, skyscrapers had a name or "anchor" tenant that occupied a few floors, and the rest of the space was filled with paying tenants. With Lever House, however, Bunshaft was freed from this constraint—only Lever's own employees would occupy the space. This meant that Bunshaft could build a short, slender tower, which he constructed on a series of stilts, or *pilotis*.* In the end, floor space on all of Lever House's 21 floors is so small that it adds up to roughly the equivalent of half of one floor in the original World Trade Center's Twin Towers [**170**].

One of the tenets of the International Style was a decisive anti-urbanism, a desire to turn away from the street rather than embrace it. Accordingly, Lever House's entrance is set back from Park Avenue and the entire building is turned perpendicular to the grid. At ground level, the bulk of the property is taken up by an expansive courtyard—originally to have been filled with sculpture by Isamu Noguchi—which is surrounded by an elevated, moatlike garden, cantilevered out from the

building's second floor. The courtyard has never functioned very well; it is one of the site's least attractive features and certainly one of the least-used public spaces in Midtown. By contrast, the light and airy second-story garden, accessible only to the building's employees, further emphasizes that the building is purposely not a part of the fabric of the neighborhood. As skyscraper historian Eric Nash neatly summarized:

> Lever was designed so that an executive could drive from the suburbs, park, have lunch in the third-floor company cafeteria, even play a round of shuffleboard on the landscaped second-floor terrace, and go home—all without ever setting foot in the dirty, chaotic city.

≈ It was soon after Lever House was finished that Samuel Bronfman, the chairman of the Joseph E. Seagram Corporation, began plans to build a Midtown headquarters for the distillery in honor of its 1958 centennial. Bronfman's daughter, Phyllis Lambert, was put in charge of the project and she, in turn, went to the Museum of Modern Art for advice. There she met architect Philip Johnson, who helped her narrow her choices down to three men: Frank Lloyd Wright, Le Corbusier, and Mies van der Rohe. In the end, Mies—a European stylist who was also closely associated with Chicago and its world-renowned skyline—may have been selected as the perfect balance between the American Wright and the Swiss-French Le Corbusier. More important, as Lambert later noted, Mies

---

*Frank Lloyd Wright, an early critic, said it looked like a "box on sticks."

was the architect that "the younger men, the second generation" were looking to for their cues.

Mies's structure is so compelling because—unlike Lever House—it doesn't struggle so hard to break free of the grid. Indeed, Mies was in love with Cartesian regularity (the measurements in the building are based on repetitions of 55.5 inches), which can be seen from the gridded façade the building presents to the street. Originally, the architect had hoped to have the building's steel frame exposed. However, since American fire regulations require steel to be coated in a fireproof material such as concrete, Mies designed the exterior skin to mimic steel slabs running horizontally between each floor. Thin bronze mullions separate the brown windows and run uninterrupted for the entire vertical length of the building. Indeed, very little interrupts the façade: the windows, for the first time ever, were designed to be floor to ceiling, with no sills or interior ledges. (And, to keep the front looking neat, Mies designed window blinds that work in only three positions: up, down, or halfway in between.) All the mechanical elements, such as the elevators and heating and cooling systems, were shunted to the rear of the building, out of sight.

The tower, opened in 1958, is not only the most successful of the first generation of postwar buildings in the city, it set the tone for all future office buildings. Lewis Mumford called it the "Rolls-Royce" of office buildings and *New York Times* critic Herbert Muschamp declared it the most important building constructed

in its millennium. Certainly, if you stand today in the plaza* and look up and down Park Avenue, you will see Seagram's children. Indeed, stand in any major city's business district and you will be surrounded—for good or ill—by imitation Seagram Buildings.

The Seagram Building

However, what was initially shocking about the building wasn't so much its glass curtain wall but its sweeping front plaza. Where Lever House hedges its bets with a protruding second-floor garden built along Park Avenue, the Seagram Plaza is gloriously empty, setting the building back from the street in much the same way that Carrère & Hastings's New York Public Library [128] is serenely set back from the flow of Fifth Avenue. However, unlike the library's plaza, which forms a popular mid-

---

*Mumford called the plaza the "motorcycle escort that gives [the Seagram Building] space and speed."

day gathering spot for office workers, Mies's plaza was originally intended to discourage congregating, and the pools were kept filled to the brim to keep people from sitting along their edges. (Philip Johnson later reported that Mies was surprised when office workers took to sitting on the steps and ledges anyway.)

Johnson helped Mies design many of the signature elements of the building, including customized mail chutes, door handles, and brass screws. (Johnson also contributed the design of the famed restaurant, the Four Seasons.) Indeed, Mies's maxim "less is more" is belied by this building, which has so much detailed, handmade work such as terrazzo floors in the elevators and magnificent oak-paneled walls in the offices, that influential critic Henry Russell Hitchcock later remarked, "I've never seen more of less."

159 Frank Lloyd Wright's Guggenheim Museum

In 1943, Solomon R. Guggenheim hired Frank Lloyd Wright to design a permanent home for his collection of non-objective art on Fifth Avenue. Two years later, Wright announced his now-famous spiral helix, a building that he later wrote "destroys everything square, rectilinear."

Wright, who was known to be generally hostile to paintings, seemed like an odd choice to build a museum, and despite his comments about "a new unity between beholder, painting and architecture," many outside observers were quite certain that the building would fail.

Innumerable delays meant that construction did not begin until 1956 and the museum did not open until three years later, by which time Wright had passed away, making the building his last major work. Immediate critical reaction was mixed; many praised the building but deplored it as a showcase for art. The general public compared it to everything from a bathtub to a battleship to a Jell-O mold. But no matter what their opinion, they gathered: over 10,000 people showed up for the opening day and many had to be turned away. Today, while some feel that the building is still too strong an architectural statement, competing with any art displayed inside, it has become one of the most visited museums in the city.

≈ It is often thought that the Guggenheim is the only place to see Wright's work in New York, but that is not true. In 1959, "Prefab No. 1," a home in Staten Island, was erected; it also was finished after Wright's death. (This is still a private house—recently renovated—and casual visitors are discouraged from dropping by.)

Four years earlier, Wright had designed the Hoffman Auto Showroom on Park Avenue at 56th Street, now occupied by Mercedes-Benz. The room can show only five cars at a time, but does so on an innovative spiral ramp that bears similarities to both the Guggenheim and what is now the V. C. Morris Gift Shop in San Francisco, which Wright designed in 1948.

Lastly, the living room of the Francis Little house, a 1912 home built in Wayzata, Minnesota, now resides in the American Wing of the Metropolitan Museum of Art [80], where it has been painstakingly re-created.

160 Fidel Castro Goes to Harlem

In September 1960, Fidel Castro arrived in New York to address the United Nations [156], just a year after his successful overthrow of the Batista government in Cuba. He and his giant entourage checked into the Shelburne Hotel in Murray Hill. However, soon after they'd arrived, Castro carped that the hotel's manager was making, in Castro's words, "unacceptable cash demands." (The management of the Shelburne complained that Castro's party were cooking in the rooms, that their chickens were making a racket, and that they'd already incurred $10,000 in damages. The hotel later auctioned off some of the chicken feathers from the Cuban party's rooms.)

When Castro left the Shelburne, the Fair Play for Cuba Committee contacted the Hotel Theresa on 125th Street and negotiated an $800 daily rate for 80 rooms on two upper floors. Castro noted in an interview that he'd "always wanted to come to Harlem" and that he felt "very warm" there. Castro met with Malcolm X during his stay, along with foreign heads of state also in town for the UN meeting, including Nikita Khrushchev and Jawaharlal Nehru.

The Theresa, built in 1913, was for years the tallest building in Harlem and one of the few hotels in the city that welcomed a black clientele; it came to be known as the Waldorf-Astoria of Harlem. Guests included boxing greats Sugar Ray Robinson, Joe Louis and Muhammad Ali, musicians Louis Armstrong, Lena Horne, Dinah Washington, and even Jimi Hendrix. It was also home to the offices of Malcolm X [163], whose Organization of Afro-American Unity occupied one of the first-floor suites. Future commerce secretary Ron Brown grew up in the hotel (his father was the manager) and young Charles Rangel, who would go on to be Harlem's long-serving congressman [see 171], had an early job as a desk clerk.

Castro's visit was to be the last hurrah for the hotel, which lost money throughout the 1960s and closed its doors in 1970. (Today it is an office building.) However, less than a month after Castro had checked out, John F. Kennedy staged a campaign event in front of the hotel. Kennedy spoke from a dais filled with heavy-hitting Democrats, including Eleanor Roosevelt and Adam Clayton Powell, Jr., declaring his solidarity with the neighborhood, saying, "I am delighted to come to Harlem and I think the whole world should come here." But more than showing his delight with Harlem, Kennedy was trying to reposition the Theresa in the minds of voters as a bastion of the Democratic Party, and not the place where Castro met with Khrushchev.

161 Bob Dylan Debuts at Café Wha?

January 1961 found New York City in the middle of what the "*New York Times* said . . . was the coldest winter in seventeen years"—or so Bob Dylan remembered in his song "Talkin' New York" from his debut album recorded just ten months later. When Dylan arrived, on or around January 24, he headed immediately to Greenwich Village [136]. There, on MacDougal Street, he found himself at Café Wha?, a hangout for what he described as "collegiate types, suburbanites, lunch-hour secretaries, sailors and tourists." In the evening, the club, run by Manny Roth, featured some of the more successful up-and-coming acts, including Richie Havens, comedian Noel Stookey—who would soon change his name to Paul and become part of Peter, Paul and Mary—and singer Louis Gossett, Jr., who gave up his burgeoning folk career altogether to concentrate on acting. The club was so popular, in fact, that Roth decided to keep it open during the day and singer Fred Neil presided over a variety show of oddball acts. It was here, just after his arrival in the city, that Dylan made his debut. Though the story in its many retellings often has Dylan performing a set of traditional folk songs or Woody Guthrie numbers, the singer denies it. In his autobiography, *Chronicles, Volume 1*, he writes emphatically, "I never played any of my own sets. I just accompanied Neil on all of his and that's where I began playing regular in New York."

By the end of the week, Dylan had accomplished his other great goal in coming to New York: meeting Woody Guthrie, his hero, who he knew was dying of Huntington's disease. Guthrie was at that point staying with friends in East Orange, New Jersey, though he would soon enter the Brooklyn State Hospital, where he spent the rest of his life. Dylan visited Guthrie frequently, playing him songs from his growing repertoire of covers and originals.

By summer, Dylan was a regular on the scene in the Village, hanging out in Izzy Young's Folklore Center (across the street from Café Wha?),

and lining up gigs at other venues, none more important than the Gaslight, also on MacDougal Street, and Gerde's Folk City on West 4th Street. Dylan also began to get paying gigs in the recording studio, backing Harry Belafonte on harmonica on "Midnight Special." At recording sessions for Carolyn Hester, Dylan met John Hammond of Columbia Records and over the course of two days in November, Dylan recorded his eponymous debut, which featured all traditional folk songs fleshed out with two originals: the sardonic "Talkin' New York" and his moving ode to Guthrie, "Song to Woody." While the album, released in March of 1962, failed to sell many copies, it established Dylan as a recording artist, and his next album—*The Freewheelin' Bob Dylan*, which showcased his writing talents on songs like "Blowin' in the Wind"—was a much bigger success.

Many of the places associated with Dylan from this early era, such as Izzy Young's and the Gaslight, are long gone. However, the cover shot of *The Freewheelin' Bob Dylan* shows Dylan and his girlfriend, Suze Rotolo, strolling down Jones Street in the West Village toward West 4th Street, along a streetscape that is little changed today.

162 Robert Moses 3: Lincoln Center for the Performing Arts

In 1957, *West Side Story* debuted on Broadway, telling the tale of the new Puerto Rican immigrants who were then moving in large numbers into the area of the West 60s known as San Juan Hill. By the time the film was shot four years later, San Juan Hill had been cleared out—the movie was actually filmed in the empty streets and tenements—in anticipation of a west side revitalization project, Lincoln Center for the Performing Arts.

The history of the Upper West Side was tied, like that of so many neighborhoods, to developments in transportation. The coming of the elevated railroad in the 1870s [81] took primarily undeveloped land and turned it into a bedroom community of brownstone townhouses. The IRT subway in 1904 [119] created a boom in apartment construction (such as the Ansonia [116]) and established the area as a bastion of upper-middle-class sensibility. However, the Depression took its toll on the neighborhood—in terms of development and the relative prosperity of its residents—and by the late 1950s, a preferred designation for the neighborhood was "shabby."

In 1956, John D. Rockefeller III was tapped to lead the Lincoln Square Urban Renewal Project, part of Robert Moses's effort—as head of the Mayor's Committee on Slum Clearance—to gentrify the declining neighborhood (and, many lamented, to push the black and Latino residents farther away from the city's economic

center). Moses began soliciting ideas from Wallace K. Harrison, the architect whose connection to the Rockefeller family went back to Rockefeller Center [149] and included work at the United Nations [156]. Together, Harrison, Rockefeller, and Moses put together a plan for a massive complex in San Juan Hill that would include the Metropolitan Opera (which was to have been the original anchor ten-

The Metropolitan Opera House and central fountain at Lincoln Center

ant of Rockefeller Center), the New York Philharmonic—which had lost its lease at Carnegie Hall—the New York City Ballet, and The Juilliard School.

Area residents and urban preservationists immediately rebelled. Jane Jacobs, author of *The Death and Life of Great American Cities* and one of Moses's most vocal opponents, denounced the project, noting that it was "planned on the idiotic assumption that the natural neighbor of a hall is another hall." However, Moses prevailed and in 1959, President Dwight D. Eisenhower broke ground for the center. In 1962, the first of the center's buildings, Philharmonic Hall—by Harrison's partner, Max Abramowitz—opened to mixed reviews. (The acoustics had been designed by noted engineer Leo L. Beranek; against his wishes, the hall was enlarged to accommodate more patrons, thus nullifying his acoustical ideas. In 1976, Avery Fisher, head of Fisher Electronics, paid for a complete acoustical refit that solved some, but not all, of the problems.)

In 1964, the New York State Theater by Philip Johnson (who had worked on the Seagram Building [**158**]) opened on the opposite side of the plaza as the home of the New York City Ballet; the building also houses the New York City Opera. That same year Wallace K. Harrison's monumental 3,800-seat Metropolitan Opera Building opened at the apex of the plaza. Taken together, these three buildings form not only the center of the complex but also the most significant statement of late International Style architecture in the city.

Lincoln Center also features a Broadway theater, the Vivian Beaumont, designed by Eero Saarinen (in a building that now also houses an Off-Broadway house), The Juilliard School, Alice Tully Hall, and a host of smaller spaces. Jazz at Lincoln Center, led by Wynton Marsalis, moved off-campus in October 2004 to a custom-built theater in the Time Warner Center [**182**].

While the project did displace 7,000 people—who were not all adequately rehoused, despite Robert Moses's promises—the complex succeeded in revitalizing the neighborhood. Where Jane Jacobs was afraid that the cultural complex would suck life and energy out of the surrounding streets, the area has turned into a thriving mixed-use commercial and residential neighborhood, especially along the Broadway corridor. Lincoln Center, meanwhile, has become the largest performing arts venue in the country.

163 The Assassination of Malcolm X

Born Malcolm Little in 1925, the man who would later be most famously known by his Nation of Islam name, Malcolm X, had a tragic childhood. The mangled body of his father, Earl, was found across the streetcar tracks near the family's home in Lansing, Michigan. Although his death was officially ruled a suicide, the family was certain that Earl had been killed by white supremacists for his Marcus Garvey–inspired views on black nationalism. Malcolm's mother, Louise, was declared insane and the Little children were sent to foster homes. A gifted student, Malcolm was asked by a teacher what he wanted to be when he grew up. As he later noted in *The Autobiography of Malcolm X* (co-written with Alex Haley), he responded "a lawyer," and the teacher replied:

> Malcolm, one of life's first needs is for us to be realistic. Don't misunderstand me, now. We all here like you, you know that. But you've got to be realistic about being a nigger. A lawyer—that's no realistic goal for a nigger.

In the early 1940s, Malcolm split his time between New York City and Boston, holding a variety of jobs and committing a series of petty crimes. In 1946, he was arrested for breaking into a pawnshop and sentenced to 8 to 10 years in Massachusetts State Prison; in prison he first began following the teachings of the Nation of Islam and its leader, Elijah Muhammad. Upon his release in 1952, he changed his name to Malcolm X, repudiating his slave surname and acknowledging the fact that his real family name was forever lost.

Malcolm X quickly grew to be the Nation of Islam's most prominent and charismatic leader. In 1954, he was appointed the head of Temple No. 7 on Lenox Avenue in Harlem [see 153] and brought in thousands of converts, none more prominent than boxer Cassius Clay, who became Cassius X and then Muhammad Ali.

However, disagreements between Malcolm and Elijah Muhammad led to a split between the two men in 1964 and one month later, Malcolm headed to Mecca to perform the hajj, the most sacred ritual among Muslims. It had a profound effect on him and he wrote back to his followers in New York:

Never have I witnessed such sincere hospitality and the overwhelming spirit of true brotherhood. . . . There were tens of thousands of pilgrims from all over the world. They were of all colors, from blue-eyed blonds to black-skinned Africans. But we were all participating in the same ritual, displaying a spirit of unity and brotherhood that my experiences in America had led me to believe never could exist between the white and the non-white. . . . We were truly all the same.

In honor of his conversion to Sunni Islam, Malcolm again changed his name, calling himself El-Hajj Malik El-Shabazz. Alas, Malcolm did not get much chance to preach his message of brotherhood. On February 14, 1965, the family's home in Elmhurst, Queens, was firebombed and burned to the ground. A week later, Malcolm was appearing at a rally at the Audubon Ballroom in upper Manhattan. In a carefully planned diversion, two men in the back of the auditorium began scuffling and a loud explosion rang out from the rear of the room. As all attention turned to the back, a man in the front row stood, pulled out a sawed-off shotgun, and fired twice into Malcolm's chest. He fell to the stage and two other men jumped onto the rostrum, filling his body with bullets. Just two days earlier, Malcolm had remarked, "It is a time for martyrs now, and if I am to be one, it will be for the cause of brotherhood. That's the only thing that can save this country."

The question of who killed Malcolm X has always been shrouded in controversy. Three members of the Nation of Islam—Talmadge Hayer, Norman 3X Butler, and Thomas 15X Johnson—were ultimately convicted of the crime; Hayer, however, was the only one arrested at the scene and denied the involvement of the other two, later naming four other members of Nation of Islam's Newark Temple who were his accomplices. Those men have never been apprehended.

164 Andy Warhol's Exploding Plastic Inevitable

In the late 1960s, 19–25 St. Mark's Place was the central destination in the new East Village. The term "East Village" was coined by real estate agents after World War II to try to raise the rents in what had traditionally been considered a part of the immigrant Lower East Side (Andy Warhol called it "Babushkaville"). Earlier, St. Mark's Place had been an integral part of Kleindeutschland [91].

These buildings were home to three related, and overlapping, music scenes: the Dom, the Electric Circus, and Warhol's Exploding Plastic Inevitable. In the 1880s, they had housed the German social organization called Arlington Hall; in the 1920s, the hall was bought by the Polish National Home as a public gathering space, bar, and restaurant. Then, in the 1960s, the bar was taken over by Stanley Tolkin, and the upstairs ballroom became a dance club called the Dom (the Polish word for "home"), known for its good jukebox and its racially integrated crowd. Meanwhile, Stanley's Bar, downstairs, played host to bands like the Fugs, one of the most politically active and influential groups in their day.

In April 1966, Andy Warhol rented the building and completely restyled its interior. He installed a rotating, mirrored ball, resuscitating the long-dormant dance floor accessory that later would come to define the age of disco. When he was done with his renovations, a month-long party began that he dubbed the Exploding Plastic Inevitable. Warhol had recently taken over the management of the Velvet Underground, which he made the Exploding Plastic Inevitable's house band and main attraction.

Warhol soon took the party on the road, and other cities had their own Exploding Plastic Inevitable—stripped down to a more manageable rock show. When they returned to New York, the Dom had become the Balloon Farm, which was soon transformed into the Electric Circus, which asked its patrons to "play games, dress as you like, dance, sit, think, tune in and turn on." Influential bands such as the Grateful Dead played the Electric Circus, but in 1970 a small bomb went off on the dance floor and by 1971 the club had closed.

The building today has been expertly renovated and houses a number of retail shops, including, for a short time, a gift store for the defunct punk club CBGB's, which—in its home on the Bowery—launched the careers of such influential bands as the Ramones, Blondie, and Talking Heads.

165 The Public Theater and *Hair*

Since the late 1950s, Joseph Papp had been presenting free Shakespeare in the Park to ever-growing audiences. The series began on the Lower East Side and then moved to the Great Lawn in Central Park [151], where Papp famously feuded with Robert Moses about whether or not he'd have to charge admission for his free theater. (Papp won and ultimately

The Public Theater (depicted here when it was still the Astor Library)

had a permanent theater, the Delacorte, built for him at the edge of the Great Lawn.)

Innovative as Shakespeare in the Park was, it focused almost completely on a classical repertory, so when Papp was presented with the opportunity to move into the recently vacated Astor Library [see 33],* he wanted to do so in a way that completely differentiated his new venture, dubbed the Public Theater, from his work in the park. And, he reasoned, if it really was to be the public's theater, it should reflect what was happening in the East Village, which surrounded the theater's new home.

The first show at the theater was *Hair*, billed as a "tribal, love-rock musical." It opened for a six-week run on October 17, 1967, and despite mixed reviews, was a sellout. People were drawn to Galt MacDermot's pop-rock score, its multiracial cast of hippies, including lyricist Jerome Ragni, and—not least—the full-frontal nudity of the cast at the finale of Act I.

After a brief stop at a Midtown disco, the show was retooled and opened on Broadway in 1968, adding to the cast lyricist James Rado and a young Diane Keaton—who notably refused to disrobe, despite the $50 bonus the actors were paid. It became the first Off-Broadway musical to transfer successfully to Broadway and coined the term "rock musical," a form that has influenced New York theater ever since.

The Public Theater, meanwhile,

*The Astor Library had moved out when it merged with the New York Public Library [128]; the building had been home to other tenants, most famously the Hebrew Immigrant Aid Society [see 99].

had cemented its reputation as a pioneer and a hitmaker. Over 50 of its productions have ultimately moved to Broadway, but none is more famous than *A Chorus Line*, which opened at the Public in May 1975. It transferred to Broadway two months later and ran for 6,137 performances—a record that held until 1997, when it was surpassed by *Cats*.

166 The Columbia Campus Takeover

As the war in Vietnam escalated in the late 1960s, protests on university campuses grew more heated. In New York, this was nowhere more apparent than on the campus of Columbia University [101], where students protested against the ROTC (which practiced on South Field, in front of Butler Library), against other military and government recruitment on campus, and against Columbia's affiliation with the Institute for Defense Analysis (IDA), a federally funded military research think tank. In March 1968, six members of Columbia's branch of Students for a Democratic Society (SDS) attempted to present a petition against IDA to Columbia's administration. In response, Columbia suspended the students.

At the same time, work was progressing on a new school gymnasium in nearby Morningside Park [73]. In 1959, the university had begun planning a state-of-the-art facility for the school and, lacking space on campus to accommodate it, had negotiated a 50-year lease on a section of the park. A small but vocal group of community activists immediately questioned the wisdom of ceding a public park for private use. Columbia responded by adding a community gym to the plan, but this did little to help. Building a gym in the park—with a tall back wall facing the Harlem community—gave the appearance that Columbia was trying to wall itself off from its surroundings. More to the point, the topography of the site meant that Columbia students would enter the building from a front door at the top of the Morningside cliff and that Harlem residents would enter via a back door in the basement of the facility. Students began crying "Gym Crow!"

Following the April 4, 1968, assassination of Rev. Martin Luther King, Jr., tensions on campus escalated. On April 23, students marched from campus to Morningside Park and tore down some of the fence surrounding the site in an attempt to halt construction. After an altercation with police at the park, where one student was arrested, the remaining protesters returned to campus and, under the direction of SDS leader Mark Rudd, decided to occupy Hamilton Hall.

During the night, SDS and the other mainly white-run organizations agreed to vacate Hamilton and leave it occupied by the Student Afro-American Society, which felt that the protests against the racism at the gymnasium site should be separate from SDS's larger issues with Columbia. The white groups moved into various campus buildings the next morning; Mark Rudd led SDS students to Low Library (the university's administration building) and took over President Grayson Kirk's office. The occupation lasted a week until police busted into Low Library on April 30, hauling the protesters to jail. Occupants of other campus buildings got into bloody clashes with the police, and over 150 people were treated for their injuries. In the end, over 700 people were arrested that day.

For the next few weeks, outdoor "Liberation" classes replaced the normal class schedule and two more protests—one at a nearby apartment building and one at Hamilton Hall—resulted in more arrests. Students left the June graduation ceremony en masse for an "anti-graduation" of their own.

In the end, the goals of the takeover were realized: Columbia scrapped its gymnasium plans, ultimately building the underground Dodge Physical Fitness Center on the main campus, and the school ceased its affiliation with IDA. However, it took decades for the school to recover, losing prestige—and alumni dollars—in the process.

The events at Columbia in 1968 had a profound effect on other college campuses, and over the next few years campus activism increased throughout the country. Mark Rudd and other leaders of the SDS further radicalized their views, eventually founding the Weatherman organization, who were briefly the most feared domestic terrorist group in America.

167 Robert Moses 4: The Lower Manhattan Expressway

By the late 1960s, Robert Moses's influence in New York was on the wane. His last big project in the city had been the 1964 World's Fair in Flushing Meadows, Queens, and he had retired from most of his official positions. What ended up as his last great fight was the battle of the Lower Manhattan Expressway (sometimes called LOMEX), a road that had first been proposed in 1929 and did not ultimately go down in defeat until 1969.

The purpose of the expressway was to relieve downtown traffic and connect the Williamsburg and Manhattan bridges to the Holland Tunnel. By the 1940s, Moses was proposing an eight-lane elevated highway roughly following the paths of Broome and Delancey streets across the island. To Moses and other urban planners, the area that LOMEX would traverse—not yet called "SoHo," a moniker that would come into use in the late 1960s—was the definition of urban blight. Though their structures still stood, famed department stores like E. V. Haughwout [60] were long gone. In their place, the buildings had become factories [see 126] and in the era following World War II, which saw a decline in Manhattan's primacy as a shipping port, those factories moved to places where they could be better connected to the nation's transportation infrastructure.

Enter Jane Jacobs. By 1962, Moses had already lost one battle to Jacobs, who lived in the West Village in an area that Moses—as head of the Mayor's Committee on Slum Clearance—had deemed worthy of a federally funded urban renewal project. Jacobs quickly formed a Committee to Save the West Village and fought a vigorous, yearlong battle that exposed secret deals between the city and a developer and that nearly cost Mayor Robert Wagner reelection. In January 1962, the city's Planning

Commission officially rescinded the "slum" designation for Greenwich Village.

Soon thereafter, however, the City Club, a good-government group, published *The Wastelands of New York City*, a scathing document about the "South of Houston Industrial Area" that bluntly stated, "There are no buildings worth saving." In the wake of this report, Moses began pushing hard for the Lower Manhattan Expressway as the savior of the area, promising that it would not only rid the city of the decaying 19th-century manufacturing buildings, but would add much-needed parking, a speedier commute across the city, and an impetus for new residential and retail establishments. As he later wrote in his autobiography, "When you operate in an overbuilt metropolis you have to hack your way with a meat ax."

Indeed, a primary reason for the area's perceived blight stemmed from zoning; as solely a manufacturing district, the buildings could not legally be used for anything else. This did not stop a number of artists, however, from moving in. The abandoned loft spaces were cheap and provided plenty of room to both work and live. According to SoHo historian Richard Kostelanetz, a few artists who were already living in the neighborhood in the 1950s appealed to Mayor Wagner to help them circumvent the nonresidential zoning. Wagner agreed that as long as no more than two artists lived in a building—and that they clearly posted a sign that read "AIR" (artist in residence) and a floor number so

that they be rescued in case of fire—they could stay.

Fresh from her victory in the West Village, Jane Jacobs brought together a Joint Committee to Stop the Lower Manhattan Expressway, which in December 1962 convinced the city's Board of Estimate not to fund the project. And yet the project refused to go away. In 1965, Moses continued to press for the project and in 1968 Mayor John Lindsay threw his weight behind the proposal, which had now expanded to 10 lanes and a price tag of $150 million. In 1968, Jane Jacobs was arrested at a particularly heated public meeting where she rushed the stage in protest.

By this point, the project was on its last legs. One of its selling points had always been the relief of traffic congestion in Lower Manhattan, but a spurt of development downtown (which would culminate with the World Trade Center [**170**] a few years later) had not significantly added to the number of cars on the street. More important, by 1968, when the "South of Houston Industrial Area" was shortened to SoHo,* the neighborhood had become a place where people lived and worked and could no longer be considered a slum—if it had been one in the first place. In 1969, the Board of Estimate officially "demapped" the Lower Manhattan Expressway. Just four years later, in a major victory for preservationists—none more prominent than *New York Times* architecture critic Ada Louise Huxtable—SoHo was designated the Cast Iron Historic District, thus preserving its remarkable architectural heritage.

---

*SoHo is a contraction that stands for SOuth of HOuston Street; it is borrowed from London's Soho, which is SOuth of HOlborn.

168 June 27, 1969: The Stonewall Rebellion

At the beginning of the 20th century, at the same time that Greenwich Village was becoming increasingly bohemian and radical [136], it was also identified as the country's most gay neighborhood. A number of residents, such as novelist Willa Cather, were openly gay—at least within the relatively safe environs that the Village offered.

Prohibition [139], which brought drinkers of various social spheres together into illicit speakeasies, had relaxed many previous moral norms. However, the law's repeal in 1933 actually had the effect of driving gay nightlife further underground. Soon after Prohibition ended, the State Liquor Authority consolidated its power and passed regulations forbidding the sale of alcohol to known homosexuals. In Greenwich Village, gay bars were often owned by the Mafia, who could circumvent the liquor laws or knew which members of the Sixth Precinct to pay off to ensure they stayed open. Even after the prohibition on selling alcohol to gays was rescinded in 1967, a host of other laws—including a ban on same-sex kissing and a law that required at least three pieces of gender-appropriate clothing to be worn at all times—made it easy to shut down gay bars.

In the 1930s, two former 19th-century stables on Christopher Street were joined together and their interior space converted into a restaurant; the restaurant closed in the mid-1960s, and in 1967 a gay bar and dance club called the Stonewall Inn opened in its place. Its principal owner, "Fat Tony" Lauria, was tied to the Genovese crime family. Lauria did little to create any ambience. A gay guidebook from 1969, *The Homosexual Handbook*, noted that it "seems to have only recently been converted from a garage into a cabaret in about eight hours and at a cost of under fifty dollars."

The Stonewall Inn

Since clubs did not need liquor licenses if the members supplied their own alcohol, the Stonewall went through the pretense of being a private club: there was no cash register and in case of a raid, the bartenders were instructed to remove bottles from behind the bar and then to mingle with the crowd. "Members" were screened at the door and forced to sign in. Fearing that the membership rolls would fall into the wrong hands, patrons often signed in as Judy Garland* and Donald Duck.

Even with Mafia protection and police payoffs, gay bars were still subject to occasional raids. What exactly sparked the Stonewall rebellion in the summer of 1969 remains unknown. The raid appears to have been instigated by the NYPD's First Division—not the local Sixth Precinct—and may have been tied to rumors of extortion or bootlegging at the club. In turn, the First Division may have been getting heat from Mayor John Lindsay, who was running for reelection, to crack down on illegal enterprises and thus burnish his law-and-order reputation.

At about 1:20 on the morning of June 28, eight plainclothes police officers entered the bar. They asked patrons for their ID cards; those who had them were told to leave. However, curious bystanders and ousted patrons began gathering outside the bar and the crowd swelled to perhaps 400 people. When police vans showed up to arrest those still inside who could not produce proper ID, the crowd began pelting the officers with bottles and loose change. The police and the crowd began to fight, and a number of people were beaten. As the crowd grew angrier, the eight original police officers retreated into the bar and barricaded themselves inside, along with some patrons and some people from the crowd. This only increased the fury of the crowd, which battered in the door and smashed the bar's plate-glass window. Eventually, the fire department and the police Tactical Patrol Force—dressed in complete riot gear—managed to extricate the police from inside the bar and disperse the crowd.

The next day, word spread throughout the city of a gathering outside the Stonewall. Hundreds—perhaps thousands—of gays and their supporters filled the streets around Christopher Park (across the street from the Stonewall) chanting slogans such as "Gay power!" and "Liberate Christopher Street!" By 2:00 a.m., the crowd had grown so large that it was impeding traffic and the Tactical Patrol Force was called in again; it took them two hours, but they eventually managed to quell the disturbance. The next night saw crowds gather again and then, after two nights of rain, a third gathering came together on July 2 to confront the police one final time.

What followed was an unprecedented wave of organized gay

---

*June 27, the day the Stonewall riots began, was also the day of Judy Garland's funeral. While some riot participants say there is a connection between the two (since emotions were running high because of Garland's passing), historian David Carter argues in his book *Stonewall: The Riots That Sparked the Gay Revolution* that the club kids at the Stonewall were too young and from too many diverse backgrounds for Garland's death to have affected them much. At best, Carter writes, Garland's death can be seen as the end of one era and the Stonewall riots as the beginning of the next.

groups standing up for their rights and individuals publically declaring themselves as "out." A year later, on June 27, 1970, a rally was held to celebrate Christopher Street Liberation Day. The march began at the Stonewall and headed up Seventh Avenue to Central Park. By the next year, the term "Gay Pride" had been attached to the event, and it has become a worldwide celebration in June of gay rights. In New York, the parade—which now boasts about 500,000 participants and is probably the largest in the city each year—is held on the Sunday closest to the anniversary of the Stonewall riots.

In Christopher Park, a white-painted bronze monument by George Segal, *Gay Liberation*, marks the importance of the area to the gay rights movement. The veterans of Stonewall are currently campaigning to erect a second statue to commemorate the people who participated in the riots themselves.

169 The Apollo Astronauts and the Ticker Tape Parade

On October 28, 1886, the ceremonies to open the Statue of Liberty [93] concluded with a parade up Broadway from Battery Park. The parade route was lined with financial companies and from the windows of one building, an enterprising clerk began throwing out used ticker tape as confetti. Thus was born an enduring New York City tradition, the ticker tape parade.

(The stock ticker was invented in 1867 to send stock prices to subscribers via telegraph. The name of the machine is onomatopoetic: it literally went *ticker, ticker, ticker* all day long.)

By the 1920s, ticker tape parades had become a relatively frequent occurrence, mostly honoring foreign dignitaries and aviation pioneers. Indeed, walking up Broadway today from Battery Park and reading the sidewalk plaques that commemorate these parades is a telling reminder of just how fascinated people were with feats of flight. Many famous aviators, such as Amelia Earhart, Wiley Post, and Charles Lindbergh, were given parades, but so too were more obscure people like Amy Johnson and James Mollison, the first married couple to fly across the Atlantic. (The only person ever to be honored with three ticker tape parades was Admiral Richard E. Byrd, the famed polar explorer.)

When aviation became more routine in the jet age, public attention turned to America's astronauts. What was referred to at the time as the largest ticker tape parade ever held took place on August 13, 1969, when Neil Armstrong, Buzz Aldrin, and Michael Collins were honored upon their return from the Apollo 11 mission to the moon. Officials estimated 4 million people along the parade route. It was also one of the *fastest* ticker tape parades. The astronauts started at Bowling Green [13] at 10:17 a.m. (about half an hour ahead of schedule) and arrived on the steps of City Hall [26] just 14 minutes later! Many people who showed up for the parade were disappointed to discover that the astronauts had already passed them by.

However, unlike a traditional ticker tape parade, which would have ended with a City Hall ceremony, the Apollo 11 astronauts returned to their motorcade and the parade continued uptown to Times Square. As the *New York Times* noted, the confetti in Midtown was "made up more of paper towels and pages from telephone directories than tickertape" and that it grew "so dense that the astronauts could hardly see."

By 1:15 p.m. the astronauts were back at Kennedy Airport to go to Chicago. They ended the day with festivities in Los Angeles. Having just been to the moon and back, a quick one-day jaunt across North America must not have seemed like such a big deal.

170 The World Trade Center Opens

Hanover Trust, Rockefeller Center's "XYZ" buildings across Sixth Avenue from the original development, and Fifth Avenue's Steuben Glass Building came to define Midtown as the place for new commercial architecture.

To stem the defection of businesses to Midtown and to bolster the Financial District's profile, David Rockefeller's Chase Manhattan Bank hired Skidmore, Owings & Merrill in 1957 to build a new Chase Manhattan Building on Liberty Street. At the same time, Rockefeller created the Downtown-Lower Manhattan Association to promote building in the area. Skidmore, Owings & Merrill created a master plan for the Financial District, which included a "World Trade Center" on the East River, which would host office space,

The World Trade Center's Twin Towers (WTC 1 and WTC 2) standing high above the Lower Manhattan skyline

By the mid-1960s, the business district in Manhattan had firmly shifted from the Financial District to Midtown. In the wake of the opening of Lever House and the Seagram Building [**158**], other buildings such as Park Avenue's Manufacturers

a hotel, a convention center, and a new home for the New York Stock Exchange [**114**].

The idea of a World Trade Center had been simmering since the end of World War II, when the state legislature authorized a World Trade Center

Corporation to investigate the possibility of creating an economic center in New York that would be similar to the United Nations, which at that time was being wooed to come to the city [156].

When the New York Stock Exchange nixed the idea of moving, David Rockefeller approached the Port Authority, the bi-state agency that ran New York and New Jersey's sea- and airports. After much negotiation, the Port Authority and both states agreed to a west side project, to be built on top of the old Hudson & Manhattan Railroad terminal. The H&M—soon to be renamed Port Authority Trans Hudson (PATH) Train—provided a vital link for commuters from New Jersey, though its ridership had been declining since World War II. The Port Authority promised to take over the ailing train system and use the World Trade Center to create jobs for New Jersey residents and New Yorkers alike.

In 1962, the Port Authority hired Minoru Yamasaki to create plans for the center. He ultimately settled on two large towers (originally each to be 80 stories tall) surrounded by a few smaller buildings. (Yamasaki deemed a single tower too tall; many towers of the same height, he feared, would look "like a housing project.") However, because the Port Authority wanted 10 million square feet of office space—a figure seemingly pulled from thin air, as no one at the time thought they had a prayer of renting out so much space—Yamasaki's towers were upgraded to 110 stories each. This would also make them the world's tallest, besting the Empire State Building [148], which had held the title since 1931.

Work on buying up and demolishing the existing properties—in a part of the Lower West Side then known as Radio Row—began in 1965. Construction on the complex started a year later with the 65-foot-deep "bathtub." Because the construction site was almost entirely on landfill, the bathtub was created to keep the Hudson River at bay while excavating deep enough to find bedrock. World Trade Center 1 (the north tower) was topped out in 1970 and began accepting tenants immediately. Its companion, WTC 2, topped out a year later. Towers 3–6 were completed during the 1970s and a seventh building, across the street from the original complex, was added in the 1980s.

Upon their completion, the Twin Towers (as they immediately came to be known) quickly became the most hated structures in the city. Architecture critic Paul Goldberger denounced them as "boring, so utterly banal as to be unworthy of the headquarters of a bank in Omaha" as well as "pretentious and arrogant." (He later softened this view—somewhat—to acknowledge that the towers "did have a certain value as minimalist sculpture" that "did wonderful things in the light.")

However, the towers also quickly came to symbolize New York: they appeared on everything from ashtrays to snow globes. The observation deck, opened in December 1975, was one of the city's top tourist attractions. Aerialist Philippe Petit walked between the towers in 1974, adding to their allure, and King Kong even climbed them in the 1976 remake of the movie—a film that launched the career of Jessica Lange, but did little else worth remembering.

Engineers were fascinated by the

buildings, since they were built in a way never seen before—or since—with the exterior frame of the buildings bearing each tower's entire load. This meant that Yamasaki could eliminate interior columns and maximize rentable floor space; each floor had approximately an acre of usable space, which meant that just one of the Twin Towers had more office space inside than most medium-sized American cities. By the 1990s, when the bulk of the offices were rented out, over 50,000 people worked in the towers each day, with thousands more occupying the surrounding buildings.

171 "Keep the Faith, Baby": Adam Clayton Powell, Jr.

In 1934, Adam Clayton Powell, Jr., the son of the influential pastor of Harlem's Abyssinian Baptist Church [**152**], emerged as a strong voice in the struggle for equality for the city's black residents.

The main thoroughfare of the neighborhood, 125th Street, was home to the Apollo Theater [**see 153**], the Hotel Theresa [**160**], and many of the area's prominent department stores, including Blumstein's, Koch's and Kress. These Jewish-owned stores were proud that they had broken the color line and allowed black people to freely patronize their stores. But their black customers knew better. While black women were allowed to shop at Blumstein's, they weren't allowed to try on the clothes. And none of these stores would hire a single black employee.

Adam Clayton Powell, Jr., then an assistant pastor at his father's church, initiated a boycott that he labeled "Don't Shop Where You Can't Work."* By the end of the year, the pressure had forced Blumstein's to hire over 30 black salesclerks and other floor employees. Powell soon organized the Coordinating Committee for Employment and gained similar concessions from other 125th Street merchants.

In 1937, Powell succeeded his father as pastor of Abyssinian Baptist and four years later became the first black City Council member in New York City. In 1944, he was elected to serve as Harlem's congressman, making him the first black person to do so and one of only two black members of the House of Representatives at the time. Powell was reelected every two years for the next 24 years and was one of the staunchest supporters of the civil rights movement in Congress, helping to craft legislation to desegregate schools, to outlaw lynching, and—in the far-reaching Powell Amendment—to outlaw racial discrimination in federally funded projects. He was known as "Mr. Civil Rights" and his catchphrase "Keep the faith, baby!" became a mantra for the disenfranchised who turned to him to help them improve their lives.

Powell's personal life, however, was nearly his undoing. A dubious fact-finding cruise to Europe—in the company of two young women and at taxpayer expense—along with his increased absenteeism prompted Congress to launch an investigation

---

*Powell was following the lead of Rev. John H. Johnson, the priest in charge at St. Martin's Episcopal Church in Harlem, who had started a similar boycott.

into possible misconduct. When Powell was reelected in 1966, the House voted to bar him from his seat. This automatically triggered a special election in Harlem to select his replacement. Powell ran for his own vacant seat and won easily. Meanwhile, the Supreme Court ruled that Congress had acted unconstitutionally by barring a duly elected member and reinstated Powell. The controversy, however, marked the end of his political career. In 1970, Charles Rangel challenged Powell in the Democratic primary and won; Rangel won the general election later that year and has served as Harlem's congressman ever since. Soon thereafter, Powell stepped down from the pulpit at Abyssinian Baptist and retired to his estate in Bimini in the Bahamas. He died in 1972.

Ironically, Powell is memorialized in Harlem by the massive Adam Clayton Powell Jr. State Office Building, the construction of which he adamantly opposed. When Governor Nelson Rockefeller first proposed the building in the late 1960s, Powell became its most high-profile foe, at one point declaring that if construction began, he would permanently leave the United States and take up residence in the Bahamas. When the building was opened in 1974, as simply the State Office Building in Harlem, the deceased congressman was not even mentioned.

However, in 1983, New York's state legislature voted nearly unanimously to rename the building for Powell. (The boulevard it sits on, formerly called Seventh Avenue, had

been renamed for Powell shortly after his death.) In 2005, a statue of Powell by Branly Cadet called *Higher Ground* was added to the plaza in front of the building. It shows Powell striding upward, a Bible in his hand and his coat flapping in the breeze behind him; on the base are inscribed the words "Keep the Faith, Baby!"

172 The Summer of '77

"It was so quiet in Central Park last night, you could have heard a knife drop." So joked Johnny Carson, the late-night television host who made a career out of lampooning New York City—first from an NBC studio in Rockefeller Center and then, after 1972, from the safe remove of Burbank, California. And while more people got mugged in Johnny Carson's monologue each week than actually got held up in Central Park (in the same way today that the weekly murder total on *Law & Order* outpaces the city's actual crime statistics), there was no denying that by the late 1970s, New York was in a steep decline.

Historians debate when the city hit its low point, but a good candidate is the summer of 1977, the infamous "Summer of Sam" (to borrow Spike Lee's term), which has been covered, most recently, by journalist Jonathan Mahler in his excellent book *Ladies and Gentlemen, the Bronx Is Burning.**

As Mahler points out, not only was serial killer David Berkowitz (the "Son of Sam") on the loose until

---

*Mahler reports that crime was so bad in 1976 that there were "seventy-five felonies an hour." However, in terms of robbery the worst year would not come until 1981 and the murder rate would not hit its peak until 1990.

August 10, the city was plagued by countless other problems. For one, it was nearly out of money. The famous 1975 headline in the *Daily News*—"Ford to City: Drop Dead"—summed up the city's problem in trying to secure a federal bailout. Even the election of New York–friendly Jimmy Carter in 1976 hadn't helped much. The lack of funds meant that necessary city services were always on the verge of being cut. When John Lindsay was mayor, he'd tried to brand New York "Fun City." When the city vowed to cut the police force, cops handed out flyers at the airports telling tourists it was now "Fear City." The flyers recommended tourists not go out after dark and that they not ride the subway at all. The city made cuts to the NYPD nonetheless. Thousands of other jobs were lost too. When city sanitation workers were furloughed, the entire department went on strike, causing massive amounts of garbage to pile up on city streets. Despite building projects like the World Trade Center [170], which were supposed to provide a new economic stimulus, the city had lost a record number of jobs since the early 1970s, with little end in sight.

The subways, strewn with litter and covered in graffiti, were the only affordable option for many New Yorkers. However, the budget gap meant that token prices shot up from 35 to 50 cents, a move necessary just to keep the trains running.

In the Bronx, 5,000 apartments burned down every year, the result of persistent arson. The buildings along 42nd Street that were once some of Broadway's greatest theaters [110], had instead become XXX movie parlors; indeed, the number of places to buy pornography had gone up by 2,000 percent in a decade.

Then, on the night of July 13—just as a terrible heat wave began—the power failed, plunging the city into darkness. That night, portions of the city erupted into looting and arson: over 1,000 fires were lit and more than 1,600 shops were looted. It was the worst disturbance in the city since the Civil War Draft Riots [67] and the most widespread. No borough was exempted—from the Bronx to Bensonhurst the burning and robbery lasted well into the night. In the end, a congressional committee estimated the damage at $300 million, though some guessed the real toll had been closer to $1 billion. By the time the power was restored a day later, over 3,700 people had been arrested.

Today, riding the subway—usually clean and air-conditioned—or walking down 42nd Street, which features a Disney theater and a Madame Tussauds wax museum, it's hard to conjure up what the city was like even 30 years ago. Movies capture it well, from *Midnight Cowboy* to *Taxi Driver* to *Saturday Night Fever*, but there are few physical scars. However, if you do walk down 42nd Street and turn onto Eighth Avenue, you find some of the area's few remaining XXX movie parlors, though these are a dying breed, at least in this neighborhood.

It remains to be seen what a person walking down this same street 30 years from now will see. At the rate of change in New York, it is likely that those things that define one's experience of the city today are likely to be transitory. This is often why people get nostalgic in New York, even for the bad old days. It isn't that we want the crime and the graffiti to return; instead, we simply rue the fact that in a city that never ceases to shift its identity, each day we lose a little bit that reminds us of what New York—and by extension, we as New Yorkers—used to be.

173 Saving Grand Central Terminal

In 1965, the outcry over the destruction of McKim, Mead & White's Pennsylvania Railroad Station led to New York City passing a strict new set of landmark laws. In 1967, Grand Central Terminal [131] received an exterior landmark designation, which meant its owners could not alter it without express approval from the Landmarks Preservation Commission.

This presented Penn Central, the building's owners, with a real quandary. The building was a money-los-

ing proposition and they had hoped to follow the lead of Penn Station: keep the railroad tracks intact, but tear down the structure to build a money-making venture—in this case a 55-story skyscraper by Marcel Breuer, the architect best known in New York for the Whitney Museum of Art. (Architecture critics were incensed. Ada Louise Huxtable called Breuer's plan "a grotesquerie" and Sybil Moholy-Nagy—noting the effect that Breuer's tower would have when combined with Walter Gropius's Pan Am Building just to the north—labeled the two "Hitler's Revenge.")

Preservationists waged a 10-year battle to save the terminal. The notoriously publicity-shy Jacqueline Kennedy Onassis became the public face of the campaign, and Penn Central was sued. The case made its way to the U.S. Supreme Court in 1978. Penn Central argued that the landmark designation had devalued its property by 75 percent. Preservationists argued that the terminal itself was priceless.

Mercury, god of commerce, atop Grand Central Terminal

In the end, the preservationists prevailed; the court ruled that New York City had not acted outside its authority and affirmed that the city's right to preserve a building trumped the owners' right to tear it down.

The ruling had far-reaching implications both for New York and for the preservation movement throughout America. However, it did nothing to reverse the effect of years of neglect on the station. In 1983, operation of the station was ceded to Metro-North, the commuter railroad, and five years later it hired noted preservationist architects Beyer Blinder Belle to prepare a master plan for restoring the terminal. In 1994, the Metropolitan Transit Authority gained the lease from Penn Central's successor and work on the restoration began in earnest.

In the terminal's Main Concourse, decades of grime were removed from the ceiling, revealing Paul César Helleu's constellation scene for the first time in memory. Today, if you visit the terminal, follow the constellations across the ceiling to the northwest quadrant, where the painted ceiling meets the wall. There you will see a dark rectangle on the ceiling: that's the grime, left there so we can see just how bad things were. Also in the Main Concourse, notice that there are two marble staircases. One leads up to the Vanderbilt Avenue exit and the Campbell Apartment (a private office that was uncovered during the restoration and which now serves as a bar.) The other staircase, on the east wall, is new, built to almost perfectly match. However, if you look closely you will see that its railings have purposely been left plain, an indicator for future generations that the staircases weren't built at the same time.

The restoration of the terminal's architecture went hand in hand with creating retail and dining spaces, and the station has become a destination for people who have no intention of taking a train. This, in turn, allows the station to make money—exactly the problem its former owners thought they couldn't solve without tearing it down.

174 The Day the Music Died: John Lennon's Murder

New York has always been proud of its adopted children. In truth, many "native" New Yorkers aren't native at all—they've moved from all corners of the globe and re-created themselves. This was certainly true of ex-Beatle John Lennon, who came to the United States in 1971, and instantly became a New Yorker.

(As Lennon gnomically told Hendrick Hertzberg in *The New Yorker*, "Everywhere's somewhere, and everywhere's the same, really, and wherever you are is where it's at. But it's more so in New York.")

He and his wife, Yoko Ono, rented a place in the West Village and soon became enmeshed in activist politics, befriending Abbie Hoffman and Jerry Rubin (both members of the Chicago Seven, who had been indicted for protesting at the 1968 Democratic Convention). Lennon composed a song to help free activist John Sinclair and followed this with an album of overtly political songs, including "Sunday Bloody Sunday," (about Ireland's 1972 Bloody Sunday massacre), "Angela" (about the imprisonment of Black Panther

Angela Davis), and—most controversially—the feminist rallying cry "Woman Is the Nigger of the World."

Around this time, Richard Nixon ordered the FBI to begin surveil-

The *Imagine* mosaic at Strawberry Fields

lance on Lennon and Yoko Ono with the hopes that he could get them deported before Lennon's popularity helped swing the 1972 presidential election in favor of Democrat George McGovern. The Lennons fought the deportation until finally being granted green cards in 1976. By that time, their son Sean had been born, Lennon had retired from active recording, and they had settled into a comfortable existence in the Dakota Apartments [**90**] on Central Park West.

In November 1980, Lennon released his first album of new material in six years, *Double Fantasy*, and immediately began recording its follow-up, *Milk and Honey*. On the night of December 8, 1980, Lennon and Yoko Ono were returning from the recording studio when Mark

David Chapman, a fan who had earlier that day waited to get an autograph, stepped out of the shadows in front of the Dakota and shot Lennon five times. Lennon was almost immediately hustled into a police car and driven to Roosevelt Hospital, but he was pronounced dead on arrival.

As word spread on television and radio, a crowd gathered in front of the Dakota to leave flowers and sing songs. When, after a few days, Yoko Ono complained that they were keeping her up at night, the vigil moved to Central Park, and on December 14, a week after the shooting, over 75,000 people gathered in the park to observe ten minutes of silence in Lennon's memory.

The New York City Council voted to memorialize Lennon in the park. Designed by Bruce Kelly, this small section of the park is named Strawberry Fields, in honor of the Beatles' "Strawberry Fields Forever." At its heart is the *Imagine* mosaic. Donated by the people of Italy and modeled on a mosaic from Pompeii, it has become the site of annual memorials in Lennon's honor and is probably the most visited spot in the park. Farther down the hill, a plaque showcases the 121 countries from around the world that donated funds to make Strawberry Fields a "Garden of Peace."

175 **Trump Tower**

Through his relentless self-promotion in books, television shows, and even board games, real estate mogul Donald Trump has made himself a symbol of modern New York City. But one needs to look behind the glitz, the gold, and the often-mocked hairdo to see the positive effect that Trump has had on the city. Nowhere is this more apparent than in the best of his large skyscrapers, Trump Tower, on Fifth Avenue.

(Because Trump has a penchant for naming things after himself, each of his buildings in the city has "Trump" in the title; however, there is only one Trump Tower, at Fifth Avenue and 56th Street.)

The tower, designed by Der Scutt and opened in 1983, rises 59 stories above Fifth Avenue. (Though it is labeled as having 68 floors, this is a marketing gimmick, as people prefer living on higher floors.) To build such a tall tower on a relatively small lot, Trump took full advantage of the city's zoning, which had been radically rewritten in the wake of the success of the Seagram Building [158] on Park Avenue. Unlike the Zoning Resolution of 1916 [135], which required buildings to have setbacks to allow light and air to circulate, the new laws emphasized plazas and public accommodation. By the early 1980s, this no longer needed to be an outdoor plaza on the Seagram model, but could be an enclosed, indoor atrium. The more public space a building provided, the more height it could ultimately add. Scutt and Trump also made the building a mixed-use structure, combining retail, residential, and office into one building, which permitted them to build taller. Though Chicago's John Hancock Center had pioneered this type of mixed commercial and residential tower, it was radical for New York and remains so; a few towers, such as the Time Warner Center [182], have embraced multiple uses, but they remain the exception.

Two elements are immediately striking about Scutt's design. On the

Trump Tower

exterior there are setbacks on the building's southwest face, which are planted with trees—an unexpected, welcome bit of life that softens the effect of the shiny glass façade. Then, inside, you are confronted with the warm glow of Breccia Pernice marble, which Ivana Trump herself selected in Italy. Along the rear wall, a giant waterfall flows down the entire atrium, bringing the organic element from the exterior trees inside, linking earth and water, and making the tower one of the most welcoming spaces along the commercial stretch of Fifth Avenue.

(There are dissonant notes: Trump's name in giant brass letters over the door—which Der Scutt joked were big and shiny so that tourists could see the name from approaching airplanes—undercuts the effect, as does the current paucity of high-end retail tenants. However, that the building still succeeds is a testament to its good design.)

176 Arturo DiModica's *Charging Bull*

On October 19, 1987, the New York Stock Exchange [114] saw the single largest one-day drop in its history. Soon dubbed "Black Monday" (after the similar day during the 1929 crash [146], the market lost nearly 23 percent of its value over the course of the trading day.

As it recovered over the next two years, artist Arturo DiModica decided the city needed a symbol of the market's resiliency and began crafting a gigantic statue of a charging bull to present to Wall Street. The symbols of the bull and the bear to represent the rising and falling market seem to have first appeared in the late 18th century, when they referred to specific types of traders. By the late 19th century the term "bull market" was well enmeshed in the popular vocabulary. When DiModica began working on his bull in 1987, there was no doubt as to what his symbol would mean.

The 7,000-pound statue was finished in late 1989. Having scoped out Wall Street to discover when the night guards at the New York Stock Exchange would be scarce, DiModica pulled onto the street in a flatbed truck on the evening of December 15, 1989, lowered the bull into place, and took off, leaving behind a sheaf of flyers telling people about his gift. To DiModica's surprise, a Christmas tree had been put up in front of the Exchange since he'd done his reconnaissance, so he was able to tuck the bull underneath the tree as a Christmas present. The flyer announced that the work attested "to the vitality, energy and life of the American people in adversity" and that it was "offered honorably"—and free— "in acknowledgment of American dynamics."

When people showed up for work the next morning, they were surprised—and many of them delighted—to discover DiModica's giant gift. However, Dick Grasso, chairman of the New York Stock Exchange, was livid and spent the day trying to get it removed. By the end of the day it had been taken to an impound lot in Queens and as far as anyone knew, that would be the end of it: a one-day installation of "guerrilla" art.

However, fans of the statue were already working on a way to find it a permanent home. Henry Stern, the New York City parks commissioner, was intrigued by the statue and agreed to move it—at least on a temporary basis—to Bowling Green Park, the closest city park to Wall Street. City workers installed the statue on December 20 and Stern unveiled it the next day. Now approaching 20 years in its "temporary" home, *Charging Bull* has become a worldwide symbol of Wall Street and one of the most visited spots in all of Lower Manhattan. More than once the statue, which DiModica still owns, has gone on the market—most recently with the provision that it not be moved from Bowling Green—but as of this writing there have been no serious offers.

177 The Downfall of John Gotti, "the Dapper Don"

It is unfortunate that the history of Italian-Americans is often filtered through the history of organized crime. Indeed, to many students of popular culture, Italian history in America begins with *The Godfather* and ends with *The Sopranos* (with *Saturday Night Fever*'s Tony Manero thrown in the middle for good measure).

But while the contributions of Italian-Americans [see 92]—who by the 1970s made up 1.7 million of the city's residents—are broad, it is true that what often gets covered in the media are the exploits of the Mafia. In the 1980s, no figure loomed larger than John Gotti. Known as "the Dapper Don" for his sartorial flair, he was one of the first publicity-hungry mobsters in modern history. Also

known as "the Teflon Don" because criminal charges never seemed to stick to him, he became the head of the Gambino crime family in 1985, after ordering the murder of *capo* Paul Castellano. One of Gotti's primary hangouts was the Ravenite Social Club at 247 Mulberry Street in what had once been the heart of Little Italy—by the early 1990s it was becoming known as NoLita (NOrth of Little Italy). Gotti would sometimes surprise tourists by popping out of the club to shake hands, have his photo taken, and sign autographs.

Following a series of acquittals in the mid-1980s, the FBI got warrants to install listening devices in the Ravenite. When Gotti found out, he moved his conversations into the hallway and a vacant apartment above the club, not realizing that these spaces had been bugged too. On the night of December 11, 1990, fifteen FBI agents raided the club, arresting Gotti, Sammy "the Bull" Gravano (who later turned state's evidence), and Frank Locascio. Gotti was charged with extortion, racketeering, and—for the first time—the murder of Paul Castellano. He was found guilty in April 1992 and sentenced to life in prison. He died of cancer while in a maximum-security facility in 2002.

Meanwhile, it took the federal government seven years to take possession of the building that housed the Ravenite Social Club. The faux-brick façade (which had been installed to foil listening devices) was stripped, giant glass windows were added, and the interior (which the *Village Voice* noted had been designed in the style of a "Massapequa rec room") was gutted. The space currently houses a shoe store and bears no resemblance to its former incarnation, except that the old tiled tenement floor—which predates the Mafia's connection to the space—has been retained.

178 The African Burial Ground

In May 1991, workers on a new federal office building on Duane Street unearthed the first of what would end up being over 400 distinct graves. What they had stumbled upon was the city's old Negroes Burial Ground (today called the African Burial Ground), a place known from early maps of the city but evidence of which had never been found.

In 1697, when Trinity Church [11] acquired the public cemetery at Wall Street and Broadway, an ordinance was passed forbidding black people to be buried there. It is unknown if the African Burial Ground was inaugurated then or was a preexisting cemetery; historical records of its use only date from 1713 and those records are scarce. It is likely that the executed conspirators from the alleged 1741 slave rebellion [12] would have been buried here. The burial ground closed no later than 1795, when the area was graded and surveyed for lots.

The graveyard itself was on a terrible piece of property just north of the Commons—today's City Hall Park—in a piece of land next to the Collect Pond [22] known as the Cripplebush Swamp. If you walk from Chambers Street down Elk Street to the graveyard (this little road is now also known as African Burial Ground Way), you can feel the change in topography as the street slopes down in front of you. This is the change between the relatively good, high ground of the Commons, and the swampy, low ground of the graveyard.

The area was likely appropriated by the black community because few others wanted it and it was near the tracts of land the Dutch West India Company had granted to free black people. In all, at least 15,000 people—both free and captive—are estimated to have been buried in the

Rodney Leon's African Burial Ground monument

African Burial Ground. That fewer than 435 people—only 3 percent of the burials—were exhumed during the 1991–92 excavation is likely the result of the topography; with so little good ground, many of the burials would have long ago sunk into the water table. It is equally likely that many burials were destroyed by other builders, who—knowingly and unknowingly—dug up the remains and removed them.*

The archaeological team transferred the remains to Howard University in the early 1990s, where they were studied for 10 years. It had always been the plan to reinter the remains and after the destruction of the World Trade Center [180], it was decided to cease further scientific study and give the remains a proper reburial at the site.

In 2006, the site was designated a national monument and a year later a memorial, created by Rodney Leon, opened there to serve as a reminder of New York's role in the slave trade and to honor the memory of these New Yorkers who had been so long forgotten.

179 Lin Ze Xu and Fujianese Chinatown

Today, New York is the most ethnically and culturally diverse city in the world, with residents who hail from every nation and who speak every language. (Having the United Nations [156] headquartered here doesn't hurt, but we'd probably have this sort of diversity anyway.) A defining factor of a New Yorker's existence—and one that most take for granted—is that every day you are in contact with people who are from places all over the world.

In Manhattan, the largest and the fastest-growing segment of the immigrant population is in Chinatown, where most people hail from Fujian province. This mountainous area (it is, in a typical Chinese locution, known for being "eight parts mountain, one part water, and one part farmland") spreads out from the city of Fuzhou. As Jennifer 8. Lee points out in *The Fortune Cookie Chronicles*, her study of Chinese food in America, "the most remarkable trait of that area may be that it is the single largest exporter of Chinese restaurant workers in the world today."**

In 1965, the Immigration and Nationality Act removed 40 years of immigration quotas in America. This was especially welcome news for the Chinese community, which—despite the revocation of the Chinese Exclusion Act [87] in 1943—had limited opportunities to come to the United States. At first, the new Chinese arrivals continued to be Cantonese speakers from Guangdong, the traditional home province of most Chinese-Americans. However, in the 1970s a shift began and new arrivals were from other parts of China, which meant they mostly spoke Mandarin—the more common language—and could not easily communicate with Cantonese speakers who had been in America for generations. In effect, this created two overlapping Chinatowns in Manhattan: an older, traditional Chinatown of Cantonese speakers centered on Mott Street, and

---

*There is anecodatal evidence that bodies were found during the building of A. T. Stewart's Marble Palace at the corner of Broadway and Chambers Street [50].

**As Lee also notes in her book, there are more Chinese restaurants in America than KFC, McDonald's, and Burger King combined.

a newer, Mandarin-speaking China-town stretching out from Chatham Square along East Broadway.

In 1997, in a sure sign of the Fujia-nese population's prominence, a statue was dedicated in Chatham Square honoring Lin Ze Xu, a Chinese diplo-mat who was born in Fuzhou in 1785. In 1838, Lin was appointed an impe-rial commissioner in Guangdong and charged with finding a way to keep British opium imports out of China. Since the beginning of the 18th cen-tury, the British had struggled to find ways to pay for the silk, tea, and porce-lain they exported from Guangzhou (aka Canton), the only port foreign vessels were allowed to use. Beginning in the 1780s, opium replaced silver as the common trade good, and by the 1830s, millions of Chinese were addicted. When the emperor sent Lin Ze Xu to Guangdong, Lin immediately banned the sale of opium, impounded the drug from British vessels, and wrote a sternly worded memoran-dum to Queen Victoria telling her that the British should stop paying for Chinese goods with poison.

What Lin got for his trouble was the First Opium War, in which the British East India Company—backed by the British government—seized Hong Kong and the mouth of the Pearl River. After three years of fight-ing, the Chinese capitulated, signing the Treaty of Nanking, which ceded Hong Kong to the British and opened up other ports to British trade. A Sec-ond Opium War (1856–60), further opened up China to foreign trade and legalized the opium business.

In the aftermath of the war, Lin Ze Xu was banished to Ili, a Kazakh-dominated prefecture in north-western China. However, he was eventually recalled and served in a variety of government positions until his death in 1850.

Steven Wong, a Fujianese resident of Chinatown, campaigned to erect the statue of Lin, both as a symbol of Fujianese pride and as an explicit anti-drug message. The statue gazes down East Broadway toward the heart of the Fujianese neighborhood, along its red granite base—specially quarried in Fujian—are the words "A Pioneer in the War Against Drugs."

180 September 11, 2001: The Attack on the World Trade Center

The attack on the World Trade Center in 2001 was such a crucial moment in the city's history—and will have such deep psychic and physical rever-berations for years to come—that to reduce it to a brief narrative seems nearly impossible.

But even though it is such recent history, the facts are already becom-ing blurred, and it is good to commit them to print so that we remember what transpired. For example, many people don't remember that all seven trade center towers fell that day—or even that there were seven trade cen-ter towers to begin with [170].*

---

*Since this is a book about New York City, we are only talking here about the World Trade Cen-ter. Of course, we were not alone on this terrible day—a hijacked plane flew into the Pentagon in Virginia, killing 184 people, and the passengers of United 93 heroically attempted to take control of that plane, which crashed into a field near Shanksville, Pennsylvania, killing all 40 people on board.

The trade center's north tower, also known as Tower 1 or WTC 1, was hit from the north at 8:46 a.m. by American Airlines Flight 11, a hijacked passenger jet that had taken off that morning from Boston. The impact tore a hole in the building above the 93rd floor. Eighteen minutes later, a second plane, United Flight 175 from Boston, came in from the south, hitting the south tower, WTC 2, at a point between the 77th and 85th floors. Within five minutes all New York City area airports had been shut down and by 9:40 a.m., the FAA had taken the unprecedented step of banning all flights in the United States.

At 9:59 a.m., less than an hour after it was hit, WTC 2 collapsed in about twelve seconds. Twenty-nine minutes later, WTC 1 also collapsed. The two buildings imploded due to their innovative structure: neither had load-bearing columns, making them essentially hollow steel shells. When the heat of the jet fuel combined with millions of pieces of paper to raise temperatures to the point that the floor joists melted, the buildings "pancaked" in on themselves. In doing so, they crushed WTC 3 (the Marriott Hotel), WTC 4 (called South Plaza), and WTC 6 (the U.S. Custom House). WTC 5, which caught fire, suffered a partial collapse. WTC 7, the only building not in the 16-acre superblock, also collapsed, at approximately 5:20 p.m., due to the partial destruction of its south face earlier in the day. A small Greek Orthodox Church, just south of the site, was also destroyed.

Two other buildings, the Deutsche Bank Building on Cedar Street and Fiterman Hall (a Borough of Manhattan Community College building) on West Broadway were so significantly damaged that they will ultimately be torn down, though as of this writing neither has been fully razed. Other surrounding buildings, including the World Financial Center in Battery Park City and One Liberty Plaza, were damaged but quickly repaired. Indeed, One Liberty Plaza—directly across the street from the site—reopened to tenants on October 24, only 43 days after the attack.

As of this writing, the official death toll stands at 2,750 for the victims at the World Trade Center (including those on the planes, but not including the hijackers). Of these, 343 were firefighters and FDNY paramedics; 37 were police officers from the Port Authority, the World Trade Center's owner; 23 were members of the New York Police Department; and 8 were independent paramedics.

∽ In the immediate aftermath of the attack, rescue workers—both professionals and volunteers—came to the site to help. A makeshift haven was set up for these volunteers at St. Paul's Chapel [**14**], the city's oldest church, which remarkably remained unscathed. As the city began to coordinate the grueling 8½-month recovery operation, a gigantic white tent, nicknamed "the Taj Mahal," was erected on the other side of what people had taken to calling "the pile" or "Ground Zero" to provide meals, safety equipment, and much-needed respite.

Visiting the site today, it can be hard to imagine what the towers looked like in context, as well as hard to visualize how such a tremendous amount of destruction could have been limited to so small a tract of land. The trade center site is only about 16½ acres—just slightly larger than Central Park's Sheep Meadow [151] or Midtown's Bryant Park [see 54]. As of this writing, with construction on new buildings [182] proceeding slowly, the site mostly looks like a hole in the ground, which serves as a powerful reminder of what was lost. As new towers rise, it will become easier to visualize how the old World Trade Center buildings filled the site.

In 2011 or soon thereafter, a museum will open at the site, detailing its history, the attack, and its aftermath. Until that time, to get some sense of what it was like for rescue workers, many people visit St. Paul's Chapel, which keeps on view a number of small displays illustrating its role in the recovery operation. Its fence was also the main repository for missing-persons posters and spontaneous tributes to the victims, some of which are now on view inside.

Along the Cedar Street side of the site is Engine/Ladder Company 10, the closest fire station to the World Trade Center and the first responders that morning. They lost five members of their company, who are memorialized in a plaque on the fire station's façade. Along the side wall, a 56-foot bronze sculpture is dedicated to all 343 fire personnel who died at the scene.

181 The *Sphere* in Battery Park

When the World Trade Center [170] was being planned, both the Port Authority—its owner—and architect Minoru Yamasaki realized the benefit of visually anchoring the buildings with pieces of contemporary art. To that end, they commissioned or purchased work from many prominent 20th-century artists, including Alexander Calder, James Rosati, Joan Miró, and Louise Nevelson.

For the central plaza, Yamasaki turned to German sculptor Fritz Koenig, who created a work entitled *Grosse Kugelkaryatid* ("large spherical caryatid"), that came to be known in English simply as *Sphere*. The

Fritz Koenig's damaged *Sphere* in Battery Park

work, sort of an abstract Atlas holding aloft the world, was designed to sit in a fountain and act as a central focal point of the towers. Austin J. Tobin, the head of the Port Authority during the World Trade Center's construction, thought that it was the perfect symbol of "world peace through world trade," though this had never been Koenig's intention.

When the towers fell on September 11, 2001 [180], they rained down debris onto the plaza and the *Sphere*; remarkably, however, the sculpture suffered relatively minimal damage.

Fritz Koenig arrived in New York in October 2001, to, in his words, "say farewell to my biggest child." After Koenig was allowed to see the piece in the rubble at the site, it was dismantled by rescue workers and shipped in pieces to a hangar at JFK Airport, where much of the crime scene evidence was being stored.

Though initially reluctant to see the statue put back on view, Koenig was persuaded by families of victims of the attack to help them lobby to bring the sculpture back to Manhattan as a memorial. After lengthy discussions as to the most appropriate spot in Lower Manhattan, Koenig supervised the reconstruction of the work in Battery Park. On March 11, 2002—exactly six months after the attack—the reconstructed sculpture was unveiled by Mayor Michael Bloomberg and a host of other dignitaries. (This was the same night that "Towers of Light" were first illuminated near the World Trade Center site.) On the first anniversary of the attack, an eternal flame was added and as of this writing—with the permanent World Trade Center memorial not due to open until 2011—the *Sphere* is the only memorial to all 2,750 people killed at the World Trade Center that day.

182 Reinventing the Skyline

One notable development in New York in the few years since the destruction of the World Trade Center [180] has been a blossoming of new high-rise developments. There are too many skyscrapers that have recently opened (or are soon to be built) to cover in one brief entry, but we will single out four here that are connected in one way or another to the redevelopment of the World Trade Center site. That project, which will ultimately add ten or more new skyscrapers to the Financial District skyline, is the most notable large-scale building project in the city since the first World Trade Center was constructed [170]—if not since the development of Rockefeller Center [149] in the 1930s.

The primary architect associated with the project in the public's mind is Daniel Liebeskind, who created the master plan for the site. And while Liebeskind himself is not designing any of the towers, he has had a lasting influence on the central tower at the site—WTC 1, better known as the Freedom Tower.

The architect of the Freedom Tower is David Childs of Skidmore, Owings & Merrill. The building, due to open in 2013, will stand near the northwest corner of the World Trade Center site and will rise—per Liebeskind's master plan—to a symbolic 1,776 feet from its base to the top of its spire, thus marking the year of the Declaration of Independence. The building will feature an observation deck at 1,362 feet, the approximate height of the original World Trade Center towers. The building will be clad in glass and will rise like a spiral, so that while its base and roof are square, the central point will be an octagon.

In 2004, Childs completed the Time Warner Center at Columbus Circle, a pair of twin glass towers that house an upscale shopping mall (or "vertical retail environment," as they prefer to call it); a hotel; headquarters for its anchor tenant, Time Warner,

The Time Warner Center

and its broadcast news arm, CNN; and a theater for Jazz at Lincoln Center [see 162]. Though this project was strongly denounced during its construction—mostly for fear that its towers would cast deep shadows on Central Park (which they don't)—it has quickly integrated itself into the life of the Upper West Side, which bodes well for Childs's work at the World Trade Center.

Just two blocks south of the Time Warner Center, at Eighth Avenue and 57th Street, sits Sir Norman Foster's Hearst Tower. Foster was one of the architects picked to submit proposals for the primary tower at the World Trade Center; his entry, a side-by-side pair of towers, was a public favorite, and they were soon dubbed the "Kissing Towers" after the fact that in three places the two towers—each

faced with triangular facets of glass—were joined together. In 2001, Foster had already been asked to prepare a design for the new Hearst Tower and ultimately designed a building that looks like one half of the Kissing Towers. This design, which features no vertical steel columns, reduced the material in the building by more than 20 percent when compared to a skyscraper of equal size. The tower prides itself on its environmentally friendly architecture: it used over 90 percent recycled steel and it contains energy-saving innovations such as offices that automatically dim their lights based on the amount of available daylight, and a rainwater recycling program.

Foster's work on the Hearst Tower was complicated by the fact that back in 1926, William Randolph Hearst [see 133] had commissioned a tower on the same spot from architect Joseph Urban. The project, however, was derailed after the Great Crash in 1929 [146] and all that was ever built was a six-story skyscraper base. In 1988, the base was designated a New York City landmark, which meant that Foster would have to integrate it into his new tower. While the interior is entirely Foster's design, Urban's splendid Art Deco base is entirely preserved, including wonderful pairs of allegorical statues representing Comedy, Tragedy, Printing, Science, Art, Music, Sport, and Industry.

However, while Foster did not get the commission for the Freedom Tower, he has been picked to build one of the office towers at the site, WTC 2. This building, along with towers by Sir Richard Rogers and Fumihiko Maki, will provide a wall of skyscrapers along the Church Street side of the site. Each building is a little shorter than its neighbor so that, in accordance with Liebeskind's master plan, the effect is to bring the viewer's eye down gradually from the spire of the Freedom Tower to the World Trade Center memorial—called "Reflecting Absence"—which preserves in sunken pools the footprints of the original Twin Towers.

PART 8

Walking Tours

The following 14 tours allow you to combine the chapters of this book into self-guided explorations of the city. The itineraries are organized by neighborhood, beginning at the southern tip of Manhattan and working north to Harlem and the upper reaches of the island. We've always believed that what really sets New York apart is how easy it is to walk around and we highly recommend spending some time in these neighborhoods exploring in person the places we've written about.

In each tour, we provide step-by-step directions on how to link the history to specific places. Every stop is keyed to a chapter in the book, and we'll tell you the best spot to pause and read that chapter. To help guide you, we've included maps for each tour, and for easy reference the numbers on each map correspond to chapters in the book. Some of the directions might seem a little daunting at first—in truth, they look more complicated on paper than they are in reality. Once you are in a neighborhood, you'll have street signs, obvious landmarks, and friendly New Yorkers to help you get around.

Most tours should take an hour or two to walk. If there is a building or museum along the route that we think is particularly worth a visit, we've tried to include opening hours or other relevant information. Two tours take you farther afield. The first, "The Dutch, the English, and the American Revolution in Downtown Manhattan," ends with additional information that will take you on optional excursions to the East Village and to Upper Manhattan. The last tour in the book, "Harlem and Upper Manhattan," has a compact first half in central Harlem and then guides you by subway to the northernmost parts of Manhattan.

Keep in mind that our directions were correct at the time we wrote them, but things in New York can change in an instant. (This is especially true downtown, where constant construction is a fact of life.) Use common sense—and the maps provided with each tour—to help navigate from place to place, even if our instructions need to be altered. Each tour begins and ends with directions to a subway station. If you are touring on a weekend, visit the MTA's website at www.mta.info before you begin, to make sure that the train you want to take is operating normally. If you are planning to visit one of the museums or other sites, it's always best to verify that it will be open before you set out.

As you walk, you will pass a number of noteworthy spots *not* included on the itineraries, and we encourage you to stop and explore them on your own. Many have plaques or historical markers attached that you can read, though it's a good rule of thumb to take what's written on historical plaques in New York City with a grain of salt.

Happy walking!

TOUR 4

The Dutch, the English, and the American Revolution in Downtown Manhattan

Highlights

- Fraunces Tavern
- Bowling Green
- Trinity Church
- Archaeological remains of early New York
- The site of New Amsterdam's wall
- Alexander Hamilton's grave

This tour roughly follows the chapters in the first section of the book, "The Early City: New Amsterdam, Colonial New York, the Revolutionary Era, and the Birth of the New Republic, 1608–1804," and focuses exclusively on an area that today we call the Financial District but was then the entire city of New York. For those particularly interested in the 17th and 18th centuries, there are instructions at the end of the tour on how to take the subway uptown to see what the countryside would have looked like when the entire city covered less than 1.5 square miles at Manhattan's southern tip.

Tour 2, "Wall Street and Beyond," covers the same ground from a different perspective and the two make excellent companion excursions. You might wish to do this one in the morning and follow it up with Tour 2 in the afternoon or do the tours on subsequent days.

The best place to begin this tour is in **Battery Park,** which hugs the southwestern tip of the island of Manhattan. If you are coming by subway, take the 1 train to the South Ferry station or the 4/5 train to Bowling Green. If you want to start at the very beginning, you might consider reading **Chapter 1**—which discusses Manhattan before European contact—on your way downtown, just to set the stage.

Once you are in Battery Park, position yourself so that you can see the water (you will also have great views of the Statue of Liberty, which is covered in Tour 2) and read **Chapter 2,** about **Henry Hudson's arrival in the harbor in 1609.**

From the waterfront, walk to the northeastern edge of the park near the juncture of Broadway, State Street, and Battery Place. Just inside the park here is the **Netherlands Memorial Flagpole,** a gift from the Dutch in 1926 to commemorate the 300th an-

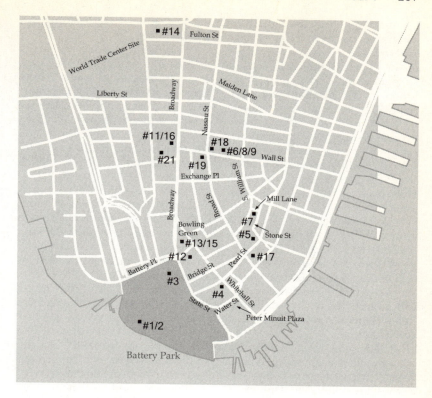

niversary of the **purchase of Manhattan Island,** which is discussed in **Chapter 3.**

Leave the park by turning right onto State Street (you'll be walking along the side of the Museum of the American Indian). You'll pass Bridge Street and Pearl Street before you see the Staten Island Ferry Terminal ahead of you. Pause at the little piece of land in front of the terminal; this is **Peter Minuit Plaza,** and some think the deal to buy the island took place here. Also, the Fighting Cocks Tavern, where the Fire of 1776 may have broken out, once stood near this spot. (You'll read about the fire a little later on the tour.)

State Street joins Water Street here. Continue on Water Street to the traffic light at **Whitehall Street** and turn left. Walk one block back north to Pearl Street; at the southwest corner of this intersection was the site of **Peter Stuyvesant**'s grand white mansion that later gave its name to the street. **Chapter 4** details Stuyvesant's arrival in New Amsterdam. Turn right on Pearl Street and walk east to the corner of Pearl and Broad streets. (Pearl, as you will soon read in **Chapter 6,** was the site of Native American oyster shell dumps; Broad Street was originally a canal, the Heere Gracht, that stretched from here up to Wall Street.)

At the southeast corner of Pearl and Broad streets you'll see **Fraunces Tavern.** Read **Chapter 17,** which focuses on this building's role as **George Washington's final Revolutionary War headquarters.** Continue along the Pearl Street side of 85 Broad Street—the hulking brown skyscraper opposite Fraunces Tavern—until you get to the **archaeological remains under the portico.** Read **Chapter 5** about the **Stadt Huis,** the most famous building that once stood here.

Continue counterclockwise around 85 Broad to the small staircase that leads up to Stone Street, which in good weather is lined with excellent outdoor dining options. Walk up the stairs and take Stone Street to little **Mill Lane.** Once there, read **Chapter 7** about **North America's first Jewish congregation.**

Walking the length of Mill Lane will deposit you on South William Street. Turn right and walk two-and-a-half short blocks to **Wall Street.** You have three stories to read here, so find a good place to stop—perhaps in front of **Federal Hall National Memorial** at the corner of Wall and Nassau streets—to read **Chapters 6, 8, and 9,** all of which relate to the **nine-foot-high wooden wall** that used to stand on this spot marking New Amsterdam's northern border and gave its name to the street.

If you have not yet proceeded along Wall Street to **Federal Hall,** do so, and read **Chapter 18** detailing **George Washington's inauguration,** which took place on this spot. If you don't plan on doing Tour 2, also read **Chapter 19** about the **founding of the New York Stock Exchange** (which is presently across the street, but was founded much farther east on Wall Street).

Continue west along Wall Street to the intersection of Broadway. Rising up in front of you is **Trinity Church.** It is worth looking inside as well as taking a stroll through the graveyard. Read **Chapter 11,** about the founding of the church, and **Chapter 16** about the **Fire of 1776,** which destroyed the original church structure.

Many distinguished New Yorkers are buried here, but the most famous is **Alexander Hamilton.** His grave is in the southern portion of the yard, marked by a large obelisk. Visit it and read **Chapter 21** about the famous **Burr-Hamilton duel.**

Leaving the Trinity churchyard, head north on Broadway six blocks to Fulton Street. As you go, you may notice **Maiden Lane** (discussed in **Chapter 1**) coming in from the right. In the early Federal era, Thomas Jefferson had his home on this street.

When you get to Fulton Street, enter **St. Paul's Chapel,** New York's oldest remaining church, discussed in **Chapter 14.** Because Trinity had burned down during the Fire of 1776, this was the place George Washington worshipped in New York, and his pew is preserved on the north wall.

You will also see a number of exhibits in the chapel relating to the attack on the World Trade Center; that event is discussed more in Tour 2.

Leave St. Paul's via the Broadway doors where you entered and walk back down Broadway toward Trinity. Keep going past Trinity and you'll soon pass **Exchange Place.** Near here was Hendrick Van Dyck's farm, where the **Peach War** began that you read about earlier in **Chapter 8.**

Nearby, there's a plaque on the front of 39 Broadway noting that it was the site of **George Washington's second presidential home.**

Soon you will see Broadway fork (at the famous *Charging Bull* statue). Just behind the bull is the entrance to small **Bowling Green Park,** which is still surrounded by the **wrought-iron fence erected in 1771.** Read **Chapter 13,** about the **Stamp Act protests** that took place here, and then read **Chapter 15,** which details the felling of the **equestrian statue of George III** that once stood in the small park and **the vandalism of the fence.**

To complete the colonial and early American stops downtown, stand in front of the **Museum of the American Indian** (the former Alexander Hamilton U.S. Custom House), the large Beaux-Arts building on the south side of Bowling Green Park. Read **Chapter 12,** which covers the **alleged slave rebellion in 1741.** That story makes an appearance on Tour 3, but the first of the fires it describes was set off in Fort George, which stood where the museum now stands.

↬You have now come full circle. Battery Park and the Netherlands Memorial Flagpole are just across the street. If you plan to do Tour 2, walk across State Street to the ornate, 1905 entrance to the IRT subway and start that tour there.

However, if you are interested in traveling farther afield in search of more colonial Manhattan, you may wish to head uptown to the former site of Peter Stuyvesant's farm. (If you don't want to do this now, it is also a part of Tour 7, "The East Village.")

There are a few public transportation options to get to the East Village from Bowling Green: the most straightforward (and, probably, the slowest) is to take either the R or W subway from Whitehall Street (behind the Museum of the American Indian) uptown to 8th Street.

Exit the subway and walk east along 8th Street, crossing through Astor Place, until you reach Third Avenue. Walk one short block north on Third Avenue and you'll see Stuyvesant Street coming in at a diagonal from the east. Take Stuyvesant Street to the corner of Second Avenue and the parish of **St. Mark's in the Bowery.** Make sure when you are here that you enter the graveyard to see Stuyvesant's gravestone in the church's exterior wall. Once there, read **Chapter 10** about **Stuyvesant's final days on his farm.**

To explore even more of what was then the countryside, you may want to explore some of the historic houses mentioned in **Chapter 20;** for more details, see the end of Tour 14, "Harlem and Upper Manhattan."

TOUR 2

Wall Street and Beyond

Highlights

- The Statue of Liberty
- The Shrine of St. Elizabeth Ann Seton
- The New York Stock Exchange
- Trinity Church
- Important early-20th-century skyscrapers
- The Alexander Hamilton U.S. Custom House
- The World Trade Center site

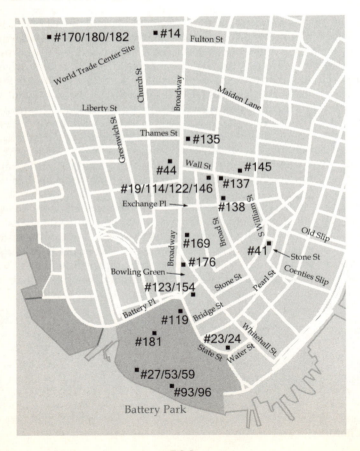

For most of New York's 400-year history, a tremendous amount of activity has taken place in the area below Wall Street. The previous tour, "The Dutch, the English, and the American Revolution in Downtown Manhattan," looked at the first 200 years of the city's development. This walk, dedicated to the 19th, 20th, and 21st centuries, presents a wide-ranging portrait of this neighborhood's importance as the country's financial center, the gateway for immigrants (nearly 20 million between 1855 and 1924), and the setting for some of New York's finest architecture.

〜 Begin in **Battery Park,** which is best reached by subway by taking the 4 or 5 train to Bowling Green or the 1 train to South Ferry. Whichever train you take, your first stop is the **IRT Control House,** just inside Battery Park near the corner of State Street and Battery Place. This 1905 structure—the oldest original shelter still in use from the **IRT subway**—is by the architects Heins & La Farge. Read about the first subway in **Chapter 119.**

Enter the park and make your way toward the harbor, following signs for the ticket office for the Statue of Liberty. You will soon come to the *Sphere*; read **Chapter 181** about this sculpture, which once stood in the plaza at the World Trade Center, the site of which you will be visiting at the end of the tour.

From the *Sphere*, continue toward the water and **Castle Clinton,** originally built for the War of 1812, but which has had many different uses over the years. If it is open, go inside and read **Chapter 27** about the **War of 1812; Chapter 53,** which details the building's life as a **theater;** and **Chapter 59** about **Castle Garden Emigrant Landing Depot.**

Leave Castle Clinton and walk to the waterfront to get views of the **Statue of Liberty** and **Ellis Island.** Pause on one of the benches here and read **Chapters 93 and 96,** which de-tail the erection of the statue in 1886 and the opening of Ellis Island a few years later. Then, walk south along the waterfront toward the restaurant Battery Gardens. Turn left here and follow the path to State Street. Across the street from you, tucked in be-tween the skyscrapers, is the red-brick **Shrine of St. Elizabeth Ann Seton.** Read **Chapter 23** about this house and America's first native-born saint. Near this spot is also where **Robert Fulton** lived when he launched his *North River Steamboat,* which you can read about in **Chapter 24.**

Turn right on State Street (it al-most immediately joins Water Street) and walk four blocks to Coenties Slip. Turn left and walk one block to Pearl Street. The large brown skyscraper ahead of you on the left is 85 Broad Street, which straddles the city's old-est paved street—**Stone Street.** Cross Pearl Street (keeping 85 Broad on your left) and you'll soon come to a short staircase leading up to the most charming block of Stone Street. This block features a well-preserved row of old countinghouses built after the **Great Fire of 1835;** for more on the fire, read **Chapter 41.** Today, the buildings host a number of restau-rants that have outdoor tables in good weather.

When you are done on Stone Street, walk back to 85 Broad Street and around the portico until you reach the Broad Street side of the building. Cross Broad Street and continue heading west on Stone Street until it dead-ends at Whitehall Street. Turn right and walk north to Bowling Green Park. Facing the park is the **Alexander Hamilton U.S. Custom House,** which today is home to the Museum of the American Indian. Stand in front of the building and read **Chapter 123** about the architecture and symbolism of the building. Then go inside (it's free) to read **Chapter 154** about **Reginald Marsh's murals in the rotunda.**

When you leave the museum, walk through Bowling Green Park to **Arturo DiModica's guerrilla art project,** *Charging Bull,* discussed in **Chapter 176.** The statue was placed here after the stock market crash in 1987.

Leave the statue and begin walking north on Broadway. You'll notice as you go the plaques inset into the sidewalk. These commemorate everyone who has been honored with a **ticker tape parade.** You can read about one of the biggest parades, **celebrating the Apollo astronauts,** in **Chapter 169.** When you reach Exchange Place, turn right and walk down the hill to Broad Street. Read **Chapter 138** about the **Curb Market,** which once made its home on this corner.

Turn left onto Broad Street and walk to stand in front of the **New York Stock Exchange** to read **Chapter 19** (about the founding of the Exchange) and **Chapter 114,** about the construction of this building. The Stock Exchange has been on this spot since the 1860s and has weathered many financial storms, including the **Panic of 1907** (read **Chapter 122**) and the **Great Crash of 1929** (read **Chapter 146**).

The building opposite the New York Stock Exchange (on the southeast corner of Wall and Broad streets) was **J. P. Morgan's bank.** Walk around to the building's Wall Street side to read **Chapter 137** and examine the shrapnel marks from **a 1920 terrorist attack.**

Across Wall Street from the Morgan bank is the Trump Building at 40 Wall Street; take a look at the building and read **Chapter 145.** Once known as the **Manhattan Company,** this was the building that was competing with the **Chrysler Building** in 1929 to be **the tallest in the world.**

Retrace your steps to Broad Street and then continue west to Broadway. Across Broadway is **Trinity Church,** the third church with this name to stand on this site and an important early example of Gothic Revival architecture. Visit the church and read **Chapter 44,** which details its construction. Then head into the northern part of the graveyard. If you walk to the rear of the graveyard, you can see the façade of the **American Stock Exchange,** which you just read about in **Chapter 138.**

Exit the graveyard back onto Broadway and walk one block north to Thames Street. Facing this small street on the other side of Broadway is the **Equitable Building** at 120 Broadway. Read **Chapter 135** about these buildings and their role in creating the **Zoning Resolution of 1916.**

Continue north on Broadway to Liberty Street. Turn left and walk down the hill one block to the **site of the World Trade Center.** (If you walk two blocks on Liberty to Engine/Ladder Company No. 10, notice the memorial to the 343 firefighters who lost their lives on 9/11 on its Greenwich Street wall.) Because of ongoing construction, you'll need to figure out where it is best to stop and read a few entries about the site: **Chapter 170** discusses the original structure; **Chapter 180** details the attacks on September 11, 2001; and **Chapter 182** talks about some of the new buildings that are being erected on this site.

A worthwhile stop near the site is **St. Paul's Chapel,** at the corner of Fulton and Church streets. It is the city's oldest church building and survived unharmed after the September 11 attacks. The church became a refuge for rescue workers and contains a number of displays that document this part of its history. Read **Chapter 14** about the church's founding and go inside to see the preserved interior and the World Trade Center commemorations.

This is the last stop on the tour. If you need the subway, just outside St. Paul's is an entrance to the 4/5 train at Fulton Street. However, the 2/3 and R/W trains are also close by.

TOUR 3
The Civic Center and Brooklyn Heights

Highlights

- The Woolworth Tower
- City Hall
- The Brooklyn Bridge
- The African Burial Ground
- Brooklyn Borough Hall
- The Plymouth Church of the Pilgrims
- Brooklyn Heights Promenade

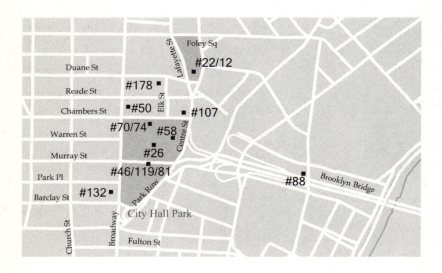

In 1883, the Brooklyn Bridge opened, linking the political hearts of two of America's largest cities: New York and Brooklyn. Fifteen years later, the bridge had created such a firm link that the pair of cities had merged into one. This tour takes you through Manhattan's Civic Center (which was also once its primary retail district), across the bridge, and into Brooklyn Heights, one of the most charming residential neighborhoods in the city.

~ Begin your tour in City Hall Park. The closest subway stations here are the R/W at City Hall; the 4/5/6 at Brooklyn Bridge/City Hall; or the 2/3 at Park Place. Go to the end of the park at the intersection of Broadway and Park Row to read **Chapter 132** about the **Woolworth Tower,** which sits on Broadway between Barclay Street and Park Place. Then walk to the center of the park, where there is an **ornate fountain, ringed with gas lamps.** Read **Chapter 46** about the original fountain on this spot and the city's water system. Underneath your feet stands the magnificent (and now closed) **City Hall station** of the **original IRT subway** discussed in **Chapter 119.** You are also very close to the site of **Alfred Ely Beach's "secret" pneumatic subway,** which you can read about in **Chapter 81.**

Exit the park on Broadway and walk north until you get a good look at the front of **City Hall,** discussed in **Chapter 26.** Then continue on Broadway to the corner of Chambers Street. Across the street (labeled in places the "Sun Building") is **A. T. Stewart's Marble Palace.** Read **Chapter 50** about this store's contributions to modern retail.

Continue north on Broadway two blocks to Duane Street, turn right, and walk to the **African Burial Ground**—you'll read about its history and rediscovery in **Chapter 178.** Continue east on Duane Street to Foley Square, once the site of the **Collect Pond.** Read **Chapter 22,** about the draining of the pond, and then read **Chapter 12** about the **alleged 1741 slave uprising.** Many of the convicted slaves were executed here.

Return to the African Burial Ground, turn left (south) onto Elk Street, and walk up the hill back to Chambers Street. Look across Chambers at the marble-columned **Tweed Courthouse,** a monument to the life and downfall of **William "Boss" Tweed.** Read **Chapters 70 and 74,** which detail his exploits.

Turn left onto Chambers, walk to the corner, and then cross Chambers Street so that you can look back at the **Surrogate's Court** and read **Chapter 107.** This building is based on a design for a new City Hall following **Five-Borough Unification.** Looking to your right, you'll also see the grand, 40-story **Municipal Building,** which houses many city offices.

Continue walking south and you almost immediately see the pedestrian entrance to the **Brooklyn Bridge.** However, before you cross the bridge, locate the nearby statue in City Hall Park of **Horace Greeley,** one of the city's great 19th-century newspaper publishers; his life is discussed in **Chapter 58.** Greeley's office once stood nearby on Park Row. (This statue is by J. Q. A. Ward, whose statue of Henry Ward Beecher you will see in Cadman Plaza, Brooklyn.)

When you are done admiring Greeley, cross Centre Street and begin walking across the **Brooklyn Bridge.** It takes about 30 to 40 minutes to cross the bridge to Brooklyn. Pause when you get to the middle to read about the bridge's construction in **Chapter 88.**

When you get to the far end of the bridge, turn right onto Tillary Street, walk one block to Cadman Plaza East, and turn left to walk to Johnson Street. Just after you cross Johnson Street, you'll see J. Q. A. Ward's handsome statue of **Henry Ward Beecher,** whose church you will visit a little

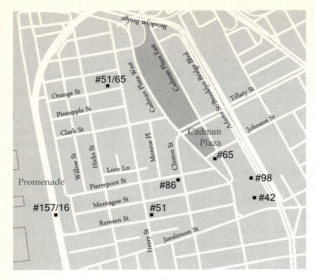

Washington oversaw the evacuation of American troops following the **Battle of Brooklyn,** which is discussed briefly in **Chapter 16.**

Take a left on the promenade and leave it one block later, turning left on Remsen Street. Walk to the corner of Remsen and Henry streets to see the **Church of Our Lady of Lebanon** (which was once the Church of the Pilgrims). Read **Chapter 51** here, which discusses both this church and Henry Ward Beecher's Plymouth Church, which you will see at the end of the tour.

Continue on Remsen Street one block to Clinton Street, turn left, and walk two blocks to Pierrepont Street. The building on the southwest corner is the **Brooklyn Historical Society,** discussed in **Chapter 86.**

Walk west on Pierrepont Street two blocks to Henry Street, turn right, and walk four blocks to Orange Street. Turn left and walk to the **Plymouth Church,** the home parish of Henry Ward Beecher. A statue of Beecher by Gutzon Borglum stands in the churchyard. You may wish to reread the relevant sections of **Chapters 51 and 65** here.

To get to the nearest subway, retrace your steps on Henry Street to the Clark Street 2/3 subway station.

later on the tour. This is a good place to read **Chapter 65** about Beecher's slave auctions.

Continue south through Cadman Plaza to the Greek Revival **Brooklyn Borough Hall** (formerly Brooklyn City Hall) and read **Chapter 42,** which is a good introduction to the borough's history.

Before you leave Cadman Plaza, notice Emma Stebbins's statue of **Christopher Columbus** in front of the Supreme Court Building. Read **Chapter 98** about the many Columbus statues—including this one—created for Central Park. Then leave Cadman Plaza heading west on Montague Street and follow it four blocks to the **Brooklyn Heights Promenade,** which offers great views of the Manhattan skyline and the Brooklyn Bridge. You can read about the creation of the promenade in **Chapter 157.** It was near this spot that George

TOUR 4

The Five Points, Chinatown, and the Lower East Side

Highlights

- The first New York City tenement
- The Church of the Transfiguration
- The main streets of Chinatown
- The Eldridge Street Synagogue
- The former home of the *Jewish Daily Forward*

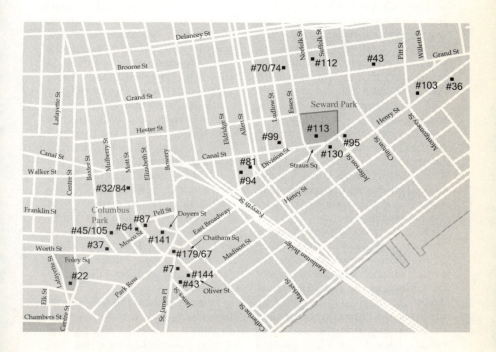

Since the early 19th century, New York's immigrant populations have centered on the neighborhoods near the East River that allowed easy access to the waterfront and its many jobs. When the area was primarily Irish, it was called Five Points—named for an intersection of streets that used to exist just behind today's courthouses. As Jewish immigrants arrived in the 1880s, they settled east of the Bowery in what we now call the Lower East Side. In between the two was Chinatown, an area that a century ago had only a few thousand residents but is currently the fastest-growing ethnic neighborhood in Manhattan.

～ This tour begins with the creation of the Five Points in what is today called **Foley Square.** The closest subway stations are the 4/5/6 at Brooklyn Bridge/City Hall or the J/M/Z at Chambers Street (which is actually one large, connected station).

Walk to the center of the square and read **Chapter 22** about the **Collect Pond,** which once stood at this site. Head to the Worth Street side of the square, turn right, and walk one block to the corner of Worth and Baxter streets. This is the only remaining "point" of the original, infamous **Five Points intersection,** discussed in **Chapter 37.**

Cross Baxter Street and enter **Columbus Park,** today a hub of the Chinese community. This is a good place to read about **Charles Dickens's visit to the Five Points** in **Chapter 45** as well as about the creation of the park in **Chapter 105.**

Exit the park on its Mulberry Street side and walk up short Mosco Street to Mott Street. Pause on the corner to read **Chapter 64** about the **Church of the Transfiguration.** Across the street and just a little up the block at **32 Mott Street** is one of the oldest shops from the heart of the original **Chinatown,** which you can read about in **Chapter 87.**

Walk north to **No. 65 Mott Street, the city's first tenement.** Tenements were the most ubiquitous form of housing in these neighborhoods; you can read **Chapter 32** about the building of this first example of the form and then read **Chapter 84,** which discusses some of the later laws intended to improve living conditions in these apartments.

Retrace your steps south on Mott Street until you reach Pell Street. Turn left on Pell Street, walk one short block to Doyers Street, and turn right. The sharp curve of this small street is the so-called **Bloody Angle** described in **Chapter 141.** Walk the length of Doyers Street to the Bowery, turn right, and walk down a block to Chatham Square. Cross the Bowery into the square (also marked "Kim Lau Square"), which features a statue of **Fujianese hero Lin Ze Xu.** Read about Lin in **Chapter 179.**

(Chatham Square connects back to the Five Points here via Worth Street, which didn't run this far east until after the **Civil War Draft Riots.** This square is a good place to find a place to sit and read about the riots in **Chapter 67.**)

Leave Chatham Square on St. James Place. As you walk down the next block, notice the small graveyard on your left. This is the first cemetery of **Congregation Shearith Israel** and was established in 1656, just two years after the congregation arrived in New Amsterdam. Pause here to read about the congregation in **Chapter 7.**

When you reach James Street, turn left and walk to the **Church of St. James, birthplace of the Ancient Order of Hibernians,** and read **Chapter 43.** Walk to the end of James Street and turn left onto Madison Street; walk one block to Oliver Street and turn left again to **25 Oliver Street, the former home of Governor Alfred E. Smith.** Smith's life and career are the subject of **Chapter 144.**

Continue on Oliver Street back to Chatham Square. Exit the square on East Broadway and walk through the heart of Fujianese Chinatown to the Manhattan Bridge. Just after you pass under the bridge, turn left onto Forsyth Street, which after one short block merges with Eldridge Street. Walk to the **Eldridge Street Synagogue** at 12 Eldridge Street and read about it in **Chapter 94.** (The synagogue is open—with paid admission—Sundays through Thursdays from 10:00 a.m. to 4:00 p.m. if you would like to visit the interior.)

When you've finished at the synagogue, retrace your steps down Eldridge Street to Division Street. Turn left and walk one block to Allen. On a ramshackle building on the west side of Allen Street (just north of Division), you can make out the faded sign of a former **elevated railroad electrical station.** (It reads—with some letters missing—"Manhattan Railway Company, Station No. 5.") This is one of the only remnants of the old elevated railroad system, which you can read about in **Chapter 81.**

Turn left and walk one block up Allen to Canal Street. As you go, try to conjure up what this street would have looked like with the elevated train rumbling overhead, plunging the sidewalks and storefronts into darkness.

When you reach Canal Street, turn right and walk two blocks to Ludlow Street and turn left. Two doors in from the corner is the **Boe Fook funeral home,** which was once the **Kletzker Brotherly Aid Association.** (Look up and you can see the name and the date of its founding in the cornice, as well as the faint outlines of a Jewish star between the upper windows.) Read about aid associations in **Chapter 99.**

Retrace your steps to Canal Street, and walk one more block east to **Seward Park;** in **Chapter 113** you can read about this park, the first municipally run playground in America. Across small Straus Square from the park is the ornate former **headquarters of the *Jewish Daily Forward.*** (You'll see that it says "Forward Building" in English directly over the door and *Forvertz* in Yiddish at the very top.) Stand in front of the building to read about it in **Chapter 130.**

Canal Street and East Broadway merge here. Keep walking east to the corner of Jefferson Street to see the **Educational Alliance,** discussed in **Chapter 95.** (As you read, make sure you notice the Seward Park Library directly across the street.) Then continue walking east on East Broadway two blocks to Montgomery Street. Turn right on Montgomery, walk one block to Henry Street, and turn left to walk to the front of the **Henry Street Settlement.** Pause here to read **Chapter 103.**

Continue east on Henry Street to look at **St. Augustine's Church** at 290

Henry Street, home of the only remaining slaves' galleries in New York, which you can read about in **Chapter 36.** The galleries are open to groups by prior arrangement with the St. Augustine's Project, www.staugsproject.org/visits.html.

When you are done here, continue east on Henry Street until it merges with Grand Street. Turn left (sort of a U-turn) onto Grand and walk back west two-and-a-half blocks to the **Church of St. Mary's** (which you read about earlier in **Chapter 43**).

Continue west on Grand Street to Norfolk Street. Turn right and walk to **Beth Hamedrash Hagadol,** the old synagogue that was once the Norfolk Street Baptist Church. Read about its most famous rabbi, Jacob Joseph, in **Chapter 112.**

Return to Grand Street and walk one block to Essex Street. In front of you is **Seward Park High School** (where such Lower East Side luminaries as Jerry Stiller, Walter Matthau, and Tony Curtis went to school). It sits on the site of the former **Ludlow Street Jail, where William "Boss" Tweed was held.** To get a sense of Tweed and his downfall, read **Chapters 70 and 74.**

This is your last stop on the tour. There are a number of Jewish shops still in this area, including the Pickle Guys on Essex Street and Kossar's Bialys on Grand Street. (And, north of Delancey Street, you'll find the area's trendier clubs and restaurants.) When you are done exploring, the closest subway is the F train at the corner of Essex and Delancey streets.

TOUR 5

Little Italy, NoLita, and SoHo

Highlights

- St. Patrick's (Old) Cathedral
- The Haughwout Building and streets of cast-iron architecture
- Mulberry Street and the heart of Little Italy
- The former site of the Ravenite Social Club
- Lombardi's: America's first pizzeria

This tour brings together two neighborhoods—Little Italy (and its northern outpost, NoLita) and SoHo—that we often think of as separate and distinct, but that are intimately connected. Before it was trendy SoHo, this was the retail and manufacturing heart of the city, and most of the people who worked here came from ethnic neighborhoods like Little Italy.

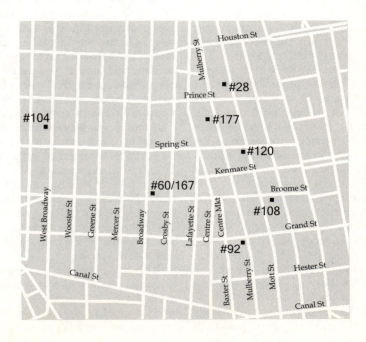

~ The tour begins at Canal and Mulberry streets. The closest subways are all along Canal Street—take either the 6, the N/R/Q/W, or the J/M/Z to get here.

Starting at Canal Street, walk two blocks north on Mulberry Street to Grand Street. You are walking through the heart of today's **Little Italy.** A century ago, this neighborhood filled 50 blocks in this area; today, Little Italy has mostly shrunk to this small strip of restaurants and shops along Mulberry.

When you reach the southwest corner of Grand and Mulberry streets, read **Chapter 92** about the **Banca Stabile.** Its former home here is now the Italian American Museum. Walk one more block north on Mulberry to Broome Street and turn right. Walk one-and-a-half blocks east to 359 Broome Street, and read **Chapter 108** about the former **Church of San Salvatore,** today a Ukrainian Orthodox church.

Retrace your steps on Broome to the corner of Mott Street, turn right, and walk north to Spring Street. At the corner is **Lombardi's pizzeria.** Read **Chapter 120** about the opening of America's first pizza parlor; it remains, in the eyes of many stalwarts, one of the best.

Walk one more block north to Prince Street and you will come to a large brick wall surrounding **St. Patrick's (Old) Cathedral.** You can reach the front gate of the church by walking just a little farther north on Mott Street. Enter the church grounds and read **Chapter 28** about the cathedral's history. The brownstone façade you see was extensively altered after an 1866 fire. The church is often open if you'd like to take a look inside.

When you are done at the church, walk along the Prince Street wall and look at the unchanged rear (Mulberry Street) façade, made of Manhattan schist. Then walk south to 247 Mott Street, a shoe store that was once the home of John Gotti's **Ravenite Social Club,** which you can read about in **Chapter 177.**

Continue south on Mulberry Street to Broome Street and turn right. As you walk west on Broome Street you'll see the grand **former headquarters of the New York Police Department**—now a luxury apartment building—on your left between Centre Market and Centre Street.

When you reach Broadway, cross the street and look back at the former home of **E. V. Haughwout's store,** one of the most significant buildings ever constructed in New York. Read about why this building is so important in **Chapter 60.** This view—and perhaps this building—would have been obliterated if the **Lower Manhattan Expressway,** discussed in **Chapter 167,** had been constructed.

Continue on Broome Street four blocks to West Broadway. As you walk, you'll be passing by a number of excellent examples of cast-iron architecture. At West Broadway, turn right and walk to **422 West Broadway,** which is not only a great cast-iron structure but, as **Chapter 104** details, a relic of the now-forgotten **South Fifth Avenue.**

This is the last stop on the tour; to reach the nearest subway, continue north on West Broadway to Prince Street, turn right, and walk back to Broadway and the R/W subway.

TOUR 6

Greenwich Village

Highlights

- Washington Square
- Café Wha?
- Charming, tree-lined streets of townhouses
- Chumley's, the city's last remaining speakeasy
- New York's narrowest home
- The site of the Triangle Shirtwaist Factory fire

Greenwich Village: depending on your age, the name may conjure up visions of rabble-rousing bohemians, long-haired troubadours, or the ladies from *Sex and the City*. This was Jane Jacobs's neighborhood, which she praised in *The Death and Life of Great American Cities*. (If you'd like, you can read more about Jacobs and her fight to preserve the West Village in **Chapter 167**, which is a stop on Tour 5, "Little Italy, NoLita, and SoHo.")

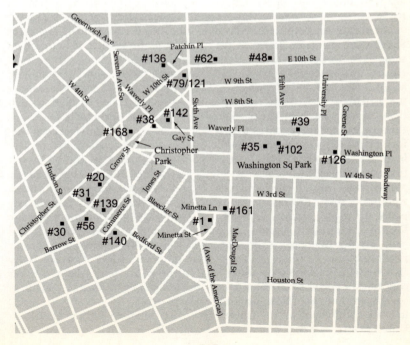

〜 If you are traveling via subway to the Village to begin this tour, your best bet is to take the 1 train to the Christopher Street station, and walk west on Christopher Street until you get to Hudson Street. This was once the last street before you reached the Hudson River—most of what you see between here and the river today is landfill. Turn left on Hudson and walk the short block to Grove. Across the street is the **Church of St. Luke in the Fields.** If it is open, there is a lovely garden surrounding the church that is worth a detour and is a great place to read **Chapter 30** about the final days of the area as an actual village.

Turn left onto Grove Street and begin walking the one block toward Bedford Street. Where Grove Street curves, you'll see tiny **Grove Court;** peer through the gate, then step back and read about these homes in **Chapter 56.**

Continue on Grove to Bedford Street. On the northeast corner stands the **wooden William Hyde House.** In **Chapter 31** you can read about this house and the origins of the neighborhood. Turn right on Bedford and walk down the block to **the nondescript entrance to 86 Bedford Street—the speakeasy Chumley's.** If Chumley's is open, be sure to pay a visit inside to see its trove of memorabilia from the literary lights who drank there. (You may wish to pause for some libations yourself.) Even if it isn't open, pause here to read **Chapter 139** on New York during Prohibition.

Once you are done at Chumley's, continue on Bedford Street to the corner of Commerce Street. Looking to your right, you'll see the **Cherry Lane Theatre,** which you may want

to take a look at up close as you read **Chapter 140.** Then head around the corner to number **75 ½ Bedford Street, the former home of Edna St. Vincent Millay and the narrowest house in the city.**

Turn and head back the way you came on Bedford Street until you reach Grove Street. Turn right at the Hyde House and walk most of the way down the block to **45 Grove Street, the former Samuel Whittemore Mansion,** the only large country home left in Greenwich Village and one dubiously associated with assassin John Wilkes Booth. You can read about this and other country mansions in **Chapter 20.**

Continue on Grove to Seventh Avenue South—if you took the 1 train to the Village, you'll be back where you started. Cross Seventh Avenue and walk through tiny Christopher Park to come out in front of the **Stonewall Inn** at 53 Christopher Street. Read **Chapter 168** about the birth of the gay rights movement here. Then cut through the park to Grove Street (pausing to look at George Segal's *Gay Liberation* monument) and turn left. Walk to the triangular point of the park and you'll see in front of you the **Northern Dispensary,** discussed in **Chapter 38.**

Walk along the front (Waverly Place) side of the dispensary, pausing to note that you've come to the intersection of Waverly Place and Waverly Place, and then continue one more block to Gay Street. Turn left and walk to **12 Gay Street, the former home of mayoral mistress Betty Compton.** You can read about her boyfriend, **Mayor James J. Walker,** in **Chapter 142.**

Continue on Gay Street to Christopher Street, turn right, and walk the short block to Greenwich Avenue, where you will see the imposing red bell tower of the Jefferson Market Courthouse to your left. Turn left onto Greenwich Avenue and walk along the side of the lovely community garden until you reach West 10th Street. Turn right and walk most of the way down the block until you see tiny **Patchin Place** on your left, once the home of revolutionary **John Reed.** Reed and other bohemian residents of the Village are the subject of **Chapter 136.**

Continue on West 10th Street to the corner of Sixth Avenue; cross the avenue and look back at the magnificent **Jefferson Market Courthouse,** now a library. Read **Chapter 79** about the building and **Chapter 121** about the murder of architect **Stanford White.** White's killer, Harry K. Thaw, was arraigned here.

Then continue on West 10th Street—one of the finest rows of townhouses in the Village—to stand in front of the Peter Warren (45 West 10th Street). This 1950s apartment building replaced the **Tenth Street Studio Building,** one of the most important artists' residences in the city; you can read about it in **Chapter 62.**

Continue along West 10th Street. Number 18 was once the home of poet **Emma Lazarus,** author of "The New Colossus" ("Give me your tired, your poor, your huddled masses . . .") You may wish to read about the campaign to erect the Statue of Liberty in **Chapter 93.** Two doors down at 14 West 10th is the home of **Mark Twain** (who was mentioned earlier in **Chapter 136**).

When you reach the corner of Fifth Avenue, you will see the **Church of the Ascension.** Read about the famous marriage of President John Tyler here in **Chapter 48.** The church is normally open weekdays from noon to 1:00 p.m. and is well worth a visit inside.

Once you have finished at the church, turn right (south) and walk down Fifth Avenue until it ends at **Washington Square Park.** Find a good place in the park to read about its history (**Chapter 35**) and the famous **Washington Memorial Arch** (**Chapter 102**). Then look at the homes at **1–13 Washington Square North, collectively known as the Row**, and read **Chapter 39.** You might wish to take a walk around the block here to see the **Washington Mews** (the service alley behind these homes). To do so, walk along Washington Square North until you reach University Place. Turn left and walk up University to the gated entrance to the mews. (A sign may read "Private," but this is a public thoroughfare.) Walk down the mews, noting the old paving stones—these are probably the oldest original Belgian Block cobblestones in the city. When you reach Fifth Avenue, turn left and head back to Washington Square Park.

Walk through the park, angling toward the exit on its east side at Washington Place. You are in the heart of **New York University**'s campus. Walk one block east on Washington Place to the corner of Greene Street. **NYU's Brown Building** on the corner here was once home to the **Triangle Shirtwaist Factory,** which you can read about in **Chapter 126.**

Retrace your steps to the park and walk to its southwest corner, where West 4th Street and MacDougal Street intersect. Turn left (south) on MacDougal and walk two blocks to the corner of Minetta Lane. As you walk, you'll pass 130–132 MacDougal Street, the house where **Louisa May Alcott wrote *Little Women.***

At the corner of Minetta Lane is **Café Wha?** You can read about the café, where Bob Dylan got his start, in **Chapter 161.**

Walk one short block west on Minetta Lane to Minetta Street and turn left. These two streets still reflect the original course of the **Minetta Brook,** which runs beneath them. Read **Chapter 1** for more information on this brook and other vestiges of ancient New York.

Walk down Minetta Street to Bleecker Street and turn right to cross Sixth Avenue. Continue on Bleecker to **Jones Street,** the site of the photo shoot for Bob Dylan's second album, *The Freewheelin' Bob Dylan* (mentioned in **Chapter 161**). Turn right onto Jones Street and walk the short block to West 4th Street. If you turn left onto West 4th Street and walk two short blocks, you will be back at Christopher Park, and the 1 train station where the tour began.

TOUR 7

The East Village

Highlights

- Grace Church
- The Public Theater
- McSorley's Old Ale House
- St. Mark's Place and the home of the Electric Circus
- Tompkins Square Park
- The remnants of the German-American neighborhood Kleindeutschland

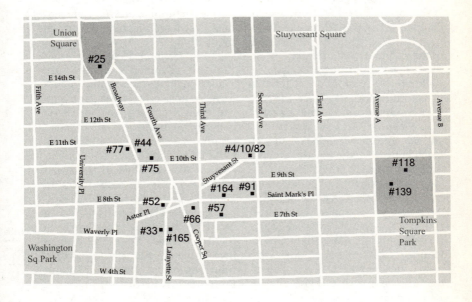

The East Village has changed so much over the years that it's been a different place for every generation: genteel residential neighborhood, German-American enclave, hippie hangout, low-rent district (think *Rent*). Before all of those things, it was the countryside, and much of the area was owned by Dutch governor Peter Stuyvesant. This tour will touch on all these eras and will take you from Broadway to the Bowery to Alphabet City.

317

Begin in Union Square, which can be reached by the 4/5/6, N/R/Q/W and L trains. Union Square is named because it is the place where Broadway and the Bowery met on the **Commissioners' Plan of 1811,** which you can read about in **Chapter 25.**

Walk south from Union Square on Broadway to the block between 11th and 10th streets and **Grace Episcopal Church** (discussed in the second half of **Chapter 44**), built by James Renwick; the church is normally open to visitors during the day. Across the street from the church, at the southwest corner of 11th Street, is the former **Hotel St. Denis.** Read **Chapter 77** about Alexander Graham Bell's successful demonstration of the telephone at the hotel.

Turn left on 10th Street and begin walking east past Grace Church's playground; this was once the site of **Fleischmann's Vienna Bakery;** read **Chapter 75** about the bakery and its famous breadline. When you reach Fourth Avenue, turn right and walk south to 8th Street. The building you'll see on the right—bounded by Lafayette Street, Astor Place, and 8th Street (with a Starbucks in the storefront)—was once the site of the now-demolished **Astor Place Opera House. The Astor Place Riot**—discussed in **Chapter 52**—was one of the largest public disturbances in the 19th century.

Head east on 8th Street. In the block between Cooper Square and Third Avenue stands **The Cooper Union.** Read about Peter Cooper and the school in **Chapter 66.** Walk to Third Avenue, turn left, and walk one block north to 9th Street. Cross Third Avenue and take Stuyvesant Street

(which comes in at a diagonal from the east) to Second Avenue and the **Church of St. Mark's in the Bowery.** On this site once stood a chapel built by **Peter Stuyvesant,** who is buried in the churchyard. (There is a plaque marking the spot on the side of the church.) Read **Chapters 4 and 10** about Stuyvesant. Then read **Chapter 82,** about department store pioneer **A. T. Stewart,** who was also once buried in this graveyard.

When you leave the graveyard, cross Second Avenue and walk east on 10th Street two blocks to Avenue A and **Tompkins Square Park.** (As you walk, you'll notice the Russian/Turkish bathhouse on your right; it is one of the few remaining bathhouses in the city.)

Walk south on Avenue A to enter the park at your first opportunity. Walk straight (east), keeping the basketball courts on your left, until you come to the entrance to a children's play area—inside this small playground is one of Manhattan's only commemorations of the *General Slocum* **disaster,** one of the worst tragedies in the city's history. Read about the disaster in **Chapter 118.**

Leave the playground and head a little bit south and west and you'll see the **Temperance Fountain,** erected here in the era before national **Prohibition;** to find about more about Prohibition, read **Chapter 139.**

Exit the park on Avenue A and begin walking back west on St. Mark's Place, which has always been the main street of the neighborhood. When you get to Second Avenue, notice the **Ottendorfer Library** and former **German Dispensary** just up the avenue from the northwest corner. Read about the German community, known as Kleindeutschland, in **Chapter 91.**

Continue west on St. Mark's Place to 19–25, a building that was once **Arlington Hall** and the **Polish National Home**, but is most famous for being home to **Andy Warhol's Exploding Plastic Inevitable and the Electric Circus,** which you can read about in **Chapter 164.** On the other side of the street, notice No. 12, the former **German-American Shooting Hall** (its name—in German—runs across the façade).

Continue west on St. Mark's Place to Third Avenue and turn left. Walk one block south, turn left onto 7th Street, and walk to 15 East 7th Street, **McSorley's Old Ale House,** discussed in **Chapter 57.** (You may wish to stop in for a drink; McSorley's only serves its own beer and only in "rounds." Order a "one and one" and you'll be given small mugs of light and dark beer.)

Leave McSorley's and retrace your steps to Third Avenue. Cross Third Avenue and walk in front of Cooper Union—you'll see a statue by Augustus Saint-Gaudens of founder Peter Cooper—and then turn right on Cooper Square to walk back to Astor Place. (The black cube in front of you is *The Alamo* by Tony Rosenthal.) Turn left onto Astor Place and then, almost immediately, turn left again onto Lafayette Street.

Stop in front of the **Public Theater** and look across the street at **Colonnade Row.** Read **Chapter 33** about the creation of this street and the row of houses; then read **Chapter 165** about **Joseph Papp and *Hair.***

When you are finished on Lafayette Place, retrace your steps to Astor Place and the 6 train.

TOUR 8

Gramercy Park, Madison Square, and Chelsea

Highlights

- Gramercy Park, the city's only private park
- The Flatiron Building
- The site of the scandalous 1906 murder of architect Stanford White
- The Hotel Chelsea
- The General Theological Seminary
- Good outdoor public sculpture

The path of this tour cuts across the island, exploring the area between 14th and 26th streets from the hustle and bustle of Union Square to the reserved propriety of Gramercy Park. It is a great tour to give you a sense of how Manhattan neighborhoods rub shoulders with each other. It is also a good tour if you like outdoor sculpture, which is well represented in the parks along the way.

The tour begins in Union Square, which is reached by a number of different subways: the 4/5/6, the N/R/Q/W and the L. However you get here, once you are aboveground, work your way to the southern, 14th Street end of the square, where a large equestrian statue of George Washington points down Broadway. This statue was erected to commemorate **Evacuation Day,** the day the British finally left New York at the end of the Revolution. Read more about Washington's return to New York in **Chapter 17.**

From the Washington statue, walk north along the Union Square East side of the park. At 16th Street, you'll come to a statue of another hero of the Revolution, the **Marquis de Lafayette;** the marquis and his eponymous street are the subject of **Chapter 33.** Continue up Union Square East until you reach East 17th Street. Turn right and walk one block to Irving Place. Take note of the plaque on the side of the small home on the southwest corner of 17th Street and Irving, proclaiming it to be the home of **Washington Irving.** It wasn't. You'll read more about Irving Place in **Chapter 40** when you reach Gramercy Park. (A bust of Irving also sits across the street in front of Washington Irving High School.)

Turn left and walk one block north on Irving Place to **Pete's Tavern,** where you can read **Chapter 139** about **Prohibition in New York.** Then continue north two blocks, where Irving Place will dead-end at **Gramercy Park,** which is closed off to the public by a wrought-iron fence. Read about the park's creation in **Chapter 40.**

The statue you see in the middle of this private park is of actor **Edwin Booth,** who lived on the park and founded the **Players** in his home at 16 Gramercy Park. Next door to the Players is the **National Arts Club,** once home to New York's governor **Samuel J. Tilden,** who was the **Democratic candidate for president in 1876.** That famously contested election is the subject of **Chapter 76.** You may also want to read about private clubs in New York while you are here (**Chapter 97**) and visit the National Arts Club, which has galleries open to the public.

Continue west on Gramercy Park South to Park Avenue South and cross to the other side. (Gramercy Park South will change its name to East 20th Street.) At 28 East 20th is the **Theodore Roosevelt Birthplace.** Read **Chapter 63** about Manhattan's only born-and-bred president. (The building is open to visitors Tuesday through Saturday, 9:00 a.m. to 5:00 p.m.)

Keep heading west on 20th Street to Broadway and turn right. Walk three blocks north and cross 23rd Street into Madison Square Park. (You'll be standing in front of a statue of **Secretary of State William Seward.** You can read more about him and his eponymous playground on the Lower East Side in **Chapter 113.**)

Turn around and you'll see Daniel Burnham's **Flatiron Building,** one of the city's most famous skyscrapers. Read **Chapter 111** about the building of this landmark and **Chapter 25** about the **Manhattan street grid;** the Flatiron's odd shape comes from Broadway's diagonal intrusion into the rectilinear street system.

Your next stop is at the northeast corner of the park, where 26th Street meets Madison Avenue. As you amble through Madison Square Park, you'll see other commemorative statuary. There's one of **Senator Roscoe Conkling** near the park's southeast corner and, near your destination, one of his protégé, **President Chester A. Arthur.** (Their power derived from New York's influential role as the home of the U.S. Customs Department. If you're curious about this facet of New York's history, read **Chapter 123** about the ornate Custom House downtown.)

At the northeast corner of 26th Street and Madison Avenue sits the **New York Life Insurance Building;** what used to be on this spot was **Stanford White's Madison Square Garden,** where he met his untimely end. Read about the murder and scandal in **Chapter 121.**

Walk along the northern edge of the park back toward Fifth Avenue. Looking north up Fifth Avenue from the corner of 26th Street gives you **one of the city's best views of the Empire State Building,** which you can read about in **Chapter 148.**

Turn south on Fifth Avenue and head back to 23rd Street, then turn right and walk two blocks west to Seventh Avenue. Cross Seventh and go to 222 West 23rd Street and the **Hotel Chelsea.** One of the first cooperative apartment buildings in New York, it is the subject of **Chapter 89.**

Continue on 23rd Street to Ninth Avenue and turn left. Walk three blocks south to the entrance, between 21st and 20th streets, of the **General Theological Seminary,** which you can read about in **Chapter 29.** To get

a real sense of the seminary, you'll want to visit the cloistered courtyard, known as the Close, which is generally open Monday through Friday, noon to 3:00 p.m. and Saturdays from 11:00 a.m. to 3:00 p.m. Photo ID is required. If it's not open when you visit, walk along the 20th Street side of the complex (toward Tenth Avenue) and you'll be able to get a glimpse through the fence.

When you are done at the seminary, walk west on 20th Street until you reach Eleventh Avenue. Cross the avenue to **Chelsea Piers,** the sports and entertainment complex, and find a place where you can get a good view of the **Hudson River.** These were once commercial piers at the heart of the shipping industry made possible by the opening of the **Erie Canal,** which you can read about in **Chapter 34.**

For your last stop, walk south on Eleventh Avenue to 16th Street, turn left, and walk back to Tenth Avenue. The building that runs the entire block between 15th and 16th streets and Ninth and Tenth avenues is today called **Chelsea Market** but was the old factory of the **National Biscuit Company (Nabisco).** As discussed in **Chapter 129,** this is the birthplace of the Oreo cookie.

This is the last stop on the tour (and a good place to find food and drink after your walk). To reach the closest subway, walk one block south to 14th Street, turn left, and walk back one block to Eighth Avenue and the A/C/E and L trains.

TOUR 9

Midtown

Highlights

- The Empire State Building
- Grand Central Terminal
- Times Square
- The Seagram Building and Lever House
- St. Patrick's Cathedral
- Rockefeller Center

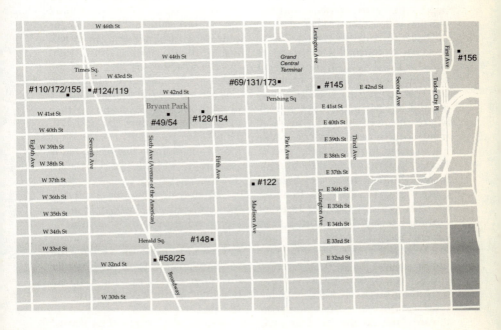

The term "Midtown" conjures up the quintessential view of New York: tall skyscrapers, blaring taxicab horns, and millions of people. You'll see all those things on this tour, but you will also experience wonderful churches, serene outdoor space, and interesting surprises, like the Shriners' former Mecca Temple.

This is a slightly longer tour than others in the book: you'll be covering over four miles and that's if you don't do the optional out-and-back to the United Nations. (If you do include the UN, it will add an additional mile to your walk.)

⌒ The tour begins at 34th Street/ Herald Square, which is served by the N/R/Q/W and B/D/F/V trains. This was once home to the *New York Herald* newspaper (a statue of bell ringers in the square is the only remnant of its building), but you are actually here to read about a different newspaper—the *New York Tribune*— which was never located here.

Because Broadway slices across the **city street grid** (when it was laid out in 1811, it did not make a provision for Broadway continuing this far north) little triangles of land appear at the intersections where the avenues and Broadway meet. Begin your tour by walking south to the 32nd Street end of Herald Square and the little triangle formally known as **Greeley Square.** Once there, read **Chapter 25** about the street grid and **Chapter 58** about **Horace Greeley.** The statue here of Greeley is by Alexander Doyle and was installed in 1890, the same year that a second statue of the famed editor was erected near City Hall.

After you've admired Greeley, return to 34th Street and walk east toward Fifth Avenue; as you walk, you will see the **Empire State Building** ahead of you. If you plan to visit the building's observatory, enter on Fifth Avenue and enjoy the spectacular view. (The observatory is open daily 8:00 a.m. to 2:00 a.m. Advance tickets are available at www.esbnyc. com.) Either way, read **Chapter 148**

about the building and its famous spire.

When you are finished at the Empire State Building, walk one more block east on 34th Street to Madison Avenue and turn left. Walk two blocks north to the **Morgan Library & Museum.** It was here that Morgan helped calm the **Panic of 1907,** which you can read about in **Chapter 122.** (The museum's hours are Tuesday through Thursday: 10:30 a.m. to 5:00 p.m.; Friday: 10:30 a.m. to 9:00 p.m.; Saturday: 10:00 a.m. to 6:00 p.m.; Sunday: 11:00 a.m. to 6:00 p.m.)

Leave the museum and walk north on Madison Avenue to 42nd Street. Turn right to see the main façade of **Grand Central Terminal.** While you are still out front, begin reading **Chapter 69;** then enter the building on 42nd Street (under the viaduct labeled "Pershing Square") to reach the Main Concourse. Once inside, read **Chapters 131 and 173.** This is also an excellent place to get food or drink from one of the many restaurants and takeout food stalls downstairs.

When you are done exploring the terminal, exit back onto 42nd Street and cross to the south side of the street before you begin walking east toward Lexington Avenue. You will have great views of the **Chrysler Building;** read about the Chrysler Building and the skyscraper race of 1929 in **Chapter 145.**

(The next stop—the **United Nations**—is an eight-block round-trip detour and you'll have to decide if it is worth your while. If you do visit, you'll walk four blocks east on 42nd Street to First Avenue and turn left to get good views of the **Secretariat** and **General Assembly** and read **Chapter 156.** Informative tours are offered most weekdays between 9:30 a.m. and 4:45 p.m. When you leave the UN, retrace your steps to Grand Central Terminal.)

Then walk west on 42nd Street to Fifth Avenue, turn left, walk one block to the front entrance of the **New York Public Library,** and read **Chapter 128.** If you are there when it's open (Monday through Saturday, 11:00 a.m. to 6:00 p.m.; Sundays 1:00 p.m. to 5:00 p.m.), make sure you go upstairs to the third floor to see **Edward Laning's WPA-era murals** (discussed in **Chapter 154**) and the famed Rose Main Reading Room.

Once you've left the library, walk around behind the building to **Bryant Park.** There is a sculpture here—near the Bryant Park Café—of **William Cullen Bryant,** the poet and newspaper publisher who first conceived Central Park. You can read about his importance to Central Park in **Chapter 49.** Bryant Park was once called Reservoir Square and was, most famously, home to New York's **Crystal Palace Exposition,** discussed in **Chapter 54.**

Leave the park at 42nd Street and Sixth Avenue and walk west on 42nd Street to **Times Square.** This is the busiest spot in New York City, and you'll need to find a place to perch to read a few different chapters. Often it is less crowded in the actual center of the square than on the surrounding streets.

The building between 42nd and 43rd streets with the electronic news "zipper" is the former **Times Tower,** which is best seen from the median in Times Square, near the Armed Forces Recruiting Station. Stand here and read **Chapter 124.** The Times Tower was made possible by the opening of the **IRT subway,** which you may also

want to read about in **Chapter 119** while you are here.

You are standing in the heart of the Broadway theater district, known as the **Great White Way.** One of the finest old theaters is the **New Amsterdam** on 42nd Street, just east of Times Square. Pay it a visit and read **Chapter 110.** (This block is also known as the New 42nd Street, a reference to the cleanup that occurred in the area in the 1990s. Times Square and environs were at their worst in the 1970s. You may want to read here about the infamous **Summer of 1977** in **Chapter 172.**) Also near here was the **Stage Door Canteen,** and Times Square is a good place to read about the city during **World War II** in **Chapter 155.**

Work your way north through Times Square to 47th Street and turn right. Walk one block east to Sixth Avenue. Cross the street and continue one more block to Fifth Avenue. This block of 47th Street is the **Diamond District,** which handles approximately 90 percent of the cut diamonds sold in the United States.

When you reach Fifth Avenue, turn left and walk north. Between 49th and 50th streets, you'll see the main entrance to **Rockefeller Center** on your left. Bypass this for a moment, and instead head to the corner of Fifth Avenue and 50th Street and **St. Patrick's Cathedral,** which you can read about in **Chapter 83.** Then, once you've finished at the cathedral, return to the main path into **Rockefeller Center** (this sloping walkway is known as the **Channel Gardens**) and walk down it to the famous **skating rink.** Take time to read **Chapter 149** and explore the center in depth. If you are in need of

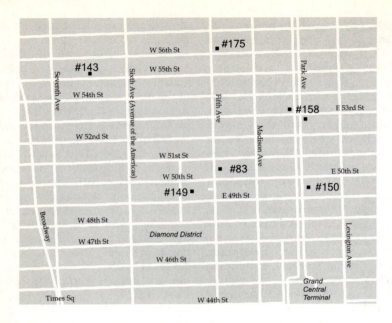

refreshment, the lower level features a number of food and drink options.

Finish your exploration of Rockefeller Center at **Radio City Music Hall,** at Sixth Avenue and 50th Street. Walk five blocks north on Sixth Avenue to 55th Street, turn left, and walk about halfway down the block to **City Center,** which was originally the **Shriners' Mecca Temple,** discussed in **Chapter 143.** Return to Sixth Avenue, cross it, and walk one block farther east to Fifth Avenue. Turn left and walk one block north to **Trump Tower.** Go inside to admire the opulence and to read about the building in **Chapter 175.**

When you leave Trump Tower,

walk two blocks east on 56th Street to Park Avenue, turn right, and walk south to 53rd Street. Diagonally across the street from each other at this intersection are **Lever House** (on the northwest corner of the intersection) and the **Seagram Building** (on the southeast corner). These two groundbreaking skyscrapers are the subject of **Chapter 158.**

To reach your last stop, continue walking south on Park Avenue to 50th Street and the **Waldorf-Astoria Hotel,** the lobby of which is open to visitors. Go inside and read **Chapter 150.**

The nearest subway is the 6 train at 51st Street and Lexington Avenue.

TOUR 10

The Upper East Side

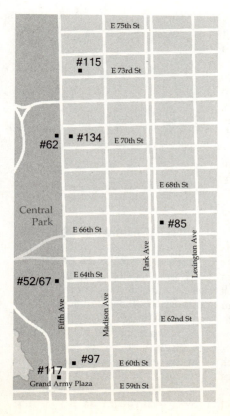

Much of this tour of the Upper East Side walks up the stretch of Fifth Avenue that has been nick-named "Millionaire's Mile" and "the Gold Coast." It features some of the spectacular mansions, private clubs, and museums for which the Upper East Side is famous.

〜 Begin the tour at Grand Army Plaza, across from the **Plaza Hotel,** at Fifth Avenue and 59th Street. The closest subway here is the N/R/W at the Fifth Avenue station.

In Grand Army Plaza, you'll see the gilded statue of **General William Tecumseh Sherman;** read **Chapter 117** about Sherman's move to New York. From Grand Army Plaza, head to the northwest corner of 60th Street and Fifth Avenue and look across the street at the **Metropolitan Club.** You can read about J. P. Morgan and the club scene in **Chapter 97.**

Continue north on Fifth Avenue; at 62nd Street, you will pass the **Knickerbocker Club,** mentioned in **Chapter 97.** When you reach 64th Street, turn left (into Central Park) and walk down the stairs to the **Central Park Arsenal,** which is discussed in both **Chapter 52** and **Chapter 67.** (The arsenal was once briefly home to the Central Park Zoo and the American Museum of Natural History; you'll read more about these institutions when you get to the Metropolitan Museum of Art.)

Return to Fifth Avenue and continue north to 66th Street. Turn right on 66th Street and walk east two blocks to Park Avenue and the **Seventh Regiment Armory,** discussed in **Chapter 85.** Today it is known as the Park Avenue Armory. Tours are available by appointment; visit www.armoryonpark.org for more information.

After you've read about the armory, walk north on Park Avenue to 70th Street, turn left, and walk back to Fifth Avenue to see **Henry Clay Frick's mansion,** now the **Frick Collection.** Read about Frick in **Chapter 134;** then check out the **Richard Morris Hunt Memorial** on the Central Park side of Fifth Avenue. You can read about Hunt in **Chapter 62.**

Walk north on Fifth Avenue to 73rd Street and turn right to 11 East 73rd Street, the **Joseph Pulitzer Mansion.** Read about Pulitzer's home in **Chapter 115.** Then return to Fifth Avenue and continue north to 82nd Street and the **Metropolitan Museum of Art.** (The grand Beaux-Arts entrance on Fifth Avenue is by Richard Morris Hunt. As you approach, look up the length of each set of columns and notice the piles of stones there—these stones were to be turned into sculptures but the project was abandoned.)

Read **Chapter 80** about the founding of this museum and its companion, the American Museum of Natural History. You may choose to go into the Met (open Tuesday through Thursday and Sunday, 9:30 a.m. to 5:30 p.m.; Friday and Saturday, 9:30 a.m. to 9:00 p.m.) If you do go inside, you can see not only the façades of earlier incarnations of the museum, but also the Frank Lloyd Wright interior discussed in **Chapter 159** (which you'll read at your next stop).

When you are done at the Met, continue north to 88th Street and the **Guggenheim Museum** and read **Chapter 159** about Frank Lloyd Wright's New York City work. Continue up Fifth Avenue to 91st Street and **Andrew Carnegie's mansion,** now the Cooper-Hewitt National Design Museum, and read about the mansion in **Chapter 109.** (The Cooper-Hewitt is open Monday through Thursday: 10:00 a.m. to 5:00 p.m.; Friday: 10:00 a.m. to 9:00 p.m.; Saturday: 10:00 a.m. to 6:00 p.m.; Sunday: noon to 6:00 p.m.)

The final stop on the tour is a little over a mile from here, so you may decide to skip it. (If you want to simply get to the closest subway station, it is the 4/5/6 station at Lexington Avenue and 86th Street.)

However, if you would like to visit **Gracie Mansion,** the city's mayoral residence, begin walking east on 91st Street until you get to York Avenue (seven lengthy blocks away). Turn right onto York Avenue, walk south one block, and turn left onto 90th Street. Walk one more block east to East End Avenue and **Carl Schurz Park.** Enter the park at 88th Street and you will be right outside **Gracie Mansion,** one of the city's old country mansions discussed in **Chapter 20.** Gracie Mansion can be visited on organized tours. Tours are offered on Wednesdays and reservations are required: 212-639-9675.

If you've come all this way, stay and enjoy Carl Schurz Park for a while and then head west to the 4/5/6 subway at Lexington Avenue at 86th Street.

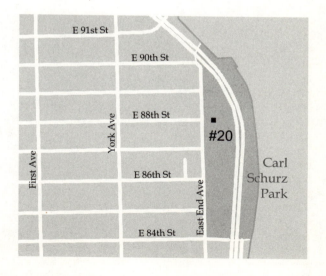

TOUR 11

The Upper West Side

Highlights

- The Dakota
- Lincoln Center
- The American Museum of Natural History
- Riverside Park
- Strawberry Fields

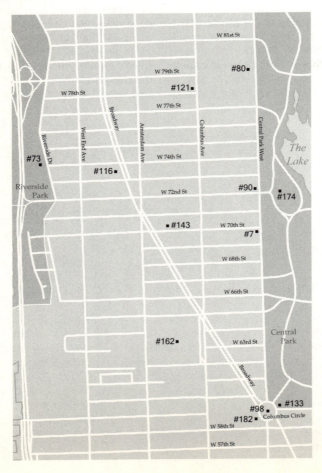

The Upper West Side is a lovely residential neighborhood that many people don't think to visit on a walking tour. However, it is rich in architecture, from grand apartments like the Dakota and the Ansonia to rows of charming townhouses. Much of the area is bounded by two parks, Central Park on the east (which you will dip into when visiting Strawberry Fields) and Riverside Park, which hugs the island's west side.

Begin your tour at the southwest corner of Central Park in Columbus Circle, which is served by the 1, A/C, and B/D subways. Here you will see some of the area's newest architectural additions, the **Time Warner Center** and (if you detour down to 57th Street and Eighth Avenue) the **Hearst Tower.** Both of these buildings are discussed in **Chapter 182.** Also notice the recently completed renovation to what was once Huntington Hartford's Gallery of Modern Art and is now the Museum of Arts and Design. (It's the building on the south side of the circle that—depending on how you look at it—appears to be saying either "HI" or "HE" on its façade.)

Also on Columbus Circle (at the entrance to Central Park) is the gold-topped monument to the **USS *Maine.*** Its creation is the subject of **Chapter 133.** In the center of the roundabout stands a tall pillar with a statue of **Christopher Columbus,** which you can read about in **Chapter 98.**

Leave the circle via Broadway and begin walking north. When you reach 63rd Street, you'll see **Lincoln Center.** As you read about the center in **Chapter 162,** take some time to explore before returning to Broadway.

Walk north to 70th Street. Turn right and walk to 135 West 70th Street, the former home of the **Knights of Pythias,** now known as the Pythian Apartments. Read about this society in **Chapter 143.**

Continue east on 70th Street to Central Park West. On the southwest corner is the synagogue of **Congregation Shearith Israel.** You can read about its founding in the 17th century—when its synagogue was in a mill in the Financial District—in **Chapter 7.**

Turn left onto Central Park West and head north two blocks to 72nd Street and the **Dakota Apartments.** Read **Chapter 90,** about the apartment building's history, before you walk into Central Park here—you'll see a sign that reads "Strawberry Fields"—to read **Chapter 174** about the Dakota's most famous resident, **John Lennon.** (Make sure you locate the *Imagine* mosaic in Strawberry Fields.)

Return to Central Park West and walk north to 77th Street, where you will see the **American Museum of Natural History** on the north side of the street. It's worth walking to the 81st Street side of the building, turning left, and walking around to the Columbus Avenue side. It is from here that you'll be able to see some of Calvert Vaux and Jacob Wrey Mould's original Gothic structure, tucked in amid later additions. As you walk through the museum's grounds, read **Chapter 80** about its creation and that of the Metropolitan Museum of Art. (The American Museum of Natural History is open daily, 10:00 a.m. to 5:45 p.m.)

When you are done at the museum, leave the grounds at 78th Street and Columbus Avenue and cross to the **Evelyn,** which is a good place to read **Chapter 121** about **Evelyn Nesbit** and **Stanford White.** Continue west on 78th Street to Broadway and turn left. Walk south to 74th Street and the **Ansonia Apartments;** the build-ing's opening is detailed in **Chapter 116.** Turn right on 74th Street and walk west to **Riverside Park,** which you can read about in **Chapter 73.**

After you've spent some time in the park, you can return to Broadway and turn south to 72nd Street and the 1/2/3 subway station.

TOUR 42

Central Park

Highlights

- Tavern on the Green
- Sheep Meadow
- Bethesda Terrace and
  The Angel of the Waters
- Bow Bridge
- The Great Lawn
- The Metropolitan Museum of Art
- Strawberry Fields and the *Imagine* Mosaic

There's no two ways about it: Central Park is huge. Measuring two and a half miles long by a half-mile wide, it covers 843 acres of land and includes over 60 miles of pathway. While this tour won't have you walk that far, it does cover two-and-a-half to three miles in the lower half of the park and is best enjoyed at a leisurely pace. For ambitious walkers, there's an add-on at the end that will take you up past the reservoir to the park's serene—but much less visited—northern end.

~ The best way to experience the park is from south to north. Our tour begins at Columbus Circle, where Eighth Avenue (which becomes Central Park West) and Broadway intersect. Before you enter the park here, take note of the **Christopher Columbus** monument in the center of the circle (he'll come up later in the tour) as well as the large gold-topped statue at the park's entrance dedicated to the **USS Maine.** Read **Chapter 133** about the *Maine* and yellow journalism.

There are a few paths that enter the park here: you want to take the one directly to the left of the *Maine* monument (the path lies between the

monument and the green concession stand). This wide path slopes downhill toward the park's old carriage road—today called the ring road or the West Drive—which is often filled with joggers and bicyclists. Cross the ring road, but please use caution and yield to oncoming traffic.

Once you've crossed the road, begin heading left (north) on the path alongside the ring road/West Drive. You'll pass over a couple of lovely stone bridges on your way to Sheep Meadow. Somewhere along here, find a nice place to perch for a few minutes and read about the creation of the park in **Chapters 49, 55, and 61.**

You'll know you've reached **Sheep**

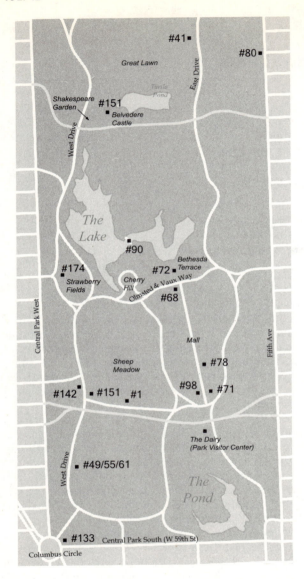

Meadow when you get to the tall chain-link fence on your right. Read **Chapter 151,** which not only discusses Sheep Meadow, but also talks about the Great Lawn, which you'll see later on the tour.

Across the ring road is **Tavern on the Green,** created when the sheep were exiled in 1934. The tavern was created in part to get rid of another Central Park restaurant, the Casino, that was the hangout of New York's playboy mayor in the 1920s, **"Gentleman" Jimmy Walker,** who you can read about in **Chapter 142.** Tavern on the Green is worth a peek if you've never been inside. Even if you're not going for a meal, there's a bar upstairs and public restrooms.

When you're done at Tavern on the Green, cross back to Sheep Meadow and walk along its southern side, outside the fence. (As you walk, the fence will be on your left.) As you reach the crest of the hill, you'll see a number of large boulders on both sides of the path. These are **glacial erratics,** left here during the last Ice Age. For more about prehistoric New York, read **Chapter 1.**

Continue east on the path, past the edge of Sheep Meadow, until you reach the ring road—here also called the East Drive. Turn left (keeping the ring road on your right) and continue to the statue of Christopher Columbus, which will be on your left. This is the beginning of the Mall.

Start with the **Columbus statue** and read **Chapter 98**; then walk around the lovely flower garden to the **statue of William Shakespeare** that stands opposite it and read **Chapter 71.**

Begin walking north on the Mall. You'll pass statues of **Sir Walter Scott** and **Robert Burns** and then you'll come to obscure American poet **Fitz-Greene Halleck.** Halleck is the subject of **Chapter 78.**

Continue farther up the Mall until you come to the broad staircase heading down to **Bethesda Terrace.** Before you go down, make sure you look at the intricate carvings on the pedestals flanking the staircase— look for the **witch on her broomstick** on the west side of the pedestal on your left, which is described in **Chapter 68.**

Now head down the stairs to the heart of the terrace and Emma Stebbins's statue *The Angel of the Waters* and read about its creation in **Chapter 72.**

To exit the terrace follow the path to your left (as you face the angel) that curves around the west side of the lake. Soon you will come to **Bow Bridge.** When you stand on the middle of the bridge and look west, you'll see the **Dakota Apartments.** Read **Chapter 90** about the Dakota, one of the most famous residential buildings in New York. (It is the low building in front of you with a three-peaked roof; it often flies the American flag from the central peak.)

Retrace your steps to leave Bow Bridge and turn right. Keeping the lake on your right, continue on the path that will soon veer to the left up a short grade to **Cherry Hill** (there's an ornate horse watering trough that look likes a fountain in the middle). From the fountain, walk down the hill on the path to your right to get to the 72nd Street Transverse. Turn right and follow the road until you reach the huge statue of **Daniel Webster** standing in front of the ring road/West Drive. Cross the ring road and you'll see a sign immediately in front of you that reads **Strawberry Fields.** Use either path to walk up the hill and you'll come to the *Imagine mosaic,* probably the most visited spot in the park. You can read about it and **John Lennon's murder** in **Chapter 174.**

When you are done in Strawberry Fields, take either path back down the hill and return to the Daniel Webster statue. Turn left, and begin walking north, keeping the lake on your right.

After about a ten-minute stroll, you will come to the **Swedish Cot-**

tage, a gift from Sweden following the 1876 Centennial World's Fair. It is now used as a children's marionette theater.

Turn right at the cottage and walk up through the **Shakespeare Garden** (which you have already read about in **Chapter 71** when you were at the Shakespeare statue). Keep heading uphill as you exit the garden and you'll reach **Belvedere Castle,** an ornate folly and—upstairs on its ramparts—the highest point in the park. You'll get a good view here of the **Turtle Pond** and the **Great Lawn,** which you read about earlier in **Chapter 151** when you were at Sheep Meadow.

When you leave Belvedere Castle, stand with the castle behind you. (In front of you will be a fenced-in area with some high-tech weather monitoring equipment.) Turn left and walk down the hill, keeping Turtle Pond on your left. The road will curve to the right as you approach the ring road/East Drive. Cross the ring road (carefully, as always), and continue heading down what is known as Cedar Hill. When you reach the first intersection on the path, turn left and walk up to the **Metropolitan Museum of Art,** which is discussed in the second half of **Chapter 80.** Turn right to exit the park here so you can walk up Fifth Avenue and past the museum's grand front entrance.

You've now covered the lower half of the park and seen many of its highlights; you may find this an excellent place to finish the tour. (The closest subway is the 4/5/6 train at 86th Street and Lexington Avenue.)

However, if you'd like to explore the northern half of the park—which has fewer landmarks and requires a good sense of direction—follow the instructions below. The second half of the tour covers an additional two-and-a-half to three miles.

〜 Continue north on Fifth Avenue past the Metropolitan Museum of Art to 84th Street. Before you cross 84th street, turn left to follow the path back into the park, keeping the museum on your left. When you get back to the ring road/East Drive, turn left onto it (into the jogging lane) and walk back to the **Statue of Alexander Hamilton,** a memorial to the **Great Fire of 1835.** (You can read about the fire in **Chapter 41.**)

Walk back on the ring road to the place where you joined it from the museum. Ahead and to your left you will see a path that leads to a small set of stairs; take the stairs and you'll see they become a bridge that leads to the reservoir. Follow the bridge and walk toward the reservoir's gatehouse. Just before you reach the stairs that lead to the gatehouse (and before you get to the narrow jogging path around the reservoir), a path will slope down to your right to take you to the wide bridle path. Take this left turn to get on the bridle path.

Then walk north about five minutes to 90th Street, where you'll see a gilded statue dedicated to John Purroy Mitchel (the "boy mayor") who was New York City's youngest chief executive. He died in World War I.

Continue walking about 8 to 10 minutes until the bridle path begins to curve to the left. A second spur of the bridle path comes in here from the right. Take this spur (making a sort of a U-turn to head away from the reservoir) and you'll soon be paralleling the ring road/East Drive as you walk north. Keep on the bridle path another 10 to 12 minutes until

Central Park North (W 110th St)

Harlem
Meer

E 108th St

#27

#155

Great
Hill

Central Park West

West Drive

#107

Fifth Ave

The
Pool

102nd St Transverse

E 102nd St

North Meadow

East Drive

East
Meadow

E 97th St

Jacqueline
Kennedy Onassis
Reservoir

John Purroy
Mitchel statue

E 90th St

Fifth Ave

East Drive

E 84th St

#41

Great Lawn

#80

Turtle
Pond

it begins to curve to the left to follow the paved 102nd Street Transverse road.

At this point, instead of following the bridle path, cross the 102nd Street Transverse. Directly ahead of you will be a path going slightly uphill and, at the top of that hill, you'll see the **Andrew Haswell Green Memorial Bench**—the only public monument to the man who created **modern New York City.** You can read about Green and his role in **Five-Borough Unification** in **Chapter 107.**

Retrace your steps back to the 102nd Street Transverse and turn right (west) to use the transverse to cut across the park. When you reach the ring road/West Drive, turn right (again, stay in the jogging lane) and begin walking up the **Great Hill,** site of an **anti-aircraft battery in World War II,** discussed in **Chapter 155.** After you crest the hill and begin to walk down, notice that the lampposts have four-digit numbers on them; directly after you get to **lamppost 0706,** you'll see a path to your right (posted with a map of the North Woods). Follow this path and you will soon come to an **1815 blockhouse fortification,** built at the tail-end of the War of 1812. Read about the city's defenses during that war in **Chapter 27.**

The best way out of the park from here is to retrace your steps back to the ring road/West Drive and head right (north) to continue down the hill. Soon you will see a path on your left—take it and at your first opportunity to turn right, walk down a set of stairs and out of the park. You are now on Central Park West at 108th Street, just two blocks south of the 110th Street station on the B and C trains.

TOUR 13

Morningside Heights

Highlights

- The Cathedral of St. John the Divine
- Columbia University
- Morningside Park
- Grant's Tomb

Morningside Heights, perched on a high plateau bounded by two great parks—Morningside and Riverside—is defined by its academic and religious institutions. It is also a very compact neighborhood, which makes it a good walk to do if you are short on time.

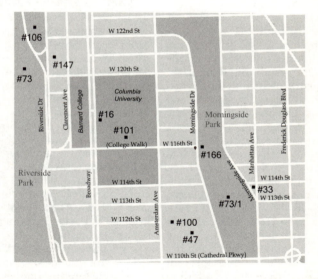

~ Begin in Morningside Park; the closest subway is the B/C at 110th Street and Central Park West/Frederick Douglass Boulevard. Walk west one block to Manhattan Avenue and **Morningside Park.** If you take a few moments to stroll in the park, you'll see outcroppings of **Manhattan schist,** the local bedrock. Find a nice

place to pause in the park and read about the park's creation in **Chapter 73,** as well as prehistoric New York in **Chapter 1.**

(If you are interested in seeing a nice statue by Frédéric Auguste Bartholdi of **George Washington and the Marquis de Lafayette,** turn right and head north on Manhattan Avenue three blocks to the small plaza between 113th and 114th streets. You can read about the marquis in **Chapter 33.** Then retrace your steps to 110th Street.)

Walk west along the 110th Street side of the park to Morningside Drive and then walk one more block west to Amsterdam Avenue. Turn right and begin walking north on Amsterdam Avenue. On your right will be the grounds of the Cathedral of St. John the Divine. Enter the grounds and begin making your way back toward the handsome Greek Revival structure attached to the south wall of the cathedral. This building is the former **Leake and Watts Orphan House** and is the oldest structure in the neighborhood; the orphanage—and the neighborhood's early history—is discussed in **Chapter 47.**

Return to Amsterdam Avenue and walk just a little farther up the street to the grand front entrance of the **Cathedral of St. John the Divine,** which is worth exploring inside and out. Read **Chapter 100** to set the stage for your explorations.

When you are done in the cathedral, continue north on Amsterdam Avenue one block to 113th Street. Turn right and walk back to Morningside Drive, passing **St. Luke's Hospital.** Turn left and walk along the park three blocks to 116th Street. There is a grand overlook here (with a statue of German politician and publisher **Carl Schurz**) that is near the spot where **Columbia proposed building a new gymnasium in 1968.** The protest and ensuing campus takeover are discussed in **Chapter 166.**

Walk west on 116th Street to Amsterdam Avenue and enter the gates of **Columbia University.** (Note that 116th Street is called College Walk as it traverses the campus.) The best place to see Charles McKim's

design is to walk to the very center of the campus and face **Low Memorial Library** while reading **Chapter 101.** (Low was the centerpiece of the campus takeover you just read about in **Chapter 166.**)

When you have finished exploring the campus, continue on College Walk to the Broadway gates, turn right, and begin walking north. After you pass the gates that lead up a flight of steps to Earl Hall, you'll see a plaque on the wall commemorating the **Battle of Harlem Heights,** one of the only skirmishes in Manhattan won by the Americans during the Revolution. You can read more about this era in **Chapter 16.**

Continue north on Broadway to 120th Street. (As you walk, you see Barnard College on the west side of Broadway, and when you get to 120th Street, the two schools flanking Broadway are the Union Theological Seminary and Teachers College. The Jewish Theological Seminary and the Manhattan School of Music are two blocks farther north.)

Turn left on 120th Street and walk two blocks to Riverside Drive. Turn right and walk along the front of **Riverside Church,** which you can read about in **Chapter 147.** Then cross Riverside Drive and finish your tour with a visit to **Grant's Tomb.** Read about the tomb in **Chapter 106** before heading inside.

You are now in **Riverside Park** (which you read about at the beginning of the tour in **Chapter 73**), and you might wish to explore a little in the park before ending the tour.

The closest subway is the 1 train at the 125th Street station. To get there, take 122nd Street east to Broadway, turn left, and walk north to the station, which is elevated above the road due to the deep, natural valley here.

TOUR 14

Harlem and Upper Manhattan

Highlights

- Hamilton Grange
- City College
- The Apollo Theater
- The Hotel Theresa
- Abyssinian Baptist Church
- The King Model Houses (Strivers' Row)

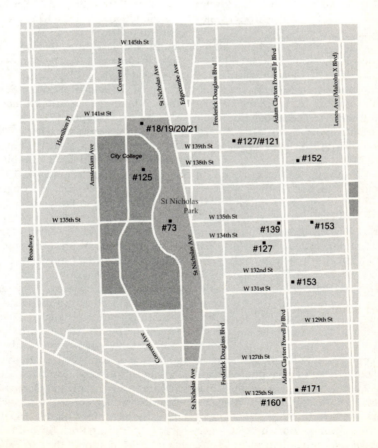

This tour is divided into two sections: a section for central Harlem, covering the area from 125th to 145th streets, which can be easily walked in an hour or two, and a second section that will take you farther afield (via subway) all the way up to Inwood Park and the island's northern tip.

◁ Begin by taking the A/C or B/D subway to 145th Street and St. Nicholas Avenue. Harlem has some of the finest townhouses in New York, and to get a good sense of them, walk one block west on 145th Street to Convent Avenue, turn left (south) and begin strolling down toward 141st Street. This is the **Hamilton Heights Historic District** and the homes you see here are mostly from the last decade of the 19th century.

When you reach 141st Street, turn left and walk down the hill to St. Nicholas Park and the entrance to **Hamilton Grange**—built in 1802, it is the oldest home in the area. To get a full sense of **Alexander Hamilton** and his importance to early American history, read **Chapters 18, 19, 20 and 21.**

When you are done at Hamilton Grange, return to Convent Avenue, turn left, and enter the campus of **City College**, discussed in **Chapter 125.** Walk through the campus on Convent Avenue until you reach 135th Street. Turn left and walk along the side of the **A. Philip Randolph Campus High School** (formerly the High School of Music & Art) until you reach the entrance to **St. Nicholas Park.** Walk down the path (it's a bit of a steep descent) to St. Nicholas Avenue. (While this particular park isn't one that we talk about in **Chapter 73,** it was born out of the same movement that created Morningside Park and Riverside Park.)

You are now on what was once known as "the Harlem plain." Back when the Dutch first settled the area (calling it New Haarlem), this was fertile farmland.

Cross St. Nicholas Avenue and walk one block east on 135th Street to Frederick Douglass Boulevard. Turn left and walk north to 139th Street. Turn right and continue east on 139th Street toward Adam Clayton Powell Jr. Boulevard. You are now in the midst of **the King Model Houses**—aka **Strivers' Row.** Read about this development in the first half of **Chapter 127.** The homes on the north side of 139th Street were designed by famed architect **Stanford White**; the end of his life is chronicled in **Chapter 121.**

To get a complete sense of the area, you should look at the houses on this block and head one block south to look at the homes on 138th Street between Frederick Douglass and Adam Clayton Powell Jr. boulevards. When you're done on Strivers' Row, exit onto Adam Clayton Powell Jr. Boulevard. Your next stop, the **Abyssinian Baptist Church,** is at 132 West 138th Street, on the other side of the boulevard, where you will read **Chapter 152.** After you've looked at the church, return to Adam Clayton Powell Jr. Boulevard and turn left. Walk south to 135th Street; at the southwest corner you'll see an International House of Pancakes—this building was the nightclub **Small's Paradise** (which you will read about in a moment in **Chapter 153**), a speakeasy during **Prohibition.** Read about Prohibition, the so-called noble experiment, in **Chapter 139.**

Today, a modern addition on top of the Small's Paradise building houses the **Thurgood Marshall Academy,** named for the Supreme Court justice who once lived nearby.

Walk east half a block on 135th Street to the **Harlem YMCA** (on the south side of the street), once home to **Langston Hughes, Ralph Ellison, Richard Wright,** and other figures associated with the **Harlem Renaissance.** You may want to read **Chapter 153** here, though it will also come up later in the tour at the Lafayette Theater.

Return to Adam Clayton Powell Jr. Boulevard, cross back to the Small's Paradise building, and turn left. Walk one block south, turn right, and walk partway down the block to **St. Philip's Episcopal Church.** Read the second half of **Chapter 127,** which discusses the church and its architect, **Vertner Tandy.** Return to Adam Clayton Powell Jr. Boulevard and continue south.

At 131st Street, in the median, stands the statue *Tree of Hope III* and on the east side of the street is the Williams CME Church, which was once the **Lafayette Theater.** If you haven't yet read **Chapter 153**—which details the Lafayette and the original Tree of Hope—do so now.

Continue south on Adam Clayton Powell Jr. Boulevard to 125th Street. The monolithic building in the plaza is the **Adam Clayton Powell Jr. State Office Building,** named in honor of the Harlem congressman in 1983. Powell was one of the most influential politicians in America, and his story is told in **Chapter 171.**

Diagonally across the intersection stands the **Hotel Theresa,** the subject of **Chapter 160.** Turn right on 125th

Street and walk about halfway down the block toward the **Apollo Theater.** Across the street is an old department store with a large sign (recently added) that reads **Touro College.** This store was originally **Blumstein's,** the object of Adam Clayton Powell, Jr.'s "Don't shop where you can't work" boycott.

You've completed the central Harlem section of the tour. If you wish to end the tour now, you are only a block and a half from the A/C B/D subway station at 125th Street and St. Nicholas Avenue.

⌒ If you want to check out some more stops in Upper Manhattan, the remainder are scattered across the rest of the island and will require a few subway rides.

Your next stop is the **Morris-Jumel Mansion** (which you read about earlier in **Chapter 20**) at 65 Jumel Terrace. To get there from the Apollo Theater, continue walking

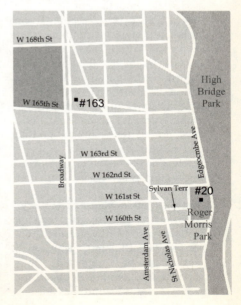

west to St. Nicholas Avenue and the A/C B/D subway station. Take the C train (the others won't stop where you're going) to 163rd Street. When you exit, walk south on St. Nicholas Avenue; in the block between 161st and 160th streets, you'll see a stone staircase on the east side of St. Nicholas Avenue. Climb these steps and you'll be on **Sylvan Terrace,** a lovely small street of what were once the Morris-Jumel Mansion's stables. Walk up Sylvan Terrace to the mansion, which is generally open Wednesday through Sunday, 10:00 a.m. to 4:00 p.m.

After you've visited the Morris-Jumel Mansion, your next stop is the **Audubon Ballroom,** where **Malcolm X** was assassinated. To get there, return to St. Nicholas Avenue and turn right (north) and walk up to 165th Street. Turn left on 165th and walk one block to Broadway and the Audubon Ballroom to read **Chapter 163.** There are also information kiosks here about the site.

Your next stop is **Fort Tryon Park.** Continue walking three more blocks north on Broadway and enter the A/C station at 168th Street. Take the uptown train to the 190th Street station. Follow the signs to the Fort Washington Avenue exit. Walk north (right) into Fort Tryon Park. Enter the main (central) path and go into the Heather Garden. Find a good spot in the park where you can look west at New Jersey's Palisades and read **Chapter 2,** which discusses Henry Hudson's 1609 voyage of discovery.

From the garden, keep walking north in Fort Tryon Park in the direction of **The Cloisters** (which will occasionally be signposted). Your goal is to find and follow one of the paths that leads behind the Cloisters

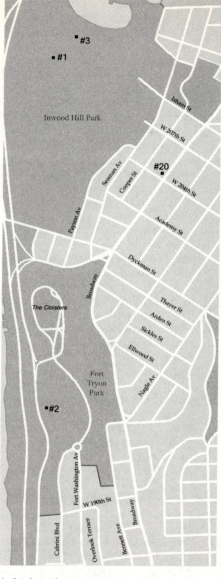

(which is the Metropolitan Museum of Art's medieval museum). Though it doesn't say anywhere that these paths bring you out of Fort Tryon Park onto Broadway, they do.

Turn left to walk north several

blocks on Broadway to 204th Street and the **Dyckman Farmhouse** (which was mentioned in **Chapter 20**). The farmhouse is open Wednesday through Saturday (11:00 a.m. to 4:00 p.m.) and Sunday (noon to 4:00 p.m.).

After you leave the farmhouse, walk two blocks west on 204th Street to Seaman Avenue. Turn right and walk two blocks north to Isham Street. Enter **Inwood Hill Park** here (on your left) and walk straight to the flagpole. Go behind the flagpole and turn right, keeping the woods on your left and the fence on your right. You'll be heading downhill. When the path forks, stay to the right. Soon you will come to a second fork; go left and follow the path to a small boulder with an attached plaque. This commemorates the **purchase of the island of Manhattan by the Dutch in 1626.** You can read about the transaction in **Chapter 3.**

After you've read this plaque, climb into the woods using one of the nearby paths. Known as the Clove, this is an old-growth forest of hickory, dogwood, and oak. Once in the woods, read **Chapter 1,** which takes you back to the earliest era in New York's history. When you are done exploring Inwood Hill Park, return to Seaman Avenue. Walk one block south to 207th Street and turn left. Walk two blocks east to Broadway and the 207th Street station on the A train.

Acknowledgments

First of all, many thanks to all of our wonderful walking tour clients through the years. We appreciate how they have allowed us to pet two cats with one hand (if we may coin that phrase) by giving us the opportunity to meet fascinating people from around the world and at the same time share our love and knowledge of New York.

Many people participated in the crafting of this manuscript, from its earliest concept to the finished product. Our thanks to Myra Manning for saying, "You should write this all down"; to Peter Lavery and Jonathan Lopez, whose comments strengthened early drafts of the proposal; to Alistair Nevius, who not only read important parts of the proposal, but would happily look at anything we sent his way, large or small; to Kelly McKinney, who literally ran hundreds of miles with us as we hashed out ideas; to Bruce Feiler for pointing us in Joy Tutela's direction; to Larry Confino for filming us on short notice; and to Erin Filner, Heather Herrera, Amanda Sutphin, Lisa Ashkenasy, Sarah Goff, Lauren Kronisch, Laura Auricchio, Cyndy Seibels, Illich Mujica, and Andrew Zeitler for their astute additions and corrections to the manuscript.

We also owe a debt of gratitude to those who tested the walking tours, both in their early drafts and as they appear here, including almost all of the people mentioned above as well as Ronnie Silverman, Devin Ratray, Samantha Greenberg, Sarah Parrish, Michael Parrish, Tanganyika Matthews, Jonathan Paisner at citylisten.com, Jenny and Mike Flores, Amina Hagan, and John Carini. Additional thanks to Jessica Goring for both testing tours and for her crucial help with *New York Times* research.

For assistance with research and acquiring prints and photographs, our thanks to David Witten, Toby Leavitt, Rohit Aggarwala, Torie and David Skoog, The Rev. Deacon Edgar W. Hopper at the St. Augustine's Project, Inc., Nicholas O'Han, Matthew Henry for sharing his original *Charging Bull* flyer, Renée M. Miscione at the GSA, and Chris Murtha at the Museum of the City of New York.

Other friends and family have been very encouraging throughout and we thank them all. Special recognition goes to: Carl Gerdau, John Kolp, Ben Parish, Monica Carson, Meg Wirth, Harvey Walters, Molly Kealy, Christine Nevius, Daniel Nevius, Elizabeth Nevius, and the late Barbara Walters.

This book would not exist without the hard work of our agent, Joy Tutela of the David Black Literary Agency, who both helped us craft the proposal and then adroitly shepherded it into the hands of Free Press. She also provided keen insights and support throughout the entire writing process and we are privileged to have her on our team.

Many thanks to everyone at Free Press: publisher Martha Levin, associate publisher Suzanne Donahue, director of publicity Carisa Hays, and editor in chief Dominick Anfuso. Our particular appreciation goes to our editor, Wylie O'Sullivan, whose questions, comments, and changes have strengthened the book immeasurably. We're grateful not only that she edited the book with such care but that she did it with such good humor. On Wylie's team, thanks to Elizabeth Perrella, J. D. Porter, and Donna Loffredo for helping us with all the pesky details. Thanks also to Shannon Gallagher in marketing, publicist Jill Browning, production editor Carol de Onís, interior designer Ellen Sasahara, and jacket designer Eric Fuentecilla.

Photograph and Illustration Credits

Illustrations on pages viii-ix, 1 (left), 4, 7, 9, 12, 13, 15, 20, 21, 22, 27, 30, 31, 35, 36, 37, 41, 45, 46, 57, 81, 93, 94, 98, 100, 119, 121, 128, 131, 133, 139, 149, 152, 169, 173, and 269 are taken from: The Memorial History of the City of New-York, ed. James Grant Wilson (New York: 1892); Volumes 1–4.

Page 1 (right): Courtesy of the City of New York.

Photographs taken by the authors appear on pages: 11, 29, 42, 49, 51, 53, 55, 65, 68, 77, 87, 89, 92, 102, 108, 109, 115, 124, 126, 135, 146, 157, 159, 161, 162, 171, 187, 190, 192, 199, 210, 211, 216, 223, 228, 229, 231, 235, 247, 257, 259, 261, 265, 273, 276, 281, 283, 284, 287, 291, and 293.

Page 26: Ives Process Company, ca. 1910; collection of the authors.

Pages 33, 111, 172 (ca. 1907), 178, 181, 201, 208 (ca. 1916): Publisher and date unknown; collection of the authors.

Page 48: Illustrated Post Card Company, ca. 1906; collection of the authors.

Page 62: Courtesy of the St. Augustine's Project, Inc. Hector Pena, photographer.

Page 75: Success Postal Card Company; date unknown; collection of the authors.

Page 78 (top): Souvenir Postcard Company, ca. 1906; collection of the authors.

Page 78 (bottom), 242, Manhattan Postcard Company, 1910; collection of the authors.

Page 84: Artist & publisher, Alfred E. Baker; 1840; Museum of the City of New York; gift of Miss Sarah Gardiner.

Page 129: Courtesy of the Library of Congress, George Grantham Bain Collection, Prints & Photographs Division, Reproduction No. LC-USZ62–88615.

Page 137: Arthur Strauss Inc.; date unknown; collection of the authors.

Page 142: The American News Company, ca. 1905; collection of the authors.

Page 144: Courtesy of the Library of Congress, Historic American Buildings Survey, Prints & Photographs Division, HABS Reproduction No. NY-6295–24.

Pages 147 and 165: Detroit Publishing Company; collection of the authors.

Page 155: A "Colourpicture" Publication; date unknown; collection of the authors.

Page 167: The Leighton and Valentine Company; ca. 1913; collection of the authors.

Page 183: Franz Huld, publisher, ca. 1902; collection of the authors.

Page 195: Courtesy of the Library of Congress, Prints & Photographs Division, Reproduction No. LC-DIG-ppmsca-12056.

Page 196: R.F. Turnbull, photographer, ca. 1907; collection of the authors.

Page 203: Valentine and Son's Publishing Co., date unknown; collection of the authors.

Page 205: courtesy of the Library of Congress, George Grantham Bain Collection, Prints & Photographs Division, Reproduction No. LC-DIG-ppmsca-05641.

Page 214: Frank E. Cooper, ca. 1938; collection of the authors.

Page 225: The American Art Publishing Company, ca. 1916; collection of the authors.

Pages 233, 238: From Empire State, 1931, a publication of Empire State, Inc.; collection of the authors.

Page 237: Published by Alfred Mainzer; date unknown; collection of the authors.

Page 240: Published by Frank E. Cooper, ca. 1939; collection of the authors.

Page 251: Carol M. Highsmith Photography, Inc., courtesy of the U.S. General Services Administration, Public Buildings Service, Fine Arts Collection.

All Tour Maps Copyright © Map Resources

INDEX

Page numbers in *italics* refer to illustrations.

About the Authors

Like many New Yorkers, **Michelle and James Nevius** each originally hail from elsewhere. Michelle was born and raised in the Baltimore area, and James lived in spots around the world as diverse as Saudi Arabia, Italy, and Utah. Since founding Michelle Nevius tours in 2000, they have led walking tours of New York City that mix architecture, history, art, and culture, with a focus on uncovering hidden history and pointing out intriguing facts and stories along the way that might not be readily apparent to the casual visitor.

For more New York City history, read the Inside the Apple blog at www.insidetheapple.net.